Nationalist Movemer

Nationalist Movement in India

A Reader

edited by

SEKHAR BANDYOPADHYAY

OXFORD
UNIVERSITY PRESS

OXFORD

UNIVERSITY PRESS

YMCA Library Building, Jai Singh Road, New Delhi 110001

Oxford University Press is a department of the University of Oxford. It
furthers the University's objective of excellence in research, scholarship, and
education by publishing worldwide in

Oxford New York

Auckland Cape Town Dar es Salaam Hong Kong Karachi
Kuala Lumpur Madrid Melbourne Mexico City Nairobi
New Delhi Shanghai Taipei Toronto

With offices in

Argentina Austria Brazil Chile Czech Republic France Greece
Guatemala Hungary Italy Japan Poland Portugal Singapore
South Korea Switzerland Thailand Turkey Ukraine Vietnam

Oxford is a registered trade mark of Oxford University Press
in the UK and in certain other countries

Published in India
by Oxford University Press, New Delhi

© Oxford University Press 2009

The moral rights of the author have been asserted
Database right Oxford University Press (maker)

First published 2009
Second impression 2010

ISBN-13: 978-0-19-569881-7
ISBN-10: 0-19-569881-9

Typeset in Nalandgaramond by Le Studio Graphique, Gurgoan 122 001
Printed in India by Ram Printograph, Delhi 110 051
Published by Oxford University Press
YMCA Library Building, Jai Singh Road, New Delhi 110 001

To
the memory of my father
Professor Nani Gopal Bandyopadhyay
(1921–2006)
a teacher, a researcher, and a nationalist

Contents

PART III
PEASANTS IN GANDHIAN MASS MOVEMENTS

PART IV
MUSLIM IDENTITY AND POLITICAL PARTICIPATION

PART V
NATION, REGION, AND CASTE

PART VI

WOMEN IN THE NATIONALIST MOVEMENT

PART VII

CAPITALISTS, WORKING CLASSES, AND NATIONALISM

PART VIII

THE RESTLESS FORTIES

Acknowledgements

The editor and the publisher acknowledge the following for permission to include the following articles/extracts in this volume:

People's Publishing House, New Delhi for Bipan Chandra, 'Economic Nationalism', from *The Rise and Growth of Economic Nationalism in India*, 1966, pp. 736–59 and Sumit Sarkar, 'Trends in Bengal's Swadeshi Movement', from *The Swadeshi Movement in Bengal, 1903–1908*, 1973, pp. 31–5.

University of California Press, Berkeley for Eleanor Zelliot, 'Congress and the Untouchables, 1917–1950', from R. Sisson and S. Wolpert (eds), *Congress and Indian Nationalism*, 1988, pp. 182–97.

American Historical Association for Sanjay Seth, 'Rewriting Histories of Nationalism: The Politics of "Moderate Nationalism" in India, 1870–1950', *The American Historical Review*, vol. 104, no. 1, February 1999, pp. 95–116.

Sage Publications India for Tanika Sarkar, 'Politics and Women in Bengal: The Conditions and Meaning of Participation', *The Indian Economic and Social History Review*, vol. 26, no. 1 and Anirudh Deshpande, 'Sailors and Crowd: Popular Protest in Karachi, 1946', *The Indian Economic and Social History Review*, vol. 26, no. 1, pp. 1–27. Both copyright © The Indian Economic and Social History Association, New Delhi, 1988. All rights reserved. Reproduced with permission of the copyright holders and the publishers, Sage Publications India Pvt. Ltd, New Delhi.

Manohar Publishers, New Delhi for Mushirul Hasan, 'The Muslim Breakaway', from his *Nationalism and Communal Politics in India, 1885–1930*, 1991, pp. 282–93; Dwijendra Tripathi, 'Congress and the Industrialist 1885–1947', from his edited, *Business and Politics in India: A Historical Perspective*, 1991, pp. 86–123; and Vinay Bahl, 'Attitude of the Indian National Congress Towards the Working Class Struggle in India, 1918–47', from K. Kumar (ed.), *Congress and Classes: Nationalism, Workers, and Peasants*, 1988, pp. 1–33.

Centre for Studies in Social Sciences, Calcutta for Gyanendra Pandey, 'The Indian Nation in 1942', from his edited, *The Indian Nation in 1942*, K.P. Bagchi & Co., 1988, pp. 1–17.

Asian Studies Association of Australia for Shahid Amin, 'Waiting for the Mahatma', from Robin Jeffrey (ed.), *India: Rebellion to Republic, Selected Writings, 1857–1990*, Sterling Publishers, 1990, pp. 83–96.

Cambridge University Press for Judith Brown, 'The Mahatma and Modern India', *Modern Asian Studies*, 1969, vol. 3, no. 4, reproduced with permission, © Cambridge University Press, pp. 321–42.

Economic and Political Weekly for Madhu Kishwar, 'Gandhi and Women's Role in the Struggle for Swaraj', vol. 20, no. 40, 5 October 1985, pp. 1694–1702; Sumit Sarkar, 'Popular Movements and National Leadership, 1945–47', Annual Number, April 1982, pp. 677–89 and M.S.S. Pandian, '"Denationalising" the Past, "Nation" in E.V. Ramaswamy's Political Discourse', vol. 28, no. 42, pp. 2282–7.

Preface

This book in various forms has been in my mind for a long time—almost since I started teaching history of Indian nationalist movement more than three decades ago. Over these years this field has been enriched by exciting new research, using new methodological tools and exploring new archives, and stoking new debates on theory and ideology of nationalism. In my view what has become clear by now is that Indian nationalism had many faces, as different social groups, classes, and regions responded differently to foreign rule and had different understanding of nationalism. The central aim of this book is to present and highlight this pluralist nature of the Indian nation and its struggle for independence. The essays in this book—some of them classics, others more recent—have been selected to familiarize the readers with these debates, which have been further discussed in details in the introduction. The introduction will also provide a broad historical outline of the nationalist movement in the post-1857 period, highlighting its various complexities and internal contradictions, and contextualizing the essays included in the volume. At the end of it there is a select bibliography to help readers intending to know more about this complex story of the nationalist movement in India.

I have incurred many debts while planning and producing this book. My first and foremost debt is to my students of the last thirty years at the University of Calcutta and Victoria University of Wellington in New Zealand, who have enriched my understanding of Indian nationalism by constantly challenging me to think in different and newer ways. I am also grateful to the staff of the library of the Victoria University of Wellington for their ungrudging help, and to the Faculty of Humanities and Social Sciences of my university for supporting my academic ventures with generous research leave and funding. I am also grateful to Professor Robin Jeffrey and the Research School of Pacific and Asian Studies at the Australian National University for offering me a Visiting Fellowship and thus giving me precious time to organize this book and write the introduction, using the rich South Asia collection of the ANU library. An earlier draft of the first section of the Introduction was presented as my professorial inaugural lecture at Victoria University of Wellington and as a paper at the Humanities Division of the Curtin University of Technology in Perth. I wish to thank all those who made valuable comments.

I am also immensely grateful to all the contributors and their publishers for giving me permission to reprint excerpts from their articles or book chapters. A separate note is added to acknowledge them separately. I would certainly not be able to finish this book on time without the assistance of my former student Craig Watterson—a very warm thank you for him. Finally, I remain immensely grateful to Oxford University Press for encouraging me to compile this collection and then helping me with the publication process.

My family has supported my work in more ways than I can acknowledge here and I need not thank them publicly. I would like to dedicate this book to the memory of my father. He was not just an inspirational figure for me, but with him I incessantly debated the nature of Indian nationalist movement, in which he was a minor participant making a major personal sacrifice. As usual, all the errors are mine.

SEKHAR BANDYOPADHYAY

INTRODUCTION

Nationalist Movement in India
Historiography and History[*]

Sekhar Bandyopadhyay

IN SEARCH OF A NATION

In this age of globalization, ironically, but not unexpectedly, nationalism has once again become a major political force all over the world.
And these recent debates over nation and national identity reveal the
inner contradictions of present-day nation-states. 'The world is divided
into territorial *states*', writes Anthony D. Smith. It is 'similarly divided
into *nations*; that is, named populations possessing a historic similarity,
shared myths and historical memories, a mass, public culture, a single
economy and common rights and duties for all members, which are
legitimized by the principles of *nationalism*'. Smith also observes that
'states, nations and nationalisms do not often coincide ... it is the aim of
all nationalists to create the conditions for a greater congruence between
state, nation and nationalism. In this quest they have been only partly
successful; but this serves merely to spur nationalists to greater efforts'.[1]
It is perhaps fair to argue that this task is even more difficult in postcolonial
nations where ethnic, religious, and linguistic diversities are too firmly
entrenched in history, and the search for 'congruence' can be counter-
productive if pushed too hard, and therefore, we should look for new
ways to conceptualize nation, disentangled from the unitary structures
of nation-states.

In recent years, as consumer goods and labour travel more freely
across the national boundaries, threaten to homogenize our consumption
cultures, and complicate ethnic structures of national communities, there
is a renewed focus on reinventing the 'congruence' between the nation,
nation-state, and national identity. In the countries of the global south
this debate has been sparked by the flooding of goods and cultural

---

[*] An earlier shorter version of the first section of this Introduction was presented
at the Division of Humanities at Curtin University in Perth.

artefacts from the north and in the north it is the influx of labour from the developing countries that has unsettled the established cultural boundaries of nations. Cultural and political anxieties created by such globalizing trends foreground another important fact that nationalism itself was homogenized as a global phenomenon during a previous era of globalization, that is, the era of European imperialism. And not just that, the way the histories of the postcolonial nations have been written bears the continuing evidence of Western intellectual hegemony that puts the modern nation-state at the centre of any historical discussion of nationalism. Instead of that, it can be reasonably argued that the history of the people in these postcolonial societies can be better understood if we give up the futile search for artificial 'congruence between state, nation, and nationalism', and discursively disengage the history of nation from the history of the state. Indian history is a major field where a complex historiography of nationalism has flourished, indicating that different readings of the history of India can suggest a number of alternative ways of conceptualizing nation. However, these alternative possibilities were lost in the modernist project of the western-educated elites of colonial India who were more attracted to the nation-state model of the West. We can discuss here a few of those ideas.

In terms of general theory of nationalism, there is a greater consensus among historians now that nation is a collective mental construct, it is not something naturally given. Benedict Anderson has given us a powerful definition of nation by calling it an 'imagined political community' living in a 'homogenous empty time', and constructed through the influence of print capitalism, that is newspapers and novels, and by such other politico-cultural apparatus of modernity as census, maps, and museums.[2] Eric Hobsbawm has called nationalism an 'invented tradition'.[3] What Anderson, Hobsbawm, and others have done is to unmistakably entangle the history of nationalism with that of modernity. Nationalism is now widely recognized as a 'modern' phenomenon, inspired by Enlightenment and Romanticism, incubated in an economic environment enriched by industrial capitalism and as the product of particular historical processes in Europe in the eighteenth and nineteenth centuries which led to the transformation of the absolutist dynastic empires into democratic nation-states. Nations and nationalism in Europe thus came to be integrally associated with the notions of self-determination, states, and sovereignty. This post-Enlightened European modernity travelled to Asia and Africa through the pathways of empires. But the boundary lines of these new geo-political constructs had very little 'congruence' with the pre-existing lines of ethnic, racial, or religious communities in these continents. It was in this state of historical confusion that the process of nation building started here. The liberal expectation of men like John Stuart Mill was that the colonized people of the empire would get their self-government when they had made sufficient progress in civilization.[4] But neither the Indians waited that long, nor the demission of empires had ever been voluntary, and Afro-Asian nationalisms were born essentially through anti-colonial resistance movements.

But there were problems in imagining nations in these regions, as their own histories differed from those of the European empires. First of all, these empires contained myriad groups of people. In the British Indian Empire, for example, there were numerous languages and castes and two major religious groups, the Hindus and the Muslims, besides a host of other minor religions. Other colonies like British Burma or Malaya, Dutch East Indies or French Indochina had equally diverse populations.[5] If we look at the pre-colonial history of state formation in these regions, what we find is that unlike Europe, sovereignty was not conceptualized as centralized absolute power; it was always shared with the periphery. In the Mughal Empire, as the recent historiography shows, the Emperor negotiated and shared his power with the regional polities.[6] Sugata Bose has recently argued that pre-colonial Indian and the Indian Ocean polities 'had looser, cascading political structures and espoused layered and shared sovereignty with lower level leaders. The formalities of precolonial empire, unlike those of the colonial type, envisioned incorporation, not subordination, of lesser sovereigns, and this distinction was much more than a matter of rituals or political semantics'. In such a political system, it was difficult to imagine firm territorial boundaries of states drawn across the maps. 'A generalised cartographic anxiety over territorial possession', Bose further argues, was new to the area and was spread only through colonialism.[7] There were of course maps in pre-colonial Asia, but the political boundaries were fuzzy and porous, and ever changing. Irfan Habib, the modern cartographer of Mughal India, admits that the administrative and political boundaries of the Mughal Empire were altered so frequently that taking the most recent one gives 'a false picture of exactitude'.[8] As Joseph Schwartzberg has speculated, until the exposure to European cartography in the seventeenth century, fixed boundary lines demarcating named territories for political domination was unknown in South Asia.[9] And therefore, it was hard for peoples to think of themselves as territorially-anchored populations which could become core groups for imagining modern nations.

As for India, many imperial observers like Valentine Chirol believed that India was a 'mere geographical expression'—and one might add, that too was the creation of the British Empire. It was, as Chirol wrote in 1910:

> inhabited by a great variety of nations ... there are far more absolutely distinct languages spoken in India than in Europe; that there are far more profound racial differences between the Maharatta and the Bengalee than between the German and the Portuguese ... and that caste has driven into Indian society lines of far deeper cleavage than any class distinctions that have survived in Europe.[10]

Some of the early Indian nationalists, like Surendranath Banerjea, accepted that and described India as 'a nation in making' (sic).[11] This 'making' process, as Benedict Anderson would suggest, was facilitated by the colonial regime, which brought to the colony Western education and print capitalism and created an intelligentsia who had been crucial to the process of imagining a nation. They were helped by several institutions of the colonial state: colonial cartographers drew their territorial boundaries; the census operations counted them, transforming the 'fuzzy communities' into 'enumerated communities';[12] and the colonial museums reinvented their antiquities. The colonial intelligentsia chose their models, Anderson claimed, from the 'official nationalisms' of European or American histories, which 'were copied, adopted and improved upon'.[13] Even before Benedict Anderson formulated his theory of western influences behind Asian nationalisms in his 1983 book, many historians of Indian nationalism had been writing in this same vein.[14] It is this claim which has been contested in recent historiography.

Partha Chatterjee in his 1993 book observed with sarcasm that if the West crafted our colonial subjection, imagined our anti-colonial resistance, and designed our postcolonial misery, then what was left for us to do? 'Even our imaginations must remain forever colonized', he says.[15] So the question is, in what ways Indian nationalism could claim its difference from the western model? We can address that question by raising several related queries regarding how this nation was imagined. The most important problematic of Indian nationalism was that the nation here did not evidently inhabit the 'homogenous empty time', but rather the 'heterogenous time of modernity', to use Partha Chatterjee's expression. Here the working classes did not internalize the ethos of capitalism and the peasants, even when they participated in nationalist events, had very different understandings of those events derived from their dissimilar life experiences. 'Politics here does not mean the same thing to all people'.[16] In a situation like this where the vast majority of the population were so unevenly touched by modernity, did education and print capitalism play the same role in nation building as envisaged by Anderson or before him by Ernest Gellner?[17] If not, then what was this process and how did it differ from Anderson's modernist rational process of imagination? Second, how did this Indian concept of nation relate to territory and the inherent pluralism of the population contained therein?

To begin with our first question, Chatterjee has sought to answer it by dividing the nation's space into an inner spiritual space where the colonized nation seeks its sovereignty in spite of subjection in the outer public space where it surrenders to Western modular influences.[18] As another postcolonial historian Dipesh Chakrabarty argues, nation is thus spiritually experienced in this inner sphere, rather than mentally or rationally imagined.[19] According to these historians, it was through such modes of spiritual imagination that Indian nationalism could permeate across various levels of popular consciousness. This can be illustrated by looking at the nationalist iconography of *Bharat Mata* or Mother India. Perhaps the first time the idea of Bharat Mata appeared in the public space was through the performance of a play at the Hindu *mela* on 19 February 1873, by a group involving Jyotirindranath and Satyendranath Tagore, Kiran Chandra Banerjee, and Sisir Kumar Ghosh.[20] Then in 1882 Bankim Chandra Chattopadhyay in his Bengali novel *Anandamath* more directly introduced the powerful imagery of the mother goddess into the discourse of nationalism. He painted with emotive words three images of Mother for her disciples—the Mother as she was, Mother as she is, and Mother as she will be and wrote a song 'Hail Mother' (*Bande mataram*) that eventually became the anthem of Indian nationalism. In the Hindu mythology the Mother goddess is imagined in two forms— *Kali* and *Durga*—both representing primal power. Mother is responsible for procreation as well as protection of the world from all evils. The nationalists in the first decade of the twentieth century extensively used this imagery of mother goddess in both these two forms for appealing to the masses. But then in 1905 Abanindranath Tagore, the illustrious nephew of Rabindranath Tagore, drew the famous water colour image entitled 'Bharat Mata', thus introducing a new form of mother goddess now expressly representing the motherland.[21] In the subsequent years this image of Bharat Mata was represented in multiple forms, but most importantly, she was inserted into a map of India, thus explicitly connecting her to the territory and thus transforming, as Sumathi Ramaswamy has argued, the disenchanted cartographic space of India, delineated by colonial rule, into a sacred geo-body of the nation, or motherland, for which her devotees were now expected to give their lives.[22] In the subsequent years these images were reproduced in millions in various art forms, and almost in every regional language songs were written in her praise.[23]

Such imageries are not absolutely rare in the history of nationalism.[24] In India too a significant amount of literature has been produced on this nationalist icon; here we may go into only a selected few. Tanika Sarkar has called Bharat Mata a 'cultural artefact' of nationalism, which also reflected the patriarchal anxieties of a male-dominated colonial society.[25] Indeed, in Tagore's representation mother appears to be more vulnerable—she is no longer the protector but requires protection by her patriotic sons. Sugata Bose on the other hand has argued that Bharat Mata was not an artefact or a rational construct, rather it naturally emanated from a centuries-old Hindu tradition of regarding earth or *Prithvi* as mother. This religio-mythological concept of mother–nature equation was naturally extended to cover motherland.[26] For Dipesh Chakrabarty, this spiritual aesthetic of visualizing nation as a nurturing mother—or this 'seeing beyond the real' is different from the rational or 'mentalist' process of imagination that Anderson speaks of. This iconic representation of nation bridged the gulf between the literate elites and illiterate masses in a way that no print capitalism could ever achieve.[27] Because, as Christopher Pinney has argued, this iconography of Bharat Mata provided 'a space where national feeling can make itself "felt"'.[28]

Yet, other historians like Sumathi Ramaswamy consider Bharat Mata and similar other nationalist imageries as 'products of a modern imagination', which had nothing in common with the Puranic Hindu mythological concepts of Kali, Durga, or Prithvi. In the subsequent representations of Bharat Mata, the way she was dressed up and placed on the map of India, amounted to what Ramaswamy calls 'territorialization of the goddess' or 'somaticization of the motherland'. In it she sees the 'cunning of modernity' as this transforms the nation into a kin group by making all its citizens sons of the same mother.[29] It is a fact that the way Bharat Mata was represented in the later nationalist iconography of the 1940s it is difficult to miss the obvious modernist elements like the flag and the map. But then it will be simplistic to describe this symbolic representation of a spiritual nation as purely modern; more appropriately we should recognize its hybrid nature, because the evidence of cultural alterity in this nationalist imagination is too obvious to miss. There were of course maps, but some of the maps did not even indicate any boundary lines, thus leaving us not with the representation of a territorial nation-state that the British left for us, but with images of a cultural space—the more traditional idea of *'a-samudra-himachal-Bharat Barsha'* (Bharat or India that stretched from the Himalayas to the ocean)—that had been the cradle for an Indian civilization that flourished over centuries.

Such evidence of hybridity could be seen in the use of other more overtly modern symbols of nationhood as well, namely, the 'flag', which was evolving in nationalist imaginary since 1905, acquiring a concrete shape through Gandhi's intervention in 1920, when he inserted the *charkha* (spinning wheel) into the middle of the tricolour flag, in which the saffron and green represented the Hindus and the Muslims respectively, the white standing for all other communities. This was the flag which the Congress adopted in 1931 as the 'national flag', the most modern symbol of national sovereignty, challenging the legitimacy of the Union Jack with the Star of India. However, as Arundhati Virmani has argued, what we also find in this nationalist imaginary is the transformation of 'an ancient implement, characteristic of an Indian culture and economy destroyed by colonial domination, into a powerful symbol of colonial resistance'.[30]

One could argue that it was in this innovative use of culture and civilization as inclusive tropes for nation that Indian nationalism could claim its difference from the Western territorial concept of nation. This broad universalist concept was spelled out more clearly in the early twentieth-century writings of Rabindranath Tagore. In a poem in *Geetanjali*, he described India as a civilization—a meeting ground for various kinds of humanity—rather than simply a country or a territorial unit. In another seminal essay called 'History of India', written in 1902, he argued that India had been subjected to a series of foreign invasions by Greeks, Scythians, Parthians, Shakas, Hunas, Arabs, Persians, Afghans, and Mongols. But many of the foreign invaders eventually embraced this land and in course of time were themselves 'Indianized' and left their mark on Indian art and culture, further enriching its immense diversity. It was in this assimilative power of Indian civilization that India could claim her difference from Europe, because here the idea of 'India' developed more as an inclusive civilizational community, rather than as a political-territorial state. Indeed, the whole of India was never politically unified until the late seventeenth century, as the various regional groups continued to maintain their political autonomy and local patriotism, and continuously fought with each other. Tagore dismisses that 'political' history of territorial warfare as a dark history of nightmares. He privileges instead the other more inclusive history of social assimilation which internalized even the invading outsiders. It was in this assimilative spirit, Tagore argued, that the true essence of Indianness, her national identity was to be found. This essence could not be rationally defined or described, but like life in a body, it needed to be felt or experienced.[31]

Mahatma Gandhi was also developing the idea of a civilizational nation when he was working for the rights of the Indians in South Africa. In *Hind Swaraj* (1909) in response to the question 'Who is the nation?', Gandhi wrote: 'It is only those Indians ... who conscientiously believe that Indian civilisation is the best...' This civilization flourished in a geographical space that was linguistically differentiated. But we learned each other's language, he argued, and visited each other's regions as pilgrims. And this civilization was not exclusive, as he went further: 'The introduction of foreigners does not necessarily destroy the nation, they merge in it. A country is one nation only when such a condition obtains in it.'[32]

One of the stalwart theorists of nationalism, Elie Kedurie has argued that nationalism is a combination of patriotism or love for the country and xenophobia or dislike for outsiders.[33] In other words, it is a process which is inclusive and exclusive at the same time. In this sense Tagore's and Gandhi's concept of nation was certainly different, because here the core of the nation was a civilization, not any 'sacred national ethnos', to borrow an expression from Arjun Appadurai.[34] Ashis Nandy has therefore described them as 'counter-modernist critic(s)' of the imperial West, who offered an alternative model of nationalism and nationhood, which could unite India at a social rather than political level by creatively using this difference.[35] We should remember, however, that neither Tagore nor Gandhi rejected modernity as a package, but made a case for an alternative modernity, which would be modern but not Western.[36] Nor did they reject the idea of nation, but suggested ways to conceptualize it outside the political exclusivity of territorial states. Nandy is however right when he asserts that the educated Indian middle classes and their party, the Indian National Congress, did not accept Tagore and Gandhi's universalist concept of nationhood, and adopted instead the narrower western political model of nation-state. However, this civilizational concept of nation also raises two uncomfortable questions, one about the antiquity of the putative nation, and the other about the limits of the assimilative power of this civilization.

It seems as if Tagore and Gandhi, and after them Jawaharlal Nehru in his book *Discovery of India* (1945), were pushing back the history of the Indian nation to 3000 BCE when the Indus valley civilization flourished in the north-western parts of what constituted British India or at least to 1500 BCE when the *Rig Veda* the earliest text of the Aryan civilization was believed to have been composed. Historians have questioned such retrospective biographies of nation. One of the well known postcolonial historians, Prasenjit Duara, who in 1995 published a book with a provocative title, *Rescuing History from the Nation*, critiqued such formulations as 'teleological model of Enlightenment History' that has tended to give the 'contested and contingent nation' a false sense of history.[37] However, one may argue that what Tagore, Gandhi and Nehru were looking for in the past was not a modern territorial nation, but a pre-modern civilizational core that could transform itself into nationhood.

In European historiography this debate over the antiquity of nation was renewed in 1990 when Walker Connor wrote a seminal essay called 'When is a nation?' reiterating the modernity of the idea. All people who call themselves nations, he argued, acquired their national consciousness in the late nineteenth and early twentieth centuries.[38] This position was contested in 1999 by Anthony Smith who published a new book *Myths and Memories of the Nation* to explore what he called 'the pre-modern bases of nationhood in the earlier manifestations of ethnic community'.[39] His primordialist approach was critiqued by a number of modernist historians and the debate between Smith and his detractors led to a special issue of the journal *Nations and Nationalism* in 2004. What is interesting however is that almost at the same time, and without any reference to the European history debate, a new set of books came out in India questioning the modernity of the Indian nation and trying to trace the pre-colonial roots of Indian nationality.

The discussion on the 'pre-history' of Indian nationalism was initiated by C.A. Bayly in his 1998 book, where he argued that nationalism in India was not a derivative discourse from the West, but rather it built on a pre-existing sense of territoriality, a traditional patriotism rationalized by indigenous ideas of public morality and ethical government.[40] This thread of discussion has been further developed in two recent books, Rajat K. Ray's *The Felt Community: Commonality and Mentality before the Emergence of Indian Nationalism* (2003) and Irfan Habib (ed.), *India—Studies in the History of an Idea* (2004),[41] both of which have tried to trace the etymology of the word 'India' and its indigenous equivalent 'Bharat' and 'Hindustan' and their history of development as a geo-cultural space, rather than a geo-political construct, since at least 1500 BCE, that is the period of the *Rig Veda*. 'A longer view of history',

Ray argued, 'reveals the process by which this civilization effected its transition to nationhood'. An important watershed in this process of transition was the revolt of 1857, when the rebels constantly referred to the people of India as the 'Hindus and Mussulmans of Hindustan'. This was not a modern post-Enlightenment concept of nationalism, Ray agrees, but in it he sees the inchoate ideas of a confederate nation. In his own words, 'It signified a confederation of two separate peoples bound together as one political unit by the shared perception of Hindustan as one land'.[42]

In this idea of confederate nation Indian nationalism could also claim its difference. Indeed this was not an idea that died with the suppression of the revolt of 1857. In the 1890s, as David Lelyveld has shown, Sir Syed Ahmed Khan visualized India as a confederate nation of *qaums* or communities based on common descent, where entitlements and rights would be determined by community identity rather than by the western notion of individual citizenship.[43] Sir Muhammad Iqbal, who is often described as the originator of the idea of Pakistan, said in 1930:

> The units of Indian society are not territorial as in European countries ... The principle of European democracy cannot be applied to India without recognizing the fact of communal groups. The Muslim demand for the creation of a Muslim India within India is, therefore, perfectly justified...[44]

Iqbal in 1930 was not demanding a separate sovereign nation-state for the Muslims or partition of India, but recognition of a confederate nation.

Gandhi too believed in this idea when he gave leadership to the Non-Cooperation–Khilafat Movement in 1920. But he seemed to have changed his vision subsequently to declare that 'we are Indians first and Hindus, Mussulmans, Parsis and Christians after'.[45] Indianness thus does not any more co-exist with, but takes precedence over all other identities. It was 1922 and since then the Indian National Congress whole-heartedly embraced the Western concept of nationhood based on individual citizenship. The ultimate goal of this nationalism was to achieve sovereignty for the Indian nation-state. It was also expected that this nation would speak in one voice, which would provide legitimacy to the nation-state. All other heterogeneous voices that could be allowed by the civilizational or confederate models of nation, were now delegitimized. However, as history of Indian nationalism suggests, it was difficult to muffle all those discordant voices, which questioned not only the official nationalism of the Congress—like the Muslim breakaway politics after 1937—but also the alternative nationalisms as well. Among such dissident voices were those of the Untouchables or the *Dalit* (oppressed) and the regional-linguistic politics of south India.

The Dalit leader Dr B.R. Ambedkar in a hard-hitting treatise in 1936, called *Annihilation of Caste*, questioned the very inclusive nature of Indian civilization. In his perception of history the foundational principle of this civilization was caste exclusion or the *varnashram dharma*, which condemned several million Untouchables into the status of social outsiders in their own land. Tagore and Gandhi accepted that untouchability was a blot on Indian civilization and needed eradication, but they considered it as a distortion or aberration rather than the foundational principle of the civilization.[46] Amdedkar rejected their reformist solution, branding it as a deliberate attempt to obfuscate the real issue of empowering the Dalit, and wrote in 1945 another hard-hitting book *What Congress and Gandhi have Done to the Untouchables*. He was not opposed to *swaraj* or self-rule, but he asked: 'Tell me what share I am to have in the Swaraj'.[47] In other words, he was not questioning Indian nationhood and did not claim a separate sovereign state for the Dalit; he was concerned about their rights of citizenship and their location within the immanent power-structure of the new Indian nation-state. Similarly concerned were the non-Brahmans of western and southern India, the latter in a more articulate way than the former.[48] They believed that the Indian civilization was essentially the Brahmanical culture of north India which spread to the south to subjugate and hegemonize the autochthonous southern Dravidian culture and the Tamil language. In other words, the so-called inclusivism of Indian civilization was actually hegemonic. The language devotion of the Tamils, as Sumathi Ramaswamy has argued, was much more than could be accommodated within the available category of nationalism, but they in the end opted for the existing certitude of linguistic nationalism.[49] Yet, Tamil separatism did not actually claim sovereignty for a separate Tamil land, not withstanding the DMK's radical political rhetoric or metaphoric claims.[50] What they really demanded was recognition of their distinctive voices and culture within the 'nation-space', to use Homi Bhabha's terminology.[51] Besides, as Rick Weiss has argued, while Dravidian movement remained powerful in the urban areas, in the countryside Tamil popular culture and religious practices continued to borrow and perform aspects of Brahmanical religion and Sanskritic culture of the north.[52]

Apart from the distinct voices mentioned above, there were multiple other voices in the history of nationalist movement in India and that makes the application of the standard modern definition of nation problematic. One of the modernist expectations is that, as Walker Connor put it, 'national consciousness is a mass, not an elite phenomenon', and it was not a nation if the 'elites' conception of the nation did not ... extend to the masses'.[53] It takes us back to the question where we had started. In a country where people spoke in so many languages, where the majority of the population were illiterate peasants, where print capitalism did not work effectively to communicate ideas, how would you homogenize the 'elites' conception of nation'? Those who came to see Gandhi in his numerous mass meetings were inspired equally, if not more, by rumours about his supernatural powers, as by his message of non-violence or universal nationalism. They envisioned their own nation, deriving meanings from their day-to-day experiences. Their notion of what it meant to be an Indian most often differed from those of their nationalist leaders.[54] The masses in their millions participated in Congress-led movements for national liberation, but the forms of these movements varied so widely from region to region, that apart from their simultaneity, it is sometimes difficult to recognize them as one movement.[55] If the Congress leaders wanted to achieve a nation-state, their peasant followers often dreamed of a utopian Gandhi Raj, where there would be no taxes, no landlords, no rents, or no moneylenders. Bharat Mata became a hybrid symbol of this nationalism. As Jawaharlal Nehru found it, however much he would prefer to see a secular modern nation in India, his rural followers would still be defining nation in religious terms or would be in immense difficulty when asked what their Bharat Mata actually stood for.[56] This nation and its nationalism therefore defy the modernist definition based on the experiences of European history.

So how do we resolve this conceptual problem? Aditya Nigam has recently argued that 'in a sense, the project of Indian nationhood was/is an impossible project. For nations, if they are to be nations, must become so by creating a homogenous cultural identity'.[57] And homogenous certainly it was not, and so G. Aloysius has talked about *Nationalism Without a Nation.*[58] On the other hand, sociologists S.L. Sharma and T.K. Oommen have defined India as a 'multi-national state'.[59] Both these positions assume that a nation has to be homogenous and it has to speak in one voice—otherwise, it is not a nation. Sunil Khilnani recognizes that Indian nationalism was not homogenous, but plural—'a dhoti with endless folds'. Behind this expression there is an obvious assumption that all those folds arise from the same piece of cloth—which is its underlying unity, 'the idea of India'. In other words, he too is looking for underlying unity because the nation needs to be put into the mould of a nation-state. For Khilnani this unity lay in the common democratic experience shared by all sections of the Indian population.[60] But in India democracy functioned at many levels in the political life of the nation: to use Homi Bhabha's discursive categories, one was the 'pedagogic' level of the educated elites and the other the 'performative' level of the masses.[61] In view of such complexities, Ramchandra Guha has recently described India as an 'Unnatural Nation'. It is '*un*natural' because it does not fit into any available political models derived from the experience of European history.[62] But it is a nation nonetheless.

So we need to conceptualize nation in a different way—as a nation with many voices. If we discursively disengage the history of the nation from the history of the state, then we need not expect that a nation has to speak in only one voice and should have a homogenized identity, which is required to provide legitimacy to the state. This disengagement will allow us to recognize the multiple voices of a nation. This recognition will not endanger the state; as Gyan Pandey has argued, to talk about the fragments is not to advocate the fragmentation of India.[63] Because, not all of these voices claim sovereignty, they only seek recognition within the broader 'nation-space'. In other words, instead of searching for a homogenous nation, or its underlying unity, we should celebrate its diversity; we should consider nation—to use Ania Loomba's expression— as 'a ground of dispute and debate, a site for the competing imaginings of different ideological and political interests'.[64] It is indeed this recognition of 'competing imaginings' that can take us away from the known trajectories of European history trying to discover homogenous nations within the constrictive perimeters of nation-states. As Sanjay Seth argues in his essay in this book, it is time that we 'embrace the possibility of many histories, and thus also of many ways of being Indian'.[65] It is only by recognizing these 'many histories' that we will be able to avoid the risk of homogenizing a majoritarian discourse of national identity. This is not to advocate or foretell the demise of nation-states; but in the twenty-first century, instead of nations being homogenized to fit into the unitary structures of nation-states, as Gurpreet Mahajan has advised, the 'nation-states [will] have to learn to live with diversity; they have to innovate and think of ways in which different communities may co-exist as equals'.[66]

NATIONALIST MOVEMENT AND THE COMPETING IMAGININGS

In this scenario, the historian's challenge is to find the abstract notion of a pluralist nation in the actual empirical history of its struggle for liberation and selfhood. The nationalist movement in India has been described as 'one of the biggest mass movements (sic) modern society has ever seen'.[67] But, as we have discussed above, the Indian masses were never a homogeneous entity and nationalism had different meanings for different groups of people. These competing perceptions and aspirations were actually reflected in a nationalist movement, which we usually conceptualize as 'one' movement acting as a ground for breeding homogeneity. The central theme of this nationalist movement was a contingent political unity against colonial rule, yet persistent resistance to any elision of the distinctiveness of its various constitutive elements and differences in their sense of history. In other words, Indian nationalism represented the myriad voices of different social groups, classes and regions, which responded differently but conjointly to foreign rule from their variegated understanding of nationhood. There were indeed many movements, which we usually group together under one rubric, either for analytical convenience or for political expediency. The essays selected for this anthology will explore this multifaceted process of nation-building in colonial India by highlighting certain major themes.

When did modern nationalism begin in India? This is a subject of major controversy. Not ignoring the importance of the recent debates on the pre-history of nationalism and the historicity of the concept of 'India', which have been briefly alluded to in the preceding section, and the extensive re-examination of the revolt of 1857 by Gautam Bhadra, Ranajit Guha, Rudrangshu Mukherjee, Rajat Ray,[68] and others in recent years,[69] we will begin with the conventional wisdom that nationalism in a 'modern' sense began to appear from the late nineteenth century with a growing sense of selfhood, with an accompanying demand not to get rid of British rule, but to have a greater share in the governance of their own country. In view of this professed 'loyalism'—both as a strategy and as a matter of faith—whether or not this politics should at all be labelled as 'nationalist' is a legitimate question that Sanjay Seth has raised in his essay in this book. However, this was only one trend visible among an emergent middle class that had been organizing political protests against certain specific aspects of colonial rule and were seeking to construct a modern nation on the European model. Side by side, there have always been parallel trends of peasant movements which rejected the colonial state, its new legal apparatus, and its new posse of oppressive agents. Although these two strands were never two hermetically sealed autonomous domains of politics, the major challenge of the Indian nationalist leaders was to reconcile the contradictions arising from this apparent hiatus. Because, for them, for a nation to be legitimate in a European sense, the elite's ideas needed to be extended to the masses.

But first, were these educated middle classes just imitating a Western model or could they also imagine their own autonomous domain of sovereignty? Partha Chatterjee's chapter in this book argues that the process of the nation's imagining its own cultural domain of autonomy started long before its political movement began in 1885. He strongly refutes the idea of 'modular influences' of the West in conceptualizing the nation, and as it has already been mentioned above, has suggested the existence of an inner spiritual domain where the nation was already sovereign, despite its surrender to colonial rule and its modernizing influences in the public domain. Whether or not we can compartmentalize the life of a nation into two autonomous domains precluding possibilities of interaction and interfaces is open to question. But there is a greater consensus now among historians across the political spectrum that the early nationalists were trying to imagine a modern nation, but that modernity was to be rooted firmly in a reinvented tradition that would mark out their difference from the domineering presence of a colonial rule.[70] They could not visualize complete separation from the empire, even some of them believed in the providential nature of colonial rule as the harbinger of modernity; yet, their most important contribution was the formulation of an economic critique of colonialism, which Bipan Chandra's chapter in this book discusses. The historical veracity of their 'drain theory' and the concept of 'deindustrialization' have come under close scrutiny in recent years,[71] but have not been discarded yet as totally fictive. However, more important is the historical context of this economic critique, which raised questions about colonial rule being unmixed blessing for the Indians and this questioning of the notion of improvement, however limited that might be, weakened the very ideological foundations of the Raj.

However, these early Congress leaders—or 'Moderates'—also suffered from ideological dilemmas which prevented them from transforming this economic critique into a full-scale attack on the colonial rule. Sanjay Seth in his chapter discusses these dilemmas of moderate politics. Modesty of goals and moderation of aims, as well as their loyalism and faith in the western model of development as the prescribed path for India's escape from poverty, were some of the characteristic features of this politics. But what made this politics 'moderate', argues Seth, was their conscious acceptance of the hiatus between the elites and the masses, or in their imagining a nation which included people—the masses—who were not yet considered to be ready, in terms of education, for the enjoyment of self-government, and were therefore to be represented by their elite countrymen.

However, the non-elites of India—the peasants and the tribals—had their own understanding of colonial rule, arising from their grievances against its land revenue policies, legal system, new property relations, forest and game laws that resulted in either their loss of occupancy rights in land or exclusion from their natural habitats and natural rights in the resources of the forests and the consequent sense of loss of their familiar world. This often resulted in violent fracas with the colonial regimes or against its more localized hierarchies of power, represented by the new agents of oppression, for example, the planters, *zamindar*s (landlords) and *sahukar*s (moneylenders). In the second half of the nineteenth century the educated metropolitan elites often sympathized with the peasants and often tried to connect their localized movements to the broader arenas of organized politics, as it happened during the indigo rebellion (1859–60) and the Pabna riots (1873) in Bengal[72] or the Deccan riots in Maharashtra (1875).[73] But these educated middle classes, wedded as they were to the western idea of capitalist development, did not want to see their familiar world turned upside down through violent peasant upsurges. Their influence therefore was often of a moderating nature and did not result in anything more than limited reforms. Their political demand for greater Indian representation in the governance of their country was also largely ignored by the colonial government and it was this failure which led to the emergence of an 'Extremist' critique of Moderate politics in the late nineteenth century.

This Extremist politics became powerful in three regions, Bengal, Maharashtra, and Punjab, but they too did not ultimately succeed in bridging the political gap with the masses, despite their reliance on Hindu revivalist trends and the overt and extensive use of Hindu symbols like mother goddess in Bengal,[74] cow in north India,[75] or Lord Ganapati in Maharashtra[76]—as means to communicate with their uneducated masses. An ideal example of how they tried to overcome their ideological dilemmas is the Swadeshi movement in Bengal. As Sumit Sarkar points out in the chapter included in this book, it started in response to the arrogant administration of Lord Curzon, but more particularly to his decision to partition Bengal in 1905. It was initiated by the Moderates, who gave a call for the boycott of British goods; this was indeed their first attempt to reach out to people outside the ranks of the educated classes. However, it was soon taken over by the Extremists, but extremism here had two distinct trends: one was the non-political trend of constructive work for the development of *atmasakti* through *samitis* or local associations and the other was political Extremism that focussed primarily on passive resistance and boycott of British goods and institutions and developing their swadeshi or indigenous alternatives. In this way they anticipated Gandhian mass movements, of course, without Gandhi's insistence on non-violence. But in the end, despite their heavy reliance on Hindu symbols, the movement failed to appeal to either the Muslim and Dalit peasants of eastern Bengal[77] or the urban working classes, and by 1908 lapsed into terrorist violence, which did not need a mass following, but only a few dedicated volunteers. The hiatus between the nationalism of the educated elites and the politics of the uneducated masses thus remained there as an uncomfortable reminder of the lack of homogeneity in India's nationalist movement. The Home Rule Leagues, started in 1916 by Annie Besant in Madras and by Bal Gangadhar Tilak in Maharashtra, made further attempts to mobilize the masses, but with no appreciable success.[78]

So we had to wait for the arrival of Mahatma Gandhi from South Africa in 1915 for a long desired transformation of the political nation through an expansion of its mass base. But how did the common people interpret his message and why did they—particularly, the peasants and the tribals—respond to his appeal are some of the contentious issues of the historiography of Indian nationalism. Judith Brown on the one hand has emphasized Gandhi's effective role as a 'mediator' between competing groups of leaders and masses, and the contribution made by the local leaders—Gandhi's 'subcontractors'—in mobilizing the people from the top. Shahid Amin on the other hand has argued about the numerous ways the masses interpreted their Gandhi—his spiritual appeal, his occult powers, and his symbolism as a beacon of hope for the empowerment of the powerless. The local leaders had limited control over this mass imagination of their Gandhi maharaj and on how they would respond to him or why often they would cross the limits of Gandhian politics at different stages. Indeed, several articles in this book (by Hardiman, Ray, Arnold, and Stoddart), show how diverse were the movements that are often analytically and somewhat arbitrarily clustered together under the broad category of Gandhian movement. From the Rowlatt Satyagraha of 1919 through the Non-cooperation–Khilafat movements of 1921–2 to the Civil Disobedience movement of 1929–34, Gandhi organized several rounds of mass movements, where the peasants and tribals participated from a variety of motivations, ranging from scarcity and high prices of daily necessities, local grievances about municipal politics or temple management, the fate of the Ottoman emperor, forced labour, restrictive forest laws, or high land revenue demands. Along with people's motivations, the intensity of the movements varied widely from region to region. Yet, everything happened in Gandhi's name and this became amply clear by the time of the Quit India movement of 1942. As Gyanendra Pandey argues, in this movement everything happened in his name, yet he had so little control over what actually happened. In other words, what appears in nationalist teleology as one homogenous movement leading to the birth of a nation-state in 1947 had actually within it several distinct strands. They all fought for the liberation of 'India', but what it meant to be an Indian as well as the meaning of liberation differed widely among various groups of her future subject-citizens.

This main story, where the centre stage was always taken by the Indian National Congress, need not be taken as the only story of Indian nationalist movement. For, as Partha Sarathi Gupta reminded his colleagues in his Presidential Address at the Indian History Congress in 1998, we should 'not equate the history of one all-India party with the history of the nation'.[79] There were also several other side stories in the history of nationalist movement in India, involving groups whose interests and concerns remained peripheral to the thoughts of the Congress leaders who proposed to define the nation for them. There were social groups which looked at nationalism from different perspectives, such as the Muslims who represented the only dissenting voice that demanded sovereignty, but not until the very end of colonial rule. Why were they alienated from the mainstream nationalism of the Congress, and why their community-centric anxieties got stigmatized and 'othered' as 'communalism' are issues discussed here by Mushirul Hasan and Ayesha Jalal. What we witness in India after the demise of the Khilafat movement in around 1924 is the emergence of a religiously informed cultural identity politics among the Muslims on the one hand and a more aggressive variety of religious nationalism among the Hindus, as espoused by the formation of the All India Hindu Mahasabha and the Rashtriya Swayam Sevak Sangh.[80] Congress's inability to maintain a distance from the Hindu cultural nationalism and its obduracy against sharing power with the Muslims after the election of 1937 led to Muslim anxiety about being dominated by a majoritarian rule. How this precipitated the partition of India remains outside the ambit of this book, as already there exists an excellent reader on this theme, edited by Mushirul Hasan.[81] We may only mention here that the journey of the Muslims from their modest demand for 'a Muslim India within India' in 1930 to the declaration of separate nationhood in 1940 and the achievement of a sovereign state in 1947 was long and complicated. And as Achin Vanaik has argued, 'the Congress-led National Movement cannot escape most of the responsibility' for this alienation of the Muslims of India.[82] The chapters by Hasan and Jalal in this book look at some of the aspects of this alienation process from different historiographical viewpoints.

The non-Brahman and the Dalit concerns for citizenship as opposed to Congress's obsession with sovereignty constitute complex themes of Indian nationalist movement. In Tamil Nadu, as the Justice Party, which initially proposed to represent the non-Brahmans, began to lose interest in the reform agenda and its popularity declined after its spectacular victory at the election of 1920. But its place was taken over by the more radical Self-respect movement that started in 1926 and the Dravida Kazhagam founded in 1944. E.V. Ramasamy, the leader of both these movements, offered an alternative ideology of nationalism, as M.S.S. Pandian argues in his chapter. Freed from the nationalism versus colonialism binary, he privileged the notion of equal and substantive citizenship for the subordinate groups of Indian society—the Sudras, Dalits, and women. Instead of locating the nation in the past or in the history of what he thought to be the Brahmanical civilization of the north, he placed his nation in the anticipatory mode of relentless struggle for the emancipation of the subordinate groups. This 'Dravidian' politics was not restricted by any notion of territoriality, but raised a millenarian hope of a society freed of caste and gender discrimination.[83]

The Dalit oppositional politics which came to be symbolized by a confrontation between Ambedkar and Gandhi has been discussed in this book by Eleanor Zelliot. Ambedkar and his followers' lukewarm responses to mainstream nationalist movement were not because they were against *swaraj*, but because they were more concerned about claiming their rights of citizenship, which the Congress failed to guarantee, despite Gandhi's reformist endeavours. Congress from the very beginning avoided social issues like untouchability which could be divisive for an incipient nation. And if Gandhi foregrounded the issue of untouchability, his secular followers attached little importance to this cause and Gandhi's religious approach to the question failed to satisfy the concerns of the Dalit leaders who wanted to see Dalit empowerment through a political solution of the problem. At the dawn of independence Ambedkar's appointment as the Chair of the constitution drafting committee and the new constitution outlawing untouchability signified a brief moment of harmony, but that as we all know was short-lived, indicating an unresolved issue of nation-building.

Gandhi's intervention, as Madhu Kishwar's chapter tells us, also brought in significant developments in terms of women's active citizenship through participation in the struggle for liberation of their nation. Yet, as Tanika Sarkar argues, this participation in Gandhian movements and the politicization of some women, mostly urban but also some belonging to middle peasant castes, did not lead to any social emancipation of women in India because of the very overt religious orientation of the way that role was conceptualized. However, it is also true that although the majority of women remained within the socially constituted boundaries, a few women were rewriting the history of liberation by participating in terrorist movements, in communist-led peasant movements, or simply by silently pushing the boundary of feminine behaviour sanctioned by the nationalist patriarchy.[84] Yearning for freedom thus had different ramifications for different groups of people.

This difference is also manifested in the stories of the two new emergent classes in Indian society, namely the Indian capitalists and the industrial working classes. The Indian businessmen, as the chapter by Dwijendra Tripathi shows, did not completely embrace the Congress and its particular variety of nationalist ideology, particularly as they feared the rise of socialism; yet they kept strategic relationships with it and participated in the Congress movements as and when it suited their specific class interests. In other words, they had their own visions and strategies of liberation, which sometimes coincided with those of the Congress, sometimes it did not.[85] The industrial working classes on the other hand, as Vinay Bahl argues, always proved a problem for the Congress leaders trying to mobilize the masses without endangering their preferred broad nationalist coalition in which the capitalists had become a major partner by the mid-1920s. Gandhi's theory of 'trusteeship' and his preference for a harmonious capital–labour relationship created problems in the way of mobilizing industrial workers in support of the nationalist movement. As a result, the interests of the workers were often sacrificed in the interest of the nation. However, as Rajnarayan Chandavarkar has shown in his two seminal books, the workers too participated in the nationalist movement, often garnering it to strengthen their own struggles for better wages and conditions. In other words, their participation was on their own terms, in spite of the ambivalent attitudes of the Congress high command, particularly after the 1930s.[86]

   This pluralism of the Indian nationalist movement becomes even more glaring when we focus on the mass movements of the late 1940s—many of them taking place outside the organizational structures of the Congress—creating a political context that forced the Raj to expedite the transfer of power.[87] In the wake of the Quit India movement (1942), when the conservative leaders once again took control over the Congress and were looking forward to the real possibilities of a peaceful transfer of power, the INA [Indian National Army] trials in Delhi and the outbursts of popular protest all over India, the RIN [Royal Indian Navy] mutiny, the strikes in the RAF [Royal Air Force], the communist-led violent peasant movements in Bengal (Tebhaga) and Telengana turned India into a boiling cauldron of popular unrest. As Sumit Sarkar argues in his chapter, the volatile political environment of the period was too much for the Congress leadership to handle, which was fast becoming the new Raj and was not willing to risk another round of mass movement and the uncertainties involved in it. They were now more eager to negotiate for freedom.

   Anirudh Deshpande's chapter in this book presents a detailed case study of one such outburst of popular protest in the city of Karachi in the wake of the naval mutiny that started in Bombay but then spread to many other port cities. It shows how rumours galvanized an irate crowd into attacking some of the more prominent symbols of alien rule and thus challenging the Raj in the last days of its precarious existence. Yet, in the same city almost simultaneously another form of mass mobilization along religious lines was taking place, resulting in a few months' time in Karachi becoming a part of Pakistan. In other words, Karachi in 1946 represented both the mass power as well as the contradictions of the Indian nationalist movement. When freedom finally arrived, the euphoria and rituals of independence—the celebration of the coming of the nation-state—were marred by the pain, agony, and melancholy associated with partition and the accompanying violence. These experiences of partition have been studied in several recent publications,[88] but for reasons mentioned earlier, they remain outside the purview of the present volume.

   The central aim of this book is to present and highlight the pluralist nature of the Indian nation and its struggle for independence. 'British Indian empire', wrote Partha Sarathi Gupta, 'was conducive to securing the greatest measure of anti-imperial consensus'.[89] But the struggle against it did not resolve all the debates and conflicts within the putative nation, and in independent India, as Ramchandra Guha has recently reminded us, there remained several 'axes of conflict', namely, caste, religion, language, class, and gender. Yet, disproving doomsday predictions of many political pundits, India has survived as one nation, because it has respected this pluralism.[90] Indeed, the nation became vulnerable only at those historical conjunctures when there had been attempts to impose or universalize any majoritarian discourse of nationalism. This theme and the associated issues outlined above are subjects of intense controversy and debate. The essays in this book—some of them classics, others more recent—have been selected to provide a comprehensive view of the debates on different aspects of the pluralist nature of the Indian nation and its struggle for independence.

Notes

1. Anthony D. Smith, 'Theories of Nationalism: Alternative models of nation formation', in Michael Leifer (ed.), *Asian Nationalism*, London, Routledge, 2000, p. 1.
2. Benedict Anderson, *Imagined Communities: Reflections on the Origins and Spread of Nationalism*, London, New York, Verso, new edition, 2006 (first published 1983).
3. Eric Hobsbawm, 'Introduction: Inventing Traditions', in Eric Hobsbawm and Terence Ranger (eds), *The Invention of Tradition*, Cambridge, Cambridge University Press, 1983.
4. See Eric Stokes, *English Utilitarians and India*, Oxford, Clarendon, 1959, pp. 298–9.
5. For Southeast Asia, see Nicholas Tarling, *Southeast Asia: A Modern History*, Melbourne, Oxford University Press, 2001, pp. 360–96.
6. See Muzaffar Alam and Sanjay Subramanyam (eds), *The Mughal State, 1526–1750*, New Delhi, Oxford University Press, 1998.
7. Sugata Bose, *A Hundred Horizons: The Indian Ocean in the Age of Global Empire*, Cambridge, Mass., London, Harvard University Press, pp. 43, 55–6, 69–70.
8. Irfan Habib, *An Atlas of the Mughal Empire*, New Delhi, Oxford University Press, 1982, p. X.
9. Joseph E. Schwartzberg, 'South Asian Cartography', in J.B. Harley and D. Woodsward (eds), *Cartography in the Traditional Islamic and South Asian Societies*, Chicago, Chicago University Press, 1992, pp. 408–9, cited in Sumathi Ramaswamy, 'Visualising India's geo-body: Globes, maps, bodyscapes', in S. Ramaswamy (ed.), *Beyond Appearances? Visual Practices and Ideologies in Modern India*, New Delhi, Thousand Oaks; London, Sage Publications, 2003, p. 160.
10. Quoted in Rajat K. Ray, 'Three interpretations of Indian nationalism', in B.R. Nanda (ed.), *Essays in Modern Indian History*, New Delhi, Oxford University Press, 1980, p. 37, n. 3.

11. Surendranath Banerjea, *A Nation in Making: Being the Reminiscences of Fifty Years of Public Life*, London, Oxford University Press, 1925

12. I take these terms from Sudipto Kaviraj, 'The Imaginary Institution of India', in P. Chatterjee and G. Pandey (eds), *Subaltern Studies VII: Writings on South Asian History and Society*, New Delhi, Oxford University Press, 1993, pp. 1–39.

13. Benedict Anderson, *Imagined Communities*, ch. 7, quotation from p. 140

14. See for details, Rajat Ray, 'Three interpretations'; for a more recent account of this historiography, see Sekhar Bandyopadhyay, *From Plassey to Partition: A History of Modern India*, New Delhi, Orient Longman, 2004, pp. 184–91.

15. Partha Chatterjee, *The Nation and Its Fragments: Colonial and Postcolonial Histories*, Princeton, Princeton University Press, 1993, p. 5.

16. Partha Chatterjee, *The Politics of the Governed: Reflections on Popular Politics in Most of the World*, New Delhi, Permanent Black, 2004, pp. 7, 12.

17. Ernest Gellner, 'Nationalism and Modernization', in John Hutchinson and Anthony D. Smith (eds), *Nationalism*, Oxford, New York, Oxford University Press, 1994, pp. 55–63.

18. Partha Chatterjee, *The Nation and Its Fragments*.

19. Dipesh Chakrabarty, *Provincializing Europe: Postcolonial Thought and Historical Difference*, Princeton and Oxford, Princeton University Press, 2000, pp. 172–9.

20. Christopher Pinney, '"A secret of their own country": Or, how Indian nationalism made itself irrefutable', in S. Ramaswamy (ed.), *Beyond Appearances? Visual Practices and Ideologies in Modern India*, New Delhi, Thousand Oaks, London, Sage Publications, 2003, p. 125.

21. Tapati Guha-Thakurta, *The Making of a New 'Indian' Art: Artists, Aesthetics and Nationalism in Bengal, c. 1850–1920*, Cambridge, Cambridge University Press, 1992, p. 255.

22. Sumathi Ramaswamy, 'Visualising India's geo-body', pp. 152–89.

23. For a recent comprehensive discussion on this art form, see Erwin Neumayer and Christine Schelberger, *Bharat Mata: India's Freedom Movement in Popular Art*, New Delhi, Oxford University Press, 2007.

24. A lot of studies have been done on Marianne of France. See for example, Maurice Agulhon, *Marianne into Battle: Republican Imagery and Symbolism in France, 1789–1880*, Trans. Janet Lloyd. Cambridge, Cambridge University Press, 1980.

25. Tanika Sarkar, 'Nationalist Iconography: Image of Women in 19th Century Bengali Literature', *Economic and Political Weekly*, 21 November 1987, 22 (47), p. 2011.

26. Sugata Bose, 'Nation as Mother: Representations and Contestations of "India" in Bengali Literature and Culture', in Sugata Bose and Ayesha Jalal (eds), *Nationalism, Democracy and Development: State and Politics in India*, New Delhi, Oxford University Press, 1997, p. 54.

27. Dipesh Chakrabarty, *Provincializing Europe*, pp. 174–5.

28. Christopher Pinney, '"A secret of their own country"', p. 142.

29. Sumathi Ramaswamy, 'The Goddess and the Nation: Subterfuges of Antiquity, the Cunning of Modernity', in G. Flood (ed.), *The Blackwell Companion to Hinduism*, Oxford, Blackwell Publishing, 2003.

30. Arundhati Virmani, 'National Symbols under Colonial Domination: The Nationalization of the Indian Flag, March–August 1923', *Past and Present*, 164, August, 1999, pp. 171, 178, 180.

31. Rabindranath Tagore, '*Bharatbarsher itihas*', Bhadra 1309 [1902], *Chirantan Rabindra Rachanabali*, CD-ROM version.

32. M.K. Gandhi, *Hind Swaraj and Other Writings*, edited by Anthony J. Parel, Cambridge, Cambridge University Press, 1997, pp. 52, 115–16.

33. Elie Kedurie, 'Nationalism and Self-determination', in John Hutchinson and Anthony D. Smith (eds), *Nationalism*, Oxford, New York, Oxford University Press, 1994, pp. 49–50.

34. Arjun Appadurai, *Fear of Small Numbers: An Essay on the Geography of Anger*, Durham, Duke University Press, 2006.

35. Ashis Nandy, *The Illegitimacy of Nationalism: Rabindranath Tagore and the Politics of Self*, New Delhi, Oxford University Press, 1994.

36. For a discussion on Gandhi's idea of 'alternative modernity', see David Hardiman, *Gandhi: In His Time and Ours*, New Delhi, Permanent Black, 2003, ch. 4.

37. Prasenjit Duara, *Rescuing History From the Nation: Questioning Narratives of Modern China*, Chicago and London, Chicago University Press, 1995, p. 4.

38. Walker Connor, 'When is a nation?', *Ethnic and Racial Studies*, 13 (1), 1990, pp. 92–103.

39. Anthony D. Smith, *Myths and Memories of the Nation*, Oxford, Oxford University Press, 1999; 'History and National Destiny', *Nations and Nationalism*, 10 (1/2), 2004, pp. 195–209, quotation from p. 196.

40. C.A. Bayly, *Origins of Nationality in South Asia: Patriotism and Ethical Government in the Making of Modern India*, New Delhi, Oxford University Press, 1998.

41. Rajat K. Ray's *The Felt Community: Commonality and Mentality before the Emergence of Indian Nationalism*, New Delhi, Oxford University Press, 2003; Irfan Habib (ed.) *India—Studies in the History of an Idea*, New Delhi, Munshiram Manoharlal, 2004.

42. Rajat K. Ray, *The Felt Community*, pp. 537, 543, 545.

43. See, David Lelyveld, *Aligarh's First Generation: Muslim Solidarity in British India*, Princeton, NJ, Princeton University Press, 1978.

44. Quoted in Syed Sharifuddin Pirzada, *Evolution of Pakistan*, Lahore, The All-Pakistan Legal Decisions, 1963, pp. 123–4.

45. See, Gyanendra Pandey, *The Construction of Communalism in Colonial North India*, New Delhi, Oxford University Press, 1990, p. 233 and passim.

46. For discussion on Tagore's ideas on caste, see Sekhar Bandyopadhyay, *Caste, Politics and the Raj: Bengal 1872–1937*, Calcutta, K.P. Bagchi & Co., 1990; for discussion on Gandhi's ideas on caste and untouchablity, see Bhikhu Parekh, *Colonialism, Tradition and Reform: An Analysis of Gandhi's Political Discourse*, New Delhi, Newbury Park, London, Sage Publications, 1989.

47. Quoted in Gail Omvedt, *Dalits and the Democratic Revolution: Dr Ambedkar and the Dalit Movement in Colonial India*, New Delhi, Thousand Oaks, London, Sage Publications, 1994, p. 216. For more on Ambedkar's philosophy, see M.S. Gore, *The Social Context of an Ideology: Ambedkar's Political and Social Thought*, New Delhi, Thousand Oaks, London, Sage Publications, 1993.

48. The non-Brahman movement in Maharashtra began its career in 1873 on a radical dissident note through the formation of the Satya Sodhak Samaj under the leadership of Jyotiba Phule. However, in 1938 the movement merged with the Congress, providing the latter with a broad mass base. See Rosalind O'Hanlon, *Caste, Conflict and Ideology: Mahatma Jotirao Phule and Low Caste Protest in Nineteenth Century Western India*, Cambridge, Cambridge University Press, 1985; Gail Omvedt, *Cultural Revolt in a Colonial Society: The Non Brahman Movement in Western India: 1873 to 1930*, Bombay, Scientific Socialist Education Trust, 1976.

49. See, Sumathi Ramaswamy, *Passions of the Tongue: Language Devotion in Tamil India, 1891–1970*, Berkeley, University of California Press, 1997.

50. See, Eugene Irschick, *Politics and Social Conflict in South India: Non-Brahman Movement and Tamil Separatism, 1916–29*, Berkeley and Los Angeles, University of California Press, 1969.

51. Homi Bhabha, 'DissemiNation: Time, Narrative, and the Margins of the Modern Nation', in H. Bhabha (ed.), *Nation and Narration*, London and New York, Routledge, 1990, pp. 291–322.

52. See, Rick Weiss, 'The Limits of Inventing Tradition: The Dravidian Movement in South India', *Australian Religious Studies Review*, 20 (1), 2007, pp. 59–75.

53. Walker Connor, 'The timelessness of nations', *Nations and Nationalism* 10 (1/2), 2004, p. 41.

54. For a discussion on how the Indian masses interpreted the Gandhian message, see Shahid Amin, *Event, Metaphor, Memory: Chauri Chaura 1922–92*, New Delhi, Oxford University Press, Paperback edition, 1996.

55. Some of the recent regional studies on nationalist movement are Gyanesh Kudaisya, *Region, Nation and 'Heartland': Uttar Pradesh in India's Body Politic*, New Delhi, Thousand Oaks, London, Sage Publications, 2006; D.E.U. Baker, *Baghelkhand, or the Tigers Lair Region and the Nation in Indian History*, New Delhi, Oxford University Press, 2007. These regional variations have also been shown in details in Sekhar Bandyopadhyay, *From Plassey to Partition*.

56. Jawaharlal Nehru, *The Discovery of India*, New Delhi, Jawaharlal Nehru Memorial Fund/Oxford University Press, 2002 [first published 1946], p. 60.

57. Aditya Nigam, *The Insurrection of Little Selves: The Crisis of Secular-Nationalism in India*, New Delhi, Oxford University Press, 2006, p. 16.

58. G. Aloysius, *Nationalism without a Nation in India*, New Delhi, Oxford University Press, 1997.

59. S.L. Sharma and T.K. Oommen (eds), *Nation and National Identity in South Asia*, New Delhi, Orient Longman, 2000.

60. Sunil Khilnani, *The Idea of India*, London, Hamish Hamilton, 1997, pp. 6ff.

61. See Homi Bhabha, 'DissemiNation'.

62. Ramchandra Guha, *India after Gandhi: The History of the World's Largest Democracy*, London, Macmillan, 2007, pp. xvii, xxi, 744–57, 771.

63. Gyanendra Pandey, *Routine Violence: Nations, Fragments, Histories*, Stanford, Cal., Stanford University Press, 2006, pp. 45–9.

64. Ania Loomba, *Colonialism/Postcolonialism*, London and New York, Routledge, 1998, p. 207.

65. For reasons of space many parts of this essay have been cut out from this book, including this passage. Readers may look at the original essay: Sanjay Seth, 'Rewriting Histories of Nationalism: The Politics of "Moderate Nationalism" in India, 1870–1905', *The American Historical Review*, 104(1), February 1999, pp. 95–116.

66. Gurpreet Mahajan, 'Reinventing Democratic Citizenship in a Plural Society', in M. Hasan and A. Roy (eds), *Living Together Separately: Cultural India in History and Politics*, New Delhi, Oxford University Press, 2005, p. 115.

67. Bipan Chandra, *India's Struggle for Independence*, New Delhi, Penguin Books, 1989, p. 13.

68. Gautam Bhadra, 'Four Rebels of Eighteen-Fifty-Seven', in R. Guha (ed.), *Subaltern Studies IV: Writings on South Asian History and Society*, New Delhi, Oxford University Press, 229–75; Ranajit Guha, *Elementary Aspects of Peasant Insurgency in Colonial India*, New Delhi, Oxford University, second impression, 1994; Rudrangshu Mukherjee, *Spectre of Violence: The 1857 Kanpur Massacres*, New Delhi, Viking, 1998.

69. The 150th anniversary of the revolt has resulted in the publication of several volumes on the subject. See for example, Sabyasachi Bhattacharya (ed.), *Rethinking 1857*, New Delhi, Orient Longman Ltd 2007; Biswamoy Pati (ed.), *The 1857 Rebellion*, New Delhi, Oxford University Press, 2007; *1857: Essays from Economic and Political Weekly*, New Delhi, Orient Longman Ltd 2008; Som Prakash Verma, *1857 An Illustrated History*, New Delhi, Oxford University Press, 2008.

70. See for example, Sudipto Kaviraj, *The Unhappy Consciousness: Bankimchandra Chattopadhyay and the Formation of Nationalist Discourse in India*, New Delhi, Oxford University Press, 1995; Tapan Raychaudhuri, *Perceptions, Emotions, Sensibilities: Essays on India's Colonial and Post-colonial Experiences*, New Delhi, Oxford University

Press, 1999; Rajat K. Ray, *Exploring Emotional History: Gender, Mentality and Literature in the Indian Awakening*, New Delhi, Oxford University Press, 2001.

71. For example, the nationalist economic theory has been questioned in B.R. Tomlinson, *The Economy of Modern India 1860–1970. The New Cambridge History of India*, III. 3, Cambridge, Cambridge University Press, 1993; Tirthankar Roy, *The Economic History of India, 1857–1947*, New Delhi, Oxford University Press, 2000.

72. For indigo riots, see B.B. Kling, *The Blue Mutiny: The Indigo Disturbances in Bengal 1859–62*, Philadelphia, University of Pennsylvania Press, 1966; for Pabna riots, see B.B. Chaudhuri, 'Agrarian Economy and Agrarian Relations in Bengal (1859–85)', in N.K. Sinha (ed.), *The History of Bengal (1757–1905)*, Calcutta, Calcutta University Press, 1967, pp. 237–336; K.K. Sengupta, *Pabna Disturbances and the Politics of Rent 1873–85*, New Delhi, Peoples' Publishing House, 1974.

73. For Deccan riots, see Ravinder Kumar, *Western India in the Nineteenth Century*, London: Routledge and Kegan Paul, 1968; David Hardiman, *Feeding the Baniya: Peasants and Userers in Western India*, New Delhi, Oxford University Press, 1996.

74. See for details, Tanika Sarkar, 'Nationalist Iconography: Image of Women in 19th Century Bengali Literature'; and Sugata Bose, 'Nation as Mother: Representations and Contestations of "India" in Bengali Literature and Culture'.

75. See for details, J.R. McLane, *Indian Nationalism and the Early Congress*, Princeton, NJ, Princeton University Press, 1977; Anand A. Yang, 'Sacred Symbol and Sacred Space in Rural India: Community Mobilization in the "Anti-Cow Killing" Riot of 1893', *Comparative Studies in Society and History*, 20, 1980, pp. 576–96; Peter Robb, 'The Challenge of Gau Mata: British Policy and Religious Change in India, 1880–1916' *Modern Asian Studies*, 20 (2), 1986; Peter Van der Veer, *Religious Nationalism: Hindus and Muslims in India*, Berkeley, Los Angeles, London, University of California Press, 1994.

76. Richard Cashman, 'The Political Recruitment of God Ganapati', *The Indian Economic and Social History Review*, 7 (3), 1970, pp. 347–73.

77. For Muslim politics in Bengal during this period, see Refiuddin Ahmed, *The Bengal Muslims 1871–1906: A Quest for Identity*, New Delhi, Oxford University Press, paperback edition, 1996; for Dalit politics, see Sekhar Bandyopadhyay, *Caste, Protest and Identity in Colonial India: The Namasudras of Bengal, 1872–1947*, Richmond, Surrey, Curzon Press, 1997.

78. For Home Rule Leagues, see H.F. Owen, 'Towards Nationwide Agitation and Organisation: The Home Rule Leagues, 1915–18', in D.A. Low (ed.), *Soundings in Modern South Asian History*, London, Weidenfeld and Nicolson, 1968, pp. 159–95.

79. Partha Sarathi Gupta, *Power, Politics and the People: Studies in British Imperialism and Indian Nationalism*, New Delhi, Permanent Black, 2001, p. 41.

80. For Hindu religious nationalism see, Peter Van der Veer, *Religious Nationalism;* Christophe Jaffrelot, *The Hindu Nationalist Movement and Indian Politics 1925 to the 1990s*, London, Hurst & Company, 1996.

81. Mushirul Hasan (ed.), *India's Partition: Process, Strategy and Mobilization*, New Delhi, Oxford University Press, 1993.

82. Achin Vanaik, *The Furies of Indian Communalism: Religion, Modernity and Secularization*, London, New York, Verso, 1997, p. 31.

83. See also, M.S.S. Pandian, 'Notes on the Transformation of 'Dravidian' Ideology: Tamilnadu, c. 1900–40', *Social Scientist* 22 (5–6), 1994, pp. 84–104; '"Nation" from Its Margins: Notes on E.V. Ramaswamy's '"Impossible" Nation', in R. Bhargava, Amiya Kumar Bagchi, R. Sudarshan, (eds), *Multiculturism, Liberalism and Democracy*, New Delhi, Oxford University Press, 1999, pp. 286–307; V. Geetha, and S.V. Rajadurai, *Towards a non-Brahmin Millennium: From Iyothee Thass to Periyar*, Calcutta, Samya, 1998, pp. 514, 523.

84. For more discussion on the women's question, see L. Kasturi and V. Mazumdar (eds), *Women and Indian Nationalism*, New Delhi, Vikas, 1994; Geraldine Forbes, *Women in Modern India, The New Cambridge History of India*, IV. 2. Cambridge, Cambridge University Press, 1998; Sujata Patel, 'Construction and Reconstruction of Woman in Gandhi', in A. Thorner and M. Krishnaraj (eds), *Ideals, Images and Real Lives: Women in Literature and History*, Hyderabad, Orient Longman, 2000, pp. 288–321; K. Lalita, Vasantha Kannabiram, Rama Melkote, Uma Maheshwari, Susie Tharu, Veena Shatrugna—Stree Shakti Sanghatana, *'We Were Making History...' Life Stories of Women in the Telengana People's Struggle*, London, Zed Books, 1989.

85. For more on the politics of the Indian capitalist class, see Sabyasachi Bhattacharya, 'Cotton Mills and Spinning Wheels: Swadeshi and the Indian Capitalist Class, 1920–22', *Economic and Political Weekly*, 20 November 1976, 11 (47), pp.1828–32; A.D.D. Gordon, *Businessmen and Politics: Rising Nationalism and a Modernising Economy in Bombay, 1918–33*, New Delhi, Manohar, 1978; Rajat K. Ray, *Industrialization in India: Growth and Conflict in the Private Corporate Sector 1914–47*, New Delhi, Oxford University Press, 1979; Claude Markovits, *Indian Business and national Politics, 1931–9*, Cambridge, Cambridge University Press, 1985; Aditya Mukherjee, 'The Indian Capitalist Class: Aspects of Its Economic, Political and Ideological Development in the Colonial Period, 1927–47' in S. Bhattacharya and R. Thapar (eds), *Situating Indian History for Sarvepalli Gopal*, New Delhi, Oxford University Press, 1986, pp. 239–87.

86. See for more details Rajnarayan Chandavarkar, *The Origins of Industrial Capitalism in India: Business Strategies and the Working Classes in Bombay, 1900–40*, Cambridge, Cambridge University Press, 1994; *Imperial*

Power and Popular Politics: Class, Resistance and the State in India, c. 1850–1950, Cambridge, Cambridge University Press, 1998.

87. This period has been studied in details in A.K. Gupta (ed.), *Myth and Reality: The Struggle for Freedom in India, 1945–7*, Delhi, Manohar, 1987; Biswamoy Pati (ed.), *Turbulent Times India 1940–44*, Mumbai, Popular Prakashan, 1998; Sucheta Mahajan, *Independence and Partition: The Erosion of Colonial Power in India*, New Delhi, Sage Publications, 2000.

88. See for example, Urvashi Butalia, *The Other Side of Silence; Voices from the Partition of India*, Delhi, Penguin Books India, 1998; Ritu Menon and KamlaBhasin, *Borders and Boundaries: Women in India's Partition*, New Brunswick, Rutgers University Press, 1998; Gyanendra Pandey, *Remembering Partition: Violence, Nationalism and History of India*, Cambridge, Cambridge University Press, 2001; S. Kaul (ed.), *The Partitions of Memory: The Afterlife of the Division of India*, New Delhi, Permanent Black, 2001. As we have mentioned already, the partition stories remain outside the ambit of this book, interested readers may look at Mushirul Hasan (ed.), *India's Partition*.

89. Partha Sarathi Gupta, *Power, Politics and the People*, p. 41.

90. Ramchandra Guha, *India after Gandhi*, pp. xvii, xix–xx, 744–67.

Part I

The Educated Classes and Modern Nationalism

1   Whose Imagined Community?*

Partha Chatterjee

[...] [N]ot many years ago nationalism was generally considered one of Europe's most magnificent gifts to the rest of the world. It is [...] not often remembered today that the two greatest wars of the twentieth century, engulfing as they did virtually every part of the globe, were brought about by Europe's failure to manage its own ethnic nationalisms. Whether of the 'good' variety or the 'bad', nationalism was, entirely a product of the political history of Europe. Notwithstanding the celebration of the various unifying tendencies in Europe today and of the political consensus in the West as a whole, there may be in the recent amnesia on the origins of nationalism more than a hint of anxiety about whether it has quite been tamed in the land of its birth.

In all this time, the 'area specialists', the historians of the colonial world, working their way cheerlessly through musty files of administrative reports and official correspondence in colonial archives in London or Paris or Amsterdam, had of course never forgotten how nationalism arrived in the colonies. Everyone agreed that it was a European import; the debates in the 1960s and 1970s in the historiographies of Africa or India or Indonesia were about what had become of the idea and who was responsible for it. These debates between a new generation of nationalist historians and those whom they dubbed 'colonialists' were vigorous and often acrimonious, but they were largely confined to the specialized territories of 'area studies'; no one else took much notice of them.

Ten years ago, it was one such area specialist who managed to raise once more the question of the origin and spread of nationalism in the framework of a universal history. Benedict Anderson demonstrated with much subtlety and originality that nations were not the determinate products of given sociological conditions such as language or race or religion; they had been, in Europe and everywhere else in the world,

* Originally published in Partha Chatterjee, *The Nation and Its Fragments*, Princeton, Princeton University Press, 1993, pp. 3–13. In the present version some portions of the text have been removed. For the complete text see the original version.

imagined into existence.[1] He also described some of the major institutional
forms through which this imagined community came to acquire concrete
shape, especially the institutions of what he so ingeniously called 'print-
capitalism'. He then argued that the historical experience of nationalism
in Western Europe, in the Americas, and in Russia had supplied for all
subsequent nationalisms a set of modular forms from which nationalist
elites in Asia and Africa had chosen the ones they liked.

　　Anderson's book has been, I think, the most influential in the last
few years in generating new theoretical ideas on nationalism, an influence
that of course, it is needless to add, is confined almost exclusively to
academic writings. Contrary to the largely uninformed exoticization of
nationalism in the popular media in the West, the theoretical tendency
represented by Anderson certainly attempts to treat the phenomenon as
part of the universal history of the modern world.

I have one central objection to Anderson's argument. If nationalisms in
the rest of the world have to choose their imagined community from
certain 'modular' forms already made available to them by Europe and
the Americas, what do they have left to imagine? History, it would seem,
has decreed that we in the postcolonial world shall only be perpetual
consumers of modernity. Europe and the Americas, the only true
subjects of history, have thought out on our behalf not only the script of
colonial enlightenment and exploitation, but also that of our anticolonial
resistance and postcolonial misery. Even our imaginations must remain
forever colonized.

　　I object to this argument not for any sentimental reason. I object
because I cannot reconcile it with the evidence on anticolonial
nationalism. The most powerful as well as the most creative results of
the nationalist imagination in Asia and Africa are posited not on an identity
but rather on a *difference* with the 'modular' forms of the national society
propagated by the modern West. How can we ignore this without
reducing the experience of anticolonial nationalism to a caricature
of itself?

　　To be fair to Anderson, it must be said that he is not alone to blame.
The difficulty, I am now convinced, arises because we have all taken
the claims of nationalism to be a *political* movement much too literally
and much too seriously.

　　In India, for instance, any standard nationalist history will tell us
that nationalism proper began in 1885 with the formation of the Indian
National Congress. It might also tell us that the decade preceding this

was a period of preparation, when several provincial political associations were formed. Prior to that, from the 1820s to the 1870s, was the period of 'social reform', when colonial enlightenment was beginning to 'modernize' the customs and institutions of a traditional society and the political spirit was still very much that of collaboration with the colonial regime: nationalism had still not emerged. This history, when submitted to a sophisticated sociological analysis, cannot but converge with Anderson's formulations. In fact, since it seeks to replicate in its own history the history of the modern state in Europe, nationalism's self-representation will inevitably corroborate Anderson's decoding of the nationalist myth. I think, however, that as history, nationalism's autobiography is fundamentally flawed.

By my reading, anticolonial nationalism creates its own domain of sovereignty within colonial society well before it begins its political battle with the imperial power. It does this by dividing the world of social institutions and practices into two domains—the material and the spiritual. The material is the domain of the 'outside', of the economy and of statecraft, of science and technology, a domain where the West had proved its superiority and the East had succumbed. In this domain, then, Western superiority had to be acknowledged and its accomplishments carefully studied and replicated. The spiritual, on the other hand, is an 'inner' domain bearing the 'essential' marks of cultural identity. The greater one's success in imitating Western skills in the material domain, therefore, the greater the need to preserve the distinctness of one's spiritual culture. This formula is, I think, a fundamental feature of aniticolonial nationalisms in Asia and Africa.[2]

There are several implications. First, nationalism declares the domain of the spiritual its sovereign territory and refuses to allow the colonial power to intervene in that domain. If I may return to the Indian example, the period of 'social reform' was actually made up of two distinct phases. In the earlier phase, Indian reformers looked to the colonial authorities to bring about by state action the reform of traditional institutions and customs. In the latter phase, although the need for change was not disputed, there was a strong resistance to allowing the colonial state to intervene in matters affecting 'national culture'. The second phase, in my argument, was already the period of nationalism.

The colonial state, in other words, is kept out of the 'inner' domain of national culture; but it is not as though this so-called spiritual domain is left unchanged. In fact, here nationalism launches its most powerful, creative, and historically significant project: to fashion a 'modern' national culture that is nevertheless not Western. If the nation is an imagined community, then this is where it is brought into being. In this, its true and essential domain, the nation is already sovereign, even when the state is in the hands of the colonial power. The dynamics of this historical project is completely missed in conventional histories in which the story of nationalism begins with the contest for political power.

[...] [In this chapter] I wish to highlight here several areas within the so-called spiritual domain that nationalism transforms in the course of its journey. I will confine my illustrations to Bengal, with whose history I am most familiar.

The first such area is that of language. Anderson is entirely correct in his suggestion that it is 'print-capitalism' which provides the new institutional space for the development of the modern 'national' language.[3] However, the specificities of the colonial situation do not allow a simple transposition of European patterns of development. In Bengal, for instance, it is at the initiative of the East India Company and the European missionaries that the first printed books are produced in Bengali at the end of the eighteenth century and the first narrative prose compositions commissioned at the beginning of the nineteenth. At the same time, the first half of the nineteenth century is when English completely displaces Persian as the language of bureaucracy and emerges as the most powerful vehicle of intellectual influence on a new Bengali elite. The crucial moment in the development of the modern Bengali language comes, however, in mid-century, when this bilingual elite makes it a cultural project to provide its mother tongue with the necessary linguistic equipment to enable it to become an adequate language for 'modern' culture. An entire institutional network of printing presses, publishing houses, newspapers, magazines, and literary societies is created around this time, *outside* the purview of the state and the European missionaries, through which the new language, modern and standardized, is given shape. The bilingual intelligentsia came to think of its own language as belonging to that inner domain of cultural identity, from which the colonial intruder had to be kept out; language therefore became a zone over which the nation first had to declare its sovereignty and then had to transform in order to make it adequate for the modern world.

Here the modular influences of modern European languages and literatures did not necessarily produce similar consequences. In the case of the new literary genres and aesthetic conventions, for instance, whereas

European influences undoubtedly shaped explicit critical discourse, it was also widely believed that European conventions were inappropriate and misleading in judging literary productions in modern Bengali. To this day there is a clear hiatus in this area between the terms of academic criticism and those of literary practice. To give an example, let me briefly discuss Bengali drama.

Drama is the one modern literary genre that is the least commended on aesthetic grounds by critics of Bengali literature. Yet it is the form in which the bilingual elite have found its largest audience. When it appeared in its modern form in the middle of the nineteenth century, the new Bengali drama had two models available to it: one, the modern European drama as it had developed since Shakespeare and Molière, and two, the virtually forgotten corpus of Sanskrit drama, now restored to a reputation of classical excellence because of the praises showered on it by Orientalist scholars from Europe. The literary criteria that would presumably direct the new drama into the privileged domain of a modern national culture were therefore clearly set by modular forms provided by Europe. But the performative practices of the new institution of the public theatre made it impossible for those criteria to be applied to plays written for the theatre. The conventions that would enable a play to succeed on the Calcutta stage were very different from the conventions approved by critics schooled in the traditions of European drama. The tensions have not been resolved to this day. What thrives as mainstream public theatre in West Bengal or Bangladesh today is modern urban theatre, national and clearly distinguishable from 'folk theatre'. It is produced and largely patronized by the literate urban middle classes. Yet their aesthetic conventions fail to meet the standards set by the modular literary forms adopted from Europe.

Even in the case of the novel, that celebrated artifice of the nationalist imagination in which the community is made to live and love in 'homogeneous time',[4] the modular forms do not necessarily have an easy passage. The novel was a principal form through which the bilingual elite in Bengal fashioned a new narrative prose. In the devising of this prose, the influence of the two available models—modern English and classical Sanskrit—was obvious. And yet, as the practice of the form gained greater popularity, it was remarkable how frequently in the course of their narrative Bengali novelists shifted from the disciplined forms of authorial prose to the direct retarding of living speech. Looking at the pages of some of the most popular novels in Bengali, it is often difficult to tell whether one is reading a novel or a play. Having created a modern prose language in the fashion of the approved modular forms, the literati, in its search for artistic truthfulness, apparently found it necessary to escape as often as possible the rigidities of that prose.

The desire to construct an aesthetic form that was modern and national, and yet recognizably different from the Western, was shown in perhaps its most exaggerated shape in the efforts in the early twentieth century of the so-called Bengal school of art. It was through these efforts that, on the one hand, an institutional space was created for the modern professional artist in India, as distinct from the traditional craftsman, for the dissemination through exhibition and print of the products of art and for the creation of a public schooled in the new aesthetic norms. Yet this agenda for the construction of a modernized artistic space was accompanied, on the other hand, by a fervent ideological programme for an art that was distinctly 'Indian', that is, different from the 'Western'.[5] Although the specific style developed by the Bengal school for a new Indian art failed to hold its ground for very long, the fundamental agenda posed by its efforts continues to be pursued to this day, namely, to develop an art that would be modern and at the same time recognizably Indian.

Alongside the institutions of print-capitalism was created a new network of secondary schools. Once again, nationalism sought to bring this area under its jurisdiction long before the domain of the state had become a matter of contention. In Bengal, from the second half of the nineteenth century, it was the new elite that took the lead in mobilizing a 'national' effort to start schools in every part of the province and then to produce a suitable educational literature. Coupled with print-capitalism, the institutions of secondary education provided the space where the new language and literature were both generalized and normalized— outside the domain of the state. It was only when this space was opened up, outside the influence of both the colonial state and the European missionaries that it became legitimate for women, for instance, to be sent to school. It was also in this period, from around the turn of the century, that the University of Calcutta was turned from an institution of colonial education to a distinctly national institution, in its curriculum, its faculty, and its sources of funding.[6]

Another area in that inner domain of national culture was the family. The assertion here of autonomy and difference was perhaps the most dramatic. The European criticism of Indian 'tradition' as barbaric had focused to a large extent on religious beliefs and practices, especially those relating to the treatment of women. The early phase of 'social reform' through the agency of the colonial power had also concentrated on the same issues. In that early phase, therefore, this area had been identified as essential to 'Indian tradition'. The nationalist move began by disputing the choice of agency. Unlike the early reformers, nationalists were not prepared to allow the colonial state to legislate the reform of 'traditional' society. They asserted that only the nation itself could have the right to intervene in such an essential aspect of its cultural identity.

As it happened, the domain of the family and the position of women underwent considerable change in the world of the nationalist middle class. It was undoubtedly a new patriarchy that was brought into existence, different from the 'traditional' order but also explicitly claiming to be different from the 'Western' family. The 'new woman' was to be modern, but she would also have to display the signs of national tradition and therefore would be essentially different from the 'Western' woman.

The history of nationalism as a political movement tends to focus primarily on its contest with the colonial power in the domain of the outside, that is, the material domain of the state. This is a different history from the one I have outlined. It is also a history in which nationalism has no option but to choose its forms from the gallery of 'models' offered by European and American nation-states: 'difference' is not a viable criterion in the domain of the material.

In this outer domain, nationalism begins its journey (after, let us remember, it has already proclaimed its sovereignty in the inner domain) by inserting itself into a new public sphere constituted by the processes and forms of the modern (in this case, colonial) state. In the beginning, nationalism's task is to overcome the subordination of the colonized middle class, that is, to challenge the 'rule of colonial difference' in the domain of the state. The colonial state, we must remember, was not just the agency that brought the modular forms of the modern state to the colonies; it was also an agency that was destined never to fulfil the normalizing mission of the modern state because the premise of its power was a rule of colonial difference, namely, the preservation of the alienness of the ruling group.

As the institutions of the modern state were elaborated in the colony, especially in the second half of the nineteenth century, the ruling European groups found it necessary to lay down—in lawmaking, in the bureaucracy, in the administration of justice, and in the recognition by the state of a legitimate domain of public opinion—the precise difference between the rulers and the ruled. If Indians had to be admitted into the judiciary, could they be allowed to try Europeans? Was it right that Indians should enter the civil service by taking the same examinations as British graduates? If European newspapers in India were given the right of free speech, could the same apply to native newspapers? Ironically, it became the historical task of nationalism, which insisted on its own marks of cultural difference with the West, to demand that there be no rule of difference in the domain of the state.

In time, with the growing strength of nationalist politics, this domain became more extensive and internally differentiated and finally took on the form of the national, that is, postcolonial, state. The dominant elements of its self-definition, at least in postcolonial India, were drawn from the ideology of the modern liberal-democratic state.

In accordance with liberal ideology, the public was now distinguished from the domain of the private. The state was required to protect the inviolability of the private self in relation to other private selves. The legitimacy of the state in carrying out this function was to be guaranteed by its indifference to concrete differences between private selves— differences, that is, of race, language, religion, class, caste, and so forth.

The trouble was that the moral-intellectual leadership of the nationalist elite operated in a field constituted by a very different set of distinctions—those between the spiritual and the material, the inner and the outer, the essential and the inessential. That contested field over which nationalism had proclaimed its sovereignty and where it had imagined its true community was neither coextensive with nor coincidental to the field constituted by the public/private distinction. In the former field, the hegemonic project of nationalism could hardly make the distinctions of language, religion, caste, or class a matter of indifference to itself. The project was that of cultural 'normalization', like, as Anderson suggests, bourgeois hegemonic projects everywhere, but with the all-important difference that it had to choose its site of autonomy from a position of subordination to a colonial regime that had on its side the most universalist justificatory resources produced by post-Enlightenment social thought.

The result is that autonomous forms of imagination of the community were, and continue to be, overwhelmed and swamped by the history of the postcolonial state. Here lies the root of our postcolonial misery: not in our inability to think out new forms of the modern community but in our surrender to the old forms of the modern state. If the nation is an imagined community and if nations must also take the form of states, then our theoretical language must allow us to talk about community and state at the same time. I do not think our present theoretical language allows us to do this.

Writing just before his death, Bipinchandra Pal (1858–1932), the fiery
leader of the Swadeshi movement in Bengal and a principal figure in the
pre-Gandhian Congress, described the boardinghouses in which students
lived in the Calcutta of his youth:

> Students' messes in Calcutta, in my college days, fifty-six years ago, were
> like small republics and were managed on strictly democratic lines.
> Everything was decided by the voice of the majority of the members of the
> mess. At the end of every month a manager was elected by the whole
> 'House', so to say, and he was charged with the collection of the dues of
> the members, and the general supervision of the food and establishment
> of the mess....A successful manager was frequently begged to accept re-
> election; while the more careless and lazy members, who had often to pay
> out of their own pockets for their mismanagement, tried to avoid this
> honour.
>
> ...Disputes between one member and another were settled by a 'Court'
> of the whole 'House'; and we sat night after night, I remember, in examining
> these cases; and never was the decision of this 'Court' questioned or
> disobeyed by any member. Nor were the members of the mess at all helpless
> in the matter of duly enforcing their verdict upon an offending colleague.
> For they could always threaten the recalcitrant member either with
> expulsion from the mess, or if he refused to go, with the entire responsibility
> of the rent being thrown on him. ... And such was the force of public
> opinion in these small republics that I have known of cases of this
> punishment on offending members, which so worked upon him that after
> a week of their expulsion from a mess, they looked as if they had just
> come out of some prolonged or serious spell of sickness....
>
> The composition of our mess called for some sort of a compromise
> between the so-called orthodox and the Brahmo and other heterodox
> members of our republic. So a rule was passed by the unanimous vote of
> the whole 'House', that no member should bring any food to the
> house...which outraged the feelings of Hindu orthodoxy. It was however
> clearly understood that the members of the mess, as a body and even
> individually, would not interfere with what any one took outside the house.
> So we were free to go and have all sorts of forbidden food either at the
> Great Eastern Hotel, which some of us commenced to occasionally
> patronize later on, or anywhere else.[7]

The interesting point in this description is not so much the exaggerated
and obviously romanticized portrayal in miniature of the imagined
political form of the self-governing nation, but rather the repeated use
of the institutional terms of modern European civic and political life
(republic, democracy, majority, unanimity, election, House, Court, and
so on) to describe a set of activities that had to be performed on material

utterly incongruous with that civil society. The question of a 'compromise' on the food habits of members is really settled not on a principle of demarcating the 'private' from the 'public' but of separating the domains of the 'inside' and the 'outside', the inside being a space where 'unanimity' had to prevail, while the outside was a realm of individual freedom. Notwithstanding the 'unanimous vote of the whole House', the force that determined the unanimity in the inner domain was not the voting procedure decided upon by individual members coming together in a body but rather the consensus of a community—institutionally novel (because, after all, the Calcutta boardinghouse was unprecedented in 'tradition'), internally differentiated, but nevertheless a community whose claims preceded those of its individual members.

But Bipinchandra's use of the terms of parliamentary procedure to describe the 'communitarian' activities of a boardinghouse standing in place of the nation must not be dismissed as a mere anomaly. His language is indicative of the very real imbrication of two discourses, and correspondingly of two domains, of politics. The attempt has been made in recent Indian historiography to talk of these as the domains of 'elite' and 'subaltern' politics.[8] But one of the important results of this historiographical approach has been precisely the demonstration that each domain has not only acted in opposition to and as a limit upon the other but, through this process of struggle, has also shaped the emergent form of the other. Thus, the presence of populist or communitarian elements in the liberal constitutional order of the postcolonial state ought not to be read as a sign of the inauthenticity or disingenuousness of elite politics; it is rather a recognition in the elite domain of the very real presence of an arena of subaltern politics over which it must dominate and yet which also had to be negotiated on its own terms for the purposes of producing consent. On the other hand, the domain of subaltern politics has increasingly become familiar with, and even adapted itself to, the institutional forms characteristic of the elite domain. The point, therefore, is no longer one of simply demarcating and identifying the two domains in their separateness, which is what was required in order first to break down the totalizing claims of a nationalist historiography. Now the task is to trace in their mutually conditioned historicities the specific forms that have appeared, on the one hand, in the domain defined by the hegemonic project of nationalist modernity, and on the other, in the numerous fragmented resistances to that normalizing project.

[...]

NOTES

1. Benedict Anderson, *Imagined Communities: Reflections on the Origin and Spread of Nationalism.* London: Verso, 1983.
2. This is a central argument of my book *Nationalist Thought and the Colonial World: A Derivative Discourse?* London: Zed Books, 1986.
3. Anderson, *Imagined Communities.* pp. 17–49.
4. Ibid., pp. 28–40.
5. The history of this artistic movement has been recently studied in detail by Tapati Guha-Thakurta, *The Making of a New 'Indian' Art: Artists, Aesthetics and Nationalism in Bengal, 1850–1920.* Cambridge: Cambridge University Press, 1992.
6. See Anilchandra Banerjee, 'Years of Consolidation: 1883–1904'; Tripurari Chakravarti, 'The University and the Government: 1904–24'; and Pramathanath Banerjee, 'Reform and Reorganization: 1904–24', in Niharranjan Ray and Pratulchandra Gupta (eds), *Hundred Years of the University of Calcutta.* Calcutta: University of Calcutta, 1957, pp. 129–78, 179–210, and 211–318.
7. Bipinchandra Pal, *Memories of My Life and Times.* 1932; reprint, Calcutta: Bipinchandra Pal Institute, 1973, pp. 157–60.
8. Represented by the various essays in Ranajit Guha (ed.), *Subaltern Studies,* vols 1–6. New Delhi: Oxford University Press, 1982–90. The programatic statement of this approach is in Ranajit Guha, 'On Some Aspects of the Historiography of Colonial India', in Guha (ed.), *Subaltern Studies I.* New Delhi: Oxford University Press, 1982, pp. 1–8.

2   Economic Nationalism*

Bipan Chandra

The fact is, you cannot both be a conquering nation and a benevolent nation at the same time.

—*Amrita Bazar Patrika*, 12 February 1892

You announce yourself as a sincere supporter of British rule; you vehemently denounce the conditions and consequences which are inseparable from the maintenance of that rule.

—George Hamilton

I. ANALYSIS OF THE NATURE AND PURPOSE OF BRITISH RULE IN INDIA

The attitude that the Indian national leadership of the period under study adopted towards British rule was ultimately determined by their understanding of its nature and purpose. In the case of most of them this understanding was not derived from theoretical reasoning or *a priori* assumptions: practice was the hard school in which they were brought up. One such field of their education was that of economic policies. Debate and discussion between Indians and Indians, on the one hand, and between Indians and their rulers, on the other, over nearly every economic issue that arose in contemporary administration and politics had some bearing on this basic political understanding. In the end, the multifarious controversies over economic policies, and, in particular, over the causes of India's poverty and the consequent remedies, led large sections of the nationalist leadership to believe—sometimes hesitantly and even confusedly, as in the case of G.K. Gokhale, G.V. Joshi, Surendranath Banerjea, D.E. Wacha, and R.C. Dutt, but often in a clear cut manner, as in the case of Dadabhai Naoroji, B.G. Tilak, G. Subramaniya Iyer, the *Amrita Bazar Patrika*, the *Mahratta*, and numerous other

* Originally published as a chapter in Bipan Chandra, *The Rise and Growth of Economic Nationalism in* India, New Delhi, People's Publishing House, 1966, pp. 736–59. In the present version some portions of the text and notes have been removed. For the complete text see the original version.

nationalist papers—that, on the whole, British rule was economically injurious to India and that perhaps it was designedly so.

To many of the Indian leaders, particularly to those who later came to be known as Moderates, British rule held for long a great promise. They were dazzled by the initial impact on India of Britain, the most advanced nation of the contemporary world. To them, law and order and a modern centralized administration, coming as they did after the near-political anarchy of the eighteenth and early nineteenth centuries, the spread of modern education and through its medium of Western democratic thought and enlightenment, the introduction of the freedom of speech and the Press and of social liberty, but perhaps most of all the process of the welding of the people of India into one common nationality, the consequent growth all over the country of the feeling of belonging to one common entity, and the birth of a new political life—all seemed to follow in the wake of, and were therefore the accomplishments of British Raj and heralded the coming dawn. In the realm of economics, it was the prospect of rapid industrial development that attracted them. Western science and technique and economic organization and the example of vigorous European enterprise, they hoped, would reclaim the country from the slough of economic backwardness and stagnation. The railways, roads, and canals, the link with the flourishing markets of the world, the early textile industry, and the foreign commercial, industrial, and plantation enterprises appeared to be a preparation for, and a prelude to, the coming industrial revolution whose first signs were already visible.[1]

It was not as if the early nationalists were not aware of the prevalence of poverty and other economic disabilities. But they believed that the credit side of British rule outweighed the debit side, and they hoped that with the passage of time disabilities would become less and less and the benefits realized more and more. In other words, in the material field, they were attracted more by the potential than the real, more by the hope than the fulfillment.[2]

With the passage of time, however, and as they waited—some patiently, others impatiently—for the tide of progress to rise ever higher, however slowly, they found that their expectations remained unrealized and even appeared to recede farther and farther; they were filled with disappointment and dismay, and their image of British rule began to take on darker hues. As far as economic life was concerned, progress appeared to be halting and too slow, and some even felt that, on the contrary, the country was economically regressing. In course of time, the evidence of India's dismal poverty began to overshadow their entire economic outlook. The one ray of hope was the growth of modern industry and here it appeared to them that official economic policies were perhaps the most important road-block.

And so gratefulness and praise began to give way to constant carping and grieving so far as economic issues were concerned;[3] and the Indian leaders began to complain that poverty was stalking the land, the peasant was rack-rented by the revenue authorities, indigenous industry had been ruined, and modern industry was deliberately discouraged or at least not sufficiently encouraged, essential food supply of the country was being exported, currency policy was manipulated against the interests of Indian industry and peasantry, Indian labour was being enslaved in foreign-owned plantations, railways were being extended in neglect of Indian revenues and the needs of agricultural development, the burden of taxation was crushing and the public revenues were diverted from nation-building departments to serve non-Indian interests and to wage unnecessary and expansionist wars, and lastly—the heaviest complaint of all—India was being drained of its wealth and capital. And all these economic evils, they came to feel, were the direct or indirect consequences of British economic policy in India: if 'the Indian economic world was out-of-joint', the responsibility was largely that of Britain. Thus, in the eyes of the nationalist leaders, all the other advantages of British rule in the past and the present paled before its economic disadvantages.[4] And, in course of time, this 'decadence of faith' led to the questioning not only of the results of British rule but also of its very whys and wherefores: Why had India not progressed materially and why had not the early promise in this respect been realized? Who was responsible for this failure? Was the injury done to India inadvertent or deliberate? In other words, what was the real purpose of British rule and, as a corollary, could their own faith in its 'Providential' character be reconciled with their current belief that the rule had been materially injurious to India?

As is well known, a large number of Indian leaders believed for many years that the material injury to India was the result of lack of proper understanding of the Indian situation on the part of the British people, parliament, and government—or, at the most, of the exigencies of party politics in Britain—and of the consequent mistakes of policy and of faulty implementation of even correct policies by the bureaucracy in India or the party leaders at home. In other words, ignorance and errors of judgement on the part of the rulers or at the most the frailties of democratic politics and not any deliberate policy or intention were responsible for India's economic backwardness. Hence, for these nationalist leaders, the chief consolation lay in an abiding faith in the sense of justice and fairness and generosity of the people of Britain, that is, in 'the conscience of England'. They, therefore, felt that if the Governments of India and England and the British public and parliament only came to know and grasp the real facts of the situation, the needful would be done. Consequently, they made all possible attempts to impart the needed instruction.[5] But their educational campaigning, their economic analysis, and their political agitation to awaken the British conscience failed in getting their economic grievances redressed in the way they desired. And slowly their faith was being shattered, their confidence in the sense of justice of their rulers shaken, and the seed of distrust sown deep.

Gradually, and in course of time, agitation on concrete economic issues, in particular those relating to tariff policy and the drain, tended to convince wider and wider strata of Indian people and leaders[6] that the goodwill of individual Englishmen and administrators and statesmen notwithstanding, the economic policies of British Raj sprang from its very nature and character, that poverty and economic backwardness were perhaps not so much the product of the rulers' well-intentioned mistakes as the concomitants of their rule, that this rule was fundamentally rooted in a desire to exploit India economically and was therefore harmful to India's economic growth, that Britain's sense of justice and generosity were overcome by the desire to utilize the economic resources of India for its own advantage. [...][T]he Indian leaders came to be discontented with particular measures of official economic policy and in nearly every instance many of them arrived at the conclusion that Britain was ruling India for British and not Indian purposes. Here it may only be added that many of them reached this conclusion even at the level of generalization.[7] In the Press, this generalization found expression in the frequent reference to India as the 'kamdhenu' or the milch cow of England.[8]

To be able to place in better historical perspective the realization of the exploitative character of British rule on the part of the Indian leaders and their later propagation of it, three other factors may be kept in view. Firstly, an important section of the Indian leadership, consisting primarily of some of the nationalist newspapers, at no stage believed in the benevolent intentions of the rulers; it consisted of people who were described by A.O. Hume in 1888 as 'this objectionable fringe' who 'rail at and abuse the best and friendliest of our rulers and who *sneer, snarl,* and *snap* at everything Government does, good, bad or indifferent'.[9] Secondly, the speeches and writings of many of them continued to abound in the paradox of faith in British benevolence, on the one hand, and assertion of British selfishness, on the other. Sometimes, in the same breath they highlighted British selfishness and reaffirmed their faith in the uplifting mission of the British. They did not find the contradiction between their political belief and their economic understanding to be irresoluble. Dadabhai Naoroji, for example, resolved it by calling British rule in India unBritish.[10] Thirdly, the newspapers invariably gave a more open and direct and bold expression to the feelings of the rank and file of national leadership than the public men did, and played an important part in developing and moulding popular nationalist sentiment on economic questions and their political bearings.

In any case it may be suggested that ultimately it was the agitation around economic policies that was carried out unremittingly by *all* sections of the national leadership which dispelled the halo of beneficence around British rule as far as the vast majority of the Indian leaders and people were concerned.[11] As many British statesmen and Indian nationalist leaders fully recognized, the secret of British power was not only physical force but also moral force; this power was based not only on the sword with which the land was conquered but also on the continuing acquiescence of the people.[12] Mere political and sentimental appeals, however, might not have succeeded in undermining the moral foundations of British rule. They might have at the most led to the condemnation of the rule as a benevolent despotism.[13] In fact, many British administrators and statesmen willingly acknowledged and defended the despotic character of their rule; they only claimed that despotism of the rule—Macaulay's 'firm impartial despotism'—or 'paternalism' as it popularly came to be known, was essential for its benevolence which might not exist without its 'strength'.[14] In any case the absence of political independence was there for all to see, but why this absence was a political evil had to be demonstrated to the unsophisticated who might not be able to see it as 'an evil-in-itself'. Hence, the historical importance of the nationalist agitation around economic policies which tended to corrode popular confidence in the benevolent character of the British Raj, that is, in both its good results as well as good intentions. The corrosion inevitably spread to the field of political loyalty which could not coexist, at least in the popular mind—whatever the more sophisticated leaders might say—with the type of charges that were made in the course of this agitation.[15] And in this agitation leaders belonging to all shades of political opinion from the moderate Dadabhai Naoroji, Ranade, Dutt, Gokhale, and Joshi to the extremist Tilak, brothers Sisir Kumar and Motilal Ghose, and numerous nationalist newspapers played an equal part. In this sense, it may be justifiably said that all the nationalist leaders sowed in the land the seeds, if not of sedition, at least of disaffection. Perhaps the only real difference between them was that while some were consciously 'disloyal', others professed, preached, and protested their loyalty and their desire to perpetuate British rule, that is, remained subjectively loyal to the end of their days, though objectively they too cut at the roots of the empire they considered Providential— they were in fact the fountainheads of 'disloyalty'. And this was one of the major reasons why the period from 1880 to 1905 became a period of intellectual unrest and of spreading national consciousness—the seed-time of modern Indian national movement.

[...]

II. Opposition to Economic Imperialism

The nature of economic policies advocated by the Indian national leaders from 1880 to 1905 gave to these years the character of being the period of economic nationalism. The most important problem which, according to them, faced the Indian people was the economic one, namely that of poverty. It was moreover a national problem, that is, a problem that embraced the interests of all sections of Indian society. Furthermore, the national leaders cast the blame for this poverty not on nature or the people but on the alien rulers. They suggested certain remedies which were not accepted. This led many of them to doubt the bonafides of the rulers and to feel that if the country was not economically progressing it was only because of 'the presence and the policy of the foreigner' and that perhaps there could be no national economic regeneration 'except by their getting rid in the first instance of their European rulers'.

The nature of the remedies the Indian leaders suggested, or of their economic policies, was basically anti-imperialist. They demanded fundamental changes in the existing economic relations between India and Britain. Even when their political demands were moderate, their economic demands were radically nationalist. A study of their economic policies brings out that they had gradually acquired a deep understanding of the complex economic mechanism of the system of British domination over India or of modern imperialism—an understanding they derived by taking in the entire range of economic issues and studying them in their relationships and in their totality within the framework of economic development—and that they opposed nearly all of the important official economic policies based on this system. They took note of all the three forms of contemporary economic exploitation, that is, through commerce, industry, and finance, and they clearly grasped that the essence of British economic imperialism lay in the subordination of Indian economy to Britain's. They vehemently opposed the attempt, on the part of the alien rulers, to develop in India the basic characteristics of a colonial economy, namely, the transformation of India into a supplier of raw materials, a market for British manufactures, and a field of investment for foreign capital. They criticized the official tariff, trade, transport, and taxation policies as obstructing in place of helping the growth of industry and as bringing about the increasing de-industrialization of the country. Most of them opposed, both on economic and political grounds, the large-scale import of foreign capital in railways, plantations, and industries and the facilities afforded to it by the government. In their attack on the expenditure on the army and the Civil Service they challenged the very material bases on which British supremacy ultimately rested. In attacking the official land revenue and taxation policies they tended to undermine the financial basis of British rule. They condemned the use of Indian army and revenues for purposes of British expansion in Asia and Africa as being another form of economic exploitation. Some of them even went to the extent of questioning the propriety of placing on Indian revenues the entire burden of British rule itself. In the drain theory, they called into question the very economic essence of the imperial idea, and gave to the popular mind a simple yet powerful symbol to mark foreign economic exploitation.

All their economic demands were ultimately rooted in the desire for a genuine national economic policy which would be determined by the interests of India and not of England. Moreover, in every sphere of economic life, they advocated the lessening and even severance of India's economic dependence of England. Even when they depended upon the British Indian administration or the British public and parliament to achieve their economic objectives the ultimate end was to lay the foundations of an independent economy. Acceptance of their demands would have gradually, but inexorably, undermined Britain's privileged economic position in India.

[...]

[...] [T]hey adopted a national approach towards economic develop-ment; their total concern was with the general welfare of the community and they, therefore, tried to represent the interests of all classes of Indian society. They pleaded for an equitable system of taxation in which the burden of public revenues would be borne by those who could afford to do so; in particular, they continuously agitated for the reduction of land revenue and the salt tax. They pressed for rapid industrialization so that the sources of national income might be enlarged. They pleaded for expenditure of public revenues in such a manner as to lead to the greatest good of the greatest number. It is true that they did not take up the class demands of the peasantry or the working class. They neither asked for a reform of the existing system of land tenures nor espoused the cause of factory labour. This was to prove a major weakness of the nationalist movement, even in the later period. But, then, theirs was a consciously national approach since they believed that all classes of Indians suffered economically under British rule and that all of them stood to gain under the broad programme of national economic regeneration for which they were agitating.[16] They felt that while they were engaged in the struggle for getting economic justice and equality for the entire nation they should not take up the fight for justice and equality between classes. They decided not to carry on any activity which would tend to divide the people at a time when the need of the hour was to unite them into a nation. This perspective, essentially correct, made them ignore other aspects of contemporary reality. The brilliance of their grasp of the essential weaknesses of India's economy arose from the fact that they focused all their thought and attention on India's colonial structure. But then precisely for that reason the weaknesses of India's internal institutional structure tended to escape their attention, at least in the first flush of intellectual illumination. And so they did not realize that even within the limits of a national approach they could do far more to protect the interests of the downtrodden groups and classes. This is not to say that they did nothing in this direction. Within the national limits they imposed on themselves they did actively agitate for the particular welfare of the peasantry and the working class. For example, they carried on a veritable political campaign to get due protection for plantation labour—no clash with any other Indian interests being involved since the employers of labour in this case were foreigners. It may also be noted that already by the end of the nineteenth century new pro-labour attitudes were discernible in the outlook of several nationalist leaders. In the case of peasantry, they continuously, and in the end with some success, agitated for the lowering of land revenue and for its permanent settlement. Many of them also pleaded for safeguards against tenants being rack-rented by landlords.[17] Moreover they believed that their chief concern was with the poverty of the peasant who was, in fact, present as the 'invisible man' in nearly the whole of their economic agitation. There were perhaps few nationalist demands which were not ultimately designed to help the peasant. In any case, he would, the nationalist leaders believed, be the chief beneficiary of national economic development just as he was the chief victim of the policies of economic imperialism. All the same, the agrarian outlook of the early Indian leaders remained perhaps the main weakness of their economic policies.

At the same time it may be kept in view that, the Indian leaders refused to espouse the class interests of the peasant and the worker, they also showed a high degree of altruism in proposing policies which went against the narrow interests of that section of the society to which most of them belonged, namely, the urban, educated middle class. In other words, their economic policies were not guided by the interests of a 'job-hungry' middle class. This has been amply borne out by our study of their economic policies. To sum up in brief: they opposed the removal of cotton import duties though the 'middle class' was the chief consumer of foreign cloth; they supported protection for industries even though its price would be ultimately borne by this class; many of them supported the countervailing duties on beet sugar even though beet sugar was consumed mostly by this class; they preached swadeshi though foreign goods were cheaper; they supported the falling rupee even though it meant that as buyers of imported goods the members of this class had to pay more and as earners of fixed income the educated employed stood to gain from any increase in the purchasing power of the rupee and to lose by a decrease in it; most of them supported the income tax and opposed the salt tax; they wanted reduction of high salaries and the raising of the salaries of *chaprasis*, constables, soldiers, and low-paid clerks; for promotion of industry and welfare activities, they were willing to advocate higher taxation; they criticized railway development which increased the comfort of the 'middle class' and favoured irrigation and industrial development instead; many of the nationalists opposed the development of the country by foreign capital, even though such development opened out new avenues of employment for the educated Indians; they actively agitated for the replacement of the British-created courts, which led to the ruin of the ryots through litigation by conciliation courts or by a revival of the old panchayat system. It is of course true that they took up some of the demands of the urban lower, middle, and upper middle classes. But this was done as part of the all-round agitation around the economic demands of all sections of the Indian society.

The mistake that is often made in this respect by writers, both Indian and foreign, is that of looking upon the early Indian nationalist writers, public men, journalists, and thinkers as a class—'the middle class'—instead of seeing them as the intellectual representatives of new Indian classes and of Indian nationalism. As intellectuals some of them might, and did, represent different interest, classes, or groups; at the same time, because they were intellectuals, their thinking was guided, at the level of consciousness, by thought and not by interests. A thinker, a philosopher in the wider sense of the term, an intellectual, can and does often rise above the narrow group into which he is born and represents the interests of a class or a group or even a nation other than his own. This is in particular true of times of rapid social change and of disruption of old socio-political structures and of birth of new classes and economic and political systems. Like the best and genuine intellectuals the world over and in all history, the Indian thinkers and intellectuals of the nineteenth century too were philosophers and not hacks of a party or a class. It is true that they were not above class or group and did in practice represent concrete class or group interests. But when they reflected the interests of a class or a group, they did so through the prism of ideology and not directly as members, or the obedient servants, of that class or group. In other words, they did all their thinking subjectively from the national point of view; only it so happened that objectively and outside the framework of their conscious beliefs their thinking coincided not only with national interest, which it did, but also with the interests of particular groups and classes. The point is that the thinking and actions of the Indian nationalist leaders and writers have to be *concretely* studied and analysed to see what they wanted and whom they were intellectually representing. It is nothing but sheer crude mechanical materialism (also crude use of sociology) to mainly look at the class or group origins of a political leadership or practising intellectuals and then brand them as *being* this class or that. In fact the early Indian national leaders did not, and could not, constitute a class. Their response at the level of economic ideas and policies, as well as at other levels, was that of ideologues and not that of an educated group concerned with its own narrow self-interest.

The economic outlook of the Indian national leadership was basically capitalist. In nearly every aspect of economic life they championed capitalist growth in general and the interests of the industrial capitalists in particular. But, if at times it seems that the Indian leaders were focusing too large a part of their attention on the interests of the industrial capitalist class, it was not because their vision was limited by the narrow interests of this class but because of their belief that industrial development along capitalist lines was the only way to regenerate the country in the economic field, or that, in other words, the interests of the industrial capitalist class objectively coincided with the chief national interest of the moment. They were pro-capitalist because they believed that this class alone could accomplish in practice what they proposed in their speeches and writings, namely, rapid industrialization. They represented the industrial capitalist class only in the sense that their economic thinking and programme did not go beyond the limits which industrialization along capitalist lines imposed in practice.

[...]

In time, their economic agitation led the Indian national leaders to put forward political demands as they came to realize that economic policies could best be influenced from the seats of political power. They began to look at political questions from the point of view of their effect on the growth of an independent industrial economy. Of course, the demand for political concessions also arose independently of their economic bearings. However, one of the important reasons for their demands for the reform of the administration and for a share in political power was their desire to make the administration a better instrument of economic development and welfare. As has been shown earlier, nearly every important economic question was linked, by one section or the other of the national leadership, with the politically dependent status of the country and with the question of political autonomy or at least with Indian people's right to share in political power.[18] In the end, many of the national leaders were even led to conclude that since the British Indian administration was 'only the handmaid to the task of exploitation'[19] the country would be economically developed only if and when unadulterated British rule gave way to a political order in which Indians played the dominant role.

[...]

The important point is that by posing the main economic issues in such a way as to highlight the clash between the economic interests of India and Britain, pointing out that the most important political and economic aspect of the Indian reality was that India was being ruled by a foreign power for the purpose of economic exploitation [...] and pointing out that control over political power was essential for the implementation of nationalist economic demands, they created a situation in which antagonism between the rulers and the ruled went on developing and a struggle for political power and independence became more or less inevitable. [...]

It may also be pointed out that the political activity of nearly all of the national leaders of this period was consciously designed to impart political education to the people and prepare them for *modern* political and nationalist thinking and activity. The Indian leaders fully recognized that their work was preparatory to a later period of active political struggle. [...]

The accomplishments of the national leaders of this period are many, provided success is not measured in terms of immediate gains. They made the people of India conscious of the bond of common economic interests and of the existence of a common enemy and thus helped to weld them in a common nationalism. They made the people conscious of their economically precarious and degraded position and of the possibility of improvement. They gave a precise nationalist form to the incoherent economic aspirations of the people and spread ideas of economic development. They inculcated among the people the desire to increase the economic wealth of the country, showed them the ways of doing so by putting forward a well-rounded programme of economic development, and pointed out the obstacles, both economic and political, that needed to be overcome if the economic objectives were to be realized. In accomplishing these tasks all the national leaders, both Moderates and Extremists, contributed alike, displaying in the process a high quality of the power of economic analysis and deep patriotism. We would not be far wrong in concluding that, in spite of their many failures, they laid strong and enduring foundations for the national movement to grow upon and deserve a high place among the makers of modern India. [...]

NOTES

1. See, for example, Dadabhai Naoroji, *Essays, Speeches and Writings*, edited by C.L. Parekh, Bombay, 1887, pp. 26–7; and M.G. Ranade, *Essays on Indian Economics*, Bombay, 1898, pp. 23, 65–6, 118–19.
2. See, for example, Naoroji, *Essays*, pp. 37, 131–5; 'The Exigencies of Progress in India', *JPSS*, vol. XV, no. 4, Apr. 1893, pp. 15–16.
3. So much so that, in 1904, Edward Law, Finance Member, cried out in exasperation against the constant criticism by G.K. Gokhale, the mildest of the Indian leaders of the day: 'When he takes his seat at this Council table he unconsciously perhaps adopts the role and demeanour of the habitual mourner, and his sad wails and lamentations at the delinquencies of Government are as piteous as long practice and training can make them...' [*Abstract of the Proceedings of the Council of the Governor-General*

of India, assembled for the purpose of making Laws and Regulations (Anuual), 1877–1905, vol. XLIII, 1904, p. 542, *hereafter LCP*].

4. For example, Dadabhai Naoroji wrote: 'It is useless and absurd to remind us constantly that once the British fiat brought order out of chaos, and to make that an everlasting excuse for subsequent shortcomings and the material and moral impoverishment of the country. The Natives of the present day have not seen that chaos, and do not feel it; and though they understand it, and very thankful they are for the order brought, they see the present drain, distress, and destruction, and they feel it and bewail it' (Dadabhai Naoroji, *Poverty and Un-British Rule in India,* London, 1901, p. 219, hereafter *Poverty*). Similarly, R.C. Dutt wrote: 'British rule has given peace; but British Administration has not promoted or widened these sources of National Wealth in India' (R.C. Dutt, *Economic History of India in the Victorian Age,* 6th edition, first published in 1903, London, p. vii, hereafter *EHII*). And *Kesari* wrote in its issue dated 31 March 1903: 'There is unity and equality among the Indians, but it is the same kind of unity and equality as is found among the servants of a common master or the flock of a shepherd. Our rulers are not willing to entrust us with responsible duties or to admit us to partnership in trade and industry' (*Report on the Native Press for Bombay (weekly), 1870–1905,* 4 April 1903, hereafter *RNPBom.*). Also see, for instance, Naoroji, *Poverty*, pp. 209–12, 224–8, 579, 652–3, quoted in R.P. Masani, *Dadabhai Naoroji: The Grand Old Man of India,* London, 1939, pp. 443, 447, in Congress Presidential Address, (hereafter *CPA*), p. 22; *Bengalee,* 10 May 1884; A.L. Roy's article in *Mahratta,* 6 June 1886; L.M. Ghose in *CPA,* p. 762; R.N. Mudholkar in *Indian Politics,* p. 37; G.S. Iyer, *Some Economic Aspects of British Rule in India,* Madras, 1903, p. 330, hereafter *EA*.

5. Interestingly enough, not only the Moderates but the *Amrita Bazar Patrika* and B.G. Tilak also emphasized the need of winning over British public and parliamentarians to India's cause. See for example, *Amrita Bazar Patrika,* Calcutta, 1870–1905, hereafter *ABP,* See *ABP,* 8 October 1874, 26 April 1883; Tilak, *Indian National Congress Reports (Annual), 1885–1905,* hereafter *Rep. INC*), see *Rep. INC for 1904,* pp. 150–1, and quoted in G.P. Pradhan and A.K. Bhagwat, *Lokamanya Tilak,* Bombay, 1958, p. 80.

6. It may be kept in view that different leaders acquired this conviction at different points of time and in relation to different issues. For R.C. Dutt, for example, the transition came in the short period between 1897 and 1901, that is between the years of publication of *England and India* and the first volume of the *Economic History of India.*.

7. Naoroji, *Poverty,* pp. v, vii, 211, 224, *Speeches,* pp. 142, 227–8, 276–8, 328, 396, in *Statesman,* 19 January 1898, and in *India,* 7 August 1903, p. 67; G.V. Joshi, *Writings and Speeches,* Poona, 1912, pp. 674–7; Prithwas Chandra, Ray, *The Poverty Problem in India,* Calcutta, 1895, pp. 37–9; P. Mehta, *Writings and Speeches,* edited by C.Y. Chintamani, Allahabad,

1905, p. 815; G.S. Iyer, *EA*, title page and pp. 116–7, 123–5, 239, 329, and in *East and West*, 1903, vol. II, p. 888; R.C. Dutt, *Economic History of India-Early British Rule*, 1956 impression of the edition first published in 1901, London, p. xviii, hereafter *EHI*, (in fact, both volumes of his *Economic History* are permeated with this feeling); Tilak, quoted in Pradhan and Bhagwat, *Lokamanya Tilak*, p. 72; L.M. Ghose in *CPA*, p. 761; G.K. Gokhale, *Speeches*, published by G.A. Natesan, 2nd edition, Madras, 1916, pp. 1084, 1156–7; A.L. Roy's article in *Mahratta*, 30 May, 6 June 1886. For newspapers, see, for example, *Hitechchu*, 25 March (*RNPBom.*, 3 April 1880); *ABP*, 19 October 1882, 4 January 1883, 7 October 1886, 12 February 1892, 20 May 1896; *Mahratta*, 21 December 1884, 30 December 1894, 30 October 1904; *Ananda Bazar Ptrika*, 31 March (*Report on the Native Press for Bengal (weekly), 1870–1905* (hereafter *RNPBeng.*), 5 April 1884); *Navavibhakar*, 21 April (ibid., 26 April 1884); *Sadharani*, 15 June (ibid., 21 June 1884); *Samaya*, 30 November (ibid., 5 December 1885); *Shams-ul-Akhbar*, 12 April (*RNPM*, April 1886); *Khasm-ul-Akhbar*, 17 June (ibid., June 1886); *Dhumketu*, 20 May (*RNPBeng.*, 28 May 1887); *Bangabasi*, 30 June (ibid., 7 July 1888), 14 June (ibid., 21 June 1890); *Tohfa-i-Hind*, 13 August (*RNPN*, 19 August 1891*)*; *Hitakari*, undated (*RNPBeng.*, 17 December 1892); *Bangabasi*, 1 September (ibid., 8 September 1894); *Poona Vaibhav*, 15 March (*RNPBom.*, 21 March 1896); *Jami-ul-Ulum*, 14 April (*RNPN*, 21 April 1897); *Indu Prakash*, 8 August (*RNPBeng.*, 13 August 1898); *Bengalee*, 9 April 1900; *Kesari*, date missing (*RNPBom.*, 18 January 1902); *Indian People*, 27 February 1903; *Hindu*, 13 October 1903; *Hind Vijaya*, 8 February (*RNPBom.*, 21 February 1905).

8. For example *Arunodaya*, 15 May (*RNPBom.*, 21 May 1881); *ABP*, 19 October 1882, 13 February 1894; *Som Prakash*, 21 August (*RNPBeng.*, 26 Aug. 1882); *Hindi Pradip*, January–February (Report on the Native Press for Punjab, North–West Provinces and Oudh (after 1902-UP) (weekly), 1888–1905, (hereafter *RNPN)*, See *RNPN*, 8 June 1901); C.Y. Chintamani in *Hindustan Review* and *Kayastha Samachar* (known as *Kayastha Samachar* from 1899–1902), Allahabad, 1899–1905, hereafter *HR*, See February 1903, p. 233.

9. A.O. Hume, *A Speech on the Indian National Congress and its Origins, Aims, and Objects*, delivered at a public meeting held at Allahabad, 30 April 1888, p. 16.

10. Pherozeshah Mehta put the sentiment in another way by describing nationalist agitation as an effort to raise British rule's 'nobler from its grosser part' (P. Mehta, *Writings and Speeches*, p. 483).

11. This was put in a very interesting manner by Lal Mohan Ghose, President of the Congress in 1903, as follows: '... may we not ask whether we are to believe that the policy which many years ago killed our indigenous industries, which even only the other day and under a Liberal Administration unblushingly imposed excise duties on our cotton manufactures, which steadily drains our national resources to the extent

of something like 20 millions sterling per annum, and which, by imposing heavy burdens on our agricultural population, increases the frequency and intensity of our famines to an extent unknown in former times,—are we to believe that the various administrative acts which have led to those results *were directly inspired by a beneficial Providence?*' (in *CPA*, p. 743) (Emphasis added).

12 For the British view, see, for example, George Hamilton's views, quoted in Eric Stokes, *The English Utilitarians and India,* Oxford, 1959, p. 300; Lord Curzon, *Speeches Vol. I,* Calcutta, 1900, p. vi. For the Indian view, see Naoroji, *Speeches,* pp. 123, 332, *Essays,* p. 36, *Poverty,* p. 216, in *CPA,* p. 181; Dr R.B. Ghose, *Speeches and Writings,* 3rd edition, Madras, undated, p. 152; A.M. Bose in *CPA,* p. 436; 'The Broken Pledge and its Consequences', *JPSS,* July 1879, vol. II, no. 1, pp. 43, 46; *Mahratta,* 6 November 1881; R.C. Dutt, *England and India,* London, 1897, p. 118.

13. See, for example, Gokhale, *Speeches,* p.1079.

14. For example, Curzon, *Speeches Vol. II,* Calcutta, 1902, p. 91, and *Speeches Vol. III,* Calcutta, 1904, p. 98; J. Strachey, *India,* new edition, 1894, and revised edition 1903, London, pp. 495–6; General George Chesney, *Indian Polity,* 3rd edition, London, 1904, pp. 390, 394, 398–9. For a detailed discussion of this view, see Stokes, *The English Utilitarians and India,* p. 65 and Chapter IV. For James Mill's views, see William Digby, *'Prosperous' British India,* London, 1901, p. 264. According to Dufferin, the foundations of British rule in India were 'Our armies, which secure the submission of the uneducated and apathetic masses; and the universal conviction in the minds of the rest of the community that, whatever its shortcomings, our administration is just, impartial, and beneficient, and that the only alternative to it would be either the revival of a Mahomedan tyranny, anarchy, or a Russian conquest' (Dufferin to Secretary of State, 9 July 1886, *Dufferin Papers,* microfilm copies in the National Archives of India, New Delhi). Similarly, the *Times* of 30 December 1897, after boasting that 'There is no achievement in the history of their race in which men of British blood took more pride than in their government of India. In none have the best qualities of rulers—courage, justice, foresight, and self-sacrifice—been more constantly or more nobly displayed... Whatever criticism may be made upon particular points, the main facts are too manifest for reasonable challenge', declared that the principles of parliamentary government were not applicable to India. 'To do so', it wrote, 'would be a short cut to anarchy. The masses of the Indian population are absolutely incapable of self-government in any shape, and they would not quietly submit to be governed by natives'.

15. In 1887, J.B. Piele had remarked in a letter to Dufferin that, 'In fact there is not in India any grievance such as incites men to throw away the comfort of peace and draw the sword against their rulers' (2 October 1887, *Dufferin Papers*). The economic agitation of the early nationalists created precisely this sense of grievance.

16. For example, Dadabhai Naoroji laid stress on this fact in 1893 in his Presidential Address to the Indian National Congress: 'We may, I am convinced, rest fully assured that whatever political or national benefit we may acquire will in one or the other way benefit all classes, the benefit of each taking various forms. The interests of us all are the same. We are all in the same boat. We must sink or swim together....If the country is prosperous, then if one gets scope in one walk of life, another will have in another walk of life. As our Indian saying goes: "If there is water in the well it will come to the cistern." If we have the well of prosperity we shall be able to draw each our share of it. But if the well is dry we must all go without any at all' (in *CPA*, pp. 180–1). Also see Joshi, *Writings and Speeches*, pp.748–9; R.M. Sayani in (*CPA*, p. 309).

17. It may be noted that the lowering of land revenue was the only agrarian demand that was taken up for active agitation by the National Congress during its more vigorous phase during the 1920s and 1930s. The protection of the rack-rented tenant was left to the individual efforts of the Congressmen till 1936 when the Congress for the first time demanded a thorough change of the land tenure and revenue systems' and 'immediate relief to the smaller peasantry by a substantial reduction of agricultural rent and revenue' (Indian National Congress, *Resolutions on Economic Policy and Programme 1924–54*, New Delhi, 1954, pp. 12–13). The only agrarian demand that the Eleven Points put forward by Gandhiji as the price for calling off Civil Disobedience included was reduction of land revenue (B. Pattabhi Sitaramayya, *The History of the Indian National Congress, 1885–1935*, Madras, 1935, p. 619).

18. Interestingly enough, when R.C. Dutt pleaded for the inclusion of at least one Indian in the Viceregal Executive Council, he also suggested that the Indian member should be assigned the departments of Land Revenue, Industries, and Agriculture (in *CPA*, pp. 497–8).

19. *Indian People*, 27 February 1903. [...]

3   Rewriting Histories of Nationalism*
The Politics of 'Moderate Nationalism' in India, 1870–1905

Sanjay Seth

[...] What is [...] distinctive about narratives of nationalism is that [...] the process of constituting a historical narrative lends itself to a certain circularity. The identification/selection of what is part of the story of nationalism necessarily occurs at the level of ideas and consciousness; but this consciousness or sentiment has then to be situated, and is often explained, in terms of the social forms and practices in which it was embodied [...].

[...]

[...] It is this form of explanation, characteristic of the history of nationalism, that this essay seeks to call into question. It does so not by denying that nationalism is both material and discursive, and certainly not by seeking to reverse the causal order, but rather by problematizing the distinction between the social or material and the discursive.

I offer for this purpose an examination of Indian nationalism, more specifically of what in the historiography of Indian nationalism is usually characterized as an early, or beginning, period. I concentrate on early or 'moderate' Indian nationalism because its claim to being part of the story of nationalism is already problematic; how it comes to be written into the history of Indian nationalism brings out clearly the principles of selection involved in narrating the history of nationalism and the sort of historical problems this narrative sets itself. This essay, then, offers an alternative or supplementary reading of a period in the history of Indian nationalism and, in so doing, also seeks to problematize the narratives of Indian nationalism. It is an essay in history, as well as on historiography.

Most accounts of Indian nationalism include, or begin with, the last two or three decades of the nineteenth century. They do so despite the fact

* Originally published in *The American Historical Review*, vol. 104, no. 1, February 1999, pp. 95–116. In the present version some portions of the text and notes have been removed. For the complete text see the original version.

that in the pre-Congress era, as in the early years of the Indian National Congress (INC), the goal of Indian nationalists fell well short of full national independence, and the methods they employed in pursuit of their goals included neither mass mobilization nor the extra-constitutionalist methods that were later to be characteristic of the Congress. Why this should qualify as part of the story of Indian nationalism at all is, therefore, itself a question. Part of the answer is simply that for many historical accounts the history of Indian nationalism is synonymous with the history of the Indian National Congress, and therefore all activities associated with the Congress form part of the history of nationalism. This is either taken to be so self-evident as to require no argumentation; or else the equation is justified by the claim that the Congress was the first body organized on an all-India scale, and that sought to speak for Indians, rather than (as with earlier organizations) Bengalis, landholders, Hindus, or Muslims, or their caste brethren.[1]

[...]

Below, I offer a different reading of Moderate Nationalism [...]. As a first step, I identify the key elements of moderate nationalism; the individual elements that collectively constituted the discourse of Moderate Nationalism, and constituted it as 'moderate'.

First of all, this was a nationalism that raised very modest demands. The main demands articulated at the annual sessions of the Congress in its early years had to do with expanding the powers of the Provincial and Central Councils and introducing elected members into them, holding the civil service examination in India as well as England, separating the judicial and executive functions, extension of trial by jury to areas not covered by this, reduction of the increasing burden of the 'Home Charges' (particularly those charges debited to India that arose out of British military adventures), income tax reform, opposition to increases in the salt tax, extension of Permanent Settlement, reform of the police, and repeal of forest laws. The issue of 'poverty' was central to the concerns of the Congress, and resolutions to do with it generally expressed concern at the dimension of the problem and advocated measures—Permanent Settlement, Indianization of the civil service, reduction in Home Charges, the introduction of responsible government—that either by reducing the colonial drain of wealth or facilitating industrial development would alleviate the problem.

In general, this nationalism sought reform of the bureaucracy that ruled India, the key elements in such reform being Indianization of the

Indian civil service and the introduction of some measure of responsible government. Surendranath Banerjea, two-time president of the INC [Indian National Congress] and frequently the one to move resolutions on the twin issues of civil service reform and responsible government, explained in his autobiography that he felt that these 'lay at the root of all other Indian problems, and their satisfactory settlement would mean the solution of them all'.[2] In particular, it was argued that such administrative/political reforms were the key to economic improvement. Dadabhai Naoroji, three-time INC president in 1895 and the energetic propagator of the theory that England was 'draining' India of wealth, told the Congress that Indianization of the civil service 'will go far to settle the problem of the poverty of the Indian people'.[3] In a similar vein, Gopal Krishna Gokhale, INC president in 1905, declared, 'It is with me a firm conviction that unless you have a more effective and more potent voice in the government of your own country, in the administration of your own affairs, in the expenditure of your own revenues, it is not possible for you to effect much in the way of industrial development'.[4] Such a link was asserted by the Congress as a body from the beginning; its first resolution on the question of poverty, adopted at its 1886 session, immediately went on 'to record its fixed conviction that the introduction of Representative Institutions will prove to be one of the most important practical steps towards the amelioration of the condition of the people'.[5]

Such goals were modest enough. They were 'nationalist' almost by default, inasmuch as the petitioners were Indian and the petitioned British. Leading Moderates frequently referred to the 1833 Government of India Act and the royal proclamation of 1858—both of which had stated that natives would not be debarred from holding office in the bureaucracy that governed India—professing to desire nothing more than what was promised in those documents but had not in fact been granted.[6] The Congress did imply that, some time in the future, India would be ready for self-government. This was not very radical an expectation, for the idea that the British were 'preparing' Indians for eventual self-government was gaining some strength even in official circles, especially since William Gladstone's return as prime minister in 1880 and Lord Ripon's viceroyalty.[7] But all the Moderate leaders agreed that for the moment this was impractical, and what the Congress sought was much less. As Banerjea put it at the fourth annual session of the INC, at Allahabad, 'The people of India are, at present, neither asking for, nor thinking of, representative government, but what they do insist on is, that an appreciable portion of the advisers of Government should be their elected representatives'.[8]

Second, the means by which such goals were pursued were also exceedingly moderate. Indeed, it was this above all else that led to sharp criticism and charges of 'mendicancy'. The Moderate leaders prided themselves on, and reiterated at every opportunity, the gradualist and constitutionalist nature of their political activity. When the Congress adopted its first (short-lived) constitution in 1899, this declared, 'The object of the Indian National Congress shall be to promote by constitutional means the interests and well-being of the people of the Indian Empire', and the provincial units of the Congress were to engage in political activity 'on the lines of general appreciation of British rule and of constitutional action for the removal of its defects'.[9]

Thus Congress resolutions opposing government action or inaction would not 'condemn' but rather 'regret'; and resolutions proposing some course of action or remedy to the government would not 'demand' but rather 'suggest' or, at the most, 'urge'. More generally, the style of functioning of Moderate Nationalism was one that some came to find lacking in self-respect—Aurobindo Ghose, one of the early and trenchant 'Extremist' critics of the INC, referred to 'the general timidity of the Congress, its glossing over of hard names ... its fear of too deeply displeasing our masters'.[10] Moreover, a great deal of Congress activity in the years immediately before and after 1892 (the year Councils reform was enacted by the British parliament) was centred in England and directed at persuading the English. Congress speeches, even when addressed to an Indian audience, seemed to presume a second, English audience.[11] Thus an essential device in this art of persuasion was extensively to quote English and Anglo-Indian officials in support of any argument—in the speeches of many Moderate leaders, such quotes often constituted one-third or more of the text. In 1917, that eminently moderate body the Deccan Sabha, in an address to the secretary of state for India, Edwin Montagu, and the viceroy, Baron Chelmsford, acknowledged 'the frequent reproach that Indian politicians are too fond of quotations', and went on to explain why that was so:

> First, that we can never command the weight and authority of your great men; secondly, that neither the strong language nor the stronger arguments used by British Statesmen may be permissible to Indian Politicians; and third that the quotations may enable the statesmen and rulers of the present day to mark the departure from great traditions which we in India have so much reason to regret and to deplore.[12]

In the three sentences of this justification were summed up some of the defining features of the Moderates—the self-abnegation that was to distress many other nationalists, but then, in the second sentence, an admission that this was in part, at least, tactical, and, finally, the strategy underpinning all this revealed—to 'hold' the English to their own promises and 'traditions'.

If modesty of goals and moderation in aims were two factors constitutive of the Moderates' moderation, an active loyalism was a third, and one that underwrote the other two. However, to see this loyalism simply as a contingent 'limit' to their nationalism (and hence as something that could later easily be transcended) would be to miss an important aspect of Moderate Nationalism.

Loyalism was, among other things, an important part of the discursive strategy of Moderate Nationalism. Loyalty was frequently invoked to answer or preempt British accusations of disloyalty. Thus Congress leaders would avow that they were fully conscious of the benefits of British rule, and often proceed to enumerate these. Against the charge that the Congress represented a small and unrepresentative elite that had become disaffected with British rule, Badruddin Tyabji in his 1887 presidential address to the Madras Congress countered that it was this elite that was most conscious of the blessings of British rule: 'Who ... will better appreciate advantages of good roads, railways, telegraphs and post-offices, schools, colleges and universities, hospitals, good laws and impartial courts of justice?—the educated natives or the ignorant peasants of this country?'[13]

[...]

[...]Not all Congress leaders were as sanguine about, say, 'British justice' in India as their public pronouncements sometimes suggested. All had bitter experiences of European racial arrogance, and there is no doubt that such rhetorical excesses as those quoted above arose, in part, out of a desire to defuse the suspicion and antagonism of an autocratic colonial state that could at any time shut down the operations of the Congress and wreak its revenge upon what it perceived as a disloyal babu elite.

Nonetheless, Moderate leaders did believe in the 'providential' nature of British rule, if not in the justice of all particular facets and mani-festations of it. After enumerating its various benefits, as above, they would frequently seek to clinch the argument by declaring that they and the INC, far from being sources of sedition, were themselves the product of British rule—shining examples of its virtues, proof of its beneficial effects. As Banerjea put it, in a representative statement, 'The National Congress is the outcome of those civilizing influences which Macaulay and his co-adjutors were instrumental in planting in the government of this country'.[14] Such loyalism was neither purely tactical, nor was it merely a contingent 'limit', the point at which the nationalist imagination faltered and began to peter out. It was rather a constituent element of this nationalism, one of its structuring principles. It did indeed place a limit to criticism, *but it was also the very ground from which criticism became possible.*

Hence the characteristic form, as well as limit, of Moderate Nationalism—it criticized British rule for failing to live up to its own promise. To urge the British to live up to their mission and their promises was part of the function of the INC—as Banerjea told the Pune Congress in 1895, 'In this Congress from year to year we ask England to accomplish her glorious work'.[15] Naoroji in his magnum opus, *Poverty and Un-British Rule in India*, attacked 'un-British' rather than British rule, declaring that 'a truly British course can and will certainly be vastly beneficent both to Britain and India'.[16] In his case as in others, Moderate Nationalists assailed the colonial connection for failing to fulfil its historic mission as the bearer of liberal and 'modern' institutions and values in India. British rule had been instrumental in the planting of some modern liberal institutions and values in India, and in the development of an elite class of educated Indians who had imbibed these values. However, Britain was failing to complete its appointed role, as evidenced by its selfish economic and political policies in India, and by its distrust of the very class that it had brought forth.

The fourth characteristic feature of moderate nationalism was an almost obsessive invocation of Indian poverty. It is indeed curious that a privileged elite should have been so preoccupied with the issue. For the last three decades of the nineteenth century, and into the twentieth, 'poverty' was the biggest stick with which the Congress beat the British. Apart from Naoroji's relentless publicizing of Indian poverty and the 'drain of wealth' from India to England,[17] there was a veritable flood of literature investigating the subject. Some of the landmarks in this included P.C. Ray's *The Poverty Problem in India* (1895), William Digby's '*Prosperous' British India* (1901), Romesh Chandra Dutt's *England and India: A Record of Progress during a Hundred Years* (1897), his monumental two-volume *Economic History of India* (1901–3), and Subramanya Iyer's *Some Economic Aspects of British Rule in India* (1903). In the press and in books, in Congress speeches and resolutions, India's poverty and the 'drain of wealth' were constantly discussed and the blame laid at Britain's door.

There is no counterpart for such an obsessive concern with poverty in the history of the European bourgeoisie's struggle for power, and thus it is not surprising that this should be seen by some historians as the 'immoderate' or radical face of moderate nationalism, or even interpreted, as Bipan Chandra does, as evidence for how a colonial elite, because it too laboured under the disadvantages of colonialism, cast its lot with 'the people'.[18]

Before we accept any such readings, however, we would do well to pause and consider the meaning and significance of this preoccupation with poverty, given that it was not accompanied by any equivalent concern for *the poor*. The evidence on this is overwhelming. With a few exceptions—such as its sympathy for peasant protests at revenue enhancement, which affected the British Indian government rather than Indian landlords (and opposition to which fitted in neatly with the theory of a 'drain of wealth')—the Congress in these early years was either uninterested in or opposed to government measures purportedly directed at protecting and improving the lot of rural cultivators or urban workers. Thus the Congress expressed alarm at the cadastral survey being undertaken in Bengal at its 1893 and 1894 sessions, describing measures directed at granting tenants greater security as 'interference' and 'a national catastrophe'.[19] Similarly, the Congress expressed its opposition to the Punjab Land Alienation Bill at its 1899 session and opposed the Bombay Land Revenue Code Amendment Bill of 1901. So, too, with legislation seeking to regulate and protect the rights of industrial workers, except where such legislation would strike primarily at British interests— as when the Congress called for an increase in the wages of Assamese coolies at its 1901 session. However, the Indian Factories Act of 1881 was condemned by the *Journal of the Poona Sarvajanik Sabha*, and on this occasion *The Hindu* went so far as to declare that 'all the so-called hardships of the factory men are a fiction'.[20] In 1900, the INC passed a resolution opposing those sections of the Indian Mines Bill that sought to regulate the employment of child and female labour.[21]

All this is well known, and the point here is not the polemical one that the Congress put a class interest before the national one. It is perfectly true that the Congress was composed of a privileged elite with little experience of how the lower orders lived,[22] but that only makes their concern with the issue of poverty all the more remarkable. The point is rather that genuine preoccupation with *poverty* did not translate, by and large, into practical efforts to assist and protect the *poor*. What, then, did this concern with the question of poverty signify?

To answer this question, it is necessary to determine what it was that poverty was contrasted with; what was the desired state that poverty fell short of or negated? There are at least two ways of conceiving of poverty. One is as a brute, palpable reality, absolute or relative, which derives its force from a contrast with plenty. The other is to place it within a continuum, where it signifies not so much sheer lack as incompleteness. This narrative is a historically recent one. Its name is progress, its end point, modernity, and its engine or driving force, economic 'development'.

This, I suggest, was what poverty signified for the moderate nationalists; it functioned as a metaphor for backwardness, which under colonial conditions meant powerlessness and humiliation. Thus it was that the solution the moderates advocated for poverty was not direct amelioration of the lot of the poor but rather economic and industrial modernization—a goal that could be seen to conflict with, and where it did so was seen as prior to, measures aimed at improving tenant security or labour conditions.[23] This explains why neglect of the poor was combined with such concern with poverty, and why economic reform, and in particular industrialization, was repeatedly invoked as the antonym of and solution to poverty.[24]

The image of modernity that the Indian elites had in mind was Europe, more specifically England. England was seen to have conquered India partly because England was industrialized and economically 'strong', as India was not. Mahadev Govind Ranade, a social reformer and founding member of the INC, remarked, 'Commercial and Manufacturing predominance naturally confers Political ascendancy'.[25] Banerjea spelled out why the Congress devoted so much attention to economic issues: 'Ours is a political organization; but we cannot overlook considerations which affect the development of our industries and our manufactures. The economic condition of a people has an intimate bearing upon their political advancement'.[26] To become modern and strong, India had to emulate England—and the unspoken question behind the poverty debate was, 'Why, after more than a century of British rule, has India not become wealthy and powerful like Britain?' This is what gave the debate on poverty its sharp edge, its critical potential—in India, it was the colonial elite that reproached the metropolitan bourgeoisie for failing to modernize and transform India, and this bourgeoisie that invoked the peculiarities of Indian 'culture' and the Indian character as excuses for its inability, or unwillingness, to do so.

However, if this lent a cutting edge to the poverty debate, making it a crucial part of the nationalist critique of British rule, it also served to give this nationalism its specifically moderate character. England served not only as a model to be emulated but, more important, was seen as the font from which modernity must needs radiate outward, until it reached even the colonies. Ranajit Guha's remark in a somewhat different context also applies here—Indian nationalists 'put their faith in the universalist pretensions of British capital'.[27] Doing so decisively shaped the character of their nationalism; however sharp the criticisms, this enterprise shared much with and expected much of its target.

These, then, were the four constituent elements of Moderate Nationalism. In summary, one could say that it was at once nationalist and liberal. It was nationalist in that the goals Moderate leaders sought were sought in the name of India and the Indian people. It was liberal and modernizing because these national aspirations would be expressed through liberal and representative institutions and because Indian interests were to be furthered by the development of a modern and industrialized economy.

Was it *because* it was liberal that the nationalism of the late nineteenth century was 'moderate'? That is, did its liberalism compromise its nationalist militancy? This suggestion was made by contemporary critics and has often been made since. The Moderate leaders' adulation of British institutions and ways, so the argument runs, blunted the sharp edge of their nationalism. Since the liberal political life they sought was also seen by them to be a product of British (or European) culture and history, any politics predicated on this was bound to be imitative and timid.

There is obviously considerable truth in such an assessment. Inasmuch as the Moderates aspired to institutions and a political culture they saw as rooted in European soil, their nationalist politics could not but be imitative, and inasmuch as such institutions were seen to lie within the gift of the British, they were bound to plead rather than demand. But this is still only part of the story, even if the most often told part.

To understand the meaning of Moderate Nationalism, it is not enough to identify liberalism as lying at the heart of its nationalist project, and thereby constricting its militancy. For it is not just that the nationalism of the Moderates was timid or partial because of their liberalism but also that their liberalism itself was of a peculiar and weak sort, a fact connected, among other things, with how they conceived the people who constituted the Indian nation and perceived their own relation with them.

When the Moderate leaders imagined, and spoke of and to, an Indian 'public', this public was a body considerably smaller than the people of India; most of the rural population, all women, and a large section of the urban population were not included.[28]And when they asked for representation on the governing or advisory bodies of state, they were not, as we have seen, asking for fully representative government. Nor was the 'responsible government' being sought to be based on an extensive male suffrage (as was the case in Britain). At its first session in 1885, the Congress called for an expansion of the advisory councils and for the introduction of an elective principle. Since the viceroy's and the Provincial Councils were only advisory, this fell well short of a call for representative government. The following year, elaborating on this, the Congress also made it clear that the 'elective principle' it championed was 'to be conferred only on those classes and members of the community, prima facie capable of exercising it wisely and independently'.[29] [...]

Thus the degree of representation desired as well as the suffrage on which it was to be based were to be limited. The reason—one that seemed so obvious to Moderate leaders that they seldom bothered to spell it out—was that India was not, in their view, yet 'ready' for fully representative self-government, based on an extensive (male) franchise, as in Britain. That 'India' was not ready meant that some Indians were not ready; needless to say, the Indians not able to cast a vote and exercise power 'wisely' and 'responsibly' were not Indians drawn from elite groups [...]

What, in the perception of the moderates, was the nature of the gulf separating them and their class from the masses, a gulf, one effect of which was that the elite were fitted for representative institutions, while the masses were not? What, more generally, was the attitude of the politically active elite toward the poor, and what place, if any, did they occupy in the discourse of Moderate Nationalism?

For the elites who constituted the bulk of the INC (and in this period they were primarily an urban, British-educated and English-speaking elite), the 'poverty-stricken masses' of India were something of an unknown quantity, a rhetorical abstraction. The divide between the nationalist elite and the bulk of the Indian population was real and vast. Recognizing this, the historiography of Indian nationalism has sometimes characterized this gap as the 'alienation' of the nationalist elite from the lower orders,[30] and pointed to this as the explanation for many of the characteristic features of early Indian nationalism. In this 'sociological' reading, of which there are many versions, a cause external to the actual discourse of moderate nationalism is invoked to explain the 'timidity' of that discourse. Versions of this historiographical approach differ precisely in that they identify different causes: class distinction between the elite and masses may be seen as the essence of alienation and hence of moderation, or else a cultural divide between an 'anglicized' leadership and a pre-modern population. In all cases, this gap and the inability of the nationalist elite to bridge it are cited as the explanation for the hesitancies and half-heartedness of moderate nationalism.

I do not wish to displace such explanations, for to varying degrees, they are persuasive. I do wish, however, to problematize the sharp distinction between the social and the discursive on which such explanations are premised, and which allow for the former to stand as cause and the latter as effect. Let us then note, first of all, that it is not that the nationalist elite 'failed' to bridge the gap between itself and the masses, for it never sought to do so. Aurobindo Ghose's trenchant indictment was precisely that the Congress 'has never been, *and has made no honest endeavour to be*, a popular body'.[31] While the Congress made some efforts to involve non-English-speaking elites in its activities, it made next to none at mobilizing non-elite groups. [...]

The Congress made no such efforts because it believed that the gap between it and the peasant masses was too vast to bridge through its efforts. Such bridging would require a great deal of time and would be effected not through overtures from the Congress but rather through the civilizing impact of British rule. Prolonged exposure to the rule of law, to good government, and the extension of education would enlighten and uplift the masses, raising them closer to the level of the elite. In the meantime, it was in fact necessary to convince the foreign rulers that their regenerating mission would be better accomplished if the educated Indians who comprised the nationalist elite were to be involved in the governance of the country. Thus the nationalist elite were not only aware of the division between themselves and the mass of their countrymen, they constantly drew attention to it.

This is the second complication: the gap between the moderate nationalist elite and the mass of Indians was not simply a social cause, operating from 'outside' the discourse of nationalism to shape it but rather was very much present 'in' that discourse. It was a central theme of this nationalism that the nationalist elite be accorded a more important place in affairs of state because it occupied a halfway point between the British and the natives. [...] Consequently, they were better able to explain the intentions and procedures of the foreign ruler to the masses than that ruler was. On the other hand, they were closer to their fellow countrymen in manners, dress, religion—closer to them, in short, in 'sentiment'. As a result, they were much better fitted than the British to recognize the needs and aspirations of India's masses and transmit these to their foreign rulers. [...] Naoroji told those attending the second session of the Congress, 'we, the educated classes, have become the true interpreters and mediators between the masses of our countrymen and our rulers'.[32]

The idea that the new elites would function to translate and disseminate the British mission was one that in ruling circles was at least as old as Thomas Babington Macaulay's Minute on Education (1835). Almost thirty-five years after Macaulay's Minute, Lord Napier was to tell the graduates of Madras University that Macaulay had succeeded: 'you, the adopted children of European civilization, are the interpreters between the stranger and the Indian, between the Government and the subject'.[33] However, soon after the founding of the Congress, official circles began vigorously to deny the obverse: the idea that these elites could lay any claim to representing the peasantry. Indeed, it became a standard means of dismissing Congress criticism of the British administration to declare that the Congress only spoke for a small, sectional class interest. [...] The rejoinder of Pherozshah Mehta, eminent Indian lawyer and Moderate leader, was representative: 'the microscopic minority can far better *and far more intuitively* represent the needs and the aspirations of their own countrymen than the still more microscopic minority of the omniscient District Officers'.[34]

The gap between the nationalist elite and the masses will not, then, serve to explain fully the character, and limits, of this nationalism. This gap did not simply operate as an external cause, shaping the discourse of moderate nationalism; it occupied a prominent place *in* that discourse. Drawing attention to the gap was part of the discursive strategy of moderate nationalism; it was part of the nationalist case as to why British rule needed to take a different form, one in which the Indian elites would play a greater role in administering the country.

We must look, therefore, not only to the relation between 'moderate' discourse and the 'social' but the place of the social in that discourse, not only to the relation of the nationalist elite to the masses but to its perception of that relationship. We know that the elite that made up the Congress in this period made a point of sharply distinguishing between itself and the masses, and we know further that it was integral to moderate nationalist discourse to declare that the masses could not represent themselves but needed to be represented. We need now to find what precisely it was that, in the eyes of this elite, made it an elite, very different from the rest of its countrymen, and also why in its view its countrymen could not represent themselves but needed the good offices of the elite to do so for them.

[...]

Homages to English education were staple fare of the nationalist rhetoric of this period. R.C. Dutt's remark—'Western education is perhaps the greatest of blessings India has gained under British rule'—was but one of a great number in this vein.[35] Histories of the introduction, progress, and effects of English education abounded, each of which hypostatized its object, so that sometimes education appeared not so much as an aspect of British rule but rather British rule as the necessary precondition to the introduction of English education. One of the earliest and more sober of these histories began as follows: 'The origin, rise and progress of English education in India ... constitute[s] one of the most significant episodes, not only in the annals of India, but in the history of the civilised world'.[36]

What led to such encomiums was the perception that education was not just the transmission of skills or literacy—indeed, it was hardly that, given the small numbers affected by it[37]—but rather the means to a much greater end, namely the transformation and regeneration of India. There were, of course, other aspects of British rule that were pointed to by Indians as well as their rulers as having the effect of 'regenerating' and civilizing India. Good government, which India was held to have lacked, was frequently pointed to as both evidence of India's regeneration and the necessary frame for further advance. In a similar vein, the 'rule of law', which had replaced arbitrary and despotic rule, was pointed to as an advance that paved the way, or provided the necessary conditions for, India's regeneration. Representative institutions and a free press were frequently singled out as providing the necessary framework for that 'material and moral progress' of India that was annually charted by its rulers. If out of all these, education was often singled out, as in R.C. Dutt's case, as 'perhaps' the greatest of all the blessings of British rule, it was because it was seen as that which enabled the other blessings to fully function. English education, and higher education in particular, was seen as structurally different from the other benefits of British rule, and hence especially important. Whereas the latter transformed the political and other structures of India, education created the people capable of understanding and operating these institutions; while the rule of law and bureaucratic government created new 'public' spaces, education created the public to occupy these spaces. As Banerjea explained to the Congress in 1902,

> The three great boons which we have received from the British Government are High Education, the gift of a Free Press and local Self-Government ... But high education is the most prized, the most deeply cherished of them all. It is high education which has made local Self-Government the success that it is admitted to be. It is again high education which has elevated the tone of the Indian Press.[38]

The institutional changes effected by British rule transformed India 'externally', but this would have remained purely external had not education created a class of Indians capable of 'internalizing' the regenerative effects of British rule. [...]

Education, then, occupied a special place in the discourse of moderate nationalism and, indeed, elite nationalism more generally. The dissemination of European knowledge was accorded a privileged role in the 'regeneration of India', because it 'generated' a new class of Indians, Indians who had imbibed the spirit that animated all institutional and other transformations effected by the British. [...] Education, which gave access to the spirit animating the transformation of India, consequently gave those who possessed it 'voice' in the new institutions of that new India. By that same logic, it rendered many others, who did not have access to this new spirit and these skills, mute; or, if they were the many without voice or influence even in pre-British India, rendered them further mute.

Thus it was that education came to be singled out for special attention in elite nationalist discourse. It served, on the one hand, as an important factor that, in the domain of a new 'public' life dominated by British-created institutions, distinguished elite from the non-elite. Further, the grounds of the distinction were such that distinguishing between elite and masses on the grounds of education simultaneously explained why the latter could not represent themselves but needed to be represented; education gave voice, and thus the 'dumb masses' could not speak for themselves but needed the elite to do so.

The nation, Benedict Anderson tells us in his work of the same title, is an 'imagined community'. Once a nationalism has made good its claim that a certain 'people' exists, by founding a state, a particular form of national imagining comes to be officially sanctioned and embodied in numerous practices and institutions—in constitutions, a parliament that represents the people and pursues the national interest, in tombs of unknown soldiers, in museums of national art and culture, in public holidays such as 4 July or Republic Day. Other forms of imagining the community continue to exist, of course;[39] but one mode of imagining the nation is given official sanction and material embodiment, and is to that extent the most visible and dominant form. By contrast, where nationalism is oppositional, where its longings have not yet yielded its own state but where, as in colonial India, it faces a hostile, colonial state, the 'evidence' for the existence of nationalism, and therefore that which allows us to write its history, can only be found in the diverse imaginings of national community: in nationalist organizations, in programmes, in literature and songs—in short, in all that which can plausibly be construed as expressing a national imagining.

The first task of the historiography of nationalism, in this latter instance, is to identify its object, which it can only do by identifying what it takes to be genuine, and socially significant, expressions of a will-to-nationhood. Its second task—logically distinguishable from the first but not separable from it—is to distinguish and connect the inevitably numerous and varied forms of national imagining. These may be characterized as 'moments' in the natural unfolding of nationalism, or as competing tendencies, or as temporal phases or stages in the evolution of a movement; in all cases, to connect these is part of the process of transforming a chronicle of nationalist happenings into a historical narrative of nationalism.

Nationalist historiography homogenizes the history of nationalism, either because it stumbles over the first step—its blinkered vision results in its only identifying one form of imagining the nation—or because, in telling the story of Indian nationalism, it assimilates all other forms of national imagining to this one form. A much superior historiography is one that is more sensitive to the varieties of imaginings of the nation and is particularly interested in the social and material circumstances in which these were embedded. However [...] having identified certain forms of imaginings, this historiography then takes the circumstances in which they are embedded to be the explanation, or even the cause, of what is imagined. In the case of Moderate Nationalism, for instance, the fact that this was an elite nationalism is quite correctly pointed out (because it serves to characterize this nationalism): but it is then made to double up as an explanation or cause for its moderation.

In this essay, I have sought to show the difficulties such a procedure encounters in writing the history of Moderate Nationalism. The loyalism of Moderate Nationalism cannot simply be explained as an externally imposed limit to the nationalist imagination, because it was part of the rhetorical and political strategy of this nationalism; the incessant invocation of the 'poverty of India' resists explanation in terms of the class origins of the nationalist leadership, given the privileged status of Moderate leaders, but it also resists explanation as evidence of their identification with the poor; and the distance between elite and masses, while real enough, was not simply the cause of a discursive consequence but present in that discourse as an important, structuring element. I have instead offered another account, in which the moderation of Moderate Nationalism lay not in a failure to imagine the nation, in an insufficiency or lack of nationalism to be explained by an external cause, but rather in the fact that its imagination was one in which the 'nation' included people unfitted for political rights, in which politics was identified with that domain of public life created and made possible by British rule, in which the inadequacies of 'the people' were measured by their distance from this domain, in which the educated elites had to represent the poor, rough, and ignorant masses, and where the *continuation* of British rule was necessary for its eventual supersession.

[...]

Notes

I am grateful to Ranajit Guha, Sumit Sarkar, and Tanika Sarkar for their comments on an earlier version of this essay; to Michael Grossberg and the anonymous readers of the AHR for their suggestions; and to Gyan Prakash and Vanita Seth for their comments on the penultimate draft. A special thanks to Dipesh Chakrabarty for engaging with successive versions.

1. For a recent example, see B.N. Pande, gen. ed., *A Centenary History of the Indian National Congress, 1885–1985*, 4 vols, New Delhi, 1985, vol. 1, especially the 'Foreword' by the then Prime Minister of India, Rajiv Gandhi.
2. Surendranath Banerjea, *A Nation in Making: Being the Reminiscences of Fifty Years of Public Life*, 1925; rpt edn, Bombay, 1963, p. 126.
3. Banerjea, Nation in Making, p. 17.
4. 'Our Political Situation' (public address, Madras, 25 July 1904), in *Speeches and Writings of Gopal Krishna Gokhale*, D.G. Karve and D.V. Ambekar, eds, 3 vols, London, 1966, vol. 2, p. 178.
5. A. Moin Zaidi and Shaheeda Zaidi (eds), *The Encyclopaedia of the Indian National Congress*, New Delhi, 1976- , vol. 1, p. 138.
6. Daniel Argov points out that, until 1908, all Congress reports had a cover sheet consisting of quotes from these acts and from British officials, under the title 'Some of England's Pledges to India'. Argov, *Moderates and*

Extremists in the Indian Nationalist Movement, 1883–1920, Bombay, 1967, p. 39 (the cover sheet is reproduced on 38).

7. See Sarvepalli Gopal, *British Policy in India, 1858–1905*, Cambridge, 1965, pp. 144 and following.

8. Zaidi, *Encyclopaedia of the Indian National Congress*, vol. 1, p. 249.

9. Ibid., vol. 3, p. 479.

10. Aurobindo Ghose, *New Lamps for Old* [1893–94], Pondicherry, 1974, p. 11.

11. Douglas E. Haynes makes the point that, before the advent of a Gandhian style of politics in Surat, 'public meetings were means of presenting a cause to the colonial rulers rather than a method of stirring popular enthusiasm': Haynes, *Rhetoric and Ritual in Colonial India: The Shaping of a Public Culture in Surat City, 1852–1928*, Berkeley, California, 1991, p. 221.

12. 'Address of the Deccan Sabha', mimeographed, Nehru Memorial Museum and Library, New Delhi, p. 20.

13. '1887 Presidential Address', in A. Moin Zaidi (ed.), *Congress Presidential Addresses*, 5 vols, New Delhi, 1985–89, vol. 1, p. 44.

14. '1895 Presidential Address', in Zaidi, *Congress Presidential Addresses*, vol. 1, p. 223.

15. Ibid., p. 286.

16. Dadabhai Naoroji, *Poverty and Un-British Rule in India* (London, 1901), p. v. A few pages later, Naoroji declared (pp. xii–xiii), 'My whole object in all my writings is to impress upon the British People, that instead of a disastrous explosion of the British Indian Empire, as must be the result of the present dishonourable un-British system of government, there is a great and glorious future for Britain and India to an extent unconceivable [sic] at present, if the British people will awaken to their duty, will be true to their British instincts of fair play and justice, and will insist upon the faithful and conscientious fulfilment of all their great and solemn promises and pledges'.

17. The economic complaints of the nationalist elite—over excessive taxation, wasteful government expenditures, military adventures paid for by India—were knitted together by Dadabhai Naoroji into a more comprehensive and damning claim, namely that England was enriching itself at the expense of India, via a 'drain of wealth'. For a good summary and appraisal of Naoroji's economic theories, see Birendranath N. Ganguli, *Dadabhai Naoroji and the Drain Theory*, New Delhi, 1965. See also Bipan Chandra, *The Rise and Growth of Economic Nationalism in India*, New Delhi, 1966.

18. See Chandra, *Economic Nationalism*.

19. John R. McLane, *Indian Nationalism and the Early Congress*, Princeton, New Jersey, 1977, p. 236.

20. Quoted in Chandra, *Economic Nationalism*, pp. 334, 336.

21. Chandra, *Economic Nationalism*, p. 353.

22. On the social background of Congress leaders in this period, see McLane, *Indian Nationalism and the Early Congress*.

23. Thus opposition to regulation of land tenure, factory hours, and so on was usually voiced on the grounds that it would throttle infant Indian industries; and, moreover, that this, rather than philanthropy, was behind such government measures.

24. By the 1890s, almost every presidential address to the Congress dilated, usually at length, on the importance of industrial development. Lord Curzon was to complain that the twin subjects of technical education and industrial development had 'an extraordinary fascination for the tongue in India'; quoted in N.G. Chandravarkar's presidential address at the 1900 (Lahore) Congress, in Zaidi, Congress *Presidential Addresses*, vol. 1, p. 495. M.G. Ranade, one of the most articulate and influential champions of industrialization, flatly declared, 'there can be no doubt the permanent salvation of the Country depends upon the growth of Indian Manufactures and Commerce'. Ranade, *Essays on Indian Economics*, Bombay, 1899, p. 121.

25. Ranade, *Essays on Indian Economics*, p. 186.

26. '1895 Presidential Address', in Zaidi, *Congress Presidential Addresses*, vol. 1, p. 257.

27. Ranajit Guha, 'Dominance without Hegemony and Its Historiography', in Guha (ed.), *Subaltern Studies VI*, Delhi, 1992, p. 227.

28. Haynes makes the same point in relation to the municipal politics of Surat—that when the educated elite spoke of the public, 'No one ... suggested that the public meant anything as broad as the entire urban population'. *Rhetoric and Ritual*, p. 157.

29. Quoted in Sarkar, *Modern India, 1885–1947*, p. 90.

30. See, for instance, Sumit Sarkar, *'Popular' Movements and 'Middle Class' Leadership in Late Colonial India*, Calcutta, 1983, p. 35.

31. Ghose, *New Lamps for Old*, p. 26 (emphasis added).

32. '1886 Presidential Address', in Zaidi, *Congress Presidential Addresses*, vol. 1, p. 26.

33. Lord Napier, Speech at 12th Convocation of Madras University, in K. Subba Rao, ed., *Convocation Addresses of the Universities of Bombay and Madras* (Madras, 1892), p. 53.

34. '1890 Presidential Address', in Zaidi, *Congress Presidential Addresses*, vol. 1, p. 88 (emphasis added).

35. Romesh Dutt, *The Economic History of India in the Victorian Age*, 7th edn, London, 1950, p. 198. Half a century later, an 'Address' to Montagu and Chelmsford delivered by a delegation of the All-India Congress and Muslim League, including Banerjea, Bal Gangadhar Tilak, and Mohandas Gandhi, described 'liberal English education' as 'Britain's most imperishable monument in India'. Mimeograph, Nehru Memorial Museum and Library, New Delhi, p. 1.

36. Syed Mahmood, *A History of English Education in India: Its Rise, Development, Progress, Present Condition and Prospects* (1895; rpt edn), Delhi, 1981, p. 1.

37. In 1901–2, the total number of students in colleges in India was only 17,148. *Progress of Education in India, 1897/8–1901/2*, Calcutta, p. 81. In 1928, only 4.51 per cent of the total population was enrolled in any educational institution, at any level. *Progress of Education in India, 1927–32*, 2 vols, Delhi, 1934, vol. 1, p. 15.

38. '1902 Presidential Address', in Zaidi, *Congress Presidential Addresses*, vol. 2, p. 118.

39. Not least of all in South Asia, where the elites who sought to lead the struggle against colonialism sometimes secured dominance but never hegemony. See Guha, 'Dominance without Hegemony'.

4 Trends in Bengal's Swadeshi Movement*

Sumit Sarkar

The politics of the Bengal's swadeshi age at first sight appears to present a fairly simple picture of a united movement against the partition gradually splitting up into 'moderate' and 'extremist' (or 'nationalist') currents, with the second trend eventually developing into 'terrorism' (or what Dr R.C. Majumdar likes to call 'militant nationalism'). This is the framework accepted by most historians of the period,[1] and I began my own work with similar ideas.

In course of my research, however, I began to find it increasingly difficult to fit the extremely rich ideological controversies of the age concerning objectives, techniques, and social ideals into this threefold scheme. I also came across some contemporary evidence indicating an awareness of a more complicated situation. The Editorial Reflections entitled 'The "Moderates" and the "Extremists"' in Prithwischandra Ray's *Indian World* of March–April 1907 note three subdivisions within each of the above of two broad categories. The moderates all share an 'attachment to the British connection' and consider colonial self-government to be the ultimate goal, but include subgroups of loyalist aristocrats, very cautions politicians of the Mehta Gokhale brand, and the Bengal variety. The last-named no longer have much faith in the British, but still desire the continuance of British rule purely on grounds of expediency; they are supposed to stand for 'a most active and persistent policy of passive resistance'. The extremists in their turn are divided into the 'Tagore group' advocating selfhelp and autonomous development ignoring British rule; those who feel British rule to be 'incompatible with our national progress' and want to '*prepare*' for its overthrow; and those wanting to force the British to 'clear out of India *at once*'.

Not all the subgroups seem equally important or relevant for a study of Bengal during the years 1903–8. Loyalists pure and simple demand

* Originally published in Sumit Sarkar, *The Swadeshi Movement in Bengal, 1903–1908*, New Delhi, People's Publishing House, 1973, pp. 31–5.

little attention in an analysis of nationalist trends. The distinction between the Bengal moderates and the Mehta group has some basis. Bepinchandra Pal in an article (1909) on Krishnakumar Mitra remarked thankfully that there were no Gokhales or Mehtas in Bengal;[2] Hemendraprasad Ghosh mentions two reconciliation bids by Bhupendranath Bose in 1908 after the Surat spilt which were spurned by Pherozeshah Mehta;[3] and that some kind of a united platform was still possible in Bengal was indicated by the Pabna and Hooghly provincial conferences of February 1908 and September 1909.[4] But this distinction is not very important in a study deliberately confined to Bengal alone. The statement that men like Surendranath were standing consistently for passive resistance is rather dubious, and it probably reflects the writer's eagerness to make this trend—which he obviously prefers—more acceptable in an increasingly radical Bengal. The distinction between the last two extremist subgroups remains vague, but perhaps may be interpreted as a tactful way of referring to the difference between advocates of passive resistance and believers in armed struggle or 'terrorism'.

A fourfold classification thus begins to emerge—moderates; the trend towards selfdevelopment without inviting an immediate political clash (which I have decided to call 'constructive swadeshi' for want of a better name); political extremism using 'extended boycott' or passive resistance in addition to selfhelp efforts; and terrorism. The *India World* analysis was made by a friend of Surendranath, but it is interesting that the article was summarized within a few weeks in the pages of the *Bande Mataram*, the newspaper representing the opposite end of the political spectrum.[5] Even more significant is the fact that Aurobindo's brilliant series of articles on passive resistance[6] seem to assume a similar frame of reference. Here the programme of the 'new party' is sharply demarcated not only from 'petitioning' but also from mere 'selfdevelopment and selfhelp'—the latter being criticized for ignoring basic political realities.[7] Aurobindo also distinguishes between the present programme of passive resistance and 'aggressive resistance' culminating in 'armed revolt'—the latter is not ruled out in principle if repression gets more intense, but will obviously be quite a distinct method. Finally, the revolutionary Bhupendranath Dutta in an account written in the 1920s and revised in 1949 made the categorical assertion that the opponents of moderate 'mendicancy' in swadeshi Bengal—all too often mistakenly considered to be part of a single camp—in reality included three distinct groups: the followers of 'Rabi Babu's Swadeshi Samaj movement', the extremists led by men like Pal, and the revolutionaries.[8]

The contemporary confusion noted by Bhupendranath and perpetuated by historians has led to the virtual ignoring of the autonomous stature of constructive swadeshi as one kind of reaction against moderate politics. There has been a strong tendency also to consider the extremism of the 1905–8 period as merely a kind of preparation for that revolutionary terrorism which has such glamour in Bengal even today. Thus while the theoretical contributions of Pal and Aurobindo to the techniques of passive resistance are fairly well known, relatively little attention has been paid so far by historians to the practical application of these methods in the swadeshi period. The shift to methods of individual violence is regarded as a matter of course, an inevitable reflex of British repression—the crucial question left unasked is why a sustained mass movement could not develop on the basis of passive resistance techniques (as happened later in the Gandhian era) despite repression.

Another important but neglected theme is the ideological conflict between modernism and traditionalism—between an attitude which broadly speaking demands social reforms, tries to evaluate things and ideas by the criteria of reason and present-day utility, and bases itself on a humanism seeking to transcend limits of caste and religion; and a logically opposite trend which defends and justifies existing social mores in the name of immemorial tradition and the glorious past, and which tends to substitute emotion and faith for reason. This is a conflict which can be traced right through the nineteenth century from the days of the Atmiya Sabha and the Dharma Sabha,[9] and it continued at the heart of the swadeshi movement just as in the 'renaissance' which had preceded and prepared the way for it. In so far as the swadeshi age saw a determined though not entirely successful effort to give the national movement a solid mass basis, the period can be regarded as a sort of test for the relevance of these opposed ideological trends in the work of national awakening.

A study of a period which tries to distinguish trends always runs the risk of becoming too mechanical or schematic. Clarity demands the isolation of logically distinct tendencies, the 'ideal-types' of Weberian jargon, but these do not necessarily or even usually imply clear-cut groups. Contradictory attitudes within a single man at different times (or sometimes even simultaneously) are not uncommon. The elements of unity also must not be ignored—thus almost all groups of Bengal patriots during 1905–8 opposed partition, supported boycott at least for a time and economic swadeshi throughout, participated to some extent in the national education movement, and talked (even if many often did not

act) in terms of self-reliance. I would like to add that the four trends
which I have distinguished were not successive temporal stages; they
may be found side by side with each other throughout the swadeshi
age. But—and that is the vital point—their relative importance varied
greatly with time. Thus mendicancy definitely predominated before 1905,
terrorism become the most significant kind of nationalist activity after
1908, while the brief but fascinating intervening years saw the first try-
out of the techniques of passive resistance in India. The whole framework
should be regarded as a kind of abstract model, relevant only at a high
level of generalization, but useful perhaps in an exploration of those
shifts within the movement, which in their totality reveal the inner logic
or dynamics of the age.

NOTES

[A first draft of this chapter was published in the *Bengal Past and Present*,
January–July, July–December 1965.]

1. Cf. for instance, the numerous writings of Haridas and Uma Mukherji;
   R.C. Majumdar's *History of the Freedom Movement*, vol. II, 1963; Amales
   Tripathi's *The Extremist Challenge*, 1967; and Daniel Argov's *Moderates
   and Extremists in the Indian Nationalist Movement*, 1967. Bimanbihari
   Majumdar in his *Militant Nationalism in India*, 1966, has referred to
   Prithwischandra Ray's classification of the extremists into three categories
   in 1907, p. 75, but he has not tried to develop this interesting hint.
2. Reprinted in Aurobindo Ghosh, *Character-Sketches*, 1957.
3. Hemendraprasad Ghosh, *Congress*, 1921, pp. 216–23.
4. For the decisions of the Pabna Conference, see Home Political Proceedings
   A, March 1909, n. 10, Annexure B; and for an account of the Hooghly
   Conference, Home Political Proceedings B, November 1909, n. 103–4.
5. *Bande Mataram*, 21 May 1907.
6. Ibid., 9–23 April 1907—reprinted in Aurobindo Ghosh, *Doctrine of Passive
   Resistance*, 1948.
7. '...to attempt social reform, educational reform, industrial expansion, the
   moral improvement of the race without aiming first and foremost at
   political freedom, is the very height of ignorance and futility'.—Aurobindo
   Ghosh, *Doctrine of Passive Resistance*, p. 3.
8. Bhupendranath Dutta, *Bharater Dwitiya Swadinata Sangram*, 3rd edn,
   1949, pp. 50, 158.
9. For an interpretation of the Bengal renaissance in terms of such an
   underlying ideological conflict, see S.C. Sarkar, 'Rabindranath Tagore and
   the Renaissance in Bengal', *Enquiry*, no. 5, 1961.

PART II

THE COMING OF
MAHATMA GANDHI

5   The Mahatma and Modern India*

Judith Brown

[...]. M.K. Gandhi [...] was by common consent one of the greatest leaders Asia has produced in an era of colonial nationalisms and decolonization, who in his own life time was called a saint and a machiavellian politician, and who has become in independent India both a national myth and an embarrassment. Accounts of the importance of Gandhi in modern India tend to fall into two main categories. There are those who dismiss him, often regretfully, as an idealist whose utopian plans for a democracy of village commonwealths and a non-violent society have collapsed in the face of economic and political necessity and the machinations of unscrupulous politicians. In the words of Jayaprakash Narayan, 'If you consider the political ideologies attaining in India today, you would find that somehow one who is called the Father of the Nation is completely missing from all of them'.[1] Such pessimism assesses Gandhi as if he had been solely a dispenser of blue-prints for a brave new world, and fails to see him as a dynamic leader whose greatest influence flowed from the type of movement he led and the techniques he used, rather than from the peculiarly personal ideals he held. On the other hand, there are those who hail him as the Father of India and try to draw direct causal connexions between his ideals and many of the major changes which have occurred in India since 1947, particularly the official abolition of Untouchability and the institution of *panchayat raj*. But this is the perspective of the biographer. It underrates the complexities of politics and society and their interaction, and turns a blind eye to the innumerable cross currents which make up the main stream of Indian social and political activity.

Bearing in mind these types of analyses and their weaknesses, I have limited the scope of this article to two objectives. Firstly, I trace some of the main ideas Gandhi put forward, discuss influences which coincide with or militate against these ideas, and investigate their fate in

* Originally published in the *Modern Asian Studies*, © Cambridge University Press, vol. 3, no. 4, 1969, pp. 321–42. In the present version some portions of the text and notes have been removed. For the complete text see the original version.

modern India. I conclude that generally it is fruitless to look for the Mahatma's influence in contemporary India in terms of direct 'legacies'. This may seem a rather negative undertaking; but it clears the ground for the second, more positive part of my argument—that to see the influence of Gandhi on India's development it is more fruitful to look at his leadership of the national movement, in which he was manifestly powerful, than to search for Gandhian 'legacies' in solutions to social and political problems. For in such cases, despite the myth of the Mahatma, his ideals are only one of many contributory and competing factors in modern India.

[...]

[...] Gandhi's ideals have often left little mark on Indian society and politics; and where they have been influential they have often been distorted in practice by social conditions. What is left by the Mahatma in modern India is not a social and political reformation, but merely a tiny group of devoted Gandhians. Some, under the leadership of Jayaprakash Narayan, preach the doctrines of *Sarvodaya*, the welfare of all. Like Gandhi, they believe that the future of India lies with village communities and the end of party politics and factional strife. Others, led by Vinoba Bhave, have since 1952 toured the country, asking for gifts of land and goods to form the basis of cooperative village communities on the Gandhian model.[2] Their political power in terms of numbers and institutions is minimal. But they have caught the public imagination by sounding a note of simplicity and tradition in a period of rapid change and deviation from traditional paths. In a strange way they provide a focus for much of the current political discontent in India, even though many of their ideas are virtually impossible to enact. They are present as a constant reminder of the heroic days of the nationalist movement, and are a standing critique of any Indian government.

But surely it is to the days of the nationalist movement that we must turn if we are to see the influence of Gandhi on modern India? To look for direct causal links between his ideals and what is happening in contemporary politics and society is really to pose the wrong questions. Gandhi was not a formulator of constitutions or a planner of economies; nor even a full-time politician, since for long periods he would retire almost completely from politics, and devote himself to the service of the Untouchables and to filling India with spinning-wheels. The concrete preparation for the government of independent India was done by the Nehrus and Patels of the national movement. They were the creators of a party machine and the architects of the new state, and one could rightly ask what their direct legacy was to modern India in terms of policies and institutions. Gandhi provided the inspiration and the dynamic leadership, particularly at critical moments in the movement, and it is his leadership which has left indelible marks on contemporary India rather than 'his specific plans for social and political reform.

Gandhi's role as a leader can be described as essentially that of a mediator between various groups and forces. In the first place, though on occasion not even a Congress member, he became the acknowledged leader and symbol of the anti-British agitation. As such, he held together a group of political leaders, mediating between their diverse ideologies and aims. His very rise to power in 1920 was based on this mediatory function. The Congresses held at Calcutta and Nagpur in 1920 completely reversed the earlier Congress policy of cooperating in the Montagu–Chelmsford constitutional reforms. The reason for this dramatic revision lay in the political forces Gandhi controlled, and the way he used them. Congress from its inception until 1920 had been the preserve of educated groups, predominantly Hindus of high caste, who came from the three Presidencies which had been longest under British influence. They alone were equipped by their education to fence with the raj in western-style institutions for political power: they alone had the qualifications which would make them the beneficiaries of the concessions of place and powers in government service and the Legislative Councils which were the heart of their political demands. Standing outside this tiny, sophisticated world of the professional politicians were vast groups, areas and communities whose aims might be very different if their political potential was ever released. It was this potential which Gandhi began to release in 1920. His strength, as shown in the voting patterns at Calcutta and Nagpur, lay in the support of sections of the Muslim community, roused to activity in the Khilafat movement, in the support of representatives from regions which had previously played a peripheral part in politics—Bihar, U.P., the Punjab, Gujarat and the Hindi-speaking parts of C.P.—and in the support of merchant groups whose loyalties had previously lain with the raj. It was not that Gandhi completely swamped the older style politicians, but rather that this novel support made him the most dangerous opponent and the most powerful potential ally in the political situation of 1920.[3] Even B.G. Tilak, in the weeks before he died, was acutely aware that his followers were faced with a critical decision by Gandhi's increasing power. According to a contemporary report, one of 'Tilak's last coherent utterances during his final illness' was 'that Gandhi should be regarded as a political power

and not be lightly thwarted or opposed by the Nationalists lest they should
find themselves in a minority and lose their lead in politics ...'.[4] The
Presidency politicians realized their predicament and many of them
turned to Gandhi at the end of 1920 rather than slide into obscurity;
while Gandhi for his part mediated between them and his own supporters
so that the older politicians retained influence, if not leadership, in the
national movement. One Bombay politician put the situation neatly:

> We have expressed our differences as regards the programme of Non-
> co-operation to Mahatma Gandhi recently and he has conceded Provincial
> autonomy so far as it agreed with the fundamental principles of his Non-
> co-operation and thus we are now in a position to work out the programme
> as it may suit us best.... The time is ripe for us all now, reserving the right to
> ourselves to express our differences amongst ourselves whenever a proper
> occasion arrives, to close up our ranks and offer a united front to the
> Government under the guidance of the only man—Mahatma Gandhi—
> who can be somewhat of a leader to us, under the present circumstances.[5]

But precisely because of the increasing diversity of those who had begun
to participate in politics with their own particular aims under Gandhi's
leadership, his mediation between the different groups had on occasion
to be dictatorial. One of the earliest examples of this occurred in June
1920 at a meeting of the All-India Khilafat Conference, when Gandhi
was trying to ride both Hindu and Muslim horses. Congress had deferred
a decision on non-cooperation over the Khilafat issue until the special
session in September, and Gandhi's unenviable task was to keep the
Muslims sufficiently happy and under his control so as not to alienate
the Hindus by wild speeches or actions. He did this by delivering an
ultimatum to the Muslims: they could have his mediation and a potential
Hindu alliance on his terms only, otherwise he would retire. The Governor
of Bombay reported this incident:

> He informed the Khilafat Committee that in order to carry out his programme
> it would be necessary that an internal committee of two or three of which
> he should be the dictator (he used this word) should be formed, and he
> proposed that this should be styled the Martial Law Committee of the Khilafat
> Movement. He explained the choice of this name by saying that just as
> ordinary law was suspended in the use of Martial law, so in the case of the
> Khilafat Committee its power of action and criticism should be suspended
> *pro tem.*, if they desired his co-operation, in favour of himself and his
> 'committee'. This was silently accepted.[6]

Both the mediation and the dictatorial tendency were present from then
throughout Gandhi's career. There were those who refused to accept

both. Most spectacular was the refusal of the Muslim community after the brief rapprochement with Congress on the Khilafat issue, despite Gandhi's insistence that his life's work was to bring together Hindus and Muslims. Some Hindus as well turned against him, particularly those under the influence of Subhas Chandra Bose, and the members of the Hindu Mahasabha. But on the whole the Hindu politicians preferred to stick together under Gandhi and preserve a united anti-British front in a Congress which became a coalition of different interests.

One writer has gone so far as to call the modern Congress an entire party system in itself, in which conflicting groups and interests find expression, conciliation, and compromise.[7] This process could be seen until recently not only in the central Congress party, where Nehru continued Gandhi's mediatory activities after the Mahatma's death, but also in the localities. At the local level Congress success in retaining power and insuring unity has rested very largely, too, on its power as the Government party to mediate between local groups, and to provide them with means of expression and roads to power.[8] The inclusive, synthesizing nature of Congress has undoubtedly contributed to the comparative stability of Indian politics in the two decades since independence, and the successful working of elected, parliamentary forms of government—phenomena rare in the post-independence history of Asian and African states. Modern India owes much to the Mahatma for this, because the nature of Congress was very largely determined by his ideal of it as the voice of all India, and by the mediatory qualities of his own leadership.

In a second way Gandhi was a mediator during the national movement—between the educated, high caste groups who had moved easily in politics since the late nineteenth century, and the wider social groups which have moved into politics since the First World War. It is often said that Gandhi was instrumental in creating mass political awareness and participation in India, and that from 1920 onwards he harnessed together the feelings of the masses and the ambitions of an elite. As more work is done on the actual mechanics of Gandhi's political leadership it becomes clear that this is an over-simplification. It is quite true that Gandhi moved with ease in the club-rooms of the Indian Bars and the political associations of the professional politicians, as well as in the market towns and villages, interpreting the different groups to each other. But it was between the politicians and those whom one might call rural and small town elites that Gandhi acted as political mediator, and rarely between the politicians and the masses. The legend of the

Mahatma's success in making mass political contact makes this sound like heresy beside the dogmas of Indian nationalist history; and of course there were occasions when Gandhi had direct political influence on ordinary villagers with no claims to the status of an elite group. For example, during the 1920 elections in one U.P. village not a single person voted after Gandhi had visited the district the previous day.[9] Occasions like this doubtless multiplied with the years as he became a truly all-India figure. But generally speaking to the really poor and illiterate Gandhi's message and appeal was social and religious. To the more prosperous peasants, and the traders and professional men of small towns his appeal became more overtly political: while at the highest levels of political participation he could couch demands in the language of legislatures and constitutions. It was between these latter groups that Gandhi acted as a political mediator.

This process can be traced in Gandhi's career right from the time when he launched himself into Indian politics with the Champaran *satyagraha* of 1917. In Champaran, though he moved through the villages, his key men were a small group of professional men from Bihar towns, most of whom were lawyers. Among them was Rajendra Prasad from Chapra who was to become one of Gandhi's chief henchmen in Bihar. The only one of the group who had hitherto had much real political experience was Braj Kishore Prasad, who had been a member of the Bihar Legislative Council, and had attended Congress. Among Gandhi's helpers were also business men from local towns who realized that if Gandhi's campaign against the planting community was successful it might increase their own power and prosperity in the area. Of the four main peasant leaders, whom Gandhi used, the most prominent was the son of a prosperous Brahmin cultivator who had personal grievances to vent against the planters.[10] Clearly such men belonged to a rural and urban elite, and association with them was not political contact with the masses. Similarly in the Kaira satyagraha of 1918 Gandhi's work was not with the poorest peasants, but with the prosperous Patidar community of this district of Gujarat, while his most important helpers were either Patidars themselves or lawyers from Gujarati towns, working through the infant political associations they had begun, particularly the Gujarat Sabha, the Gujarat Political Conference and the local branches of the Home Rule League. Both Patidar and lawyer, Vallabhbhai Patel was the foremost of these associates.[11] The same pattern of leadership appears in the Rowlatt satyagraha of 1919 and in the non-cooperation movement begun in 1920. In every case Gandhi used a middle group between the masses and the politicians in the role of political sub-contractor. In Bihar in 1920 this middle group consisted not only of small town pleaders but also of Muslim religious leaders, particularly the *maulvis*, who were interested in the Khilafat cause.[12] In Maharashtra the police reported that the ordinary villagers understood virtually nothing of what was said at non-cooperation meetings, but that village officials like the *talatis*, *patels*, and *shroffs* did, and villagers' behaviour would depend on their bidding.[13]

But though Gandhi's leadership did not create mass political awareness as is sometimes glibly suggested without a detailed study of the mechanics of that leadership, his kind of political sub-contracting significantly extended the range of real political participation both in towns and in the countryside. This has been reflected in the changing composition of some local Congress parties, where the high caste, educated few have had to give way to, or at the very least share power with, powerful rural elites taking active part in politics for the first time. In Belgaum, for example, by the mid-1930s there had occurred a dramatic decline in the power of the Brahmins, who were the earliest leaders and participants in local politics, in the face of non-Brahmin agricultural castes, particularly the Lingayats.[14] An interesting corollary to this is the very recent indication that in some places the rural elites mobilized by Gandhi are now being displaced or challenged in politics by groups from below them in social and economic ranking—groups who were barely touched by Gandhi's leadership. In the Mahatma's home territory of Gujarat, the Patidars who followed him from 1918 onwards and effectively made up the local Congress were in 1962 defeated in Kaira district by a Bariya–Rajput alliance under the banner of a Kshatriya Sabha.[15]

From 1917 onwards Gandhi mediated between the small groups to whom politics had become a natural activity over several decades and a wider spread of groups who began to be active in politics for the first time. As he did so he trained a new kind of leader who has risen to prominence in the years since independence. The Nehrus and Patels of politics—urbane, fluent in English, often educated in England or qualified at the English Bar—are giving way to, or at least needing the assistance of, men like Kamaraj who until recently spoke no English, the late Prime Minister Shastri who had never left India until he took up office. This new style of leader is better equipped to represent and understand the rural groups whose power has increased since the introduction of adult suffrage, and to deal with local party bosses than were the political leaders of the days when politics were still the preserve of an urban elite.[16] India's comparatively smooth transition from elitist politics to a stage of far wider participation in political activity owes much to Gandhi's ability to interpret between different groups and to train new leaders who could tap a wider range of support than their predecessors. This is a political dividend of very great value to an ex-colonial territory where violence can so easily erupt from the bitterness of social, economic, and regional divisions if those divisions are reflected in a monopoly of political power.

In a third sphere also Gandhi's role was that of mediator—in matters of social and political ideology. Compared with an older generation of politicians who owed much of their political thinking to education on English liberal lines, and made progress the sober morning-dress affair that it once was, Gandhi appeared both in outward appearance and in his attitudes and arguments to be far more traditionally Indian. Indeed this was part of his strength as he stretched out to groups not yet involved in the sophisticated game of western-style politics. But in many ways he reinterpreted traditionally Indian ideas to justify more modern or western attitudes, and similarly interpreted the more modern in terms of the traditional. One of the most obvious examples of this was his attitude towards caste divisions. His egalitarian ideas owed much to his western education, but he took care always to clothe these ideas in traditional forms, stressing that *varnashrama* was a purification of corrupt Hindu practice, and not a departure from Hindu tradition. Similarly he emphasized that his criticism of the contemporary treatment of women in India was not an attack on Hinduism from outside, but a call to return to the original tenets of Hinduism.

> These statements of mine may have verbal similarity with the occasional attacks of Christians, but, apart from this similarity, there is no common ground between us. The Christians, in their attacks, seek to strike at the roots of Hinduism. I look upon myself as an orthodox Hindu and any attack proceeds from the desire to rid Hinduism of its defects and restore it to its pristine glory.[17]

In somewhat the same way Gandhi's ideal of an Indian nation, and a good Indian, at first owed much to examples of nationalism and heroism, from outside India. In South Africa he set himself the task of uniting the Indian community and educating its members in the qualities he thought made nations great, using his writings and the columns of *Indian Opinion* in particular. He drew heavily on the lives of nationalist leaders from outside India, like Mazzini[18] and Mustafa Kamal Pasha;[19] and exhorted his audience to follow men as diverse as Oliver Cromwell, George Washington and Florence Nightingale, in the belief that nations were as great as the people they contained.[20] By the time he returned to India, however, his writings were orientated far less towards western examples, and his stress fell increasingly on the traditionally Indian—hence his use of words like *swaraj* and *swadeshi,* his emphasis on vernacular education, village communities and the wearing of *khadi.* This new kind of exposition was part of the ideological structure he built up round his concept of the supremacy of satyagraha, truth or soul force. Much of that ideology and the resulting personal idiosyncrasies were rejected in India, but Gandhi's restatement of western political ideals of nationhood and independence in overtly Indian, even Hindu, terms and symbols was of great psychological importance to the leaders of the national movement. It removed the sting of the charge the British had always laid against them, that they were 'denationalized', representing nothing but themselves, a group of over-educated *babu*s. It also helped to unify the groups who participated in the movement by stressing the traditional in opposition to the divisions which British rule and influence had caused or exacerbated.[21] Even in the mundane matters of dress and language, by dressing the leaders in khadi and exhorting them to speak a vernacular, Gandhi brought them closer to the rest of the population, appearing to iron out the differences between rich and poor, educated and illiterate. Literally and metaphorically Gandhi clothed the leaders of modern India in the robes of tradition, and thus eased India's passage into the modern world.[22]

In discussing Mahatma Gandhi's influence on modern India it is misleading to study his ideals and to try to see them as legacies left to his country. [...] Society and politics are far too complex to reflect the ideals of one man, even though he was one of the greatest leaders India has produced and at times even seemed to personify the Indian nation. Only the collusion of ideals with social and economic pressures can produce radical change in traditional societies: where the ideal alone is present, in practice it is either forgotten or distorted. This can be seen in microcosm in the fate of satyagraha and its political application in non-violent passive resistance. This above all was Gandhi's message to India. It was for him the manifestation of a consuming vision of a non-violent world, as well as a superbly adaptable technique for conducting and resolving conflicts. [...]

[...]

NOTES

1. P. Mason (ed.), *India and Ceylon: Unity and Diversity,* London, 1967, p. 295.
2. For a discussion of the Sarvodaya movement, see H.P. Varma, *The Political Philosophy of Mahatma Gandhi and Sarvodaya,* Agra, 1959.

3. For an analysis of voting patterns in the Calcutta and Nagpur Congresses and an investigation of the sources of Gandhi's power, see J.M. Brown, 'Gandhi in India, 1915–20 his emergence as a leader and the transformation of politics' (Cambridge PhD dissertation, 1968), pp. 414–72.

4. Bombay Presidency Police, Secret Abstract of Intelligence of 1920, par. 1211, S.B. Bombay Presidency, Poona, 27 August.

5. M.R. Jayakar to B.S. Moonje, 5 January 1921, Jayakar Papers, Chronological Correspondence File No. 19, Serial No. 2.

6. Sir George Lloyd to E.S. Montagu, 25 June 1920, Montagu Papers, India Office Library, Mss. EUR.D.523 (25).

7. R. Kothari, 'The Party System', *The Economic Weekly*, 3 June 1961, quoted in G. Rosen, *Democracy and Economic Change in India* (Revised Edition), Berkeley and Los Angeles, 1967, p. 64.

8. M. Weiner, *Party Building in a New Nation. The Indian National Congress*, Chicago and London, 1967, pp. 469–72.

9. V. Chirol, *India Old and New*, London, 1921, pp. 201–2

10. For a description of Gandhi's associates in Champaran, see undated letter from W.H. Lewis, Subdivisional Officer, Bettiah, to the Commissioner, Tirhut Division, B.B. Misra (ed.), *Select Documents on Mahatma Gandhi's Movement in Champaran 1917–18*, Bihar, 1963, pp. 339–43.

11. J.M. Brown, 'Gandhi In India, 1915–20', pp. 207–10.

12. *Searchlight*, 29 April 1920, Government of India, Home Political, A, September 1920, Nos 100–3.

13. Bombay Presidency Police, Secret Abstract of Intelligence of 1920, par. 1491(21), Poona, 12 November.

14. Weiner, *Party Building in a New Nation*, pp. 234–5.

15. Ibid., pp. 105–10.

16. The introduction of adult suffrage hastened the process of expanding political participation, and shifted power even more quickly to the dominant rural castes in the regions, castes which then gained more power through the institution of *panchayat raj*. This shift in the balance of power to the countryside is one of the main themes dealt with in Rosen, *Democracy*.

17. Speech by Gandhi on 20 February 1918, *The Collected Works of Mahatma Gandhi*, [hereafter *CW*], which were at the time of the publication of this article in 1969 in processs of publication by the Government of India, New Delhi, vol. 14, p. 204.

18. For example, a passage in *Hind Swaraj*, *CW*, vol. 10, pp. 40–1; an article in *Indian Opinion*, 22 July 1905, *CW*, vol. 5, pp. 27–8; numerous references as in *Indian Opinion*, 27 July 1907, *CW*, vol. 7, p. 122 and *Indian Opinion*, 4 April 1908, *CW*, vol. 8, p. 175.

19. A course of articles entitled 'Egypt's Famous Leader', *Indian Opinion*, 28 March 1908, 4 April 1908, 11 April 1908, 18 April 1908, *CW*, vol. 8, pp. 166–7, 174–6, 187–8, 199.

20. *Indian Opinion,* 9 September 1905, *CW,* vol. 5, pp. 61–2; *Indian Opinion,* 27 July 1907, *CW,* vol. 7, p. 122.
21. Of course stressing the traditional and the Hindu also involved dangers. The increasingly Hindu character of the national movement helped to alienate Muslims and to push them into demands for a Pakistan where they would be free from the danger of Hindu raj. Use of vernaculars, also, was fraught with uncertainties. It might bring educated and uneducated together, but it might also emphasize the differences between the regions of India and the claims of their various vernaculars for official recognition and use.
22. This process of using tradition in the service of modernity is worked out in some detail in relation to Gandhi's leadership by the Rudolphs in a section of their recent book, entitled, 'The Traditional Roots of Charisma: Gandhi', L.I. Rudolph and S.H. Rudolph, *The Modernity of Tradition. Political Development in India,* Chicago and London, 1967.], pp. 157–249.

6   Waiting for the Mahatma*

Shahid Amin

[...]

We have had enough of what Mr X, Dr Y, and Prof. Z think of Gandhi (or why they do not think about him); it is time we figured out the Gandhi of Abdulla Julaha, Bhagwan Ahir, and Rampati Chamar—to name just three Congress volunteers of Chauri Chaura who were sent to their deaths by the High Court of Allahabad in 1923. Branding them criminals and thereby ruling them out of court will not do.

Research into this much-talked-about but little-discussed event reveals that many among the crowd that rioted on that fateful afternoon of February 4, 1922, were firm believers in the 'power' and the 'glory' of Mahatma Gandhi. Those convicted under Section 302/149 of the IPC were of the view that the repudiation of police authority—and the riot at the police station was *one extreme* case of it—was to usher in 'Gandhiji's Swaraj' which, according to the Mahatma, was to have been attained by September 30, 1921! Separating the sheep from the wolves does not help matters either: these very ideas were entertained by thousands of others who did not turn violent in the summer and winter of 1921.

Gandhi in 1921–2 touched the lives of thousands of peasants in a way that his *Collected Works* cannot affect [...] [people like us]. For, in the early 1920s, not only did the myth of the Mahatma permeate peasant conceptualization of extraordinary occurrences in everyday life, it also infused in the ordinary villagers an unusual strength, enabling them to become political actors in their own right. Hence the phenomenon of un-Gandhian acts (like the riot at Chauri Chaura) being undertaken in the name of Mahatma Gandhi. As the historian, Sumit Sarkar, has written: 'In a world largely untouched by secular creeds of progress, total breakdown involves a change of such magnitude that it can usually be conceived only in supernatural terms'.

* Originally published in Robin Jeffrey (ed.), *India: Rebellion to Republic, Selected Writings, 1857–1990*, New Delhi, Sterling Publishers, 1990, pp. 83–96. In the present version some portions of the text have been removed. For the complete text see the original version.

To probe such mythic imaginations among the people is to come to terms with their Mahatma. It is also to demythify the mystique of Gandhi. And here I prefer the words of an old war-horse to that of modern gladiators: Nirad Chaudhuri has reminded readers of the [*Illustrated*] *Weekly* that:

> Apotheosis or canonization among us is not deliberate; neither status is conferred by authority—an Emperor or a Pope. In India, the masses make a god of a great man, collectively and unconsciously, and succeed in giving to his memory a permanence which nothing else, neither ideas nor personality, can give. ('Have We Forgotten the Mahatma', October 2, 1983).

The unofficial canonization of Gandhi began in north India during the Champaran Satyagraha of 1917. Along with the usual spectacle of popular regard, we find a spate of fantastic rumours, all of them connected with the idea that Gandhi had arrived to help the Bihari peasant. Thus it was reported that Gandhi had come to Champaran at the Viceroy's or seen the King's behest to remove the grievances of the indigo peasants and that this mandate overruled all the officials and the *kachahri* (courts). More pointedly, it was believed that all the onerous obligations that the peasants groaned under were about to be abolished by Gandhi and there was no need to obey the planters any more. Faith in a saintly outside figure in direct touch with the higher authorities had given the oppressed peasants the moral strength to question the might of the *nilhe sahebs* (indigo planters).

Three years later, the scene shifted to the eastern districts of Partapgarh and Allahabad in U.P. where, as a result of the Kisan Movement led by Baba Ramchandra, the 'whole countryside', the young Nehru observed, was 'afire with enthusiasm and full of a strange excitement' (*Autobiography*). Gandhi's tour of Eastern U.P. seeking support for his non-cooperation programme, offers yet another glimpse into the popular fabrication of the Mahatma myth. An officer of the U.P. police reported to his superiors in January 1921 as follows:

> The currency that Gandhi's name has acquired even in the remotest villages is astonishing. No one seems to know quite who or what he is, but it is an accepted fact that what he orders must be done. He is a Mahatma or Sadhu, a Pandit, a Brahman who lives in Allahabad, even a *deota*. One man says that he is a merchant who sells cloth at three annas a yard.... it is a curious instance of the power of a name.

How should we interpret these sentences 60 years after their composition? Surely not in the way in which they were meant to be read by senior police officials, for we would then have stifled the enthusiasm of the rustic devotee and reproduced instead the concerns of the functionaries of the Raj.

The alternative is either to dismiss this elaborate myth-making by the unlettered as meaningless mumbo-jumbo or at best to recognize it as the *necessary price* of mass mobilization. But that would be to deny the role that popular ideas and self-mobilization played in the march of Indian nationalism. It would also amount to substituting a false clarity for a rich ambiguity. For the one thing that is clear about the early 1920s is the many layers of meanings (polysemy, as the linguists call it) that the name Gandhi and the 'Swaraj' donned during those heady days. As another historian, Gyan Pandey, puts it: 'From the standpoint of many U.P. peasants in the 1920s...there was a Gandhi different from the one we know and a promise of Swaraj also different from the one we do not so much *know as assume...*'

Despite evocative details of popular reverence contemporary nationalist accounts still manage to straitjacket peasant devotees in a rigid posture of deference to the Mahatma, denying them any freedom of movement whatsoever. Touching instances of devotion and childlike manifestation of affection are highlighted in the tour-diaries of Mahadev Desai, Gandhi's secretary during the early 1920s. And, if this spectacle of popular regard gets out of hand, it is read as a sign of the mule-like obstinacy (*satyagraha*) of the simple, guileless kisans. The sight and sound of uncouth peasants invading the train carrying Gandhi, rending the sky with cries of *jai* and demanding *darshan* at an unearthly hour, could be annoying and unnerving, but all was not yet lost for Desai because Congress leaders could be counted upon to restrain the militant exuberance of the *lathi*-wielding, torch-bearing enthusiasts. Examples of such darshan-seeking scenes could be multiplied by dipping into any standard nationalist account of this period.

However, as we probe deeper, the Gandhi-darshan motif in nationalist discourse reveals an interesting attitude towards the ordinary people or *sadharan janta*, as they are referred to in the contemporary Hindi press. To behold the Mahatma in person and become his devotees was the only role assigned to them, while it was for the urban intelligentsia and full-time Congress activists to convert this groundswell of popular feeling into an organized movement. Thus it would appear that, even in the relationship between the peasant devotees and *their* Mahatma, there was room for political mediation by the economically better-off and socially more powerful of his followers.

In anti-Congress newspapers—for instance, *The Pioneer* of Lucknow—the origin of stories about the 'powers' of Gandhi was located in a popular imagination fired by a 'nervous excitement'; their *circulation*, however, was attributed to 'agitators'. Nationalists and anti-nationalists were nevertheless at one in denying that a 'deified' Mahatma could have inspired popular actions independent of outside manipulation. Blaming *agent provocateurs* for misleading 'the poor ignorant peasants' (*pace* Nehru, *Autobiography*), in the manner of both nationalists and anti-nationalists, would be to plump for an authorized version of the Mahatma myth, which by its very nature was not one but many.

It would also be to miss out the stamp that the Mahatma rumours carried of a many-sided response by the masses to current events and their cultural, moral, and political concerns. To talk about the charisma of Gandhi should not be to limit oneself to analysing the outward attributes of this charisma but, more importantly, to track its career in popular imagination and thereby to grant a certain dignity to the 'popular mind'.

The minds of ordinary people are not like blank paper, but stocked with ideas and images which are transmitted through the many-sided channels of a rich oral tradition. Even folk-tales are not passively accepted by popular singers and their audiences. In fact, they are modified or transformed in a process which looks from above like misunderstanding or distortion, from below like adaptation to specific needs.

This process is, of course, familiar to students of popular religion. Confronted with the notion of 'popular ignorance' of the teachings of the Church in medieval England, the historian, E.P. Thompson, has remarked:

> The old English peasant who thought of God as 'a kindly old man', of Christ as 'a handsome youth', of the soul as 'a big bone stuck in the body', of the hereafter as 'a beautiful green field' where he would go if he behaved well, certainly wasn't ignorant of Christian doctrines: he simply translated them into images that corresponded to his experiences, to his aspirations, to his fantasies. Instead of harping on ignorance, shouldn't we see in this particular conception of the hereafter 'the assimilation of both death and paradise in a single image of rest from daily labour, the modest, taciturn, expectations of eternity'?

Similarly, figment of an ignorant imagination the Mahatma certainly was not. The masses did not invent a personage who not there. It was just that they perceived the saviour of India—and this is how Gandhi was projected in 1921—in terms of their harsh everyday life and their beliefs about powerful beings. An earthing, shall we say, of the Mahatma myth took place.

Let us then look at the popular reception of Gandhi as Mahatma in one specific region of North India during the winter and spring of 1921. Gandhi visited the sprawling district of Gorakhpur in North-Eastern U.P. on February 8, 1921, addressed a mammoth meeting variously estimated at between 1 lakh and 2.5 lakhs and returned the same evening to Banaras. He was accorded a tumultuous welcome in the district but, unlike in Champaran and Kheda, he did not stay in Gorakhpur for any length of time to lead or influence a political movement of the peasantry. Gandhi, the person, was in this particular locality for less than a day, but the 'Mahatma' as an 'idea' was there throughout and reworked in popular imagination in the subsequent months. Even in the eyes of some local Congressmen, this 'deification' assumed dangerously distended proportions by April–May 1921.

An explanation of this in terms of some ahistorical, innate superstitiousness of the *bhojpuri* peasant will clearly not do. Rather, it is the nature of the broad social concerns of the area, the projection of Gandhi by the local nationalists and the ways in which his message was interpreted and assimilated in popular consciousness that will enable us to place the Mahatma of Gorakhpur in a proper context.

In the 1910s, movements and organizations of Hindi, Hindu culture and social reform—*nagri sabhas*, *pathshalas*, *gaushalas*, *seva samitis*, and *sudharak sabhas* of various sorts—provided the support and the cover for nationalist activity in Gorakhpur. Each type of these socio-political movements served nationalism in its own way, but there was also a considerable overlap in their function and interests. Traditional religious discourses addressed to large congregations lasting several days often ended with the establishment of a nationalist social service league and a multi-community arbitration court (panchayat).

Caste sabhas were also undergoing interesting transformations. Thus, on December 12, 1920, a Bhumihar Ramlila Mandal was established at Bhiti village in Southern Gorakhpur; its 'object was to encourage unity and propagate satyagraha by revealing the true character of Sri Ramchandraji'.

Similarly, in a great many cases, lower and middle-caste panchayats were imposing novel dietary taboos as a part of the widespread movement of self-assertion which was exemplified also by such acts as the refusal of their women to work as housemaids or the withholding of *beggar* (forced labour) both from the *sarkar* and the zamindar. The sweepers, washermen and barbers of Naugrah, in the neighbouring Basti district, met in panchayats of their various brotherhoods on January 27,

1921. They decided that 'anyone who partook of meat, fish and liquor would be punished and would have to donate Rs 51 to the *gaushala*'. For the low castes and the untouchables to give up meat in 1920–1 was not simply an instance of 'self-purification'. Such acts on the part of the ritually impure amounted, in some instances, to a reversing of the signs of subordination.

Gorakhpur in 1920 was no stronghold of the Congress. In fact, the relative backwardness of the region was admitted in the local nationalist press and the main reason for this was thought to be the absence of an effective and dedicated leadership. Political meetings in Gorakhpur City and the market towns picked up from July–August 1920, as the campaign for council elections by the rajas, notables, and lawyers was countered by challenging the bonafides of 'oppressive landlords' and 'self-seeking pleaders'. But, increasingly, the boycott of council elections and, after the Nagpur Congress (December 1920), the propagation of non-cooperation were being written up and broadcast as a part of the spiritual biography of Mahatma Gandhi. It was to such a region that Gandhi came on February 8, 1921.

Gorakhpur in January 1921 was witness to a sense of mounting excitement at the advent of Gandhi. Advance parties of lectures were dispatched to the *tahsil* headquarters and market town of the district. At meetings held at these places, the visiting lecturers preached the doctrine of the Congress and asked for contributions to the Swaraj fund. In their turn, local residents ensured that people within a radius of 10 miles attended these public discourses on the philosophy and the advent of Gandhi. The massive attendance at the Gorakhpur sabha and the crowds that thronged the five stations on the 50-mile railway strip in the district suggest that news had spread widely enough. An index of this popular expectation was the increase in the number of rumours which assigned imaginary dates to Gandhi's visit.

The impending arrival of the distinguished visitor was announced in the local nationalist press on February 6, 1921, as follows:

Our plea is that the common people (*sadharan janta*) of Gorakhpur are only anxiously awaiting for the darshan of the Mahatma. The Mahatma will arrive, the public will have darshan and will be eternally grateful for it. There will be no end to the joy of the people when they are able to feast their eyes on the Mahatma. But what about those who are openly cooperating with the Government—i.e., lawyers, teachers, etc...do they have some duty at this juncture or not? A voice from the heart says: 'Of course!'...They should kneel before Mahatma Gandhi and pray to the

Almighty for courage to enable them to row their boats out of the present whirlpool into safety...For Mahatma Gandhi to appear (*avteern hona*) before us in these difficult times is a tremendous boon for us, our society and our country...Don't vacillate, arise to serve the oppressed brothers of your district. Blow the *shankh* (conch-shell) of Swaraj...This movement is an elixir for you. Mahatma Gandhi is offering it to you.

The sadharan janta, then, were offered darshan of the Mahatma and nothing more. They were not expected to proclaim the cause of Swaraj on their own. For the *shankhnaad* of Swaraj, the 'oppressed brothers' of Gorakhpur had to await the initiative of the elite followers of the Mahatma. The implication is that the peasants' pilgrimage to Gorakhpur and the mofussil railway stations would be useless from a nationalist perspective unless 'leaders' stepped in to channel the goodwill generated in the village as a result of Gandhi's darshan. That such a journey, often made in defiance of landlord opposition, could in itself be a political act and that Gandhi's message might be interpreted by the common villager on his own, without prompting by outsiders, were possibilities not entertained by the district leadership.

The 'fantastic flow of *bhakti*' caused by the Mahatma's visit to the district was commented upon in glowing terms in the local nationalist press. As a merchant-Congressman wrote:

A crowd of 2–2½ lakhs for the *darshan* of Gandhiji is no ordinary thing...But let no one think that this vast multitude came like sheep, inspired by blind faith, and went back empty-handed...The *janta* come with *bhakti* in their hearts and returned with *bhav*...

The people then do have a certain freedom of ideas and action. The janta does not just have bhakti; seeing and hearing the Mahatma also inspire *bhav*, a word suggestive not merely of feeling and ideas, but of urge to action as well.

Gandhi's advent was perceived as a major event by the zamindars as well, who had sought forcibly to prevent their peasants from seeking darshan. It was for them an event which stood out from the flow of quotidian existence and as such threatened to bring about displacements in the local power structures.

The enthusiasm Gandhi generated, the expectations he aroused and the attack he launched on British authority all combined to initiate a process which, given other factors, could make the peasant conceptualize the turning of his world upside down. This was an incipient political consciousness called upon for the first time to reflect—albeit vaguely and intermittently—on the possiblity of an inversion of many of those power relations deemed inviolable until then, such as British/Indian, landlord/ peasant and high caste/low caste. This process of conceptualization was set in train that spring in Gorakhpur by a clash between the ordinary and the extraordinary, a clash triggered off directly by the Mahatma's visit.

It is difficult to gauge the way in which Gandhi's pronouncements were *understood* in the countryside. But an effort must be made, for the ambiguities in what Gandhi said, or was believed to have said, had significant repercussion on peasant beliefs about the Mahatma. The main thrust of Gandhi's speech at Gorakhpur was to condemn the then recent acts of peasant violence and rioting in Southern Awadh. 'Gandhiji's utterances were devoted exclusively to the outbreaks of robbery, villainy and rioting that had taken place in U.P.', Mahadev Desai recounted in his diary.

This was indeed so, but a close reading of that speech suggested that it had enough ambiguity in it to leave room for a variety of interpretations. It is not possible in these columns to reproduce the entire speech in *extenso*. Instead a sequential summary of that speech is provided in an attempt to reconstruct the way in which Gandhi's utterance might have been discussed in the villages of Gorakhpur.

TABLE 6.1   *Main Points of Gandhi's Speech at Gorakhpur on 8 February 1921*

1. Hindu–Muslim unity.
2. What people should *not* do on their own: use *lathis*; loot bazaars and *haats*; enforce 'social' boycott.
3. What Gandhi *wants* his true followers to do: stop gambling, *ganja*-smoking, drinking, and whoring.
4. Lawyers should give up practice; Government schools should be boycotted; official titles should be given up.
5. People should take up spinning and weavers should accept hand-spun yarn.
6. Imminence of Swaraj; its realization conditional on innate strength of numbers when matched with peace, grace of God, self-sacrifice, and self-purification.

It is reasonable to assume that such discussions would have proceeded by breaking up his message into its major ideological constituents (*baat* in indigenous parlance). Without going into details, let me state that it is the conflation of baats 3 and 6 and their contextualization within existing ideas about 'power' and magic which lay at the root of some of the rumours relating to the Mahatma in Gorakhpur. It seems that the complementarity of the Dos and Don'ts in these particular messages—2 and 3—was largely lost on his rustic audiences. On the other hand, baats 3 and 6 came to be associated in the popular mind as a linked set of spiritual commandments issued by a godlike personage: in other words, it came to be believed that Swaraj will follow if people abstained from ganja-smoking, drinking, and the like and purified themselves in other ways. As such, these were consistent with those legends about Gandhi's 'divinity' which circulated at that time. The enforcement of 'social boycott' was not widespread yet; it was to pick up only from late 1921.

How the people made a Mahatma of Gandhi can best be gauged in terms of the 'stories' or rumours about his 'powers' and ritual acts which accompanied popular acceptance of these 'powers'. It is with the intervention of the supernatural in this process and the Mahatma's role in it that most of the Gorakhpur 'stories' are concerned.

To scoff at these as *mere rumours* is to miss their significance as indicators of popular perceptions about Gandhi.

Table 6.2   *Some Representative Rumours about Mahatma Gandhi
in Gorakhpur between February and May 1921*

1. Sikander Sahu of Village Mahuawa said on February 15 that he would believe in Mahatmaji when the boiling-pan in his *karkhana* split in two. The boiling-pan split in two in the middle.

2. On February 18, a Kahar of Basantpur said that he would be prepared to believe in Mahatmaji's authenticity only when the thatched roof of his hut was raised. The roof lifted 10 cubits above the wall. And fell back to its original position only when he cried and folded his hands in surrender and submission.

3. On April 13, a *karahi* was being set up as an offering to the Mahatma in village Belwa. The wife of one Thakur Saheb said that she would offer a karahi to the Mahatmaji only if there were some miracle performed. Suddenly, a *dhoti* hanging on a peg caught fire and was reduced to ashes, although there was no smell of burning whatsoever.

4. Mauni Baba Ramanugraha Das of Village Benuatikur had slandered Mahatmaji on several occasions. As a result of this, his body began to stink on its own. After some exertions in the right direction, things improved somewhat. Mauniji then made arrangements for a sacrifice.

Contd

Table 6.2 Contd

5. A Muslim toddy-tapper of Padrauna was told by a Master Saheb to give up this practice in accordance with the teachings of Mahatmaji. One day, he fell down from a tree. As a result of this incident, all the Muslims are giving up toddy-tapping.

6. A man in a sabha in village Majhwa had vowed not to smoke, but he started smoking once again. Suddenly, he was hemmed in by worms and insects from all sides. Because of this incident, people in villages far away from Majhwa have also given up intoxicants.

7. The sons of a Tamoli near Bhatni Station killed a goat and ate it up. Some people tried to dissuade them, but they paid no heed. Later, all of them started vomiting and got very worried. In the end, when they vowed in the name of Mahatmaji never to eat meat again, their condition improved.

8. In Village Deokali, as a result of *manuati* of Mahatmaji, a vessel of a Musalman, which had fallen into a well six months back, came up on its own.

9. In Village Naipura, the long-lost calf of Dalku Ahir returned to its peg as a result of the manuati of Mahatmaji. Dalku Ahir has contributed one rupee of the manuati to the Swaraj fund.

Even a cursory reading of these 'stories' suggests that two obvious processes are at work here. First, the rumours are indicative of considerable discussion about Gandhi in the villages of Gorakhpur in the spring of 1921. The recurring phrase, 'I shall believe in Mahatmaji only in the event of such an extraordinary thing happening', may be read as a dialogue between sceptics and firm believers.

Secondly, this crucial phrase also suggests that what people thought of the Mahatma were projections of existing patterns of popular belief about the 'worship of worthies' in rural North India. In the villages of U.P., the deification of such 'worthies' was based, among other things, on the purity of the life they had led and on 'approved thaumaturgic powers'.

Turning to the 'stories' themselves, we find that 1–3 are developments of the basic idea of the genuineness of the Mahatma as revealed through various tests: the person who sets the test invariably submits to the Mahatma's power. Thus the Kahar of Basantpur in 2 gets the roof of his hut back in position only after he makes amends for questioning the saint's authority by tearful repentance. The rumour about the Mauni Baba who seems to have broken his vow of silence to criticize Gandhi and the affliction it caused (4) suggest that the world of the local sadhu was no match when pitted against that of the Mahatma. His suffering was interpreted in Benuatikur and broadcast through rumour over a wide area as an obvious punishment for his anti-Gandhian stance.

There is an element which story 2 shares with 3 where the *thakurain* makes her offering to the Mahatma conditional on some miracle taking place and the latter occurs in the form of a dhoti bursting into flame. In both, it is fear which imposes faith in the non-believers. This penal motif recurs frequently in many religious ballads of Eastern India. The doubting woman and the sceptical Kahar are persuaded to join the devotees—and do so ritually in the karahi episode—in the same way as the forceful display of an offended godling's destructive powers breaks the resistance of a non-conformist in a *vratkatha* or *panchali.*

Again, 'stories' 5–7 are indicative of the way Gandhi's message was being interpreted and amplified in terms of popularly accepted notions of pollution and punishment and cause and effect. Gandhi did not press his Gorakhpur audience to forsake fish and meat. It seems that this popular emphasis on dietary purity in the spring of 1921 was an extension of the Gandhian idea of self-purification (through abstinence from ganja and liquor) to a context where the prohibition was enlarged to include meat and fish. It could here be regarded as an indicator of religiosity and lower-caste self-assertion at the same time. An example of his extension from one banned item to another is provided by the widening of the taboo against ganja to smoking, even to chewing tobacco. In 'story' 6, the violation and punishment which follow have an impact not only on the village concerned but far beyond it.

Gandhi was also fitted into the widespread practice of the taking of a vow (manuati), addressed to a god, a local godling or a saint, on condition that an affliction be removed or that a wish be fulfilled (for example, 8–9). The practice of Gandhi-manuati, of his *vrat* and *aradhana* (fast and worship), and of women begging in his name and making offerings of cooked food (*karahi charahna*) are further instances of the transference of existing worshipful attitudes and rituals into a new context.

Just as the Mahatma was associated in Gorakhpur with a variety of miraculous occurrences, so did his name lend itself as a label to all sorts of public meetings, pamphlets and, of course, to that ambiguous word Swaraj itself. Surveying the background to the Chauri Chaura riot, the judge of the Allahabad High Court found it

> remarkable...how this name of 'Swaraj' was linked, in the minds of the peasantry of Gorakhpur, with the name of Mr Gandhi. Everywhere in the evidence and in statements made...by various accused persons [they found that] it was 'Gandhiji's Swaraj' or 'Mahatmaji's Swaraj' for which they [that is, the peasants] were looking.

The popular notion of 'Gandhiji's Swaraj' took place quite independently of the district leadership of the Congress Party. The High Court judges observed that the local peasantry

> perceived of it [Swaraj] as a millennium in which taxation would be limited to the collection of small cash contributions or dues in kind from fields and threshing floors, and [in] which the cultivators would hold their lands at little more than nominal rents.

In fact, as early as March 1921, public proclamations about the advent of Swaraj were being made in the countryside, which found a ready reception in the neighbouring districts of North Bihar as well. The local pro-landlord paper drew pointed attention to such occurrences as ominous signs which bode ill for all concerned:

> One night, people from all the villages [!] kept awake and roamed over five villages each. That night, it was impossible to get any sleep. They were shouting *Gandhiji ki jai!* They had *dhol, tasa, jhal, majiras* [kettledrums and cymbals] with them. The din thus created was unbearable. People were shouting: This is the drum of Swaraj [*swaraj ka danka*]. Swaraj has been attained. The English had made a bet with Gandhiji that 'we shall grant you Swaraj if you come out of fire' [unhurt]. Gandhiji took hold of the tail of a calf and went through fire. Now Swaraj has been attained...Now only 4 annas or 8 annas a *bigha* will have to be paid in rent...

Quite clearly, this miracle (Gandhi's passage through fire) was consistent with the existing level of peasant consciousness as well as utopian hopes for a world free of rents—a far cry these from official Congress policy—which marked the eruption of Swaraj that night in Gorakhpur villages. And again, as local-level volunteer activity entered a more militant phase in late 1921, the coming of Swaraj was perceived—contrary to anything that the Congress stood for at the time—in terms of the direct supplanting of the police. Thus Sarju Kahar, a *khidmatgar* (personal attendant) at the Chauri Chaura police station, testified that 'two or four days before the affair, (he) had heard that Gandhi Mahatma's Swaraj had been established, that the Chaura *thana* would be abolished and that the volunteers would set up their own thana'.

While such action sought to justify itself by a reference to the Mahatma, the Gandhi of rustic protagonists was not as he really was but as they had thought him up. Indeed their ideas about Gandhi's 'orders' were often at variance with those of the local Congress-Khilafat leadership and clashed with the basic tenets of Gandhism.

Let me clear some misunderstandings that may have arisen at this stage. I do not wish to suggest that faith in the Mahatma was the *only* or the *real* reason for peasant politicization in Gorakhpur or the riot at Chauri Chaura. In cases such as these, it is not really possible to separate political ideology from an all-pervasive religiosity. The popular mind is not like a Faculty of Humanities where economics, politics, and divinity are kept in separate departments under different heads.

It is certainly not my endeavour either to mock or celebrate the proverbial 'idiocy' of rural life. Peasant beliefs about social, moral, and political issues, though 'traditional', are also located in time and space. In building up images about an-Other, peasants, like the rest of us, reveal a lot about themselves and about their times. A reference to Chauri Chaura or Gorakhpur (of which it is a small market-town) is then not to defile an essay on Gandhi by mentioning the unmentionable. It is to use the apparently useless to understand a Mahatma that the people fashioned after their own hearts.

PART III

PEASANTS IN GANDHIAN
MASS MOVEMENTS

Part III

Peasants & Gandhian Mass Movements

7 The Rowlatt Satyagraha*

David Hardiman

In the months after the close of the Kheda Satyagraha of 1918, the home-rulers had plenty of opportunity to demonstrate that they were the true friends of the peasants. The monsoon failed, leading to a famine, and to add to the peasants' troubles there was an epidemic of influenza in the autumn which killed nearly 24,000 people in the district.[1] Many cattle died, and hoarding by unscrupulous traders continued to send prices of essentials soaring.[2] In November 1918, the second Gujarat Political Conference was held at Nadiad, and the chief demand was that the land revenue be suspended. Although the government had insisted that political agitation had no effect on land revenue policy, it suspended the whole year's revenue demand with unprecedented speed and generosity.[3] Over the matter of relief, the nationalists proved more energetic than the government. Large sums were collected from rich industrialists of Bombay and Ahmedabad and given to the needy in the form of food and fodder.[4] During the influenza epidemic, the Nadiad Home Rule League distributed medicine to 300 villages.[5] In this manner, the home-rulers kept in touch with the villages which had been mobilized in 1918 and also spread the movement to new ones. By 1919, Kheda District probably had the strongest rural nationalist organization in India, with 3,000 Home Rule League members in 105 villages.[6]

During March and April 1919, Gandhi, who at that time controlled only the Gujarat Sabha and Gujarat Home Rule League, gained temporary control over the Bombay City Home Rule League, which was dominated by Gujaratis. As a result, the chief centres of agitation in Bombay Presidency during the Rowlatt Satyagraha of 1919 were Ahmedabad City and District, Kheda District, and Bombay City. The agitation started in February 1919 with the drawing up of a satyagraha oath in protest of the Rowlatt Acts. Within two weeks, 600 signatures to the oath had been obtained throughout India. Of these, 369 came from Bombay City, 120

* Originally published as 'The Politics of Non-Cooperation 1919–1924', in David Hardiman, *Peasant Nationalists of Gujarat: Kheda District 1917–1934*, New Delhi, Oxford University Press, 1981, pp. 129–38.

from Kheda District, and 111 from the rest of India.[7] By the end of March, about 700 people of Kheda had signed.[8]

Amongst the peasants, there was wild speculation as to the nature of the Rowlatt Acts. Essentially, they feared that the 'Black Acts' would strengthen the powers of the police by allowing arbitrary arrest and imprisonment without trial. Emotive rumours circulated: it was said that if a policeman fancied a woman he could arrest her husband under the new Acts to get him out of the way; in future, the police would be allowed to confiscate half of all private property; no more than four men would be permitted to congregate in temples; brides and bridegrooms were to be inspected by a British doctor before they could get married; and so on.[9] Posters were circulated which were of doubtful relevance to the agitation, but of relevance to the peasants. One read:[10]

> How to stop the evils of the Rowlatt Bill. If one thousand men refuse to pay revenue there is no evil therein, but if we pay revenue to the State that acts wrongfully, the state is helped and so to pay revenue is itself an evil.

During the campaign, Gandhi never suggested non-payment of land revenue, which this poster implied.

Initially, the agitation against the Rowlatt Acts was restrained. On 6 April, a *hartal* was observed in towns and prominent villages throughout Kheda. In several places, copies of the banned *Hind Swaraj* were sold. In the evening there were mass meetings, after which the crowds dispersed peacefully. There had been an impressive show of strength without one violent incident.

But in Kheda there was a mood for violence. This was expressed by a Patidar of Vaso, who wrote the following song, had it printed at Dakor, and then sent it anonymously all over Gujarat.[11]

Deen Deen Jagaro, Har Har Mahadeo

The English people are very tyrannical, they are perfidious and treacherous;
They have disgraced India by enacting Black Acts.
In the war, blood was freely shed (by Indians) and food, money and
    valuable lives were given;
And as a reward thereof Black Acts and two stones of a grinding were
    given.
Punjabi, Bengali, Deccani and Gujarat;
Why have you been asleep, you also rulers of the Native States.
Post Offices, Railways and Telegraph Offices must be destroyed first;
Police must also be destroyed to ensure a positive success.
Collectors, Commissioners and Governors in particular.
Massacre them, then only your (Indian) prestige will be saved.

To slaughter the white people take up swords;
Brave men make haste and do not delay.
If you will spare them, they will assume the tiger's form;
And will crush all, even the Indian Ruling Chiefs.
Form plots and have courage, but do not have at heart the slightest mercy;
Then only will success be achieved, understand, oh India.
Arjun too was given the same advice emphatically by Krishna;
You all too therefore act in the same way and victory in every way will
    be attained.
Nothing will be achieved by taking to Satyagraha, but by taking up arms
    victory will be had;
The English will fly and your object will be served.

                                                              Anarchist.

On the afternoon of 10 April, news arrived in Nadiad of Gandhi's arrest. The shops in the bazaar put up their shutters and crowds began to gather in the streets. The Chakalashi leader, Janardan Sharma, led a ragged procession to the two cotton mills and persuaded their two thousand workers to go on strike. The whole crowd then marched back to the bazaar, where Sharma addressed them in an excited manner and sang nationalist songs. In the evening, there was another meeting attended by about 5,000 people at which the need for non-violence was stressed.[12] Next morning, railway passengers began to bring news of the riots in Ahmedabad, where the people had risen and burnt down the government offices. Some rowdy youths of Nadiad demonstrated their solidarity with the people of Ahmedabad by pelting the Government High School and a European dairy with stones.[13] Rumours were heard that a *mukti sena*, or freedom army, was marching from Delhi to liberate Ahmedabad.[14] In the early afternoon, the telegraph operators at the station heard that a train full of troops was to come through at midnight to quell Ahmedabad. Some suggested that the train be stopped. The Gandhian leaders quickly organized a meeting, attended by about 10,000 people, at which they reiterated the need for non-violence. But few in the huge crowd could hear the speeches. On its fringes, some influential Patidars plotted to derail the troop train. Amongst them was the well-known lawyer, Maganbhai 'Raja' Patel; also Purushottam Amin, a Patidar of Vaso who managed a theatrical troupe based in Nadiad. It was his father who had written the song *Deen Deen Jagaro, Har Har Mahadeo*. Later that evening, about fifteen of these plotters went to the railway and, with some difficulty, removed a rail and threw it into a ditch. In the early hours of the next morning the train, with two hundred troops on board, crashed to a halt at the spot. Somehow, it remained upright so that nobody was injured. Within sixteen hours trains were running again.[15]

The most violent outbreak in Kheda during the Rowlatt Satyagraha was at Anand. On 11 April, there were processions in Anand with black flags in protest at Gandhi's arrest. In the evening, Janardan Sharma arrived to make inflammatory speeches accompanied by songs. Next day, the Secretary of the Anand Home Rule League, Bhagwandas Patel, led a procession to a British-owned milk factory and demanded that it close down. The British manager appeared with a gun, whereupon they left. They then marched to a government milk factory and pelted it with stones. At five in the evening there was a rumour that Gandhi was to pass through the station on his way to Ahmedabad, and the crowd, about four hundred strong, surged to the station. They discovered that refreshments were being sold in defiance of the hartal. One of the snack-sellers, Rogilal Bhaiya, was a loyalist who used to report on nationalist activities to the Europeans in Anand. He made a disparaging remark about Gandhi and there was a violent argument. The train came through without Gandhi, and in their disappointment the crowd marched to Rogilal Bhaiya's house, splashed it with kerosene and set it on fire. Next, they burnt down the house of the European station master. They then dispersed. On the following day, troops arrived to find the town quiet.[16]

In the villages, the Patidar peasants expressed their solidarity by cutting telegraph wires at four places along the main railway line between Ahmedabad and Baroda.[17] An attempt was also made to damage a railway culvert at Uttarsanda. These wirecuttings all occurred on the night of 12 April, and it seems probable that a message was passed down the line, for it is unlikely that the peasants in these villages should all have decided on their own initiative to damage railway property on the same night in largely the same fashion. The railway authorities later blamed their signallers, who were considered to be disloyal because all the best railway jobs went to Anglo-Indians.[18] The only recorded provocation was by Janardan Sharma, who on 11 April made an inflammatory speech at Anand and on 12 April praised the Nadiad train derailers in speeches at Chakalashi and Narsanda.[19]

The Patidars of Narsanda gave enthusiastic support to the Rowlatt Satyagraha from the start. On 9 March, thirteen men of the village took the satyagraha vow.[20] Meetings were held on 6 April, and on 11 April the Patidars did no work. On the twelfth, there was great excitement over the Nadiad derailment, and Janardan Sharma's speech added to the tension. People were walking around flourishing their *dhariya*s shouting

'Gandhi ki jai' and talking of cutting the telegraph wires along the nearby railway. In the evening, the two nationalist leaders of the village, Dahyabhai and Venibhai Patel, called the Patidars to the village dharmashala. About a hundred and fifty came and were told that they should cut the wires as had been done elsewhere. They were told to say nothing: if anyone was accused, the village would stand by them and collect funds for their defence. They then rounded up some Muslims and low-caste people so that other communities would be implicated in the crime. One Patidar was holding a gun, so that they dared not disobey. About two hundred men marched to the railway track, and the Muslim and low-caste people were ordered to get to work. One Baraiya who objected was beaten. They slashed and hacked at the wires and telegraph posts until a sufficient amount had been brought down. They then heard a train coming and fled back to the village.[21]

Another village which took part in the wire-cutting was Vadod. There had been a Home Rule League branch there since 1917, run by Patidar peasants. During the Kheda Satyagraha, about a hundred of these Patidars had had property confiscated from them for revenue refusal. In April 1919, fifteen Patidars of the village took the satyagraha oath. When, on 11 April, news came of Gandhi's arrest, everyone in the village stopped work and there was a procession with black flags. On 12 April, horns were blown to summon a meeting. About three hundred people turned up, to be told by the President of the village Home Rule League that they should disobey the law and the 'Black Acts' in particular. They discussed the action they should take. Some suggested causing a disturbance at a dairy managed by a British company, others wanted to derail a train, but were dissuaded lest Gandhi was on it. Finally, they decided to cut the telegraph wires. They ordered the village blacksmith to come with his tools, but he fled to his house and was only persuaded to carry out the deed after a thrashing. In the evening, the President of the Home Rule League and the village *mukhi* led about fifty to seventy-five men to the railway. At the railway, a ladder was put up against a telegraph pole and the blacksmith hacked the wires down.[22]

These attacks on railway property and minor riots represented the full extent of the Kheda disturbances of April 1919. The only serious incidents were the derailment at Nadiad, which could have caused much loss of life, and the riots at Anand. Compared with Ahmedabad, where at least twenty-four people were killed and well over one hundred injured, and Viramgam in Ahmedabad District, where six were killed and eighteen injured, this was very small stuff.[23]

During the crisis, the Bombay authorities acted with restraint, and restored order with a minimum amount of fuss. But any sympathy which they might have gained from this was soon lost when they started to arrest those responsible for the disturbances. Janardan Sharma was arrested and was found to have in his possession a copy of the seditious song *Deen Deen Jagaro, Har Har Mahadeo*. The men who derailed the train at Nadiad were arrested after one of their number confessed to the police while drunk. Purushottam Amin agreed to confess his guilt and act as a prosecution witness in return for his freedom.[24] In the villages, the police took advantage of communal rivalries to obtain evidence. The leading Muslim opponent of the Patidars in Narsanda was Faiju Umrav, who in 1906 had filed a charge against some Patidars for throwing stones at *tajiya*s during Moharram.[25] In 1919, he saw his chance to rid the village of its leading Patidars. He drew up a list of fifty-three 'wire-cutters' and handed it over to the local police sub-inspector, also a Muslim. The list included the guilty and the innocent. The sub-inspector acted in the heavy-handed manner normal to the Kheda police. Witnesses were rounded up from amongst the poor peasants with threats that they would be thrashed if they did not testify against the men on the list. They were taken to the Collector, and while they gave their forced evidence, the sub-inspector and Faiju Umrav stood at the court door listening. As a result, forty-eight leading men of Narsanda were arrested and thrown into Nadiad jail.

In May, the British decided to punish the people of Nadiad as a whole. On 16 May, Frederick Pratt, James Ker (the Collector), and the Inspector General of Police for Bombay Presidency, Robertson, met to discuss the need for extra police in Nadiad since the town had become a nationalist centre. They decided that an additional forty-five armed policemen were required, and that as the Vaniyas and Patidars of the town were the chief trouble-makers, they were to pay the Rs 15,556 needed to cover the cost of the extra policemen. This police-tax was announced on 26 May, several months before similar taxes were announced in Ahmedabad and Viramgam. In those two places there had been serious rioting. This was not the case in Nadiad, where the vast majority of the population had remained peaceful during the Rowlatt Satyagraha. In Gandhi's words:[26]

> Should these men be punished because a few ruffians in a fit of madness go to the station and pull down the rails? ...Moreover, it is dishonest to fasten the guilt of a dozen drunkards of a big town on a whole population when the real cause of the punishment is not the crime but the political activities of the people.

The police-tax caused great resentment in Nadiad.

The tribunal hearings on the disturbances in Kheda started on 22 July 1919. Vallabhbhai Patel acted as the chief defence lawyer. He was in his element, defending his caste-mates charged with criminal offences and obtaining acquittals by showing up inaccuracies and inconsistencies in the evidence of the prosecution witnesses. In the first case, Janardan Sharma was found guilty of possessing seditious literature and was sentenced to eighteen months' imprisonment.[27] The second case concerned the derailment of the troop train. In this case, many of the witnesses were bribed, for the people of Nadiad wanted to prove before the tribunal that the police-tax was not justified. One lawyer who had tampered with evidence had to be removed from the court. One prosecution witness retracted his evidence suddenly, saying that he had been drunk when he had confessed. The star witness for the prosecution, Purushottam Amin the actor, pretended not to be able to recognize any of the accused. Two of the prosecution witnesses were shown to be criminals, universally distrusted in Nadiad. Vallabhbhai proved that a spanner which, it was alleged, had been used to unscrew the bolts on the line, did not fit the bolts. As a result, the police case proved flimsy, and all except one of the accused were acquitted.[28] On their return to Nadiad, they were given a hero's welcome, being taken in a huge procession to the Santram Mandir for prayers of thanks. The drunkard who had confessed to the police in the first place was put out of caste and suffered such severe boycott that he was unable even to purchase tea or *pan-supari* in Nadiad.[29]

The next two cases concerned the wire-cuttings at Vadod and Narsanda. The police evidence came largely from Baraiyas or Muslims who had grudges against the accused. In the Vadod case, evidence from a talukdar of a neighbouring village and from local Baraiyas proved strong enough to convict twelve of the thirty-six brought to trial. The President of the Vadod Home Rule League and one other were transported for life; the rest received from three to ten years' imprisonment.[30] In the Narsanda case, Vallabhbhai Patel proved that the Muslim sub-inspector had intimidated witnesses into giving false evidence. He also showed that there were inconsistencies in the evidence of the key prosecution witness, Faiju Umrav. As a result, all the accused in the Narsanda case were acquitted.[31] The Anand riot case was heard last. Three of the nine charged were found guilty, and were given three to five year sentences. The people responsible for the riot were not caught.[32]

The events of 1919 demonstrated that sabotage was a dangerous weapon for the Patidars. The countryside was not united, and Baraiyas or Muslims could always be found to testify against Patidars. Unless the Patidars took the extreme step of starting secret societies, such forms of protest were unlikely to be effective. It was to their advantage to act within the law, except when an open protest was to be made against a specific law.

Gandhi did not see the case for passive resistance in such functional terms. He considered that the cold removal of rails and the cutting of wires by educated men was more disgraceful than the passionate rioting of ignorant Ahmedabad mill workers.[33] On 6 July 1919, Gandhi came to Nadiad. In his autobiography he writes that as he entered the district he suddenly remembered how the people of Kheda had similarly misused and misunderstood him in 1918. At the subsequent meeting at Nadiad, he used the term 'Himalayan miscalculation' for the first time to describe the Rowlatt Satyagraha.[34] As always with Gandhi, the statement was not as straightforward as it seemed, for it was in fact expedient for him to come to that conclusion at that moment. By July, he had lost control of the Bombay City Home Rule League and he needed an excuse to call off his threatened campaign of Civil Disobedience.[35] But also, his statement reflected his loss of faith in the Patidar peasants of Kheda, a loss of faith which was to tip the balance in favour of the Bardoli Taluka of Surat District when the time came to choose a locality for the launching of Civil Disobedience during the Non-Cooperation movement of 1920–2.

NOTES

1. *Census of India 1921, Bombay Presidency*, Part I, Bombay, 1922, p. 24.
2. *Land Revenue Administration Report of the Bombay Presidency, Northern Division 1918–19*, Bombay, 1920, p. 23.
3. Ibid., p. 14.
4. Indulal Yajnik, *Atmakatha*, vol. II, Ahmedabad, 1970, pp. 147–57.
5. Evidence of Gokaldas Talati, *Evidence Taken before the Disorder Inquiry Committee*, vol. II, *Bombay Presidency*, Calcutta, 1920. (Hereafter *Disorder Inquiry*.)
6. Evidence of Gokaldas Talati, *Disorder Inquiry*.
7. *Bombay Chronicle*, 14 March 1919.
8. Evidence of Gokaldas Talati, *Disorder Inquiry*.
9. These rumours were not specifically for Kheda, but are taken from a list of Rowlatt Satyagraha rumours in NAI, H-Pol. A. February 1920, 421–31.
10. *Source Material for a History of the Freedom Movement in India Collected from Bombay Government Records*, vols I and II, Bombay, 1957 and 1958, vol. III, parts I–IV, Bombay, 1965–75, (hereafter *Bombay Source Material*), vol. III, pt. 1, p. 109.

11. *Bombay Secret Abstracts*, 1920, p. 1795. *Bombay Secret Abstracts*, 1919, p. 307. The title represents Muslim and Hindu war cries.
12. Evidence of Bombay Government, *Disorder Inquiry*.
13. *Bombay Chronicle*, 25 July 1919. Evidence of N.V. Trivedi, *Disorder Inquiry*.
14. Indulal Yajnik, *Atmakatha*, vol. II. p. 179.
15. *Bombay Chronicle*, 26 July 1919. Evidence before tribunal, Nadiad derailment case, continuous in *Bombay Chronicle*, 26 July–22 August 1919. B.A.H.D. Special, 1919, File 521, part 3. Interview with Bakubhai Amin, the son of Purushottam Amin, in Vaso.
16. Evidence before tribunals, Anand arson case, continuous in *Times of India*, 3 December–15 December 1919.
17. Wires were cut at Barejadi (just over the border in Ahmedabad District), Narsanda, Anand, and Vadod.
18. *Bombay Secret Abstracts*, 1919, p. 327.
19. Evidence of N.V. Trivedi, *Disorder Inquiry*.
20. *Bombay Secret Abstracts*, 1919, p. 189.
21. Evidence before tribunal, Narsanda wire-cutting case, continuous in *Times of India*, 20 October–15 December 1919. Interviews in Narsanda.
22. Evidence before tribunal, Vadod wire-cutting case, continuous in *Times of India*, 18 August–30 October 1919.
23. *Bombay Source Material*, vol. II, p. 777. These were the official estimates or casualties. Gandhi estimated that over twice as many were killed and wounded in Ahmedabad, *CWMG*, [Collected Works of Mahatma Gandhi], New Delhi 1969, vol. 15, p. 250.
24. Evidence before tribunal, Nadiad derailment case, *Bombay Chronicle*, 26 July–22 August 1919. *The All India Reporter, 1921, Bombay Section*, pp. 3–16.
25. *Times of India*, 22 October 1919. The Patidars were fined.
26. *Young India*, 30 August 1919.
27. *Bombay Chronicle*, 26 July 1919. After his release, Sharma gave up nationalist politics and started an ashram on the banks of the Narmada river, where he remained till his death.
28. *Bombay Chronicle*, 26 July–28 August 1919.
29. *Bombay Secret Abstracts*, 1919, p. 740.
30. *Times of India*, 30 October 1919.
31. *Times of India*, 29 November 1919 and 15 December 1919.
32. Interview with Tribuvandas Patel, Anand.
33. *Bombay Chronicle*, 10 July 1919.
34. M.K. Gandhi, *An Autobiography, or The Story of My Experiments with Truth*, Ahmedabad, 1969, pp. 356–7.
35. *CWMG*, vol. 15, p. 436.

8 Masses in Politics*

Non-co-operation Movement in Bengal

Rajat K. Ray

[...]

In the aftermath of the First World War, sharply alternating cycles of boom and depression forced the pace of mass discontent in Bengal. Attracted by the expanding opportunities of employment offered by the abnormally inflated conditions of industry, a large number of workers crowded into the town from the countryside during 1919 and the first half of 1920 and were then left stranded by a depression which came all of a sudden in the middle of 1920. [...]

The economic difficulties of 1920–1 were cyclical in character. But by arousing mass discontent these temporary difficulties brought out into the open the more fundamental perceptions of economic exploitation and racial humiliation. The large number of people who participated in the non-co-operation movement in Bengal desired consciously or unconsciously to shatter the domination of colonial business interests, and inevitably this desire manifested itself in forms that were unmistakably anti-white. The initial target of attack was the interlinked complex of tea, jute, coal, oil, railway, steamer, and engineering interests. The popular hatred of white racial domination provided the bitter edge of this economic assault.

[...]

On his return from Nagpur, [Chittaranjan] Das first concentrated on organizing a student strike throughout Bengal; when the strike failed to sustain itself he began a campaign of mass mobilization. At the first the vast majority of college students in Calcutta left their classes and an epidemic of student strikes hit all districts of Bengal except Darjeeling, Jalpaiguri, and Dinajpur in the north.[1] At the height of the student unrest in Bengal in February 1921, about 11,157 students had been withdrawn

* Originally published in Rajat K. Ray, *Social Conflict and Political Unrest in Bengal 1875–1927*, New Delhi, Oxford University Press, 1984, pp. 270–310. In the present version some portions of the text and notes have been removed in this version. For the entire text see the original version.

from government and aided institutions out of a total of 103,107 pupils attending these institutions. Of those withdrawn, perhaps a third returned later, the remainder joining national schools, conducting political propaganda or doing nothing.[2] The schools and colleges reopened and the excitement died down by the beginning of March. Yet the student strikes left their mark upon the general political situation. [...]

The first tentative Congress move towards mobilizing the common people in an enmassed assault on the colonial structure of the economy occurred in February 1921 when striking students and national volunteers launched a campaign among the cultivators to boycott the cultivation of jute. The Bengali middle classes had long come to regard the production of jute as a means by which the economy was being subordinated to British capitalism, and the press had familiarized the public with the thought that restriction of the acreage for jute would result in a larger crop of food for the people. These ideas were circulated among the peasants by the striking students, but as the ruling price of raw jute was slightly higher than that of rice, the cultivators did not respond to this propaganda. However, the effect was to make the peasant think of other methods to improve his position and to prepare the way for non-payment of taxes later on.[3]

By April increasing signs of lawlessness were becoming manifest. In Dacca town there were four or five occasions on which Europeans were stoned. In the town of Comilla (Tippera district) bricks were thrown at the wife and child of the Superintendent of Police. In Howrah, a jute mill manager was beaten up because he had cut bonus from the pay of labourers observing hartal. In the interior of Mymensingh there was a general refusal to attend police investigations and a belief that the government had lost its authority. Volunteers looted and rioted in Tippera, rescued arrested persons in Barisal, and prevented unloading of Liverpool salt in Munshiganj.

In May there was a temporary but complete strike of all servants of the Europeans at Akhaura in Tippera following the slapping by a jute agency assistant of 'an insolent khidmatgar'. At the same time a more successful strike was organized in the Burma Oil Company's workshops at Chittagong, where orders prohibiting meetings and processions were successfully defied and a complete hartal was called off only on the company surrendering to the strikers.[4] On the eve of the 'coolie' exodus from the tea gardens of Assam which brought about a sudden breakdown of law and order in extensive parts of East Bengal, there was thus already much disorder in the area.

Colonial manufacturing, mining, and planting complexes provided the focal points of the seething popular discontent against imperial rule. The mills, factories, and engineering workshops in and around Calcutta were natural centres of labour unrest. Even before the Bengal Congress under the leadership of Das had embarked on a violent campaign of mass strikes, pro-Gandhi elements had started in a more quiet way organizing the workers and improving the quality of their life. C.F. Andrews, together with a batch of young Bengalis headed by Nagendranath Gangopadhyay (a son-in-law of Rabindranath Tagore, he had recently left Grace Bros so as not to serve a foreign capitalist firm drawing money out of India), was engaged in the constructive work of forming trade unions in Calcutta.[5] In the suburbs of Calcutta, similar constructive work was being done by Pandit Krishna Kumar Sastri, a disciple of Gandhi hailing from Arrah district in Bihar. In and around Titagarh, where he had settled, he was preaching Hindu–Muslim unity, forming arbitration courts and persuading mill-hands to give up toddy and liquor. His campaign had considerable success in Titagarh, Kankinara, and Kamarhati; both Hindu and Muslim mill-hands looked on him with respect and followed his instructions in social and religious matters.[6]

This pacific, constructive, and distinctively Gandhian approach in labour matters contrasted sharply with the more militant tone which the Khilafat workers and the Congress volunteers imported into the trade union movement. The Khilafat workers, who were the most active group in organizing the mill-hands, also preached Hindu–Muslim unity, abjuring of liquor and social reforms, but they did so with the more specifically political purpose of arousing anti-government feeling.[7] They were able to tap a very strong popular undercurrent of ill-feeling towards the European management of the jute mills.

[...]

Beyond Calcutta and its industrial suburbs, similar labour discontent was being fomented in the Raniganj coalfields by two Swamis, Biswanand and Darsananand, with the active help of Marwari coal traders and Bengali colliery owners who were fighting with the European managing agencies for the control of the coal trade and mining. Deputed to the coalfields by the Trade Union Congress formed at the Nagpur Congress, Swami Biswanand, Dip Narayan Singh, and Chandra Bangshi Lal Sahay formed two labour associations at Raniganj and Barakar. They were financed by rich Marwaris who were also contributing to the Barakar Bank opened by Gandhi and Swami Biswanand to promote Indian enterprise in the coalfields. Darsananand addressed a meeting of 300 upcountry workers at

Ballarpur, presided over by a local Bengali zamindar who owned some collieries, and by his remarks deliberately worked up the undercurrent of racial ill-feeling against the Europeans. At Jamuria, Darsananand delivered another speech inculcating the 'Bolshevik principle' of equity between the rich and the poor, whereupon the mechanics at Andrew Yule & Company's Sibpur Power House went on strike.

On a second visit to Jamuria, however, Darasananand told a gathering of 5,000 labourers that the real object of these meetings was 'to stop the work of the European "owned" collieries and to strengthen and enrich the collieries belonging to Indians'. He advised the workers that unless Andrew Yule, which was preventing other companies from increasing wages, granted a 100 per cent wage increase, workers should stop work at once and join the collieries owned by Indians. As a result there was a strike at six collieries of Andrew Yule, four collieries of Equitable Coal, and one of Bird, involving altogether 5,300 miners demanding higher wages and more honourable treatment from white colliery managers. The strikers were tribals and low caste villagers who looked upon Darasananand as a god come to earth who would bring blindness, barrenness of women, and flooding of pits unless they followed his instructions. At the same time there was a strike at Burn & Company's Kulti Iron Works, which was directed by men returned from the Nagpur Congress—Jagraj Marwari, Dip Narayan Singh, and Swamis Biswanand and Darsananand.[8] [...]

The labour situation deteriorated even more sharply in the tea garden area. [...] Sporadic unrest instigated by the non-co-operators continued among tea garden labourers in Darjeeling. In July there were several strikes, spontaneous and unorganized, without direction from a central agency. A special officer was deputed by the government for propaganda work in the affected area and the Indian Tea Association was asked to impress on the planters the necessity of keeping in touch with the workers.[9] Unrest had also spread further downhill to the Duars in July, and later on, in 1922, this unrest manifested itself in attempts to loot tea garden market fairs in Jalpaiguri district.[10]

In Darjeeling and Jalpaiguri, however, some sort of stability was provided by the fact that the Nepalese labour employed in the tea gardens was local. A much more serious situation developed in Assam, where the labour employed in the gardens was drawn from Bihar and UP. In May there was a sudden massive exodus of labour from Chargola valley in Assam, induced by rumours that Mahatma Gandhi was about to usher in the millennium and that a happy future awaited them in their distant homes in the west. The wages offered in the Assam tea gardens no longer offered any attraction when compared to the agricultural wages currently prevailing in their native districts in Bihar and UP. But the planters, being protected by the Inland Emigration Act of 1859, could afford to ignore this; while downcountry wages had risen everywhere, in Assam there was no increase. The planters took full and unwarranted advantage of the Act of 1859, often making illegal private arrests, a practice which continued even after it had become illegal under the amended act of 1908. The law still required discharge certificates for 'coolies' who wanted to go home, which were often refused by district magistrates on the ground that they had not fulfilled their contracts.[11]

In the summer of 1921 a strange discontent and a stranger hope seized the labourers, and refusing to obtain 'certificates', a large body of them started on the long trek for home which brought them to Chandpur in Tippera district on 15 May.[12] The local officials at first followed the policy of repatriating the labourers, but before long the Government of Bengal, influenced by the Indian Tea Association, assumed a stance of 'neutrality' between capital and labour, which really meant veiled opposition on the spot to the repatriation of labourers. This change of attitude synchronized with the arrival at Chandpur of Mr Macpherson, a representative of the Indian Tea Association who collaborated with the subdivisional officer of Chandpur to prevent labourers from boarding a steamer for the next stop on their journey, Goalando, on the night of the 21st.[13] On the following night, to prevent a recurrence of the day before's rush to the steamers, and to safeguard the railway premises, the local officials cleared the station with the help of Gurkha military police, who carried out the operation with extreme brutality.

'It was only by a miracle on that Gurkha outrage night', wrote Andrews to Gandhi from Chandpur, that the East Bengalis (who were 'highly emotional, quick tempered, hot, passionate'), 'did not go out and try to kill those Gurkhas'. In no time at all, East Bengal was 'on the very border-line of violence'.[14] On the morning after the event there was a complete hartal in Chandpur town. At Comilla the local bar left the courts in a body, schools closed down, domestic servants almost to a man deserted European masters, the bazaar refused to sell food to government servants, and for a few days the European community lived in a state of siege. Similar conditions prevailed in Chandpur, Noakhali, and Chittagong. On 24 May there was a strike on the Assam–Bengal Railway in Chittagong which rapidly became general. On 27 May a steamer strike occurred at Chandpur which in a few days spread to

Goalando, Barisal, and Khulna. Rail and river transport westwards was practically suspended by the action of local non-co-operators headed by J.M. Sengupta of Chittagong, the organizer of the railway strike. Das, who rushed by boat to Chandpur, personally directed the steamer strike at Goalando.[15] A perturbed Ronaldshay wrote to Montagu: 'The most disquieting feature is the extent of the hold which events have shown they have already acquired over large classes of people. They have been able to call strikes on the inland steamer lines and the Assam–Bengal Railway, and they have been able to call hartals in a number of East Bengal towns simultaneously'.[16]

What East Bengal witnessed in this hour of crisis was a spontaneous rising of the entire population, especially the lower classes, who expressed through the strikes their acute sense of economic exploitation and racial abasement under white rule. It was impossible to overlook that the Government of Bengal was deliberately refraining from helping the refugee labourers 'for fear of a further exodus from the gardens'.[17] Andrews was asked to act as a mediator, and with the support of the non-co-operators he made a simple proposal: government to provide to token subscription of Rs 5,000 as a mark of sympathy and the public to subscribe the rest for the repatriation of the refugees at Chandpur. He went all the way to Darjeeling, where the Government of Bengal had shifted for summer, with this proposal, but the Government, surrounded there by planters, coldly rejected it.[18] Meanwhile all transport in East Bengal had been paralysed by the organized action of the lower classes, who now gave full vent to their repressed hatred of the white ruling class. A new feature of the hartals, which profoundly disturbed the government at the beginning of June, was a deliberate attempt to boycott Europeans and loyal Indians and to intimidate their servants into leaving service.[19] The acute resentment of white economic controls reflected itself in the strike on the British Indian Steam Navigation Company's steamer lines, and predictably there were renewed proposals of a national steamer company to replace the foreign steamer services.[20]

The intention behind the strike was to force the government to repatriate the refugees.[21] The Government of Bengal, however, refused to be coerced, especially 'as the Indian Tea Association was dealing energetically with the matter'.[22] In the meanwhile cholera had broken out in the refugee camp. This confronted Das with a difficult choice. Andrews was urging the withdrawal of the strike so that the refugees could be transported home by public subscription of their steamer and railway fares. Should the non-co-operators now carry on the strike to force the government to surrender, or should they call off the strike to let the refugees go at non-official expense? Privately Das began to gather funds for repatriating the refugees.[23] He got a promise of the required sum, but was firmly of the opinion that the strike, which was 'national' in character, must not be allowed to fail.[24]

[...]

Eventually a solution was found that allowed Das both to continue the strike and to let the refugees be repatriated. Andrews, with the help of some moderate politicians and a few Marwari businessmen, collected the necessary funds and hired a private steamer to carry the tea garden labourers across to Goalando on their westward journey. Far from obstructing, the non-co-operators enthusiastically assisted the operation. Doctors and volunteers were supplied by the non-co-operators to help the refugees on the way.[25] The journey was punctuated by loud cries of 'Chittaranjan Das ki jai', to the chagrin of the officials who recalled bitterly that the money had been found by moderates.[26] In point of fact, however, Das spent no less than Rs 1.5 lakh from the Tilak Swaraj Fund for the relief of the refugees and the strikers.[27] The non-co-operators employed their extensive organization to look after the different groups of tea garden workers at every stage of their journey.[28] [...]

The root cause of the tragedy lay in the very structure of colonial domination. Tea planting and exporting was an essential part of the British economic stake in India and the 'coolie' exodus threatened this entire business. The *Mussalman* commented: 'Mr Andrews has vividly pointed out what a government not responsible to the people is capable of. European capitalists exploit the country to their advantage, and the bureaucracy helps them in every possible way'.[29] The European commercial community was now demanding firm government action. The Indian Tea Association held the view that rather than appointing an enquiry committee on labour conditions in Assam, it was more reasonable to have a committee on the reasons for the inactivity of the government in not dealing with the situation in the initial stages of the movement.[30] Under this political pressure, the earlier policy of wait and see laid down by the Government of India towards the non-co-operation movement was slightly modified, and local officers were instructed to undertake active counter-propaganda without at this stage resorting to suppression of the movement. Under this modified policy, special propaganda officers were deputed to the tea districts in Assam and Darjeeling, and in Bakarganj the district magistrate launched an anti-non-cooperation movement with useful hints from A.K. Fazlul Huq, who was now co-operating with a vengeance.[31]

As a result of this counter-propaganda by local officials, the steamer strike in Goalando suddenly collapsed on 25 June, nearly all *sèrangs* and *khalasis* returning to work. All other steamer lines resumed work in the first half of July, Khulna, Chandpur, and Goalando returning, one by one, to normal. Trouble broke out once again in Barisal upon the arrest of the local leader Sarat Ghosh, and there was a complete hartal for three days during which schools were closed, steamers were blocked, traffic ceased in the streets, and even conservancy sweepers were prevented from going to their work by the volunteers. The strike was broken by firm action, but the Assam–Bengal Railway strike in Chittagong continued until the end of August. [...]

While no deaths resulted from the Gurkha outrage which set East Bengal aflame, the railway and steamer strike certainly resulted, as Andrews pointed out at a meeting of the pro-Gandhi faction in the Indian Association Hall, in the death of many labourers whose repatriation was held up by the cessation of transport.[32] Shyamsunder Chakravarti, the chairman of the meeting, strongly supported Andrews and emphasized that strikes were no part of the non-co-operation programme as set out at the Congress.[33] [...]

Gandhi [...] came out with a strong article, entitled the 'Lessons of Assam' in *Young India*: 'Mr Andrews deplored the sympathetic strike of the steamship employees. Whoever instigated it, did an ill-service to the labourers. In India we want no political strike... We do not need an atmosphere of unsettled unrest... We must gain control over all the unruly and disturbing elements or isolate them even as we are isolating the government. The only way, therefore we can help the strikers is to give them help and relief when they have struck for their own bona fide grievances. We must sedulously prevent all other strikes. We seek not to destroy capital or capitalists, but to regulate the relations between capital and labour. It would be folly to encourage sympathetic strikes'.[34] Das and his followers were infuriated by this statement and for a time they considered breaking off from Gandhi. They were restrained from this course by the consideration that in such a case they would irresistibly gravitate towards violence.[35] But the underlying differences in Das's and Gandhi's thinking were now clear. The clash that occurred over the Chandpur crisis was due to fundamentally differing conceptions of the role of labour in politics. Gandhi and Andrews had a natural preference for constructive activity instead of strikes. They were prepared to tolerate strikes for the redress of specific grievances, but were opposed to strikes as part of the non-co-operation movement. Their attitude was that strikes and hartals brought added suffering to the lower classes and tended towards mass violence. Das, on the other hand, was prepared to take these risks of violence and suffering in a national cause. His aim was to mobilize the lower classes to create irresistible political pressure on the British. He did not believe that the only legitimate reason for strikes lay in specific grievances; and he did his best to relieve the suffering of the strikers by providing funds and volunteers to look after them.

Soon after the excitement had subsided, Gandhi came on a visit to East Bengal. He walked straight into a trap laid for him by the district authorities who were conducting counter-propaganda at Barisal. At a meeting of Gandhi in Barisal town, the district Propaganda Committee of local moderates controlled by the government from behind the scenes posed a series of questions about the late strike to which Gandhi replied with characteristic honesty, putting the local non-co-operators on the spot. To the question whether a strike for the release of the local leader Sarat Babu was justified, Gandhi replied in Urdu: 'The meaning of non-cooperation is that we want deliberately to go to jail though quite innocent... Therefore it should be *haram* for us to be sorry'. Replying to a question about the stopping of conservancy service and water supply in Barisal during the strike, he said that he did not want to get Swaraj at all if people behaved in this manner. He condemned the cry 'Gandhi Maharaj ki jai' accompanying violent actions, and advised the people not to utter such a cry, which, he said, thrust daggers into his heart.[36] [...]

Much more serious implication for the NCO movement as a whole [...] was the fact that the social and ideological contradictions in the movement were by now brought to focus by the 'Lessons of Assam' and the speech at Barisal. While the ideology of the movement, the Hind Swaraj, had no place in it for capitalism, the organization of the movement depended squarely on the financial support of native capitalists. While exhorting his people to boycott British goods, Gandhi was at the same time asking Bombay mill owners not to exploit this opportunity for making profit. He himself admitted in his Barisal speech that the mill owners were making exorbitant profits, and his solution was to advise the people not to use mill-woven cloth at all.

[...]

But in that case—asked the *Hijli Hitaishi* pertinently—why should not Indian mill-woven cloth also be boycotted?[37] Such a logically consistent move would of course have cut the financial ground from under the movement, for the interests which were patronizing the movement had no patience for 'charkha, ghani and all that'. So while the poor consumer bore the burden of boycott, the rich mill owner reaped the profit. [...] On Gandhi's return from Barisal to Calcutta, the Marwari Chamber of Commerce in September took the decision to order no more foreign cloth till the end of the year and fined Mohan Chand Gopi Kishen Rs 1,001 as being the only person to violate the agreement. As soon as the year ended, however, fifty-eight Marwari merchants entered into fresh contracts with Manchester and the boycott could no longer be enforced although a majority of the Chamber voted for it.[38]

After the excitement in East Bengal over the Chandpur incident had subsided, there was a lull in political activity in the province at the end of July, which continued through August, September, and October. Then in November there was a sudden turn in the situation towards violence. The reason for this change was to be sought in the perfecting of the volunteer organization, the opening of Congress committees and penetration of political propaganda to the interior during the lull. Though there were no widespread outward disturbances, there was no diminution in the steady stream of political propaganda. No less that 4,265 non-co-operation meetings took place between June and mid-November.[39] The reaching of remote areas in the interior by the Congress committees and volunteer corps ultimately began to produce observable effects on the unrest which had been simmering under the surface during the lull. When it burst into the open in November in both urban and rural areas, it took three forms: rioting by landless and tribal elements in rural society, peasant combinations against tax payments and settlement operations, and urban disorders, strikes, and hartals.

Trouble of the first type started in April on the lands of the Midnapur Zamindari Company in Rajshahi, where the sharecroppers refused to pay rent to the European landowning corporation, the only zamindari concern to be affected in the district. The non-co-operators sent Someswar Chaudhuri to Rajshahi to stir up trouble between capital and labour. Being proceeded against under Section 107, Someswar Chaudhuri crossed the river from Rajshahi into Nadia, where trouble simmering between the Midnapur Zamindari Company and its utbandi tenants (shifting tenants whose customary right to land could be easily denied because of the absence of permanent holdings) since 1918 broke into defiance of law and order in July and August. The utbandi cultivators proposed abolition of indigo cultivation and demanded letting out of land on terms which the Company refused. Someswar Chaudhuri held a meeting near the indigo factories with the result that they had to be closed down the next day as no one came to work. He was joined by the dismissed assistants of the concern, in whose company he visited the country of the Midnapur Zamindari Company. An attempt at compromise by the district magistrate failed and the non-co-operators addressed meetings, defied orders under Section 144, and instigated the rural police to resign.[40]

Trouble spread also in the lands of the Midnapur Zamindari Company in Murshidabad and Midnapur, the most serious disturbances occurring among the tribal Santhals and Mahatos in the western part of the latter district. There the company held extensive lands, where rent was much higher than in other areas of Jhargram Subdivision.[41] Sailajananda Sen, a schoolteacher, opened a Congress Committee at Gidni near Jhargram and incited the tribals in Pargana Silda to combine against the Midnapur Zamindari Company. Trouble started in November 1921 when looting at the weekly market fair by tribals necessitated a route march by military police through the area. At the instigation of Sailajananda Sen the tenants of the Company refused certain terms of settlement offered by the additional district magistrate who came to Jhargram to enquire into complaints of oppression. This opposition gradually degenerated into regular plunder of forests, and on some occasions more than a thousand people would combine at a time to plunder and damage the jungle. In his meetings Sailajananda Sen told the tribals that Swaraj had been obtained, the jungle and the land were theirs, and they would have to pay only four annas each to the Congress fund and nothing to the zamindars. Upon his arrest in February 1922, Murari Mohan Rai took charge of the Congress in pargana Silda, and in September 1922 the tenants at his instigation took a vow not to cut wood from any jungle leased by the Midnapur Zamindari Company to the Midnapur Mining Syndicate, with the result that all attempts by the Company to work in the jungle failed. European officials of the Company were often threatened with arrows while trying to stop jungle looting by the Santhals.

From the European zamindari of Silda the disturbances spread in April 1923 to the native zamindari of Jamboni, where a spate of fish-looting broke out, inspired by similar acts in Malda and Dinajpur by Santhals earlier in February and March. Trouble had been brewing between Jagdis Dhabal Deb of Jamboni and his Santhal tenants, instigated by a rival claimant to the Jamboni Raj, the Raja of Dalbhum, and his agent, the Mohanta of Ghatsila, with the help of some hereditary enemies of the estate—a few Satpathis (Brahmans) and Mahatos (wealthy once, broken by the Jamboni Raj). At their instigation the Santhals started looting fish and armed clashes between the servants and tenants of the Jamboni Raj followed. The zamindar lost control of the estate and his servants could not move out of fear of life. The disturbances spread to other estates, involving (1) in the north, Raipur thana in Bankura district, (2) in the central part, Silda Pargana in Binpur thana, (3) in the south-east, Jamboni thana, including the Gidni Railway station, and (4) in the south-west, the eastern portion of Singhbhum district in Chhota Nagpur. The disturbances were 'agrarian and economic in character' and 'directed against the owners of tanks and jungles in general' who had deprived the Santhals of their traditional fishing and jungle rights.[42]

More complex than these outbreaks of violence among the dispossessed aboriginal elements at the bottom of rural society were combinations of Bengali peasants, led by leading villagers of peasant stock under the direction of local lawyers and politicians. Combinations threatening to disrupt settlement operations and collection of taxes had sprung up by November 1921 in Pabna, Bogra, Birbhum, and Midnapur. Macpherson, the settlement officer for Pabna and Bogra, was actually assaulted by an unruly crowd including NCO volunteers when he went to a market fair to buy food for his staff from whom supplies had been withheld. After this assault the district magistrate and the police superintendent toured Bogra and a show of force by armed police got the settlement operations going again, but Macpherson was assaulted a second time in succession.[43] For some time Khilafat meetings had been held in the bigger market fairs in Bogra where tales of outrage against Muslim holy places had been circulated, and ordinary *maulvi*s and *mullah*s who had formerly held aloof from politics had been recently drawn into the boycott movement in East Bengal.[44]

An even more impressive peasant combination was put together in the Contai and Tamluk subdivisions of Midnapur district against newly introduced union boards by a Mahishya lawyer from Contai, Birendranath Sasmal, who had joined C.R. Das's party and was one of his three top lieutenants. This area was thickly settled by agricultural Mahishyas, led by rich agriculturists and small proprietors who had acquired 'lots' in the Sundarbans. They opened up the Sundarbans with their Mahishya dependants in Contai and Tamluk, who were moved across the river to the Sundarbans for clearing the forest. Thus this class of respectable peasant-proprietors, a considerable body in Contai and Tamluk, had an assured income. The great mass of poor peasants of the area were also Mahishyas. The homogeneity of the population in Tamluk and Contai and the caste identity of its social leadership with the rest of the people produced an extremely effective combination against payment of union board rates once it became known that these new local self-governing bodies were likely to increase the older chaukidari rates by fifty per cent. The news dashed the hopes of poor Mahishya peasants who had thought that they were electing their own village officers to the union boards who would take the place of the *Hakim*s (government officers) and administer justice to them without costly lawyers.

B.N. Sasmal, who had a personal antagonism against the sub-divisional officer Contai, Mr Dey, organized meetings all over the region with the help of Satish Chandra Jana, an educated young man of a respectable local Mahishya family. The educated people of Contai, who controlled the union boards and who might therefore have counteracted Sasmal's campaign, were split by rivalry between two sections, one consisting of the local residents and the other of people from other districts who had established a practice in the Contai courts or had flourished in other spheres. [...]

[...]

Sasmal now organized a campaign with the help of educated Mahishya volunteers which reached the remotest parts in Tamluk and Contai, and the agitation soon spilled over to Ghatal and Sadar subdivisions in Midnapur district. By November 1921 entire villages had combined in such a manner that under social pressure union board members and *chaukidar*s in many unions had resigned, union board rates had been withheld in all subdivisions of Midnapur and attempts at distraint of property in order to realize union board rates had been foiled by the fact that no purchaser was forthcoming in the seriously affected areas of Tamluk and Contai. The local officers, hoping that people might be persuaded to pay the *chaukidari* rates under the older Chaukidari Act, recommended the abolition of union boards in November as a tactical withdrawal in order to regroup against the NCO campaign in the district. In accordance with this recommendation the union boards were abolished by the government and Sasmal thus scored a complete victory. This victory was due to the combination of what was effectively the whole population of an extensive rural tract, who had implicit faith in Birendranath Sasmal, their kinsman, who had renounced a lucrative practice to serve them and who had worked with them during the last two floods.[45]

The urban unrest also reached a climax in November, and in Howrah and Calcutta the situation began to slip out of the control of the police. On the night of 4 November a procession returning from a Khilafat meeting in Howrah town attacked the police, forcing them to retire to a police station. Armed police requisitioned from Sibpur were attacked en route. They succeeded in relieving the police station, now besieged by a large mob, only by firing in order to disperse the crowd. In this action one police constable and a number of rioters were killed. A boycott of the Howrah police was put into operation by volunteers who intimidated the shopkeepers and house-holders. At the same time an attempt to break a tram strike in Calcutta by running a tram in north Calcutta led to serious disturbances in Belgachia where a deputy commissioner, an assistant commissioner, and twenty other members of the police received injuries.[46] The arrival of the Prince of Wales on 17 November provided the occasion for a striking demonstration of national solidarity all over India. Widespread riots greeted his arrival in Bombay, and for four days life in the city was disrupted. Calcutta responded in a more quiet way by the most complete twenty-four hour hartal ever seen.

[...]

To what extent was the non-co-operation movement successful in committing the body of the population to a course of opposition to government? Up to the end of 1921, when the government won the battle for Calcutta during the visit of the Prince of Wales to the city, the unrest in Bengal, as elsewhere in India, was mainly urban in character. Even during the Chandpur crisis in the predominantly agricultural area of East Bengal, it was the towns which were affected by strikes and hartals. After December 1921, when the massive application of government power began to break the organization of the non-co-operation movement in the towns, the unrest became mainly rural in Assam, Bengal, Bihar, and UP, and quickly began to go out of control of the town-based Congress and Khilafat organizations. In Bengal, administration was virtually paralysed in Contai, Tamluk, Sabong, and Ghatal in Midnapur district, Nilpahari and Fulchar in Rangpur, Laksam and Chauddagram in Tippera, and Banskhali, Satkania, and Cox's Bazar in Chittagong. The mass character of the movement, at least in its origin, was not the result of a groundswell from below, but of the reaching-down of organization from above. J.M. Sengupta's campaign in Chittagong and B.N. Sasmal's agitation in Midnapur, which brought the villages into close contact with the Congress organization and the volunteer movement for the first time, clearly showed that the movement was organized from above by means of a closer rapport between the provincial political elite and the local town and village leadership. At the beginning of 1922, however, there was a peasant movement from below, a groundswell which burst the bonds of Congress control. In Tippera, in Rangpur, and in Chittagong the Congress volunteers lost control over the rural crowds. These crowds were now composed mainly of the poorer peasants. Richer villagers, frightened off, were dropping out of the movement in some places.

The movement succeeded best in committing the mass of the people to political opposition in those areas where the tyranny of an upper cast landed gentry was relatively weak. In these areas the leading villagers, if they belonged to the majority community of the local population, were in a strong position to commit whole bodies of villagers to defiance of authority, providing of course they joined the political leaders from the towns who brought the Congress and the Khilafat organization down to them. In the case of the prosperous Mahishya farmers of Contai or the Muslim *jotedar*s of Rangpur, who locally enjoyed a good social position, there was no impediment to their joining the party of the Congress of Khilafat leaders from the towns. There was strong disincentive to join the Congress only in the case of local leaders of ritually low peasant castes like the Namashudras and the Rajbanshis, and in fact the political response from these two large peasant communities, which numbered next only to the Muslim and Mahishya communities, was weak because of their resentment of their low ritual rank. The Rajbanshi community of Rangpur under the leadership of Rai Sahib Panchanan Barman temporarily went over to the non-co-operators in July 1921, but in fact the Muslim volunteers remained the main driving force behind the movement in the district.[47]

[...]

Even in areas thinly inhabited by upper caste gentry like Midnapur and Rangpur, however, the local rich farmers did not wish the unrest to stir up the poor peasants and share-croppers to a point where their own economic interests would be threatened. There was no movement of under-tenants and share-croppers to withhold rent from zamindars, unless the landlord happened to be the government (as was the case with regard to the government *khas* estates in Contai) or a European corporation (as was the case with regard to the lands of the Midnapur Zamindari Company in Midnapur, Nadia, Rajshahi, and some other places). A small number of native landlords were affected, but in some of these cases the jotedars themselves had turned against the landlord, as in Rangpur where they were refusing to pay *abwab*s to the zamindars of Balna and the Maharaja of Kasimbazar. The most successful peasant combinations in Bengali villages were usually, but not always, led by village heads and rich farmers, who turned against the movement as soon as it began to slip out of their control.

But in spite of the control exercised by the substantial villagers, a strange unrest, usually expressed in terms of a millennial hope of Swaraj, stirred the lowest elements in Indian society. Gandhi's charismatic appeal reached deep down to the bottom layer of the deprived—the tribals, the low castes, the coolies, the landless labourers. It penetrated even into the jails of Rajshahi, Barisal, and Midnapur, where criminal elements broke out from prison, excited by the false rumour that Swaraj had been established outside by 'Maharaj Gandhi', that the Raj was over and notes and rupees were being coined in the name of Gandhi.[48] Under the impact of these strange millennial hopes, Oriya porters in Calcutta refused to carry loads of foreign cloth for Marwari merchants.[49] Santhal and Oraon tribals attacked armed police, wearing Gandhi caps supposed to give immunity from bullets, and tea garden coolies left their estates en masse to find the Swaraj that Gandhi was said to have established in their distant villages.[50] [...]

This, then, was the extent of the involvement of the masses in the political unrest of the non-co-operation movement: a millennial unrest among the lowest elements of rural society, kept in check by dominant village classes; combinations by the mass of cultivating families against payment of government taxes and, in a few districts, landlords' rents; and widespread and frequent disorders in cities, mill towns and mining areas by mill-hands, miners, carters, coachmen, and coolies, mostly upcountrymen, tribals or Muslims. Social control tended to break down more readily in those areas of life where the colonial government or foreign capital came into direct contact with large bodies of people than in areas where control was exercised indirectly through Indian intermediaries. In the case of the government these contact points lay mainly between police parties and unruly crowds in urban areas and rural markets, and between the tax-collecting machinery of the sub-divisional administration and bodies of chaukidari tax payers and government estate tenants. In the case of foreign capital the contact points were mainly those between mill managers and mill-hands, and between European land-owning corporations and dispossessed tribes. Where the machinery of social control was exercised by Indians, the power-holding groups which usually lost control of the population under them were non-agricultural moneylenders and absentee landlords. There were, however, instances of rural conflict in which the poorer peasants alienated the richer resident cultivating families. This happened in the last stage of the movement. But initially all kinds of villagers participated in village combinations against the government or the landlord over carefully chosen and limited issues.

[...]

Notes

1. Intelligence Branch [henceforth IB] 1920, 'Non Cooperation [henceforth NCO] Movement in Bengal, January 1921'; Chelmsford Collection, MSS. Eur. E. 264.26, no. 47, Ronaldshay to Chelmsford, 19 January 1921.
2. Government of Bengal [henceforth GB], Poll Dept Poll Branch, 395/1924.
3. GB, Poll Dept Poll Branch, 395/1924.
4. Ibid.
5. C.F. Andrews Papers, Andrews to Tagore, 22 March 1921.
6. IB 1920, 'The NCO Movement in Bengal, January 1921', weekly confidential report from the Superintendent of Police, 24 Parganas, 29 January 1921. [Superintendent of Police hereafter S.P.]
7. Ibid., S.P.'s weekly confidential report, 29 January 1921.
8. IB 1920, 'The NCO Movement in Bengal, January 1921', W.C.R. of S.P. Bankura, 22 January 1921 and W.C.R. of S.P. Burdwan, 29 January 1921.
9. IB 1921, 'Fortnightly Reports of the Government of Bengal on the Political Situation (1921–1922)'.
10. Ibid.
11. Indian Tea Association, *Detailed Report of the General Committee of the Indian Tea Association for the year 1922*, containing the resolution of the Govt of Assam on the Report of the Assam Labour Enquiry Committee 1922.
12. This was a spontaneous mass exodus, a virtual *hijrat*. It was not instigated, as Broomfield has alleged (*Elite Conflict [in a Plural Society: Twentieth Century Bengal, Berkeley and Los Angeles, 1968*, p. 215), by a group of Congressmen from Calcutta who moved into the tea gardens of Assam, nor did this alleged group promise the coolies transport or later on fail to keep the promise.
13 *Modern Review*, July 1921; *Bengal Legislative Council Proceedings*, 8 and 11 July 1921; Zetland Collection, MSS. Eur. D. 609.2, 'My Bengal Diary', 1 June 1921, 6 June 1921.
14. C.F. Andrews Papers, Andrews to Gandhi, 21 June 1921.
15. GB, Poll Dept Poll Branch, 395/1924.
16. Zetland Collection, MSS. Eur. D. 609.5, Ronaldshay to Montagu, 15 June 1921.
17. C.F. Andrews, *The Meaning of Non-Cooperation*, Madras, n.d., p. 16.
18. Ibid., pp. 16–18.

19. IB 1921, 'Fortnightly Reports of the Government of Bengal on the Political Situation (1921–1922)'.
20. Ibid., Hemendranath Dasgupta, *Deshabandhu Smriti*, Calcutta, B.S. 1333, p. 273.
21. Ibid.
22. IB 1921, 'Fortnightly Reports of the Government of Bengal on the Political Situation (1921–22)'.
23. GB, Poll Dept Poll Branch, October 1921, nos 11–53 (A).
24. Ibid., Broomfield writes that C.R. Das's statement about national honour infuriated C.F. Andrews and in support of this allegation he quotes from a letter from Andrews to Tagore: 'Honour is very cheap when another person has to maintain it.' Actually this letter, written one year later (dated 23 February 1922), was not about the Chandpur strike at all, but concerned the East Indian Railway strike of 1922, organized principally by the Khilafat workers. Andrews wanted to settle the strike, but was afraid that the extremists would cry out that honour was at stake. Broomfield thus uses a statement relating to a different incident.
25. GB, Poll Dept Poll Branch, October 1921, nos 11–53 (A).
26. Ibid.
27. Hemendranath Dasgupta, p. 272.
28. GB, Poll Dept Poll Branch, September 1921, nos 300–52 (B).
29. IB, 'Fortnightly Reports of the Government of Bengal on the Political Situation (1921–1922)'.
30. ITA, *Detailed Report of the General Committee of the Indian Tea Association for the year 1921*, annual general meeting, 10 March 1922, speech of Chairman.
31. GB, Poll Dept Poll Branch, 395/1924; ibid., 209/1921, 'Propaganda Work in the Bakarganj District'.
32. *Hijli Hitaishi*, 14 July 1921; *Medinipur Hitaishi*, 4 July 1921.
33. IB 1921, 'Fortnightly Reports of the Government of Bengal on the Political Situation (1921–1922)'.
34. GB, Poll Dept Poll Branch, 209/1921, 'Propaganda Work in East Bengal'.
35. Ibid.
36. IB 1921, 'The Non-Cooperation Movement in Bengal'.
37. *Hijli Hitaishi*, 16 September 1921.
38. IB Library, 'Report on the Progress of the Non-Cooperation Movement in Bengal 1922'.
39. GB, Poll Dept Poll Branch, 395/1924.
40. *Bengal Legislative Council Proceedings*, 21 November 1921, 1 February 1922.
41. *Final Report on Midnapore*, p. 69.
42. GB, Poll Dept Branch, 181/1923, 'Disturbances in Jamboni, District Midnapore'; *Servant*, 10 July 1923; *Nihar*, 14 February 1922, 15 and 29 May 1923; *Final Report on the Survey and Settlement Operations in the district of Bankura 1917–24 by F.W. Robertson*, Calcutta, 1926, pp. 11–12.

43. IB 1921, 'Fortnightly Reports of the Government of Bengal on the Political Situation (1921–1922)'; IB 1921, 'The Non-Cooperation Movement in Bengal'.
44. *Final Report on Pabna and Bogra*, pp. 93–5.
45. This account of the agitation in Midnapur is based on the 1921 issues of two Contai newspapers, *Nihar* and *Hijli Hitaishi*, and on BMP, Local Self-Government Branch, July 1922, nos 36–34.
46. IB 1921, 'Fortnightly Reports of the Government of Bengal on the Political Situation (1921–1922)'.
47. IB 1921, 'Fortnightly Reports of the Government of Bengal on the Political Situation (1921–1922)'.
48. GB, Poll Dept Poll Branch, 395/1924.
49. IB 1921, 'Fortnightly Reports of the Government of Bengal on the Political Situation (1921–1922)'.
50. C.F. Andrews Papers, Andrews to Gandhi, 21 June 1921.

9 Rebellious Hillmen*
The Gudem–Rampa Risings 1839–1924

David Arnold

If the names 'Gudem' and 'Rampa' have any meaning for the historian of modern India it may be recalled that they are hill tracts, located near the Godavari River in Andhra Pradesh, and that they acquired a brief prominence in the early 1920s because of a rising there. Existing historiography has nothing further to add, and only M. Venkatarangaiya in a collection of documents on the freedom movement in Andhra has described and attempted to explain the 1922–4 rising (or *fituri*).[1] Even he seems largely unaware that this was merely the last in a long series of disturbances and rebellions in the hills which stretch back at least to the early nineteenth century and possibly earlier.

This neglect need not surprise us. It is an indication not that there was anything peculiarly obscure about these tracts or trivial about their history but of the prevailing state of the historiography of modern India. Conventional academic wisdom about the subcontinent stresses (especially by contrast with China's massive peasant revolts and twentieth-century revolutions) fatalism and passivity, corruption and self-seeking, resignation in the face of hardship and oppression. Violent conflict is rarely seen to have been of importance—after the Mutiny and Rebellion of 1857 it is allowed significance only in the communal rioting that preceded and accompanied Partition in 1947 and in the terrorist sub-plot to the Gandhi-dominated saga of India's nationalist movement. Equally, conventional historiography has been too busy searching for what are presumed to be the grand, overarching themes of modern Indian History to concern itself greatly with the attitudes and activities of the peasants who constituted the great majority of the population. Peasants appear as the victims of history, not as its principals. They have revenue systems imposed upon them, they are invaded by the modern state,

---

* Originally published in Ranajit Guha (ed.), *Subaltern Studies I: Writings on South Asian History and Society*, paperback edition, New Delhi, Oxford University Press, 1986, pp. 88–142. In the present version some portions of the text and notes have been removed. For the complete text see the original version.

they are harangued and mobilized by the nationalist orator and activist. Rarely do they enter the pages of modern Indian history in their own right, motivated by their own interests, giving voice to their own grievances.[2] Little wonder, then, that the rebellious peasants of Gudem and Rampa, tucked away in the remote corner of the Eastern Ghats, have received no more than a cursory glance.

Quite apart from the intrinsic interest of any area of persistent disturbances and risings, Gudem and Rampa demonstrate two fundamental characteristics of subalternity in India (and perhaps in peasant societies generally). The precise forms that these took were, no doubt, moulded by the physical environment of the hills and by that almost universal antipathy which hillmen feel towards the inhabitants of the plains. But far from detracting from the basic similarity between these peasant movements and others, such factors often serve to dramatize and to highlight developments that occurred more gradually, were less starkly illuminated, in the plains.

In the first characteristic manifestation of subalternity, the inhabitants of the hill tracts were opposed to outsiders who threatened their territory and their customary ways of life. The outsiders were of several kinds—British colonial administrators, their Indian troops, police and civilian subordinates, Telugu traders and contractors moving up from the coastal plain. But this diversity did not weaken the hillman's conviction that they conspired together and had a mutual interest in oppressing and exploiting him. In the cause of resisting external interference and control, the local elite—composed of members of the zamindari and mansabdari families and their subordinate chiefs (or *muttadars*)—took a leading part, with varying degrees of popular support. As outside intervention increased in scale and intensity, and as the threat to the hillmen's old ways grew, resistance came more and more from the peasants, though with leaders recruited (sometimes under threat of violence) from the fragmented elite. It was this long-established hostility to outsiders that the rebel leader Sita Rama Raju tried to mobilize in the 1922–4 fituri in the cause of Indian nationalism. Xenophobia and peasant territoriality were thus pressed into service for a wider cause in the Gudem–Rampa hills as they have repeatedly been by nationalist and communist movements in the modern world.[3]

In the second characteristic of subalternity, the hillmen were themselves divided. On one side were the local elite with their superior wealth, social status, and political influence: on the other, the peasantry. This relationship was one of profound ambiguity and great social and cultural complexity. To summarize it crudely, for much of their lives the poorer villagers paid their lords the taxes and fees, the respect, the deference, and the social obligations, that were customary or necessary for survival. In return, hopefully, they received protection, help, and security. But this relationship did not reduce the peasants to mute and unquestioning obedience, nor did it rob them of the capacity for initiative and self-expression, though like peasants elsewhere they would prefer to till their land and leave the business of fighting and negotiating with the higher authority to those better qualified. Peasant resentment against excessive taxation might be expressed by migrating elsewhere or by open revolt; peasants might coerce a lord who was slow to move on his own account into leading their opposition to outsiders. This ambiguous relationship was further complicated in the Gudem–Rampa hills by the relative poverty and backwardness of the area which tended to limit the degree of socio-economic differentiation that was possible and, at least in the earlier part of our period, to keep the muttadars close to their villages. Hence, the lines of division were not always clearly drawn, especially when remoter members of *muttadari* families or dispossessed muttadars and their descendents were drawn back into the peasant mass. Nonetheless, in this internal tension and conflict within hill society one can see the seeds of the development of rural class identity and class conflict.

[...]

RAMA RAJU'S FITURI, 1922–4

In many respects Rama Raju's rebellion (the seventh Gudem fituri, 1922–4) followed the pattern set by the earlier ones [...]. Restrictions on *podu* and the hillmen's access to the forest, and the petty tyranny of subordinate government officials again accounted for much of the background discontent. Ex-muttadars, dispossessed landholders, and outlaws once again constituted an important leadership element: police stations were, as usual, a main target for attack. The rains, fever, and difficult terrain, the help villagers gave to the rebels and withheld from the government— these were as much a feature of this fituri as of previous ones. What is of particular interest about this final fituri is the extent to which there was a new departure. To what extent was Rama Raju, an outsider from the plains, able to adapt the fituri tradition so as to make a rising in the hills a starting point or a war of national liberation against the British?

Accounts of Alluri Sita Rama Raju's life vary slightly, but according to one official report he was born in Bhimavaram taluk, Krishna district, in May 1898. He was a Telugu Kshatriya; his father was a travelling photographer and his uncle (by the time of the rising) a deputy collector. He was educated to the fourth form at Visakhapatnam. According to this account he did not go to the Agency until 1918;[4] but Venkatarangaiya says that he was born in 1897 and went to the Agency at the age of eighteen, which would be in 1915.[5] If so, then Rama Raju may have seen something of the Lagarayi fituri of 1915–16. Even if he did not witness it in person the hills must still have echoed with rumours and reports of the fituri when he arrived.

Rama Raju travelled in the Gudem hills as a sanyasi and, according to Venkatarangaiya, his 'austerity and his knowledge of astrology and medicine and his reputed ability to tame wild animals gained for him the respect and admiration of the tribal people who credited him with magical powers'.[6] The British thought him mentally unbalanced and 'bordering on insanity' for his intense and unreasoning hatred of any thing British but then conceded that the hillmen believed him 'possessed by God'.[7] Before the rising and during it, Rama Raju made repeated use of the sorts of religious sanctions we have encountered in previous fituris. He bound his followers by oaths and (a bureaucratic innovation) recorded them in a book with the hillmen's mark or thumbprint alongside. He paid frequent visits to hill temples and shrines.[8] Following his early successes against the police, he claimed to be invulnerable to police bullets and attributed victory to divine support.[9] It may be, too, that his very name evoked in the hillmen the same associations with the Rama–Sita–Hanuman story that had figured in the 1886 fituri. That earlier rising also offers a precedent for the involvement of an outsider in the hillmen's fituris, and in both Anantayya and Rama Raju's cases it is striking that religion provided the means by which men from the plains could identify themselves with the grievances and aspirations of the local population. But whereas Anantayya was a 'rolling stone' who projected his own frustrations and ambitions onto the hillmen's revolt against their oppressors, Rama Raju seems always to have been concerned to use the hills as a base for launching a military movement to liberate India from British rule. In this respect he showed something of the romantic idealism of his class, rather than the more limited and local aims of the other *fituridars*.

In 1921 Rama Raju went on a pilgrimage to Nasik in Maharashtra, and it was perhaps in the course of this journey that he came into contact with the Gandhian movement. On returing to Gudem, he began to preach temperance and to urge the hillmen to settle disputes through their own panchayats rather than through the British courts. He adopted khadi and was said to speak highly of Gandhi, but to believe that Indian independence could be attained only by force. Such an attitude was in keeping with his own Kshatriya traditions—just as during the fituri he dyed his khadi shirt red and tucked a police pistol in his captured Sam Browne belt—as well as with the hillmen's heritage of a defiant and avenging fituri. The British claimed that Rama Raju sought to establish his own hill kingdom, but he does not seem to have adopted any regal titles and it was as a sanyasi, perhaps as a prophet armed, rather than as a king, that he was revered and followed.

Alerted by his new preaching, officials in the hills began to fear that Rama Raju might lead a new fituri, and in January 1922 he was put under police surveillance. This may have convinced Rama Raju that he would have to act quickly before the police arrested and imprisoned him. He began to promise hillmen redress for their various grievances especially against Bastian, the hated tahsildar of Gudem. He also carefully built up support among discontented and dispossessed members of the elite, men of the type that had provided the fituris of the past with so many of their leaders. [...]

[...]

Through the influence of these lieutenants Rama Raju attracted a motley band of old fituridars, ex-convicts, landless 'budmashes', men fined for forest and grazing offences, and dispossessed petty landholders. As the fituri gathered momentum and as the small rebel bands roved the hills, headmen and other villagers were drawn into the rising by supplying them with food, shelter, and information about police movements.[10] Without this assistance the fituridars would not have been able to evade the elaborate measures devised for their capture and to sustain the rebellion for nearly two years. Rama Raju did not inspire such massive demonstration of popular support as those aroused by Tamman Dora and Bhima Reddi at the height of the Rampa rebellion, but the government's attempts to crush the rebels were foiled by the villagers' reluctance to cooperate with the authorities. The imposition of a punitive police tax in March 1923 was a serious government error as it confirmed villagers' hostility to the administration without deterring them from helping the fituridars.

Rama Raju tried to develop the raiding and reprisals of earlier fituris into a more sophisticated form of guerrilla warfare. The raids on Chintapalle, Krishnadevipet, and Rajavomangi between 22 and 24 August 1922 brought into the rebels hands a rich haul of police arms and ammunition. With 26 muskets and 2,500 rounds of ammunition, Rama Raju's followers were better armed than the rebels in previous fituris and, the government conceded, better led.[11] Rama Raju followed his initial raids with two successful ambushes: in the first of these two European police officers and four Indian subordinates were killed, and six .303 rifles and a pistol were captured.[12] A number of rebels were subsequently seen in captured police uniforms, perhaps because Rama Raju wanted to dress his men up as soldiers, but it was also another expression of the triumphant inversion of roles between the hillmen and their former oppressors.

Unlike the leaders of previous fituris, Rama Raju sought to carry the rebellion into the plains, though, in actuality, government counter-measures cordoned off the hills and prevented him from spreading the revolt beyond the area of the 1879–80 rising. His base area, to which he retired for months at a time, lay in the back country between Peddavalasa, Gudem, and Darakonda. The initial raids of September and October 1922 took Rama Raju as far west as Chodavaram, but there was little support for the rebels in Rampa and the muttadars there remained loyal to the government. In June 1923 Rama Raju crossed into Malakanagiri; in September he advanced north-west as far as Paderu in Madugula before being driven back by the police. It was during a second sally into Madugula that Rama Raju was captured and shot on 6 May 1924.[13]

Rama Raju's inability to extend the fituri beyond Gudem and the neighbouring hills was not just a military failure. It also demonstrated the difficulty of trying to enlarge the fituri tradition beyond the hillmen's natural territory to encompass a national war of liberation. There had, of course, been strong anti-foreigner elements in earlier fituris, especially that of 1886. But then the aim had been only to drive the outsiders from the hills, not to seek to expel them from the plains as well or to identify the rising in the hills with a broader struggle of Indians against British. It is striking how successful Rama Raju was in impressing upon his lieutenants and followers that their war was against the white men, not against fellow Indians (Bastian would appear to have been made an exception). Although it went against the fituri tradition, there was a deliberate policy of killing only European officers and sparing their Indian subordinates. When the latter fell into rebel hands they were humiliated but not punished more severely. The old laws of discrimination (hillmen against outsiders) had been temporarily overruled.[14] But since the rebellion never spread beyond the hillmen's territory it is impossible to say how far Rama Raju would have been successful in linking the hillmen with Indian nationalists in the plains.

The evidence from the other side—of the plainsmen's attitude to the fituri—is almost wholly negative. Rama Raju tried to recruit fellow Kshatriyas and Congressmen from the plains of Andhra Pradesh, but only one Kshatriya, Aggi Raju, joined him.[15] The Congressmen not only declined to join the fituri: they threw their weight against it. Attachment to Gandhian non-violence provides a ready explanation for this attitude. The Telugu nationalist paper, *Andhra Patrika*, wrote on 17 May 1924 that the fituri was 'another illustration to show that violence is quite a useless weapon. Hence all will do well to adopt the excellent non-violent non-cooperation preached by Mr Gandhi'.[16] But a more basic reason for the hostility of the Andhra Congressmen was that they represented precisely those interests—the traders, moneylenders, contractors, immigrant cultivators, and lawyers—whose hold on the hills the fituridars were fighting to overthrow. They had, moreover, the same contempt for the 'rude Koyas' that had been exhibited by the memorialists against the Agency Land and Interest Act in 1917.[17] To the nationalists of the plains the only useful function of the fituri was the opportunities it presented to make political capital from the government's blundering attempts to suppress it.[18] For them Rama Raju's rebellion was an anachronism: it held no key to India's political future.

CONCLUSION

Over the course of the period 1839 to 1924 the fituris of the Eastern Ghats passed through three phases. In the first phase, they were primarily elite conflicts between external powers, attempting to extend their control from the plains into the hills, and the muttadars, seeking to preserve their independence and privileges. There is little evidence of popular participation in these early fituris, except in the abandonment of villages in the path of invading forces and raiding. At this stage of relations between the hills and the plains, the hillmen generally had the upper hand against the invaders. The terrain, the climate, the general hostility of the population, the paucity of exploitable resources, all helped to save the hillmen from effective control.

From the middle of the nineteenth century the relationship was changing, tilting in favour of the invaders from the plains, and the character of the fituris showed a corresponding shift. Backed by the power of the police and law courts, facilitated by the construction of roads, and spurred by the realization that the hills now had attractive economic resources to offer, outsiders began to penetrate the hill tracts and to undermine the hillmen's traditional economy and society. Both elite and subaltern hillmen were affected by this transformation. The muttadars continued to play a major role in the leadership of the risings, but pressure for a rising now sometimes came from the subalterns. The fituris took on a more popular character than formerly, especially in the widespread Rampa rebellion of 1879–80. As in many other parts of the world where a traditional society has found itself under attack from aggressive modern imperialism and capitalism, the reaction of the hillmen took two main forms. Firstly, there was the religious element (often characterized as millennialism or messianism), consisting of a wide variety of fears and expectations couched in religious terms. This religious idiom gave the hillmen a framework within which to conceptualize their predicament and to seek solutions to it. Religion, however syncretic, provided a basis for solidarity against outsiders. Secondly, there was the crime-as-protest element, which approximates to what Hobsbawm has called 'social banditry', but which includes a greater range of supposedly criminal activities than banditry. Because of the shared sense of grievance among the hillmen, an individual crime or act of revenge was interpreted as a gesture of defiance against all outsiders and oppressors. Ambivalence best describes this fluidity between crime and protest.

The third phase of the fituris represents the attempt by outside idealists, opportunists, and dissidents to convert the expanded fituri tradition of the second phase into a popular movement that could be extended into the plains. In the Rampa and Gudem tracts there was only one clear case of this—Rama Raju's fituri of 1922–4—though one might see a precedent for this in Anantayya's involvement in the 1886 rising in Gudem. Rama Raju believed that a rebellion begun in the hills could become the base for a war of national liberation against the British. There were no subsequent attempts to use the fituri tradition in this way in the Gudem and Rampa hills, but the pattern recurred in the late 1960s with the attempts by Naxalite communists to mobilize hillmen as the initial phase of rural insurrection and revolution in India. Srikakulam in Visakhapatnam was one of the centres of Naxalite activity in 1968–9, an area which had its own history of participation in the fituris of the Eastern Ghats. While risings of this type were often able to mobilize hillmen through their enduring sense of grievance and hostility to outsiders, they were gravely inhibited by the tribals' or hillmen's restricted territoriality.

Territoriality—the peasant's identification with that small territory that encompasses almost all his economic, social, and cultural ties and beyond which he begins to feel himself a stranger—has been a powerful factor in inhibiting peasant involvement in broader political movements.

It takes an exceptional set of circumstances—a flood or famine that drives him from his home, the ravages of armies, the confident belief in an imminent millennium—to lift him more than momentarily out of his intense commitment to his locality. Equally, peasant xenophobia has been a persistent factor in opposition to those outsiders who arrive to tax, to exploit, to practise their foreign faiths, to rule. Territoriality and xenophobia are to be found in many, if not most, peasant struggles in India, but they are particularly acute in the risings and rebellions of the hillmen of India, where such identities and aversions are reinforced by the cohesiveness of communities that have remained relatively isolated, the limited social differentiation they often exhibit, and above all by that exceptionally sharp divide between those who live in the hills and those who inhabit the plains. In this respect then, the Gudem and Rampa fituris represent an emphatic expression of the patterns of peasant protest and subaltern resistance found elsewhere in India, but not a wholly atypical one. Certainly it should no longer be assumed that the rebellious hillmen of Gudem, Rampa, and countless other hill tracts like them were irrelevant and unimportant in the unfolding story of modern India's political and social history.

NOTES

1. M. Venkatarangaiya (ed.), *The Freedom Movement in Andhra Pradesh, Volume III, 1921–31*, Hyderabad, 1965.
2. For some extreme statements of these views, see Barrington Moore Jr, *Social Origins of Dictatorship and Democracy: Lord and Peasant in the Making of the Modern World*, Harmondsworth, 1973, esp. pp. 202, 330–41, 378–85; Thomas R. Metcalf, 'Social Effects of British Land Policy in Oudh', in Robert Eric Frykenberg (ed.), *Land Control and Social Structure in Indian History*, Madison, 1969, pp. 145–6; Christopher Baker, 'Non-cooperation in South India', in C.J. Baker and D.A. Washbrook (eds), *South India: Political Institutions and Political Change, 1880–1940*, Delhi, 1975, pp. 98–149.
3. The classic case of this would appear to be China during the Second World War: see Chalmer A. Johnson, *Peasant Nationalism and Communist Power: The Emergence of Revolutionary China*, Stanford, 1962. The prominence Johnson gives to 'peasant nationalism' as a factor in the communists' success has been extensively criticized but not altogether denied.
4. Report of A.J. Happell, 21 April 1923, G.O. 572, Public, 23 July 1923.
5. Venkatarangaiya (ed.), *The Freedom Movement in Andhra Pradesh, Volume III*, p. 79.

6. Venkatarangaiya (ed.), *The Freedom Movement in Andhra Pradesh, Volume III.*
7. Happell's report, 21 April 1923, G.O. 572, Public, 23 July 1923; Special Commnr. for Agency Operations to Chief Sec., 22 August 1922, in Venkatarangaiya (ed.), *The Freedom Movement*, p. 367.
8. Venkatarangaiya (ed.), *The Freedom Movement in Andhra Pradesh, Volume III.*; Happell's report, 21 April 1923, G.O. 572, Public, 23 July 1923.
9. Intercepted letter, 16 September 1922, in Venkatarangaiya (ed.), *The Freedom Movement*, p. 370; Deputy Tahsildar, Malakangiri, to Agency Commnr., 13 June 1923, ibid., p. 388.
10. Venkatarangaiya (ed.), *The Freedom Movement*, pp. 368–9, 380. On 19 January 1923, for example, 8 headmen and 10 villagers were convicted for harbouring rebels and giving false information: Happell's report, 21 April 1923, G.O. 572, Public, 23 July 1923.
11. Chief Sec., Madras, to Sec., Home, Govt. of India, Home Dept, Pol., 898 of 1922, NAI, New Delhi: Happell's report, 21 April 1923, G.O. 572, Public, 23 July 1923.
12. Agency Commnr. To Chief. Sec., 26 August 1922, in Venkatarangaiya (ed.), *The Freedom Movement*, pp. 372–3.
13. See narrative in ibid., pp. 80–91.
14. See ibid., pp. 382–9.
15. Letter to Pericherla Suryanarayana Raju (alias Aggi Raju), ibid., pp. 370–1, and narrative, pp. 88, 91.
16. Cited in ibid., p. 401.
17. *Guntur Patrika*, cited in ibid., p. 389; cf. p. 30.
18. See the debates in the *Madras Legislative Council Proceedings*, 17 March 1923, vol. XII, pp. 2516–30; 25 March 1924, vol., XVII, pp. 1136–61.

10 The Structure of Congress Politics in Coastal Andhra, 1925–37*

Brian Stoddart

I

Within the framework of modern Indian nationalism there were variations of political style and agitational politics both between and within British Indian provinces. Sometimes the variations sprang from linguistic differences which British boundaries frequently ignored; sometimes from social or economic conditions which created different lifestyles in adjoining localities.

This chapter examines the pattern of agitational politics displayed by the Telugu-speaking coastal Andhra districts of the Madras Presidency during the 1930–4 Civil Disobedience campaign. The districts concerned were East and West Godavari, Kistna, Guntur, and Nellore. The emergence of a political style peculiar to those districts may be attributed to three major conditions. First, between 1925 and 1930 Congress recruited numerous supporters in the coastal districts and established a solid organizational network. This was achieved mainly by relating Congress activities to protests against increases in Kistna–Godavari land revenue rates planned by the Government of Madras. The political intermediaries who took up the land revenue issue provided the second element of a distinctive political style. Generally members of the dominant social group in their particular locality, these Congress intermediaries possessed qualities and resources which enabled them to act as political brokers between local people and politicians and the upper levels of the Congress hierarchy in Andhra. Finally, the Government's reluctance to reconsider the land revenue enhancement in light of the economic depression gave strength to and helped shape the pattern of civil disobedience in Andhra, because it complicated the official response to agitational politics as basically laid down by the Government of India.

* Originally published in D.A. Low (ed.), *Congress and the Raj*, New Delhi: Oxford University Press, 2004, pp. 109–32. In the present version some portions of the text and notes have been removed. For the complete text see the original version.

The interaction of these conditions gave coastal Andhra a different political development to that experienced elsewhere in India between 1925 and 1937. Between 1925 and 1930 Congress activities in India were at a generally low level but they were quite intense in coastal Andhra. This helped Congress in the area achieve considerable success during the first phase of civil disobedience. Local conditions, however, meant that the conclusion of the Gandhi-lrwin Pact alienated some coastal Andhra Congress supporters who considered that their major leaders had abandoned the land revenue issue. During the rest of 1931 local leadership became more important than ever as it sought to retain support for Congress. Government attention was drawn increasingly to this level of the leadership and action was taken against it. As a result, the 1932 Civil Disobedience campaign in coastal Andhra was more subdued than the 1930 campaign had been. During 1933 and 1934, though, a partial revival of the land revenue issue allowed local Congressmen to consolidate their standing in the coastal districts. Subsequently, the organization and recruitment which had occurred since 1925 gave Congress in coastal Andhra a strong base which to conduct the constitutional and electoral politics which took place between 1934 and 1937.

II

Andhra was an accepted linguistic unit of the Madras Presidency by 1925. Demands for the creation of a separate Telugu-speaking province had not been successful, but they had promoted an awareness of the area's cultural homogeneity. In 1920 the Indian National Congress confirmed Andhra's status as a Congress province under the linguistic reorganization plan. However, this cultural homogeneity was not matched by the economic structure of the area. The drier inland districts of Bellary, Kurnool, Anantapur, and Cuddapah were known collectively as the Rayalaseema. They were considerably less prosperous than the coastal districts which were divided economically between the drier upland taluks and the coastal taluks which derived a natural alluvial richness from the Kistna and Godavari river deltas. Mid-nineteenth century irrigation projects endowed the coastal taluks with an even greater prosperity. Since then, population densities and growth rates had tended to be larger in the coastal taluks, and landholdings slightly smaller. Though there were substantial zamindari holdings in Andhra, most land in the coastal Andhra districts was subject to the ryotwari land revenue system.[1]

It was Madras practice to reassess ryotwari holdings every thirty years so that their land revenue rates might reflect prevailing economic conditions.[2] A joint reassessment of the three Kistna–Godavari districts was begun in 1924 and a revised schedule of land revenue rates was to be implemented in 1930.[3] The Government of Madras recalled that there had been considerable opposition to the previous resettlement at the end of the nineteenth century. The Guntur district no-rent campaign during non-cooperation had also demonstrated the agitational potential offered by land revenue grievances.[4] The Government, therefore, named B.G. Holdsworth as Special Settlement Officer for the Kistna–Godavari operation. His qualities had been tested during his previous assignment when he had dealt capably with substantial opposition to the introduction of enhanced land revenue rates in the Tamil-speaking Tanjore district.[5]

The prospect of increased land revenue rates arose at a time of growing economic tension in coastal Andhra. Like other food grain surplus areas, it had profited from food scarcities experienced in urban centres during the post-war economic boom. Good seasons in the coastal districts had produced heavy crops which were disposed of at unusually favourable prices. A sense of economic expansion created demands for new lands as people anticipated a lucrative future in grain production. Land prices rose to unprecedented levels. Once the grain shortages eased and prices returned to more normal levels, many landholders in coastal Andhra had to meet heavy economic obligations from diminishing returns.[6] Production costs began to rise, aggravating the problem. As early as April 1926, coastal Andhra agriculturalists claimed that they faced increased costs for foodstuffs, wages, building materials, agricultural supplies, and equipment.[7]

Holdsworth, however, reported that landholding and agriculture was extremely profitable in the Kistna–Godavari districts.[8] Submitting his findings to the Government of Madras during 1927, he recommended that land revenue rates be increased by the permitted maximum of 18.75 per cent in most of the area. He noted that there were fewer landless labourers than at the previous settlement, that tenant cultivators were decreasing in numbers and that absentee landlordism was not on the increase: more landlords now cultivated their own holdings. Hold worth took this to mean that people could acquire land and make a profit from agriculture. He supported his claim with evidence concerning mortgage transactions.[...]

There was little organized opposition to the resettlement until the report appeared. Holdsworth's economic survey teams encountered little difficulty in gathering considerable information concerning mortgages, debts, land sales, leases, price-variations, and seasonal conditions.[9] The East Godavari District Association, a long-established organization which represented the proprietors of medium-sized ryotwari holdings in the district, was first to attack the report as a gross misrepresentation of economic conditions in coastal Andhra.[10]

The major organizers of opposition to the land revenue proposals, however, were political intermediaries like Dandu Narayanaraju. He was a wealthy Congressman from the Raju community, an important West Godavari landholding community which claimed Kshatriya status. During non-cooperation he had been an active Congress organizer, and in 1926 was elected to the Madras Legislative Council. He was typical of these political brokers.[11] They were usually drawn from, and had interests identical with, the main local landholding caste. They were usually involved in the politics of local and district boards which added to the strength of their connections. In a predominantly agrarian community, their continued local prominence rested largely upon a successful handling of agrarian grievances.[12] An association with Congress gave the intermediaries a dual role. By involving provincial Congress leaders with local agrarian issues they drew the local community within the ambit of Congress activity. But they had also to translate to the local communities policies formulated at the higher levels of the Congress organization. Those policies often cut across local interests. If an intermediary was also a member of the Legislative Council, as Narayanaraju was, he stood between the local community and the Government of Madras as well. To fulfil his local obligations Narayanaraju attacked the land revenue proposals when they were discussed in the Madras Legislative Council.[13]

The fundamental organization of rural discontent was directed in the affected districts by the political intermediaries who arranged meetings at the village, *firka*, taluk, and district levels. The frequency of the meetings increased early in 1928 with the approach of the Government deadline for filing objections to the reassessment proposals. Dandu Narayanaraju began his organization in Bhimavaram taluk of West Godavari where his Raju caste-fellows gave him immediate support.[14] From there he moved into neighbouring taluks. He was accompanied by Tangaturi Prakasam, a Niyogi Brahman lawyer from Guntur district who had become a leading Andhra politician with much of his work being done in Madras city.[15]

Cooperation between Prakasam and Narayanaraju on the land revenue issue demonstrated the relationship between political intermediaries and their Congress superiors. Chastening experiences with mobilizing Madras city opposition to the Simon Commission had reminded Prakasam of the need for a mass awareness of matters political.[16] In particular, work had to be done among the rural communities. The land revenue issue offered an excellent example. Narayanaraju, meanwhile, could show his immediate supporters that the interest of a provincial level politician would strengthen and give wider publicity to the campaign against enhanced land revenue rates. In important West Godavari villages like Aravilli, Tanuku taluk, and Korukollu, Bhimavaram taluk, Narayanaraju and Prakasam urged the formation of village committees and ryots' associations which might acquaint the Government of Madras with the true economic state of the Andhra delta.[17]

Most of the organization took place in deltaic taluks most subject to the rising economic pressures. These were Bhimavaram, Tanuku, Narsapur, and Tadepalligudem taluks in West Godavari; Razolu, Ramachandrapuram, and Amalapuram taluks in East Godavari; Bandar, Divi, and Gudivada taluks in Kistna. [...]

Population trends in the taluks compounded the economic problem. Attracted by the apparent post-war prosperity of the coastal taluks, people from the poorer upland areas flocked to the delta causing spectacular increases in the already high population growth and density rates. [...]These economic and social conditions helped reduce the average size of landholdings in the districts and further depressed the conditions for local landholders. Enhanced land revenue rates would cause serious economic problems for these people so they were inclined to support political organizers like Narayanaraju who promised to protest against the Government's proposals.

Narayanaraju and Prakasam advocated the use of 'peaceful and legitimate' methods to combat the land revenue proposals, but an alternative view was gaining support in the Andhra Congress ranks. Its main spokesman was Konda Venkatapayya, a middle-aged Guntur Brahman and one of Gandhi's first recruits in the Telugu country. He was a key figure during the Andhra non-cooperation campaign, believed in the value of agitational politics and retained some influence in the Andhra Congress. The most active organizer for this school of thought was Venneti Satyanarayana, another of the political intermediaries. His influence was based in East Godavari, similar to the way in which Narayanaraju was strong in West Godavari. Unlike Narayanaraju, Satyanarayana eschewed institutional politics after the suspension of non-cooperation. Venkatapayya and Satyanarayana argued that a vigorous no-rent campaign, similar to the one organized in the Bardoli district of

Bombay Presidency, should be mobilized in the Kistna–Godavari districts.[18] Venkatapayya held a 'Bardoli Day' in Guntur and his district organizers staged similar observances elsewhere in Andhra.[19]

[...]

By the end of 1928 a finely balanced political situation existed on the Andhra delta. Both Congress wings, working from similar economic and social bases, were promoting the land revenue grievance and linking it with a wider political pattern. The differences between them concerned the use of agitational or constitutional politics. Both had begun to establish organizational networks which would help them achieve their objectives. Against them were arrayed the forces of the Government of Madras which sought to prevent the land revenue issue from turning into a major political campaign.

III

The Andhra Congress enjoyed substantial success between the beginning of 1929 and the conclusion of the Gandhi–Irwin Pact in March 1931. The political intermediaries, using the land revenue issue as a basis for agitation, maintained a formidable Civil Disobedience campaign in the coastal districts for most of 1930 and the early months of 1931. The conclusion of the Pact, however, had a depressing effect on the movement and altered the political status of the intermediaries. When civil disobedience resumed in 1932, response to it in coastal Andhra was somewhat lower than in 1930.

Organization of the land revenue agitation was built up during the second half of 1928, even though its promoters were divided over the use of constitutional or agitational methods against the Government's proposals. Dandu Narayanaraju became a secretary of the West Godavari District Congress Committee and shifted the district's Congress office from Ellore to Tadepalligudem, a central town from which he might direct organization in the coastal taluks. He also founded, and became chairman of, a West Godavari Resettlement Committee.[20]

The organization of agitation also spread to Guntur and Nellore districts. At the end of July 1928 over 100 'influential ryots' attended the first-ever Kovuru taluk ryots' conference to discuss the resettlement problem. Congress intermediaries were again to the fore. Bomma Sesha Reddi was one of the organizing secretaries and became an office-holder in the permanent association set up by the conference. He was related to some of the most powerful Reddi families in the district and many of his relatives held, or had held, positions in the local Congress as well as on the taluk and district boards. He was also secretary of the Nellore District Congress Committee.[21]

The first change in the direction of this general agrarian organization occurred in the wake of the Calcutta Congress session where it became apparent that constitutional politics had lost favour with a large number of Congressmen. To prevent the Satyanarayana wing from making too much political headway, Narayanaraju moderated his opposition to agitational campaigns such as that conducted at Bardoli. In fact, he went to Bardoli with Satyanarayana to observe the movement there. The visit was sponsored by the Central Committee of Ryots' and Land-Owners of Kistna and East Godavari and West Godavari which met in January 1929.[22] Narayanaraju's concessions allowed the two wings to draw closer together and, as a result, organization of agrarian discontent became more centralized. This particular meeting drew together most district leaders and planned a series of taluk conferences which would call upon the Government to convene an economic inquiry into the land revenue issue. The meeting also agreed that each district would contribute Rs 3,000 to a central fund which would finance future organization. Venneti Satyanarayana demonstrated the power of the intermediaries when, as its President, he committed the East Godavari Congress Committee to providing the Rs 3,000 from that district.[23] Quite definite connections between Congress and the agrarian communities were established as the intermediaries built an integrated organization to contest the imposition of enhanced land revenue rates.

A surprise concession by the Government of Madras undid a little of the Congress organization. In mid-January 1929 it authorized the Legislative Council to appoint, from within its elected ranks, an Inquiry Committee to investigate the land revenue proposals.[24] By meeting one of the demands made by agitational organizers at numerous village, taluk and district meetings, the Government created a rift in the Congress coalition. Dandu Narayanaraju was elected to the Inquiry Committee and reverted to a constitutional style of politics. He made it quite clear to the All-India Congress Committee that he and his followers would work the inquiry despite Congress rulings that forbade them to do so.[25] Venneti Satyanarayana and his East Godavari followers made it equally plain that they placed little reliance on any constitutional inquiry.[26]

[...]

Congress preparations were now indeed so advanced that they were not damaged irreparably by the Government's actions. Satyanarayana, in particular, carried out some extremely efficient organization during the second half of 1929. Despite his earlier objections to the Inquiry Committee he realized its tour would attract attention to the resettlement issue. His District Resettlement Committee appointed paid workers in important villages, especially those to be visited by the Inquiry Committee, and its organizational headquarters were transferred to Rajahmundry so that the customary political activities of the district towns might be associated with the growing political organization of the rural communities.[27] Satyanarayana also formed a district Land League. It was controlled by the district's Legislative Councillors, the presidents of the district and taluk boards, the secretaries of the District Congress Committee, and the Secretaries of the East Godavari District Association.[28] An imposing piece of political organization, it gave Satyanarayana a strong hold on the district's political activity.

Satyanarayana then made an extensive tour of Ramachandrapuram, Rajahmundry, Amalapuram, and Razolu taluks.[29] Meetings were held at the village, firka, and taluk levels. Attendances were consistently good, even the smaller scale meetings attracted 500–600 people. The tone of the meetings was quite radical. In each case, the main resolution was to employ satyagraha against the land revenue proposals, with Satyanarayana being left to decide when such methods had become necessary. 'Influential' and 'rich' ryots provided a lot of support for the meetings, but the chairmen of local boards, professional men (particularly lawyers), merchants, and caste leaders were also present. Dr B. Subrahmaniam was probably the most important figure drawn into the resettlement agitation by these meetings. He was a leading district politician (as were a number of his close relatives) and had given up a medical practice to direct an *ashram* at Sitanagaram. It was from there that he helped publish *Congress*, a Telugu-language daily newspaper whose editors were steadfast supporters of direct action politics. Subrahmaniam gave full support and wide publicity to the campaign conducted by Satyanarayana, with whom he had been arrested during the non-cooperation movement. By the beginning of 1930, Satyanarayana controlled an organized, established, and widely publicized agitational force in East Godavari.

The Lahore Congress session's approval of civil disobedience set the seal on agitational organization in coastal Andhra, for it drew the two wings of Congress together again. Dandu Narayanaraju and his followers, realizing that moderate views had lost further ground, were less conspicuous organizers than Satyanarayana during late 1929 and West Godavari was not so fully tuned for agitation as was East Godavari.

However, once the Lahore decisions became known, Narayanaraju aligned himself with the agitational wing in order to protect his status as an intermediary. Venneti Satyanarayana convened an East Godavari Congress Committee meeting to ratify the Lahore resolutions and to organize a no-rent campaign against the new land revenue rates. His District Resettlement Committee complemented the Congress Committee policy by arranging for a Volunteer Corps to tour the district promoting a no-rent campaign.[30] Dandu Narayanaraju acknowledged the strength of the agitational school's position and his West Godavari Resettlement Committee also established a Volunteer Corps to prepare for a no-rent campaign.[31]

These Congress preparations for civil disobedience were assisted by the release of the Inquiry Committee's report which concluded that rural debt was high and rising rapidly, that production costs had outstripped returns and that population pressure had exacerbated the economic difficulties.[32] The organization of rural discontent in coastal Andhra was strengthened by this report and officials forecast that political activity there would sharpen once the Congress programme was finalized.[33] Gandhi's general *schema* for civil resistance was well-known by now but not his plans for this occasion, so the local Congress momentum faltered slightly.[34] Experienced British District Officers, like Scott Brown in West Godavari, realized that it was but a temporary lull for the coastal districts. The problem for local Congressmen lay not in recruiting support but in choosing sites for the first acts of civil disobedience and selecting from among the flock of volunteers.[35]

Konda Venkatapayya was appointed by the Provincial Congress Committee as director of the Andhra salt satyagraha. But the intermediaries ignored his suggestion that Andhra should stage one march, Gandhi-fashion, and launched a series of district marches without reference to any provincial Congress leader.[36] The support and organization which made it possible for the intermediaries to make this demonstration was especially evident in the coastal taluks of Kistna, East and West Godavari. But it was also present in parts of Guntur and Nellore.

Guntur underwent some rural agitational organization during 1929, mainly in taluks which abutted upon the Kistna–Godavari delta proper: Guntur, Repalle, Tenali, and Bapatla. Because these taluks had economies similar to those of the Kistna–Godavari coastal taluks, and because Guntur's land revenue rates were to be reviewed in the early 1930s, there was considerable interest in the nearby agitational activity.

N.V.L. Narasimha Rao was at the centre of the Guntur organization.
A Brahman lawyer, he controlled the Congress organization in Guntur
town and was also chairman of the municipal council. He had many
commercial and financial interests as well. These diversified connections
allowed him, despite his Brahmanic status, to make contacts with the
Reddi communities which dominated life in the fertile coastal taluks. In
this he was assisted by Unnava Lakshminarayana who was a marvellous
example of the versatile Congress organizer.
[...]
With its variety of strong connections, then, the Guntur Congress
organization was also well-prepared for Civil Disobedience.

The 1930–1 Civil Disobedience campaign in Andhra was most intense
in taluks where resettlement agitation had been most successful. The
district salt marches were extremely effective. The West Godavari march,
for example, set out from Ellore and travelled through the villages of
Kovvali, Gundugolanu and Pulla in Ellore taluk; Ungaturu,
Padamaravipparru and Ganapavaram in Tadepalligudem taluk;
Endagandi, Gollakoduru, and Bhimavaram in Bhimavaram taluk. The
marchers then divided into three groups which toured extensively in
Ellore, Narsapur, and Tanuku taluks before regrouping to break the salt
laws.[37] The East Godavari march started from the Sitanagaram ashram in
Rajahmundry taluk, marched through Rajahmundry, visited numerous
villages in Razolu taluk, and then travelled through Amalapuram taluk.[38]
Congress gained a strong image from this activity and its programme
was given solid support by the local population. Coastal villages in Guntur
district were said to be 'astir', and 'hundreds of ryots' were reported to
be active in the Congress district of East Kistna.[39] Recognizing the
organizational importance of the intermediaries, the Government of
Madras had Satyanarayana arrested on 13 April and Narayanaraju was
arrested two *or* three days later; earlier than many official provincial
organizers of civil disobedience.[40]

The Civil Disobedience movement of 1930 won, therefore, most
support amongst locally predominant landed groups which sympathized
with the land revenue agitation, and were most affected by the pressures
bearing upon coastal society: falling grain prices, rising debt, and the
inheritance of fragmented holdings as population levels rose in the coastal
districts. [...] Landless groups took little part in the campaign.

The Government lost some of its customary aplomb in the face of
this agitational anger. At first it obeyed the Government of India's policy
and virtually ignored the agitational campaign. But District Officers

doubted the wisdom of the policy, and argued that their superiors had underestimated the situation on the Andhra delta. Herbert Uzielli, Collector of Kistna, noted that 'villagers' wondered why 'agitators' were allowed to wander the districts 'breaking the law with impunity, and making speeches against the Government'.[41] Similar comments from other officers prompted Secretariat officials in Madras, many of whom considered New Delhi men to be quite remote from provincial political realities, to seek stronger measures with which to meet the situation.[42] Immediately the All-India Congress Committee was banned by the Government of India in June 1930, the Government of Madras declared the Andhra Congress Committee, its district components and some of its local organizations to be unlawful associations.[43] In the Government's view it was the end of 1930 before the situation became satisfactory in some areas of coastal Andhra.[44] Even then some officials realized that civil disobedience was subdued rather than destroyed. Sir George Stanley, the Governor of Madras, felt that official policies had not attacked the roots of the Congress organization and feared that the worst might be yet to come in coastal Andhra.[45]

It was the conclusion of the Gandhi–Irwin Pact, rather than the Government's repressive policies, which altered the Congress hold on the coastal districts of Andhra. A darkening economic horizon, preceding the full force of the depression, and a Government decision to proceed with Holdsworth's land revenue proposals had added new strength to the agitational movement in coastal Andhra. Many agitational supporters were dismayed when Gandhi agreed to the Pact and so ruled out the use of direct action politics at the time when they seemed to be most needed.[46]

The political intermediaries were in a difficult position. If they were to retain their local political credibility they had to promote the agrarian cause vigorously. Yet the terms of the Gandhi–Irwin Pact prevented the use of agitational politics. The intermediaries convened a sub-committee of the Andhra Ryots' Conference and challenged the Pact by agreeing to initiate a no-rent campaign if it became necessary. A significant feature was the continued coalition between Narayanaraju and Satyanarayana. Both appreciated the extent of agrarian unrest and the need to maintain pressure on a comparatively weak provincial leadership caught between loyalty to its district organizers and obedience to its all-India superiors. In turn, the provincial leadership realized the danger to Congress prestige if the agrarian agitation was continued independently. The intermediaries were drafted onto a land revenue committee formed by the provincial Congress organization.[47] Gandhi and Vallabhbhai Patel upset this attempt to accommodate the Andhra agrarian organization. They informed the provincial leaders that Congress should not encourage land revenue agitation while the Pact was in force.[48] Effective leadership reverted to the intermediaries who organized the discontent through their agrarian associations rather than through their Congress agencies.

During the rest of 1931 a series of local meetings were held to proclaim the agrarian cause. At the Razolu Taluk Ryots' Conference agriculturalists were urged to prepare for a no-rent campaign. Narayanaraju formed the Ellore Taluk Ryots' Seva Dal whose peasant volunteers would tour the coastal districts to campaign against the new rates.[49] A 'Resettlement Day' occasioned small hartals in the district towns and the creation of some new agrarian organizations.[50] The success of these activities revealed the extent to which a continued political dominance by the intermediaries, and by Congress, depended upon the successful resolution of coastal Andhra's agrarian grievances.

The intermediaries became so important by November of 1931 that the Government of Madras had a number of them arrested, including Dandu Narayanaraju. Many of their important taluk organizers were also arrested. Duggirala Balaramakrishnayya, for example, was a young Kamma from Gudivada taluk in Kistna district. He was an enthusiastic agrarian organizer in Angalur, a village which had given active support to civil disobedience during 1930. A number of his Telugu prose and verse works, like the ballad *Gandhi Gita*, popularized the agrarian and Congress campaigns.

These arrests attacked the foundations of rural organization, as the Government of Madras soon realized. When Gandhi resumed civil disobedience in 1932 similar action was ordered in coastal Andhra and the reservoir of local leadership was drained far more than it had been in 1930. As a result, the enthusiasm that still existed for Congress activity was not so closely directed in the localities as it had been previously.

The centres and composition of the 1932 campaign paralleled those of 1930. At Bezwada, 31 men tried in three particular cases were aged between 19 and 35 with most in their mid-20s. All but 4 were agriculturalists, and there were 15 Kammas, 8 Rajus, 4 Brahmans, 3 from lower castes and a lone Muslim.[51] Many people convicted for civil disobedience offences again came from the broad range of 'middle peasants' most affected by the economic depression.[52] [...]These were the people with small holdings which had become economically unviable, or who came from joint families with average holdings which could not now supply their economic needs, or from quite large joint families whose diversified economic interests were strained by the depression. Of course, economic stress alone did not determine their participation in agitation. However, the coastal districts' dominant agrarian communities were hard hit by the economic depression, and feared that increased land revenue rates would add to their economic problems. The political intermediaries, already in a strong position because of their work for and social identity with the dominant communities, used these mounting economic fears to bolster support for challenges to the Government.

Despite the existence of this quite extensive support, then, the 1932 Civil Disobedience campaign in Andhra was less spectacular than that of 1930. Government officials ascribed the change to the revised policies adopted towards satyagrahis, and Konda Venkatapayya agreed that hard-line action dampened the enthusiasm of many Congressmen.[53] Both views rather overlooked the fact that agitation in coastal Andhra was not swept away immediately. After the first Government onslaught, agitation reappeared at the end of February 1932 and persisted, on a small scale, until the end of the year. Lack of leadership rather than lack of enthusiasm caused the changed appearance of the movement. The political intermediaries, who had controlled developments quite skilfully before 1932, were removed from the arena and the rump of the provincial leadership could not command the same attention. Government policies and the distinctive character of the Andhra Congress had both contributed to the situation.

Once again, it was Gandhi who helped alter the political situation in coastal Andhra when, towards the end of 1932, he turned his attention almost exclusively to the plight of India's untouchables. It had been reasonably simple for the intermediaries to relate their agrarian activities to general Congress policies. Gandhi and Congress had reputations for organizing and supporting agrarian causes. Because the impetus for the agrarian campaign came from within the communities in which they worked, the intermediaries, had been able to override directions from the provincial leadership. But the campaign against untouchability emanated solely from Gandhi who worked through provincial level politicians like Venkatapayya. Because the intermediaries could not risk a complete break with Congress, they were obliged to pay more attention to the provincial leadership.

Support for the intermediaries began to fall away. The agrarian communities were preoccupied with an economic crisis and the intermediaries, who had promoted the resettlement movement during

1931 despite the terms of the Pact, were obliged to promote a social issue which was not universally popular in an area where religious orthodoxy was strong. There was a complicating factor. Most of coastal Andhra's numerous untouchables were employed as day labourers by the landholders on whose behalf the intermediaries had previously worked. It appeared as if the intermediaries had abandoned the land revenue agitation.

Meetings organized by intermediaries on behalf of untouchables were poorly attended.[54] Orthodox religious opposition to the campaign often came from areas which had given solid support to the land revenue and satyagraha movements. In Guntur district, where there was a concentration of orthodox Brahmans, the Varnashrama Dharmodharaka Sabha complained that Gandhi and the Congress had 'blackmailed' the administration into conceding undue importance to the untouchable communities.[55] Similar complaints were heard in Razolu taluk of East Godavari and Narsapur taluk of West Godavari which had both been strong agitational centres.[56] The intermediaries were losing support. The Government's counter-offensive against civil disobedience attracted people alienated from the Congress ranks, or at least faced reduced opposition from communities which had sympathized with Congress programmes.

Though the intermediaries, and Congress, might have been disappointed with the loss of support by the time Gandhi suspended civil disobedience in May 1934, they retained considerable advantages from the agitational experience. The intermediaries were recognized as extremely important political organizers at the village, firka, taluk, and district levels. Through them, the coastal communities had been involved in considerable political activity. In practical terms, a network of political associations had been established. The network had been damaged momentarily by the Government, but it could be revived. In the intense constitutional political activity which ensued, this organizational expertise proved invaluable for Congress in coastal Andhra.

[...]

V

Political development in coastal Andhra between 1925 and 1935 was influenced considerably by the fortunes of the political intermediaries. As Eric Wolf suggests, they were responsible for translating 'community-oriented' expectations into 'nation-oriented' terms. Theirs was a difficult role which highlighted the complexities of associating local grievances with nationalist ideology. In the land revenue campaign the intermediaries gained strong support from the districts. When general Congress policies made it difficult for the expectations of supporters to be met, the intermediaries were subjected to considerable pressure from the localities. With the campaign against untouchability, the pressure was applied by the intermediaries' Congress superiors whose strength was a link with Gandhi. The intermediaries could not ignore their Congress connections, so they promoted a social policy they knew to be locally unpopular.

[...]

When Congress turned to constitutional politics after the 1935 Government of India Act was passed, the benefits of the agitational experience in coastal Andhra became apparent. Congress candidates enjoyed a huge success in the area during the 1937 Madras Legislative Council elections. Many of them were the intermediaries or their district organizers who had been so active since 1925. [...] By 1940 Congress could claim to have over 60,000 primary members in East and West Godavari, 25,000 in Kistna, 41,000 in Guntur, and over 10,000 in Nellore.[57] The political intermediaries, who controlled Congress politics in the coastal districts of Andhra, were responsible for most of these considerable successes.[58]

NOTES

1. K.V. Narayana Rao, *The Emergence of Andhra Pradesh*, Bombay, 1973; J.G. Leonard, 'The Conflict of Two Nationalisms: a Study of the Formation of Andhra Pradesh', (unpublished MA thesis, University of Wisconsin, 1962); Gopal Krishna, 'The Development of the Indian National Congress as a Mass Organisation', *Journal of Asian Studies*, XXV, 3 May 1966, pp. 413–30; A.V. Raman Rao, *Economic Development of Andhra Pradesh 1766–1937*, Bombay, 1938; David Washbrook, 'Country Politics: Madras 1880 to 1930' in John Gallagher, Gordon Johnson and Anil Seal (eds) *Locality, Province and Nation: Essays on Indian Politics 1870–1940*, Cambridge, 1973; O.H.K. Spate and A.T.A. Learmonth, *India and Pakistan: a General and Regional Geography*, London, 1967, pp. 732–8; *Godavari, Kistna and Cauvery Delta and the Pennur Annicut Systems: Selections from the Proceedings of the Madras Government in the Public Works Department*, Madras, 1883; B.H. Baden–Powell, *The Land Systems of British India*, Oxford, 1892, Pt III, pp. 24,138.
2. Madras Board of Revenue [BOR] Resolution 542, 6 December 1900 in *Land Revenue Policy of the Indian Government*, Calcutta, 1920 reprint, pp. 152–243.

3. Special Settlement Officer to Special Assistant Settlement Officers, 27 April 1935, Madras Revenue Dept [Rev.] Government Order [GO] 1788, 28 November 1928, State Archives of Andhra Pradesh [APA].

4. M. Venkatarangaiya (ed.), *The Freedom Struggle in Andhra Pradesh*, Andhra, Hyderabad, 1965, vol. I, p. 97 and vol. III, ch. VII–IX; Gummidithala Venkata Subbarau, *Andhraratna D. Gopalakrishnayya: Life and Message*, Bezwada, n.d.; Hugh F. Owen, 'The Tamil and Telugu Regions and Gandhi, 1919–22', paper prepared for the IVth International Conference-Seminar of Tamil Studies.

5. Accounts of the Tanjore resettlement may be seen in Madras Rev. GO 1537, 25 August 1922 in Land Revenue and Settlement [LRS] Press 108, 2 September 1922, TNA and in Madras Under Secretary's Safe [USS] Secret File [SF] 632, 2 July 1929, TNA. A copy of this last file was obtained for me by Dr H.F. Owen. Holdsworth evidently gained himself a reputation for efficiency by his work on these two resettlement operations; see S.K. Chettur, *The Steel Frames and I: Life in the I.C.S.*, Bombay, 1962, p. 27.

6. V.V. Sayana, *The Agrarian Problems of Madras Province*, Madras, 1949, Ch VI: T. Budhavideya Rao Naidu, 'The Kistna Delta Ryot', in W. Burns (ed.), *Sons of the Soil: Studies of the Indian Cultivator*, Delhi, 1941.

7. Hindu, 24 September 1927, carries a report of the meeting at which these claims were made.

8. The following paragraph is based on the 'Resettlement Scheme Report for the Kistna, West Godavari and East Godavari Districts', Madras BOR (LRS) Proceedings 29 Press, 18 May 1937 contained in Madras Rev. GO 405, 36 February 1929, A PA.

9. The scope of the investigation is indicated in Madras Rev. GO 2502, 25 October 1928, APA, and Madras BOR (LRS) Proceedings 3287, 4 October 1928, APA.

10. *Hindu*, 11 January 1928. For some later protests, see Sec. West Godavari Resettlement Committee to Sec. Madras Rev. 19 August 1928, Madras Rev. GO 2707, 16 November 1928, APA; Sec. Ellore Resettlement Committee to Sec. Madras Rev. 15 November 1928, Madras Rev. GO 466, 6 March 1929, APA.

11. Eric Wolf provides one of the best definitions for this linking role: 'Individuals who are able to operate both in terms of community-oriented and nation-oriented expectations then tend to be selected out for mobility. They become the economic and political "brokers" of nation-community relations, a function which carries its own rewards'. See 'Aspects of Group Relations in a Complex Society: Mexico', in *American Anthropologist*, 58, 6 December 1956, pp. 1065–78. The following is a small selection of the considerable literature relating to the subject: F.G. Bailey, 'The Peasant View of the Bad Life', in *The Advancement of Science*, 23, 114, December 1966, pp. 399–409, University of Sussex, Joint Reprint, No. 7; Robert Redfield, *Peasant Society and Culture: an Anthropological Approach to*

Civilization, Chicago, 1966, ch. II; Hugh Tinker, 'Local Government and Politics, and Political and Social Theory in India', in Marc J. Swartz (ed.), *Local-Level Politics: Social and Cultural Perspectives*, London, 1969; Mark Holmstrom, 'Action Sets and Ideology: a Municipal Evaluation in South India', in *Contributions to Indian Sociology*, New Series, III, December 1969, pp. 76–93; Philip Carl Salzman, 'Tribal Chiefs as Middlemen: the Politics of Encapsulation in the Middle East', *Anthropological Quarterly*, 47, 2 April 1974, pp. 203–10; E.J. Hobsbawm, 'Peasants and Politics', in *Journal of Peasant Studies*, 1, 1, October 1973, pp. 23–62. The articles by Wolf and Bailey are reprinted in Teodor Shanin (ed.), *Peasants and Peasant Societies*, Harmondsworth, 1971. Hamza Alavi, in 'Peasant Classes and Primordial Loyalties', *Journal of Peasant Studies*, 1, 1, October 1973, pp. 23–63, sees the role of the middlemen in a slightly different way.

12. For discussions on this point see the various papers in Robert Eric Frykenberg (ed.), *Land Control and Social Structure in Indian History*, Madison, 1969.

13. See his 14 March 1938 speech recorded in *Madras Legislative Council Debates*, XLI, 2, pp. 143–7. Earlier he had raised the general question of resettlement; ibid., XXVll, 4, p. 448.

14. *Hindu*, 24 April 192B. In his fortnightly report dated 30 January 1928, the Collector of West Godavari suggested that local ryots showed 'very little interest' in resettlement activity; Madras USS SF 632, 3 July 1929, TNA.

15. Sec Prakasam's Telugu autobiography, *Na Jeevita Yatra*, Hyderabad, 1972 (translated for the author); G. Rudrayya Chowdari, *Prakasam: a Political Study*, Madras, 1971; P. Rajeswara Rao, *T. Prakasam*, New Delhi, 1972.

16. My article, 'The Unwanted Commission: National Agitation and Local Politics in Madras City 1928', in *South Asia*, No. 5, December 1975, discusses the origins and results of the boycott organized in Madras City against the Simon Commission.

17. *Hindu*, 24 April 1938. Another view of this agrarian organization is given by N.G. Ranga in his autobiography, *Fight for Freedom*, New Delhi, 1968, pp. 136–7. See also his *Revolutionary Peasants*, New Delhi, 1949, p. 83, where he estimates that agrarian associations were formed in over 300 Kistna–Godavari villages during this period.

18 See Venkatapayya's speech at the Andhra PCC annual meeting, reported in *Hindu*, 10 July 1928, and the account of an East Godavari District Congress Committee meeting, ibid.

19. Ibid., 11, 14, 16 June 1998.

20. *Hindu*, 19 July, 14 August 1928. The Collector of West Godavari reported that Narayanaraju had gathered Rs 1,100 from at least one village, but doubted that the ryots 'as a whole' were caught up in the resettlement organization: Collr West Godavari to Ch. Sec. Madras. 29 August 1928, Madras USS SF 632, 3 July 1929, TNA.

21. *Hindu*, 31 July 1928.

22. District Superintendent Police, East Godavari, Special Branch report, 5 January 1929, USS SF 632, 3 July 1929, TNA.

23. *Hindu*, 15 Jan. 1929.

24. *Madras Legislative Council Debates*, XLVI, 3 pp. 362–5.

25. Dandu Narayanaraju to Motilal Nehru, 16 June 1929, A1CC, 45/1929, NML. At least one local police officer predicted that there would be little agitation so long as Narayanaraju was involved with the inquiry; Ellore police report, 30 January 1929, Madras USS SF 639, 3 July 1929, TNA.

26. *Hindu*, 28 March 1929.

27. *Hindu*, 10 April 1929.

28. Ibid., 30 October 1929.

29. Detailed reports of these meetings may be seen in *Hindu*, 20, 28 November, 3, 6, 10, 11, 12, 23 December 1939.

30. Ibid., 3, 13 January 1930.

31. Ibid., 25 January 1930.

32. Ibid., 1 February 1930.

33. Sir George Stanley (Governor of Madras) to Irwin, 22 March 1930, IP.

34. For example, see the reports given by the following Collectors in *Civil Disobedience in Madras Presidency* 1930–31, H.R. Uzielli, A.C. Woodhouse, A.R.C. Westlake, W. Scott Brown (Uzielli Report), H. Poll 14/21/1932, K.W. Also Madras to H. Dept GoI, tel, P(Secret) 24/5, 29 January 1930, H. Poll 88/1930; Stanley to Irwin, 14 February 1930, IP. These reports concerned the celebration of Independence Day by Congress, the text for which was prepared by Jawaharlal Nehru; AICC FD-16/1930, NML.

35. Scott Brown Report.

36. F.W. Stewart Report.

37. C.H. Masterman, Collector of Salt Revenue for the Madras Presidency was cautioned in mid-Feb. 1930 by GoI's Central BOR against 'Mr Gandhi's alleged somewhat fantastic project for an anti-salt campaign'. Masterman's subsequent reports give an interesting official version of the salt campaign in Andhra. See A.L.R. Tottenham to C.H. Masterman, 51-Salt/30, 19 February 1930, H. Poll 247-II/1930; GoI Central BOR Salt-I, 14-Salt 11/30/1931; GoI Central BOR Salt-I, DOs 368-Salt 1930; H. Poll 257/13/1931. The programme for the West Godavari salt march was announced in *Hindu*, 28 March and its progress reported dally from 1 April 1930.

38. The East Godavari salt march began on 31 March 1930. Its complete programme appeared in *Hindu*, 3 April 1930, and its progress was also reported daily.

39. *Hindu*, 10 April, 5 May 1930.

40. Ibid., 19 April 1930.

41. Collr Kistna to Ch. Sec. Madras, 16 April 1930, Madras SF 686, 6 July 1930 contained in MHFSA 48/1930 pp. 1862–6, APA.

42. Madras to H. Dept GoI, tel P 349-S, 27 May 1930, H. Poll 257/III/1930. See Humphrey Trevelyan, *The India We Left*, London, 1972, p. 121 for the Madras attitude towards New Delhi.

43. Madras to H. Dept GoI, tel P 517-S, 23 June 1930, H. Poll 257/111/1930.

44. The Scott Brown Report carries a detailed account of the counter-offensive in West Godavari and reveals indirectly the persistence of Civil Disobedience in the area.

45. Stanley to Irwin, 29 June 1930, IP.

46. The government's decision was announced in Madras Rev. GO 1486 (21-S), 11 July 1931, TNA. Further clarification was given in Madras BOR (LRS) Proceedings 2889, 16 September 1931, APA. The intention to proceed with the enhancement was confirmed in Madras Rev. GO Press 2704, 22 December 1931, TNA (also in GoI EHL Lands B Proceedings 65, February 1932, NAI). The districts' economic situations are best illustrated in the statistics and graphs contained in *A Statistical Atlas of the Madras Presidency: Revised and Brought up to the End of Fasli 1350* (1940–41), Madras, 1949. A detailed analysis of the Guntur situation is provided in Madras BOR (LRS) Proceedings 2931, 5 November 1932, APA. See also 'History of West Kistna in the Freedom Struggle', MHFSA 26/1932, pp. 110–26, APA; 'Report of the 1932 Collector's Conference: the present economic situation and future prospects', Madras Pub. Dept GO 1030, 27 July 1932, TNA; Madras Rev. GO 948, 1 May 1931 (abbreviated report of the Madras Economic Inquiry Committee) in GoI Finance 17-(67)-F/1932, NAI.

47. *Ryot Patrika*, 3 July 1931, RNP, 29/1931, p. 948; *Andhra Patrika*, 4 July 1931, RNP 28/1931, p. 936; *Hindu*, 27 June, 18 July 1931; Sec. East Godavari District Association to Ch. Sec. GoI, 5 July 1931, GoI EHL Lands B Proceedings 42–46, November 1931, NAI.

48. *Deenabandhu*, 12 August 1931 and *Congress*, 18 August 1931, RNP 35/1931, p. 1146; Hindu, 6 August 1931. I.

49. *Ryot Patrika*, 17 July 1931, RNP 30/1931, p. 984; *Hindu*, 14 August 1931.

50. Ibid., 4 November 1931.

51. See cases CC 10/32, 31 July 1932, CC 12/32, 31 July 1932, CC 14/32, 14 November 1932 of the Bezwada 2nd Class Magistrate's Court, Madras Law (General Dept GO (85–S) 2016, 10 June 1933, TNA.

52. For analyses of the middle peasants' political role see Eric A. Wolf, *Peasant Wars of the Twentieth Century*, London, 1971 and Hamza Alavi, 'Peasants and Revolution', in Kathleen Gough and Hari P. Sharma (eds), *Imperialism and Revolution in South Asia*, London and New York, 1973. The definition of 'poor', 'middle' and 'rich' peasants depends largely upon the social and economic structure of a particular geographical area. For example, some of the peasants defined as 'middle' here might be termed 'rich' in other parts of India, yet impressions gained from a number of sources suggest that in coastal Andhra there were many peasants richer and poorer than these.

53. Madras to H. Dept GoI, 16 January 1932, H. Poll 5/46/1932; Madras to District Officers, DO 50-S, 15 January 1932, H. Poll 5/36/1932; Konda Venkatapayya note of 7 February 1932, AICC P-2/1932, NML. Also AICC circular of 28 March 1932 contained in Madras SF 771–B, 1 January 1932 reprinted in MHFSA 48/1930, p. 2004–39, APA. A good local view of the 1932 campaign is 'Congress Work in West Kistna District, 4 January 1932 to 6 September 1932', AICC P-2/1932, NML. For the reappearance of agitation subsequently, sec District Magistrate East Godavari to Ch. Sec. Madras 43/32, 3 May 1932, Madras Pub. Dept, Madras MS 736 (S-17) Confidential, 12 May 1932, TNA; the Andhra PCC's 'Civil Disobedience Report for the Months of January, February and March 1933', AICC 3/I/1933, NML.

54. District Magistrate Kistna to Sec. Pub. Dept Madras CI 1/33, 19 September 1932 and District Magistrate West Godavari to Sec. Pub. Dept Madras, DO 274/0, 18 September 1933 in MHFSA 19/1932, pp. 2186–7, 2185–6, APA; Madras to H. Dept GoI, 704-S, 23 September 1932 and Madras to H. Dept GoI, tel, R 35 September 1933, in GoI Reforms Office 199/R/1932, NAI.

55. Guntur District Varnashrama Dharmodharaka Sabha to the Private Sec. to V, 17 June 1933, GoI Reforms Office 51/VI/33-R/1933, NAI.

56. One consolidated list of protests against social reform proposals contains numerous petitions from coastal Andhra; H. Poll 22/18/1934. See also Ch. Sec. Madras to H. Dept GoI, 40059 A-4,6 Jan. 1933, Madras Pub. Dept GO 93, 24 January 1933, TNA; Madras to H. Dept GoI, 2-S, 2 January 1933, H. Poll 50/II/1933; Ch. Sec. Madras to Reforms Office GoI, M-S-105, 27 January 1933, GoI Reforms Office 9/I 33-R/1933, NAI.

57. AICC 65/3/1940, NML.

58. Their strength was so complete that it often caused discontent within district Congress ranks. For one account of East Godavari politics after 1936, see V. Subba Rao to President Andhra PCC, 13 October 1946, AICC P-3/1942–7, NML.

11 The Indian Nation in 1942*

Gyanendra Pandey

Quit India, the moment of India's most massive anti-imperialist struggle, provides a good opportunity for us to examine the contours of the Indian nation as it had emerged on the eve of Partition and Independence. The intensity of the Quit India Movement of course had a good deal to do with war-time conditions. Its distribution too was determined by a number of contingent factors: the 'immediacy' of the War in different parts of the subcontinent, the Government's preparedness to put down any resistance that might interfere with War supplies, the sharp difference of opinion among nationalist leaders and parties about the stand to be adopted in the face of the national and international crisis of 1942. Thus it was not without consequence that Rajagopalchari among Congress leaders, and the Communist Party among committed anti-imperialist parties, openly opposed the Quit India Movement. The growth of an independent Muslim political leadership and a separate Muslim constituency contributed its own part in the general aloofness of the Muslims from the Quit India uprising.

The broad features of the movement are now fairly well known.[1] If I refer to them here, it is partly because [...] any investigation of the boundaries of a nation must indicate the limitations of the national movement, all the more so in a historiographical context where its strengths are more readily portrayed.

The strongest centres of Quit India lay in a wide arc across northern India, stretching from Bombay, Satara, and Ahmedabad in the west, through United Provinces (UP) and Bihar in the north, to Bengal and Orissa in the east. A variety of factors appear to have been responsible for the force of the anti-imperialist upsurge in these areas. The eastern and northern states lay pretty much in the direct line of the threatened Japanese advance and the all too evident (and pathetic) withdrawal of soldiers wounded in the war and migrant labourers and merchants ejected from their sources of livelihood in southeast Asia. Some of the storm

* Originally published in Gyanendra Pandey (ed.), *The Indian Nation in 1942*, Calcutta, K.P. Bagchi and Co., 1988, pp. 1–17. In the present version some portions of the text and notes have been removed. For the complete text see the original version.

centres of the revolt in these states—Banaras and Gorakhpur, parts of
Bihar, the Medinipur district of southwest Bengal—were also the site of
prolonged nationalist agitation in the preceding decades, or areas where
the Kisan Sabhas and the Congress Socialist Party (CSP, which provided
a good deal of the local leadership in the course of the 1942 uprising)
had been especially active since the mid-1930s.[2]

The areas of western India that were to the fore in the Quit India
Movement, while far removed from the zone of military activity, shared
this tradition of a high level of nationalist activity. However, the agencies
for this were different in different places. In Satara, a new generation
of non-Brahman leaders had in the 1930s carried their non-Brahman
supporters into the Congress, and some of them had developed close
links with the CSP.[3] Bombay had been a prominent centre of nationalist
and, of course, labour agitation, inspired or guided by a variety of Liberal,
Congress, CSP, and Communist leaders. Ahmedabad, and Gujarat more
generally, was a recognized stronghold of the Gandhian Congress since
the close of the First World War.

Madras, which at one stage looked as though it might be in the
frontline of the expected Japanese invasion of India, was relatively quiet
during the Quit India Movement. This was due at least in part to factors
that we have already noticed—the open opposition of the most important
Congress leader of the south, C. Rajagopalachari.[4] In Kerala, it was
perhaps due to the opposition (or, at least, diffidence) of the Communists.
The Indian States, where the Congress had long been shy of establishing
branches and nationalist activity had been for the most part ill-organized
and fitful, were with one or two notable exceptions quiet. Punjab, which
remained a most important military recruiting ground, and where neither
the Congress nor the Kisan Sabhas had a strong base, was again
'backward' in nationalist terms; and the predominantly Muslim areas of
north-western India by and large remained withdrawn.

1942 confirmed that there had been a significant Muslim drift away
from the Congress. Of course, Muslims of many different classes and
regions were still far from being committed to the Muslim League, but
the political future appeared sufficiently uncertain for them to adopt a
policy of general detachment and caution. Even in the North-West Frontier
Province, so prominent a centre of Civil Disobedience in the early 1930s,
support for Quit India was at best lukewarm.[5] In other regions, where
Gandhi's call to 'Do or Die' evoked a more enthusiastic response, Muslim
aloofness was nevertheless marked and potentially dangerous from the
nationalist point of view.[6]

There was another large section of Indian society, not nearly so 'united' or so well organized politically as the Muslims of the different provinces, which was evidently disturbed by the emerging balance of forces within the Congress. This was the 'community' (as it was increasingly coming to be described) of 'untouchables' or *Dalits*. It was surely a statement of some moment when Ambedkar joined Jinnah in calling upon 'his' people to celebrate the resignation of the Congress ministries in October 1939 as a 'day of deliverance'.[7] At the grassroots level, Dalit groups, like others among the classes of the poorer peasants and landless and menial labourers, appear to have been somewhat hesitant about joining the rich peasants and small landlords, and the students from a rural or urban petty-bourgeois background who provided the spearhead of the nationalist uprising in 1942.[8]

One may refer to some other areas of uncertainty as well, although in the absence of more detailed research it is difficult to speak of them with much confidence. One relates to the part played by industrial labour about which we know precious little even for the first phase of urban demonstrations and *hartals*. Jamshedpur, Ahmedabad, and a few industrial centres produced extraordinary political statements, in the form of labour strikes on the single issue of the formation of a national government and of millowner support for workers who went on strike.[9]

Elsewhere, the picture is hazier. In Madras, according to David Arnold, it is not entirely clear whether the strikes in the Buckingham and Carnatic Mills in August–September 1942 were inspired by the Quit India Movement or only a new stage in an on-going worker-employer struggle.[10] In Bombay and Calcutta, we are told, industrial labour played very little part.[11] As with the militant coir workers of nothern Kerala, this may have been due in part to the restraint counselled by influential communist (and, in Calcutta, Muslim League) leaders.

Another interesting feature of Quit India was that, even when, in its second phase, it had spread out from the bigger cities and towns into the countryside and assumed the form of a mass peasant uprising in some areas, it led to very few anti-landlord actions. This was in marked contrast to the pattern of events in the earlier campaigns of mass agitation against the British launched by the Congress in 1920–2 and 1930–4. It has been attributed to the intensity of anti-British feeling in the unusual circumstances of 1942, which meant that all other contradictions were pushed into the background;[12] or, alternatively, to the fact this was a period of some prosperity for the bulk of the peasantry who were in no mood, therefore, to launch into no-rent and no-revenue campaigns.[13]

It needs to be said that sections even of the richer peasantry did, after all, hurl themselves into an all-out anti-colonial campaign which, if defeated, was liable to entail severe losses for them. The absence of anti-landlord action in 1942 may, in fact, have a simpler explanation, which is that the mass movement was not given the time nor the space in which to produce a second, more radical wave of revolt of the kind that has characterized many other peasant uprisings in India before and since.[14] Over the greater part of the country, the British Government's response was brutal, effective, and quick. And in most places where it survived, Quit India was transformed, in its final phase, into a hit-and-run guerilla campaign which lasted for many months and even years in some regions, with the emphasis on sabotage and individual punishment rather than on efforts to mobilize support for mass resistance.

No national movement can expect to gain the active support of the whole body of the 'nation' over the entire geographical area of its claimed territory; or to be wholly free from inner tensions and divisions. In the brief sketch of the geographical and social extent of the Quit India Movement presented above, I have done no more than survey the boundaries of the emerging Indian nation in the most obvious way. There are, however, other ways in which this enquiry may be pursued. One is to examine the class character of the aspirant ruling class, which Gail Omvedt explicitly and some others implicitly do [...]. Another, which the rest of this chapter will be devoted to, is to investigate the relationship between proclaimed 'citizens' and potential power-holders in the future nation-state, which may also be conceived of as the relationship between leaders and followers in the national movement. Here the evidence from Quit India is very striking indeed.

With all the variations between one region and another and the undoubted importance of many exceptional factors associated with the Second World War, two tendencies related to our subject stand out from experience of the Quit India Movement. One was the general acceptance of Gandhi as the leader of the projected 'final struggle' against the British, the person with the exclusive right to determine the timing and scope of the movement. The other was the assumption of leadership once the struggle began by men and women who were far from being Gandhian in their outlook and approach, and even by many who had little to do with the Congress organization in the past. This development, it needs to be said straightaway, was not a product solely of the fact that the bulk of the recognized Congress leadership at the national and provincial levels was arrested in one sweep on the morning of 9 August 1942.

THE INDIAN NATION IN 1942

Quit India might be fairly summed up as a popular nationalist upsurge that occurred in the name of Gandhi but went substantially beyond any confines that Gandhi may have envisaged for the movement. In this respect it revealed tensions that prevailed widely even in the earlier nationalist campaigns of Non-co-operation and Civil Disobedience. But 1942 showed them up in starker relief. Gandhi [was] the undisputed leader of a movement over which he had little command. This paradox has a good deal to tell us about the relationship between the Congress and the people in the final years of anti-colonial struggle against the British. It also helps to explain the remarkable ambivalence displayed by the Congress leadership in its response to Quit India in the months and years after August 1942.

Let us begin by examining the above proposition regarding Gandhi's virtually unchallenged position as the leader of the nation in 1942. Jayaprakash Narayan spoke for a large section of 'advanced' opinion in the country when he wrote in 1940, 'If a national struggle as opposed to sectional, factional or partial (struggles) can be launched by Mahatma Gandhi alone, it is suicidal to fight him. It is necessary to lend him our fullest cooperation and loyalty in everything that is preparatory for struggle'.[15] The feelings of ordinary folk, and of the British rulers of India, were well reflected in the air of expectancy and the considerable speculation that arose in the months before August 1942 as to 'Gandhi's next move'. To quote two reports from the Government of UP in May and June 1942, 'It is hardly profitable to speculate about Gandhi's next move, though of course there are numerous rumours'; and 'nearly every district has reported rumours, but it is not much use speculating what his final decision will be'.[16]

It is perhaps worth our while speculating a little on how this situation had come about, where Gandhi was recognized all around as the only one who could launch the struggle on behalf of the people. The simple explanation, that this was inevitable given the nature of the principal contradiction of the times—between nationalism and imperialism, is plainly inadequate. For the question remains why this particular vehicle was chosen for the expression of that anti-imperialist sentiment? The answer to this question has much to do with the history of the Congress and the forms of nationalist agitation in the 1920s and 1930s.

Gandhi had after all been the undisputed leader of all the earlier countrywide campaigns of nationalist protest against the British, in 1919, 1920–2, and 1930–4. The Non-co-operation Movement of 1920–2, which marked the transformation of Indian nationalism from an elitist into a popular or mass phenomenon, was mainly his idea. The technique of non-violent resistance or *satyagraha*, so widely adopted after 1920, of *civil* disobedience of 'unjust' laws and controlled agitation over specific issues, was his particular contribution. And if the Civil Disobedience Movement of 1930 was to a large extent thrust upon Gandhi and other senior leaders of the Congress, the Mahatma was still reckoned to be the one person who could lead the agitation: It was left to him to initiate the campaign at a time and on an issue of his choosing.

What we speak of today as the Quit India Movement was projected initially as the mass Civil Disobedience movement of 1942, with an emphasis on the 'mass' aspect to underline the change in circumstances from 1941 when the Congress had launched its strictly controlled and limited campaign of Individual Civil Disobedience. It is not without interest to note that the campaigns of 1941–2 are represented in nationalist historiography as the 'third great wave' of struggle against the British. It certainly looked like that to many observers in the early 1940s. From the writings of Gandhi on the one side to the reports of the Viceroy on the other, the surviving records from 1942 do suggest the anticipation of a movement which would be in line with those that had gone before, if rather more militant.[17]

As before, the All-India Congress Committee (AICC) left it to Gandhi to determine the 'steps to be taken' and to launch the movement at the appropriate time. Gandhi in his speech to the AICC after the adoption of the Quit India resolution on 8 August 1942 said: 'The actual struggle does not commence this moment. You have only placed all your powers in my hands. I will now wait upon the Viceroy and plead with him for the acceptance of the Congress demand. That process is likely to take two or three weeks'. He went on in the same speech to advise different sections of the society (Government servants, students, and others) as to what they should do in the period of waiting 'till the time that I frame a programme for the struggle'.[18]

Behind Gandhi stood the organizational strength and prestige of the Congress. Gandhi had himself been instrumental in giving the organization a new vitality through the new Congress constitution of 1920 and the reorganization of the Provincial Congress Committee on linguistic lines. He had also been the first to underline the fact that the Congress, if it was to be a truly national party, must move out into the villages, and become the party of the peasantry. Along with this, the sustained constructive work of the decades before the Second World War—extending from flood relief to the promotion of spinning and the *achhutoddhar*programme—and the enthusiasm generated by the Non-co-operation and Civil Disobedience Movements, had given the Congress a unique position in the country and indeed all over the colonialized world. In Ahmedabad, Gillion suggests,[19] moral authority had passed from the Government to the Congress as long ago as 1919 on account of its activities. Much the same thing was to happen in many other parts of the country, in 1919 and afterwards.

Congress, or Swarajist, participation in the provincial and national elections and the legislative councils of the 1920s and '30s had given the organization added strength. By the early 1940s, moreover, the Congress had come to be commonly perceived as the party most likely to succeed to power when the British finally left India—'the party of Government', as it came to be called. Its exceptionally good performance in the provincial elections of 1937, the formation of Congress ministries in seven out of eleven provinces, the actions taken by those ministries to show that the era of authoritarian British rule was over (however short-lived or nominal some of these proved in the end to be) and the constitutional discussions between Congress leaders and high-level representatives of the British Government to decide the political future of India, had all contributed to this result.

Along with these sources of Congress strength, one may refer to the 'weakness' of the other political elements in the country that were concerned with the mobilization of mass political support. Apart from the Muslim League, and to some extent the Hindu Mahasabha, most of the important political groupings in the country seem to have acknowledged the primacy of the Congress. This might appear unlikely in the case of the Communists. But we must remember the peculiar situation in which the Communist Party of India was placed. Relative newcomers on the political stage, committed at least theoretically to a politics based rather narrowly on the industrial working class, their ranks were further decimated by heavy state repression in the late 1920s. In the 1930s the 'united front' strategy of the Communists brought them into a position of working alongside the Congress. At this time they worked through a number of front organizations, including major bodies like the CSP and the Kisan Sabhas which openly conceded leadership to the Congress as the national party. The 'People's War' line adopted at the end of 1941, to the extent that it was accepted by Communist activists in different parts of India, was to place them at loggerheads with the Congress once again. This new line would earn them some kind of reprieve from the

Government of India, but also much unpopularity among large sections of their politically-conscious countrymen and women.

The CSP which had quickly become a party with considerable influence in scattered parts of the country, saw itself—as its name indicates—very much as a part of the Congress, and the party leadership continued to acknowledge the ultimate authority of Gandhi throughout 1942 and 1943. In an essay entitled 'Gandhiji's Leadership and the Congress Socialist Party', Jayaprakash Narayan stated the position unambiguously: 'The Congress alone is the country's salvation.'[20] In his letters 'To all Fighters for Freedom' written from the underground ('somewhere in India') and printed by the Sind Congress Socialist Group in December 1942 and September 1943, he reiterated this position: 'In August last...Congress stood in all its power at the head of the people'; 'Truly was the "Open Rebellion" envisaged by our incomparable leader, Mahatma Gandhi'.[21]

The All-India Kisan Sabha (AIKS) which became another important political platform in the 1930s, was a purely sectional movement with no pretensions to becoming the central organization of the national movement. A division appeared within its ranks in 1942 more or less along the lines of a wing that leaned towards the Communists and another that favoured the CSP. We may expect that the two wings followed these different inclinations in their response to Quit India, though again with the proviso that formal party positions and actual local behaviour frequently differed. In any case, even those AIKS leaders who opposed the Congress leadership in the later 1930s and again on the issue of a mass civil disobedience movement in 1942, recognized that the Congress had a special authority and legitimacy.

Thus during the 1937 election campaign in Bihar, Swami Sahajanand Saraswati, taunted for canvassing on behalf of zamindars seeking election to the provincial legislature when he had only a little while earlier bitterly opposed their adoption as Congress candidates, argued that it was a question of loyalty to the Congress, to which all other organizations were subordinate.[22] The pairing of 'the Congress' and 'the nation' remained a common feature of Kisan Sabha resolutions during 1942 and 1943— at the very time when it was alleged that Communists had established an excessive domination over the AIKS[23]—as in the condemnation of acts of sabotage and 'goondaism' (in Quit India) which brought shame upon the 'fair name of *our* National Congress and our country', or the declaration that the British Government would never be able to crush 'the Congress and the Indian people'.[24]

Yet, if what has been said in the preceding paragraphs expresses one truth at the level of organized politics, there are other truths that still require investigation. The history of Indian society, as Partha Chatterjee has recently written,[25] will have to be the articulation of many histories if it is to comprehend the totality of social and political developments. The foregoing pages will already have indicated the frequent gap between organized party politics and the rather differently organized sphere of popular political action. While the formal Communist Party position in 1942 was in support of British war efforts, for example, many party members supported and even took a leading role in the Quit India movement in different parts of the country. Consider only the UP Government's observation, 'Muslims except possibly Communists have taken no part and appear anxious to continue studies'.[26]

A similar breaking of rank occurred in the influential Krishak Sabha of Medinipur district [...]. The Sabha, like its parent body the AIKS, was opposed to the Quit India movement. But the majority of its cadre in the district could not escape the general mood of militancy. At a meeting of Krishak Sabha activists especially convened to hear the views of both pro- and anti-Quit India leaders, the majority of those assembled decided to discard the official policy of the Sabha and join the movement.[27]

From Medinipur in 1942, again, we obtain illustration of how local Congress politics was sometimes far in advance of the party's official position. In the eastern part of the district, local workers launched a mass satyagraha against the Government's drive to procure rice and paddy, long before the all India Congress Committee met in Bombay to pass the Quit India resolution. Congress workers and villagers seized procurement boats, offered satyagraha on the roads along which procurement carts passed, and many of them were arrested under the Defence of India rules.[28]

What all this suggests is that if there was a widespread acceptance of the primacy of the Congress at one level, there were at the same time autonomous forces at work on another level that repeatedly challenged the notion of a necessary Congress 'leadership'. These forces had their roots in the far-from-complete integration of the Indian economy, in the significant cultural divide between the elites and the masses, and not least in long-standing traditions of militant resistance to class and state oppression in one region and another. Developments in the 1930s had strengthened these traditions of local politics in many areas. Indeed, one could argue that if the 1920s was the decade of the ascendancy of the Congress, the 1930s saw that ascendancy challenged in numerous ways—by the emergence of several new political forces and the resurgence of some older ones, so that the anti-imperialist struggle once again came to exhibit a rather more different appearance.

The revival of the strength of the Muslim League, and the growing importance of other 'communalist' forces, was only the most obvious reflection of the changing situation. The establishment of the CSP and the AIKS were powerful indicators of the new trends in mass politics. And there were others too. In Kheda district, Gujarat, to take a different kind of illustration, the subordinate peasantry which had been sympathetic to the Congress movement in the 1920s and early 1930s, had since turned hostile to the Congress. Here, David Hardiman reports, a meeting of some 10,000 Baraiyas and Patanvadiyas in August 1942 resolved that they would give no support to the Quit India movement. In the Shahabad district of Bihar, likewise, the Triveni Sangh, representing the interests of the 'backward' cultivating castes—the Koeris, the Kurmis, and the Ahirs—declared its support for the war efforts of the Government of India.[29]

In some instances popular forces such as these, awakened to a new consciousness of their organized strength, found representation even within the regular Congress party. One of the more striking examples of this has already been mentioned: the Satara district in Maharashtra where the Congress was taken over by young non-Brahman leaders in the 1930s. These men, inspired by and trained in the militant non-Brahman movement of the region, now drew large sections of the *bahujan samaj* into orthodox nationalist politics. Gail Omvedt makes the point that the Satara peasantry came into the nationalist movement at this time having few organizational links with either the Congress or the 'Left'.[30] In this region, the non-Brahman Satyashodhak movement provided the base and the main striking force of the Quit India upsurge. Nevertheless, Gandhi was by now evidently an important symbol for the entire range of nationalists in Satara, and their response to his call to 'do or die' produced the *prati sarkar*—perhaps the most powerful and long-lasting of the parallel governments established during the Quit India movement.

Over most of the country, the younger and more militant nationalists found conditions congenial to their mood in the CSP, the Kisan Sabhas, and other radical organizations. Not only did these bodies succeed in raising the land question, for instance, to the level of a national debate, in drawing the Congress leadership on the question of precise social and economic content of *swaraj*, and thereby in reviving the danger of a split between Left and Right in the Congress. The CSP also won a number of dramatic victories in Congress organizational elections at the local level. In Kerala, again, it was the more radical elements of the CSP who converted the Congress into a mass organization in the mid-1930s and went on to lay the organizational base for the powerful Communist movement of the region.[31]

Such developments were indicative of a fairly general trend. It is not surprising to find that young men and women associated with the CSP and other radical organizations took such a prominent part in the Quit Indian Movement. Even in the Gandhian stronghold of Ahmedabad, where almost the entire population—minus the Muslims—was behind the Congress, and millowners gave financial assistance to the workers to enable them to prolong their strike in support of Quit India, it was a young Congress Socialist called Jayanti Thakor who became the *Shahersuba* and assumed leadership of the movement.[32]

In Medinipur district, with its own notable tradition of Congress-led satyagrahas and dynamic Congress leadership at the local level, a number of the established Congress leaders held aloof from Quit India while others hesitated initially. In the circumstances the initiative passed to militant young students, many of whom, while they were without district party affiliations, had veered towards the Forward Bloc in the late 1930s. At that time, Sanyal tells us, some of the students 'even in the remote villages' of eastern Medinipur were inspired more by Subhas Chandra Bose than by Mahatma Gandhi, whom they believed to be guilty of compromising with the British and hence a 'Rightist', although it is necessary to add that these diverse groups came together again under the Congress umbrella before the Quit India Movement caught fire in Medinipur.[33]

The question of the 'taking over' of the Congress, which we have referred to specially in the case of Satara, has another aspect which ought to be mentioned. This act of appropriation was one that occurred time and again at the level of grassroots action in the anti-imperialist struggle. The appropriation of nationalist symbols—whether 'Gandhi' or the 'Congress'—was the means by which the popular classes in different parts of the country repeatedly forced the pace of the movement and came to leave their impress on Indian nationalism.[34] The process occurred in a great variety of situations—from the *kisan* movement in northern Allahabad and Awadh, to the Assam plantation workers' agitation, to the Gudem-Rampa rising led by Alluri Sitarama Raju in the early 1920s, for example—but it was never more evident than in 1942.

We need refer only to the widespread attacks on Government installations, police *thanas*, and railway stations, and indeed the killing of police officials and stray British (or American) military personnel, all carried out in the name of Gandhi. In eastern UP and Bihar, there was long and serious contention between the so-called spirit of violence and that of non-violence—between those who believed in the capture of power, as it were, and those who still kept faith with satyagraha and the possibility of a peaceful succession. This was a contention that was very widely observed at the local level in 1942. And in many places, as some of those involved in the Quit India Movement in the Ghazipur district of UP recalled, the 'leadership' was Gandhi's but the spirit was that of Bhagat Singh.[35]

The tension between these contradictory tendencies was resolved in some places only with the open disowning of Gandhi. This is demonstrated most strikingly in the case of the legendary *prati sarkar* in Satara. Here the bulk of the activists refused to surrender even as late as August 1944, when the Quit India movement had more or less run its course and Mahatma Gandhi expressed his desire that those who were still underground should surrender: the *mantra* of 'do or die', they declared, took precedence over Gandhi's later wishes.[36] Jayaprakash Narayan, one of the acknowledged leaders of the underground movement from the end of 1942, had said the same thing somewhat earlier: 'We have declared ourselves independent, and also named the British as an aggressive power; we are, therefore, justified within the terms of the Bombay resolution itself to fight Britain with arms. If this does not accord with Gandhi's principles, that is not my fault'.[37] Let it be noted that this statement came after the massive and frequently violent rebellion that had occurred in his native Bihar, in UP, and Bengal and several other parts of the country, and Jayaprakash's own dramatic escape from Hazaribagh jail in November 1942. It was another instance of the pace being forced, and an indication of the different centres of political initiative that had emerged out of the preceding decades of militant nationalist activity.

It is in this context that we must place the equivocal response of the Congress leadership to the Quit India movement which they were and to a large extent still are presumed to have conceived and directed. The leaders sought on the one hand to claim the revolt as their own and thereby to appropriate the credit that flowed from it, an effort that was especially noticeable in the run up to the elections of 1946 and 1952. There was at the same time, however, an attempt to distance the Congress

from the 'excesses' of the movement and a plea—sometimes a warning—
to the people not to repeat these.

A resolution adopted by the Congress working committee meeting
in Pune on 14 September 1945 gives the substance of the Congress
position in 1945. It congratulated the nation for 'the courage and
endurance with which it withstood the fierce and violent onslaught of
the British power' and expressed deep sympathy with all those who
had suffered, 'during these three years [1942–45] of military, police
and ordinance rule'. The committee went on to register its sorrow at the
fact that

> in some place the people forgot and fell away from the Congress method
> of peaceful and non-violent action, but realizes that the provocative action
> of the Government in effecting sudden and widespread arrests of all
> well-known leaders, and brutal and ruthless repression of peaceful
> demonstrations, goaded them to rise spontaneously to resist the armed
> might of an alien Imperialist Power which was trying to curse the spirit of
> freedom and the passionate desire of the Indian people to gain
> independence.[38]

The hesitation implied in this Congress ratification of the rising of 1942
was stated more plainly at other times. Mahatma Gandhi's concern over
an outbreak of violence on this scale was to be expected. Writing to the
Viceroy from jail in late September 1942, he described the events of
August and September as a 'calamity' and declared that the people had
gone 'wild with rage to the point of losing self-control'.[39] While it is
possible to argue that this was only Gandhi's attempt at explaining away
the violence that had occurred and justifying the position of the Congress,
we would do well to pay attention to his language.

Similar language issued from other Congress sources who were not
writing for the benefit of the colonial regime or in the heat of the moment.
In his *Discovery of India* (1946), Jawaharlal Nehru wrote of the
'impromptu frenzy of the mob',[40] Pattabhi Sitaramayya in the second
volume of his *History of the Indian National Congress* published in 1947,
of how 'people grew insensate and were maddened with fury'.[41]

'Wild with rage', 'maddened with fury', 'frenzied', and 'insensate':
it is a collection that competes with any colonial lament over an uprising
among the Indian peasantry. The colonial regime and its representatives
had argued many times that the honest but 'primitive' peoples of the
tribal belts, or the 'simple', illiterate folk of the depressed cultivating
and labouring classes, had been maliciously, foolishly misled. The
reaction of the Congress leadership after Quit India betrayed a parallel

perception. Thus in numerous speeches and writings, Nehru referred to the Quit India Movement as the greatest event in India since the Mutiny but lamented also that 'the people forgot the lessons of non-violence which had been dinned into their ears for more than twenty years'.[42] 'Lessons' which could apparently be imparted to the masses only by being 'dinned' into their ears. The distance between the leadership and 'nation' was evident.

Some of the other implications of this distance were spelt out in statements made after the end of the War by a Congress leadership that had, so to speak, 'arrived'. Gandhi, one might add in parentheses, was fast becoming a mere father-figure of the Indian National movement, who needed to be honoured but not necessarily listened to.[43] So it is no longer 'non-violence' that appears as the critical issue in the statements of this ascendant leadership, but the question of 'discipline' and 'order' (though it is probably fair to say that even earlier, non-violence was in their eyes at least partly a weapon of political control). Addressing the Bihar Provincial Students Conference in 1945, Nehru praised the students of the province for their sterling part in the Quit India uprising, and then went on to say, 'I encourage you to have academic discussion on political matters, but warn you against taking the initiative in the political field. You must look for guidance from the accepted political party which is the Congress'.[44] The advice was in line with the Congress leader's instructions to the peasants of Awadh twenty-five years earlier to give up 'meetings' and 'disturbances' (sic) and leave it to Gandhi to win swaraj.[45]

In January 1947 Vallabhbhai Patel made the party high command's position clearer still when he wrote to Govind Ballabh Pant, Premier of UP, about some pictures of police atrocities in 1942 which had been displayed in a Congress exhibition in Banaras. He was surprised, wrote Patel, that Pant, who had inaugurated the exhibition, should have been associated in any way with an exhibition in which such pictures were displayed.

> The punishment of persons who were concerned with the 1942 atrocities is quite a different matter, and it is open to provincial Governments, it they so desire, to deal with official misdemeanour in that connection. But the caricaturing of official activities in the manner reported in the Press at a time when we are in office is open to serious objection. This is likely to affect the morale of the police force which in the present emergency can hardly be considered proper.[46]

This statement may be read as follows: The bureaucracy and the police were once again 'neutral'. The struggle for 'nation-building' was over. The task of controlling the 'nation' had begun. It betrays a perception of nationalism which was far different from that displayed by the mass of the people in the early 1920s, the early 1930s, and even in 1942 when the sole object of the uprising appeared to be to drive the British out of the country. For most ordinary Congress men and women, for students, workers and peasants, artisans and petty traders, nationalism had come to mean a society awakening, a people on the move—seeking more or less consciously to make their own history. That mood was not likely to evaporate in 1947: the effects of these different perceptions of nation-building are still with us.

NOTES

† An earlier draft of this essay was presented at seminars in the University of Tokyo and Oxford. I am grateful to the participants in those seminars, and also to David Arnold and Dipesh Chakraborty, for their response to the questions raised in it.

1. Sumit Sarkar, *Modern India 1885–1947* (New Delhi, 1983) provides the most useful summary, and the next few paragraphs follow his account closely. F.G. Hutchins, *Spontaneous Revolution: The Quit India Movement* (Delhi, 1971) and A.C. Bhuyan, *The Quit India Movement* (Delhi, 1975), among others, provide more detailed accounts. See also the useful collections of documents in N. Mansergh (ed.), *The Transfer of Power*, Volume II, '*Quit India*', London, 1971 and P.N. Chopra (ed.), *Quit India Movement: British Secret Report*, Faridabad, 1976.

2. For an illustration of the importance of events since the mid-1930s, see Chandan Mitra's contribution in G. Pandey (ed.), *The Indian Nation in 1942*, Calcutta, 1988, ch. 5.

3. See Gail Omvedt's contribution in *The Indian Nation in 1942*, ch. 8. In a similar way, the Orissa–Andhra fituri fed into the nationalist movement from the 1920s; see Biswamoy Pati's contribution in *The Indian Nation in 1942*, ch. 6.

4. See David Arnold in *The Indian Nation in 1942*, ch. 7.

5. Nevertheless, as I have already said, this was no indication of commitment to an anti-Congress position: in the 1946 elections, the Congress again won a majority in the N.W.F.P.

6. See the examples of Medinipur, Ahmedabad and eastern UP in *The Indian Nation in 1942*, chs 2, 3, 4.

7. Sarkar, *Modern India*, p. 358.

8. Evidence for this statement is scattered through this volume, but is not unambiguous. For what may be 'exceptions', see the contributions of Sanyal, Hardiman, Pati, and Omvedt in *The Indian Nation in 1942*.

9. Other examples include Dehri-on-Sone, referred to in *The Indian Nation in 1942*, ch. 4, and Coimbatore.
10. See ch. 7 in *The Indian Nation in 1942*.
11. Govind Sahai, *42 Rebellion*, Delhi, 1947, p. 89; Sarkar, *Modern India*, pp. 396–7.
12. This was one of the more contentious issues at the July 1983 seminar on the Quit India Movement held at the Centre for Studies in Social Sciences, Calcutta, where Sabyasachi Bhattacharya and Barun De, among others, pointed to the effectiveness of decades of nationalist propaganda and the united 'umbrella' character of the national movement to account for the absence of open class conflict in 1942.
13. Cf. Hardiman, in *The Indian Nation in 1942*, ch. 2; Sarkar, *Modern India*, p. 403.
14. The exceptions in Satara and Medinipur, where no-rent campaigns and other kinds of anti-feudal actions developed, would appear to support this contention, for these were precisely the isolated areas where the Quit India Movement persisted longest.
15. J.P. Narayan, *Towards Struggle: Selected Manifestoes, Speeches and Writings*, Bombay, 1946, p. 141.
16. Mansergh (ed.), *Transfer of Power*, vol. II, pp. 157, 220.
17. On 13 August and even as late as 17 August, Linlithgow was still expecting a 'formal' inauguration of 'Civil Disobedience' by the Congress; ibid., pp. 683, 734. See also India Office Library, London, L/P & J/5/271, Hallett–Linlithgow, 18 August 1942; and National Archives of India, New Delhi, Government of India, Home Deptt., Political (Intelligence) File 3/16/42 & Kw, which is entitled 'Civil Disobedience Movement 1942, "Appreciation" Telegrams'.
18. *Collected Works of Mahatma Gandhi*, vol. 76, Ahmedabad, 1979, pp. 391, 395.
19. K.L. Gillion, 'Gujarat in 1919' in R. Kumar (ed.), *Essays on Gandhian Politics: The Rowlatt Satyagraha of 1919*, Oxford, 1971, p. 143.
20. *Towards Struggle*, p. 139.
21. Reprinted in ibid. (without complete dates).
22. Sahajanand Saraswati, *Mara Jivan Sangharsh* (Patna, 1952), p. 481, cited in K. Kumar, 'Congress-Peasant Relationship in the late 1930s', in D.N. Panigrahi (ed.), *Economy, Society and Politics in Modern India*, New Delhi, 1983.
23. Indulal Yagnik, President and Vice-President of the AIKS in 1942 and 1943, resigned on this ground in August 1943; M.A. Rasul, *A History of the All India Kisan Sabha*, Calcutta, 1974, p. 107.
24. Ibid., pp. 87, 101.
25. P. Chatterjee, *Bengal 1920–1947: The Land Question*, vol. I, Calcutta, 1984, p. xii.

26. L/P & J/5/271, D.O. No. F. 2/8/42 of 19 August 1942. For other evidence of Communist participation, see A. Guha, *Planter-Raj to Swaraj: Freedom Struggle and Electoral Politics in Assam 1826-1947*, New Delhi, 1977, p. 275; A. Das, 'History in the Present Tense', *Social Scientist*, vol. 12, no. 10, October 1984, p. 61.

27. *The Indian Nation in 1942*, ch. 3.

28. Ibid., ch. 3.

29. Ibid., ch. 2 and ch. 5.

30. Ibid., ch. 8.

31. Sarkar, *Modern India*, p. 369.

32. *The Indian Nation in 1942*, ch. 2.

33 Ibid., ch. 3.

34. See, for example, article by David Arnold and G. Pandey in R. Guha (ed.), *Subaltern Studies I* (Delhi, 1982), and by Shahid Amin and Sumit Sarkar in *Subaltern Studies III* (Delhi, 1984).

35. See *The Indian Nation in 1942*, ch. 4.

36. Ibid., ch. 8.

37. J.P. Narayan, *Towards Struggle*.

38. Mansergh (ed.), *Transfer of Power*, vol. VI, pp. 274–5.

39. Ibid., vol. II, p. 1002.

40. J. Nehru, *The Discovery of India*, 1946, reprinted Bombay, 1969, p. 489.

41. P. Sitaramayya, *The History of the Indian National Congress*, vol. II, Bombay, 1947, p. 373.

42. Nehru, *Discovery of India*, p. 487; Mansergh, *Transfer of Power*, vol. VI, p. 60.

43. Cf. Partha Chatterjee's comments on the relationship between Gandhi, Nehru, and the other senior Congress leaders in the 1940s in his *Nationalist Thought and the Colonial World*, London, 1986.

44. *Selected Works of Jawaharlal Nehru*, vol. 17, New Delhi, 1983, p. 510.

45. S. Gopal, *Jawaharlal Nehru, A Biography*, vol. I, London, 1975, p. 56.

46. Durga Das (ed.), *Sardar Patel's Correspondence*, vol. 5, Ahmedabad, 1975, p. 325. (I am indebted to David Arnold for this reference).

PART IV

MUSLIM IDENTITY AND
POLITICAL PARTICIPATION

12 'The Muslim Breakaway'*

Mushirul Hasan

[...]

In explaining the 'Muslim breakaway' from the Congress—a major theme in studies on Indian nationalism—historians assume the existence of an all-India Muslim consciousness, which found organized and tangible expression in the ideological orientation of Syed Ahmad Khan and his associates at Aligarh. This, however, is a questionable assumption and this [...] [chapter] will examine why it is so. It will also try to establish that 'Muslim response' to the Congress did not crystallize at an identifiable level, and that isolated and sporadic reactions of fragmented groups must not form the basis of a highly generalized reconstruction. Bodies like the Central National Mahommedan Association and the United Patriotic Association, with their localized concerns, had no popular following and could not legitimately sustain their claim to represent Muslim interests generally.[1] Consequently, their response to the Congress, as Badruddin Tyabji perceptively pointed out, rested on 'local, special and temporary causes'.[2]

Given their different socio-economic interests there was no likelihood of a monolithic Muslim response to the Congress movement. There was none. The Congress demands affected Muslims of various classes and regions in several different ways; so, their reactions were moulded by local, regional, and sometimes class-based interests as opposed to the altruistic concerns for the larger community of Indian Islam.

This [...] [chapter] alludes to yet another contentious issue in contemporary historical writings: the part played by Syed Ahmed Khan, who is said to have orchestrated the 'Muslim viewpoint' on political matters with vigour and consistency and whipped up an anti-Congress stir among his followers. While the weight of his arguments against the Congress must be recognized, as also his influence on Muslim society, at the same time, we need to explore how a group of Muslims, imbued

* Originally published in Mushirul Hasan, *Nationalism and Communal Politics in India, 1885–1930*, New Delhi, Manohar Publishers, 1990, pp. 282–93. In the present version some portions of the text and notes have been removed. For the complete text see the original version.

with the spirit of nationalism, were beginning to work out an alternative political strategy in the last decade of the nineteenth century. Admittedly, they could not match the intellectual resources of Syed Ahmed and his disciples at Aligarh. They also did not possess the organizational strength to counter their more influential detractors. But they were not lacking in ideological conviction and consistency, a fact that enabled them to develop and pursue their nationalist aims and spearhead a pro-Congress movement in the early decade of the twentieth century. Thus, our preoccupation with Syed Ahmad's anti-Congress crusade need not lead historians to ignore alternative political currents within the Muslim community.

The mixed and diverse reactions to nationalist forces is evident from the ways in which some of the Congress demands were perceived. Most educated Muslims in Bengal and Punjab were averse to competitive examinations, because they were educationally ill-prepared to compete with the more advanced Hindus. Ameer Ali and Abdul Latif, representing two of Bengal's premier organizations, maintained that the Congress goal of a more open and competitive society, if implemented, would favour educated Hindus and accentuate existing disparities between the religious communities.[3] The same argument was echoed in upper India in order to make a case for nomination. Moreover, there was the familiar clamour for separate representation in public appointments and its extension to representative bodies, especially because many 'respected families' had been left out on account of franchise being confined to those who fulfilled property, wealth, and educational qualifications.[4]

In UP, too, the Congress faced stern opposition. Here the main apprehension was of being swamped by the so-called Hindu majority in a prospective popular government—a fear reinforced by some isolated examples in western UP. When some Muslim candidates were defeated in the municipal board elections held in 1890, the *Najmul Akhbaar* struck an alarming note: 'If the elective principle was extended to the legislative council an entire exclusion of Muslims from the council would follow'.[5] 'This is not an imaginary bugbear to scare away Muslims from the Congress camp', wrote a contributor to the *Aligarh Institute Gazette*, 'but a stubborn fact daily illustrated in the proceedings of the district and municipal boards scattered all over the country'.[6] If anything, this was a reiteration of Syed Ahmad's arguments against the Congress demand for a more representative and popular government.

Though Syed Ahmad's assault on the Congress has been interpreted in several different ways,[7] most explanations are often based on later day ideological predilections. Besides, there is a tendency—more pronounced in the subcontinent than elsewhere—to try and prove or disprove that the genius behind the founding of the Aligarh college was also the progenitor of a 'Muslim nation'. This has distorted perspectives, stimulated, somewhat needlessly, acrimonious controversies, and obscured the more vital aspects of Indian polity and society during Syed Ahmad's lifetime. So far, attempts to establish him as the architect of 'Muslim nationalism' have proved to be as unrewarding as the efforts to discover in him elements of an 'Indian nationalist'.

It is, at first, hard to make sense of Syed Ahmad's fiery denunciation of the Congress. After all, he had the required credentials to be a leading light in any nationalist organization. Hindu–Muslim unity was close to his heart and a constant refrain in his public utterances.[8] Friendship between the two communities, he said, should be a matter of course, for since 'centuries we have been living on the same soil, eating the fruit of the same land...breathing the air of the same country'.[9] In 1873, he declared that he did not care for religion to be regarded as the badge of nationhood. He advocated separation between matters religious and political. Spiritual and religious matters, he asserted, cannot have any connection with worldly affairs. A true religion only stated cardinal principles comprising ethical values and only incidentally dealt with the problems of the world. When he was a member of the viceroy's legislative council he strove for the welfare of both Hindus and Muslims: so when he toured north India in the eighties he was feted on all sides.[10] In 1884, Syed Ahmad made clear that

> by the word qaum, I mean both Hindus and Muslims.... In my opinion it matters not whatever be their religious beliefs, because we cannot see anything of it; but what we see is that all of us, whether Hindus or Muslims, live on one soil, are governed by one and the same ruler, have the same sources of benefits, and equally share the hardships of a famine....[11]

Common territory, in the eyes of Syed Ahmad, thus imposed upon Indians the obligation of mutual co-operation and unity in order to ensure the common good.

[...]

Syed Ahmad's political concerns were no less secular and there was little in his early attitudes to suggest that he wanted separate and favoured treatment for his co-religionists. He was the first to argue that the 1857 upsurge had been caused by the monumental indifference of the East India Company to the economic plight of the masses, and the failure to grant Indians some form of advisory representation in the council. He supported local self-government, the right of Indian judges to try English defendants, wrote in defence of Indians entering the covenanted civil service and revived the British Indian Association at Aligarh to join with Surendranath Banerjea in a campaign to restore the age of entrance for the Civil Service examination from nineteen to twenty-one.[12] Banerjea had attended a meeting at Aligarh in 1877. When he returned to the city in 1884 to start a branch of a new political organization, the National Fund, with Syed Ahmad as president, he was received with 'utmost kindness'. His friendly relations with the Syed continued 'notwithstanding differences of opinion, which the Congress movement subsequently gave rise to'.[13]

With a background so remarkably similar to that of any contemporary Congress leader, Syed Ahmad's December 1887 outburst at Lucknow surprised many. He sharply criticized the application of the principles of representative and parliamentary government in so diverse, so divided, and so complex a society. He also raised the spectre of Bengali dominance. 'If you accept', he said at Lucknow and repeated elsewhere, 'that the country should groan under the yoke of Bengali rule and its people link the Bengali shoes, then, in the name of God, jump into the train, sit down, and be off to Madras'. The Congress demands, he thundered, would hurt the Muslims most. The enlarged councils would have no place for them: it would be dominated by 'Babu-so-and-so Mitter, Babu-so-and-so Ghose and Babu-so-and-so Chuckerbutty'. This was not the language one associated with a man who had once held up the Bengalis as an example to be admired and imitated, and was generally known for his balanced views on so many public issues since the publication of his celebrated *Asbaab-i Baghawat-i Hind* in 1858.

It is doubtful if Syed Ahmad worked out his arguments against the Congress on his own. Though acutely sensitive to the changing climate of opinion in India in the decades after 1857, he was only superficially familiar with the intricacies of the newly-developing institutions of representative government. In such matters he was tutored by British officials in north India, whose active backing he required for his prestigious Aligarh project. The person who influenced him most was the MAO college Principal, Theodore Beck, 'a pretty young man with pink cheeks and blue eyes'. This 24-year old Cambridge undergraduate was the political mentor and ideologue of the grand old man of Aligarh.[14]

[...]

Though Beck described himself as one of 'England's adventurers', he reached the Indian shores with a clear sense of mission: to stamp out sedition in order to bolster imperial rule for the good of the Indian people.

'To have a great grievance shop, an anti-government cave of Adullum marching about the country will be bad for the peace of India',[15] he wrote with reference to the Congress. He was constantly haunted by such apprehensions. Yet he set out to counter the 'evil' influence of the Congress with an evangelical fervour. He assiduously cultivated Muslims to create a 'strong conservative school of thought' and 'complete a breach' between them and the Bengali dominated Congress.[16] He kept his students on a tight leash. The Siddons Union Club, a Cambridge-like institution, debarred discussion on sensitive political affairs. Unlike the Cambridge prototype, the Principal had the veto power over any discussion so as to prevent the Union from becoming a forum for Bengali-style 'sedition'.[17] But Beck's eyes were set on the world beyond the Aligarh college: his aim was to establish an enduring Anglo-Muslim alliance and to stiffen Muslim feelings against the 'incendiary' Congress. 'I am more excited about this blessed Congress,' he wrote to his mother in April 1888, 'than about anything else.... It seems likely this Congress will create a great stir in this part of India, and I shouldn't be surprised if some jolly good rows occur. The opposition has got well on its legs....'[18]

With his stature, influence, and connections, Syed Ahmad was an invaluable asset to further Beck's ideals. He was, therefore, goaded into taking anti-Congress postures. Beck was dutifully present whenever his 'chief' fired his shots at the Congress. After the Meerut speech, he gleefully recorded: 'We have played off our 81 ton gun against the Congress again'.[19] He encouraged the launching of an anti-Congress newspaper,[20] herded the scattered elements of opposition to the Congress into the United Patriotic Association,[21] prompted some students to congregate at the Delhi Juma Masjid to collect signatures for an anti-Congress petition to Parliament,[22] and kept on jogging up the *Pioneer* and the government with little accounts of Muslim demonstrations against the Congress.[23] Beck's intentions were clear; yet he was sometimes daunted by the outcome of his endeavours. 'It is a desperate struggle. If we relax our energies they will give us a thrashing. If we stick to it we may possibly—I say possibly, but probably—give them a desperate blow'.[24] He foresaw, thanks to his own initiatives, the emergence of a 'gigantic' Muslim organization in upper India with a distinct political creed. This would naturally suit the government, 'which will have some people to defend it, ...' 'We shall have a body of men bent on rooting out the fallacies of their [Congress] arguments'.[25]

Syed Ahmad could hardly match the young Principal's boundless energy and passion. Besides, after the initial spurt of activity he was reluctant to prosecute his anti-Congress campaign any further.[26] He bluntly said so to Beck in April 1888, just a few months after his well-publicized Lucknow speech. 'We have I think done enough in opposition to the Congress', he firmly stated.[27] In the same conversation, he recalled how during the turbulent days of 1857 the British employed brute force to crush the revolt—reminiscent of the atrocities perpetrated by Chingiz Khan and Timur. Beck was not pleased with the comparison. 'This little conversation', he noted despondently, 'has put a damper on my politics'.[28] But as one made of sterner stuff, he not only kept up the tempo of his activities but also kept the Syed on a tight leash. His perseverance paid off. Constrained by his dependence on government support for the college of his dreams and ingratiated by the honour and approbation he received from the British, the ageing Syed Ahmad relented to the charms of the young principal and lived up to his expectations of playing the anti-Congress drum loud and clear. Moreover, the rising tide of Hindu revivalism and its links with Indian nationalism reinforced his growing fears that the Congress movement was prejudicial to Muslim interests and that the 'well-being of the people of India, and especially of the Mussalmans, lies in leading a quiet life under the benign rule of the English government'.[29] Beck's aim of bringing the Aligarh reformer to the centre of the political stage was a consummate success.

There is no denying Syed Ahmad's profound impact on north Indian Muslims. He was a visible symbol of Muslim regeneration, a catalyst of social and educational reforms, a 'Notre eminent contemporain,' as Gracin de Tassy called him. His political message also carried weight: hence the Congress overtures to court his support. But his influence was by no means all-pervasive, because his anti-Congress stance did not go down well with *all* his co-religionists.[30] The United Indian Patriotic Association and the Muhammadan Anglo-Oriental Defence Association were tame affairs. They petered out, despite much fanfare, within two years of their lazy existence. Mohamed Ali, an Aligarh graduate, recalled how Syed Ahmad, his British patrons, and the college trustees got together to pass a resolution against the Congress and had it published in the *Pioneer* and the *Aligarh Institute Gazette*. 'That was all that the Mussalmans would do in those days in the field of politics'.[31]

Sustained and organized opposition to the Congress was generally confined to Aligarh and its neighbouring districts; elsewhere, there were enough Muslims who were unmoved by Syed Ahmad's political exhortations. In 1887, seventy Muslims from Awadh attended the Madras Congress. Of the 222 Muslims gathered at the Allahabad Congress a year later, ninety came from Allahabad and Lucknow districts.[32] In 1889, 254 Muslims turned up in Bombay, of whom 125 were from Delhi and UP. At least some of them were inspired by a *fatwa*, signed by over a hundred *ulama*, in support of the Congress and in opposition to the Patriotic Association. The signatories included Rashid Ahmad Gangohi, Mahmud Hasan, and several other eminent Deobandi ulama.[33] The fatwa, published under the title *Nusrat-al-Abraar*, received wide publicity. It served as a political manifesto for the succeeding generations of the ulama at Deoband.

Aligarh's first generation students, brought up under Syed Ahmad's benign influence and tutored incessantly on the virtues of loyalty to the raj, were not all cut out of same cloth. His Lucknow and Meerut speeches drew no applause from several Aligarh students, including Syed Nabiullah and Rafique, soon to be a Cambridge graduate after a brief stint with the Lucknow paper, *Advocate*. The Meerut outburst, according to another Aligarh graduate, Inayatullah, 'smacked of flattery'.[34] Rafique was equally forthright in his rebuttal. 'The prospect of a united India', he observed in one of his inspired moods, 'does seem at first utopian and impracticable. But it is an object worth striving for'.[35] In a similar vein, though with greater incisiveness, Mir Mohamed Husain told Beck in April 1888:

> As long as you talk to me about the interests of Muslims alone I won't listen to you. I will only look to the interests of the country. And by the country I mean these 90 per cent of poor peasants who live from hand to mouth. Every effort should be made to improve their condition. How? Not by trying to get more appointments for Muslims, but by trying to improve the material condition of the country—its industry and commerce. If you stir up ill-will between Hindus and Muslims you will ruin the country.... The Anglo-Indians don't like two things—union amongst us, and the improvement of material conditions.... We should have joined the Congress and opposed their bad schemes. We should have directed the attention of the Congress on improving the material prosperity of the country and bettering the conditions of these poor peasants.[36]

This was 'subversive' talk by men who, in Beck's assessment, had 'gobbled up the radicalism of England and of Young Bengal'.[37] But neither he nor the sage from Aligarh could quite foresee the course of events which would slowly but steadily lead the young English-educated Muslims, especially those trained at Aligarh, to clamour for a reordering of political priorities and autonomy of political action. The anguished successors of Syed Ahmad watched helplessly as some of Aligarh's brilliant products—Mohamed Ali, Hasrat Mohani, Zafar Ali Khan, Shaukat Ali, Raja

Ghulam Husain, Ghulam-us-Saqlain[38], and Wilayat Ali Bambooque[39]—moved into the political arena with a fresh disposition, a distinct style of politics, and a new ideological orientation. The Ali brothers—Mohamed and Shaukat—both graduates of the Aligarh college, villified Beck and his successors[40] and were at pains to establish that the radical temper of their comrades was consistent with the intentions of their mentor, Syed Ahmad. Mohamed Ali announced in an Urdu verse:

> It is you who had taught the community all this 'mischief'
> If we are its culmination, you are its commencement

Out of 1,620 individuals from UP who signed the roll as delegates to the annual Congress sessions from 1885 to 1901, 596, or slightly over one-third, were Muslims from UP [...], the province where Syed Ahmad is supposed to have exercized the greatest of influence. Their strength increased steadily from 8 per cent in 1886 to high-points of 42 per cent in 1889 and 55 per cent in 1890.[41] The delegates included members of the dispossessed nawabi elite, newspaper editors like Munshi Sajjad Husain, editor of *Oudh Punch*, and a mixed group of teachers, lawyers, bankers, and traders. Connected with secular-oriented organizations like the Rifah-i Am and the Anjuman-i Muhammadi, many of them had close cultural and professional links with Congress leaders in Lucknow and Allahabad. [...]

Six-tenths of all Muslim delegates from 1886 to 1901 came from Lucknow, the city where the composite, cross-communal traditions continued to ensure a broad secularity in public life. When the Congress met at Allahabad in 1888 and 1892, Lucknow had more Muslim delegates in attendance than the host city. There were 313 Muslims at the 1899 Congress and 288 came from Lucknow itself [...]. It was the largest Muslim attendance at any annual session before 1916.

[...]

Next to Lucknow, Allahabad, the 'city with its hoary traditions, inspiring memories, sacred associations [and] high intellectual reputation',[42] elected one-fifth of the Muslim delegates. They included some small zamindars from Daryabad, poverty-stricken Shia dependents of the old royal house of Awadh, and a group of lawyers led by Abdul Majid and Abdur Rauf who were closely tied to Ajudhia Nath Kunzru.[43] In general, however, the Shias were more numerous in the Muslim delegation. It is surprising that this was so. Their population was small, the level of political consciousness was low and, above all, there was no institutional or organizational structures to sustain their political concerns.

Their sudden, active interest in Congress affairs can only be explained in terms of their rift with the Sunnis over the *Madhe Sahaba* issue, which gripped so many cities of UP in the last quarter of the nineteenth century.[44]

Shia leaders in Allahabad and Lucknow turned to the Congress to defend their right to take out *tazia* processions and exercise control over their endowments. They seized the initiative and, in November 1888, a Khoja Muslim from Bombay, Mohammad Ali Bhimji, was invited to address a pro-Congress Shia gathering. Sunni leaders were not to be outmanoeuvred. Maulana Mohamed Husain of the Diara Shah Hujatullah, already won over by the Syed Ahmad–Beck combine, launched a counter-attack.[45] The Congress in UP was caught up in the crossfire between the Shia zealots and the Sunni orthodox opinion. Appearing to be impartial in the deepening sectarian controversies was the only way to ensure the balance of its support. Increasingly, however, Shia–Sunni conflicts, which erupted in the years 1937 to 1939, imposed severe strains on Congress' ability to maintain an equilibrium in its relationship with the two rival sects.

The social profile of Muslim Congressmen in Bengal and Punjab[46] was no different from other regions of British India. They were urban-based and connected with various professions, such as journalism and law. Shared professional experience, besides removing mutual prejudices which often stemmed from social distancing, provided the stimulus for acting in unison on contemporary political issues. This is illustrated by the career of Abdul Rasul, a prominent Congress leader in Bengal. He went to St John's College, Oxford, and was called to the Bar from the Middle Temple. On his return to India, he enrolled himself as a barrister of the Calcutta High Court, where he came in contact with leading lawyers like W.C. Bonnerjee and Lal Mohan Ghose and was much inspired by their political activities. Likewise, the social background of Abdul Halim Ghuznavi and Abdul Kaseem, founder of *Mussalman*, was decidedly important in the making of their ideological orientation. It helps to understand why they, along with Liakat Hossain, Hassan Jan, and other Muslims, marched with the opponents of the partition of Bengal and joined heart and soul in the swadeshi *tehrik*.[47]

In western India, Badruddin Tyabji, a Sulaimani Bohra, was the prized trophy of the Congress. His father Tyab Ali was not born with a silver spoon but made a neat fortune through his matrimonial links with an affluent trading family. He did not have the benefit of studying in an English school or college but saw the advantage of educating his sons in England. [...]

Tyab Ali was a devout Muslim, though not one to harp on Hindu–Muslim differences. Badruddin Tyabji was no different. His association with the London Indian Society and the East Indian Association provide enough clues to his cosmopolitan outlook and political inclinations.[48] In 1882 he was given a place on the legislative council to represent graduates and lawyers and not simply the Muslims. And in 1885 Badruddin became one of the founders of the Bombay Presidency Association which that December played host to the first Congress. Here, as elsewhere, he worked, along with two other members of the 'trio'—Pherozeshah Mehta and K.T. Telang—'not as Hindus, Mahomedans and Parsis but as soldiers in the public cause'.[49]

Given his background and concerns, Badruddin Tyabji was the obvious person to spearhead the Congress movement. It is, therefore, not surprising that W.C. Bonnerjee insisted that his friend from student days in England occupy the presidential chair at the Second Congress, and the Congress Standing Committee unhesitatingly declared in November 1887 that Badruddin was 'not only the best, but the only possible man for the post'.[50] What was surprising was how quickly his election provoked a counter-reaction. Syed Ahmad was angered. He chose the occasion of Badruddin's presidency to come out publicly against the Congress.

Badruddin rebutted the views of Syed Ahmad. The Congress, he said, should be allowed to play the major role in aggregating the Muslims' articulated interests and that Muslims could by united action confine Congress to such issues as they deemed safe for discussion. On 18 February 1888 he wrote:

My policy, therefore, would be to act from *within* rather than from *without*....
We should thus advance the general progress of India, and at the same time safeguard our own interests.[51]

Many Muslims, Badruddin claimed, recognized this and supported the Congress. Those who did not was because of 'certain special, local and temporary causes', which applied 'only to a particular part of India'.[52]

Syed Ahmad Khan did not think so. There was no such thing as 'the general progress of India' or 'India as one nation'. The different castes and creeds, he told Badruddin in January 1888, did not belong to a nation and their aims and aspirations were also not the same. 'You regard', he continued, 'the doings of the misnamed National Congress as beneficial to India, but I am sorry to say that I regard them as not only injurious to our own community but also to India at large'.[53] Small but significant gatherings of Muslims in Bombay endorsed Syed Ahmad's line of reasoning rather than Badruddin's plea for Muslim participation in Congress.[54] In October 1888, a dejected Badruddin suggested that the Congress activities be suspended for five years because 'an overwhelming majority of Mohammedans is against the [Congress] movement'.[55] Nobody took the suggestion seriously. And nobody ever agreed with Badruddin's assessment of Muslim hostility. For once the future judge of the Bombay High Court had spoken too soon.

It is worth reiterating the several different ways in which Muslims related themselves to developments around their immediate and distant surroundings. Admittedly, there was some talk of 'Muslim solidarity' and some half-hearted endeavours to steer the political discourse around religious lines, but neither Syed Ahmed nor his compatriots could translate their objectives in any tangible form. Diverse regional and local concerns, conflicting class interests and sectarian animus sharpened cleavages and impeded the growth of an all-India Muslim political consciousness. In fact, no amount of pious exhortations could bridge the wide gulf that separated, say, the East Bengal Muslim peasant from the Muslim taluqdar in Awadh. By the end of the nineteenth century, all attempts to bring about 'some degree of solidarity among the disintegrated masses of Mahomedan society' failed to achieve any measure of success.

No summing up of late-nineteenth century trends can, however, be complete without reference to the spurt in cow-protection activity and the strident demand for securing recognition of the Nagri script in government and law courts.[56] These were not isolated assertions of militant, religio-revivalist tendencies but were outward manifestations of the new and burgeoning sense of Hindu consciousness. There were similar trends among Muslims. The Graeco-Turkish War of 1897 stimulated pan-Islamic feelings.[57] Islamization in Bengal and parts of upper India, inspired by the Waliullahi traditions and bolstered by the success of the Faraizi ideology, was an equally important force. Insistence on a revitalized Islamic consciousness and identity, with its corresponding denigration of Islam's local roots, was beginning to erode the syncretistic traditions and undermine inter-religious peace and understanding.[58] The massive communal rioting in the summer of 1893 was a grim reminder to the nationalists that the fabric of Hindu–Muslim unity was too fragile to withstand the onslaught of various revitalization movements. 'If the smouldering fire of religious enmity...is not put out', warned an observer, 'it will before long be kindled into a mighty flame and destroy the noble edifice which the Congress has built up with so much pains'.[59]

The prophecy did not come true. Though relations between Hindus and Muslims were sometimes strained, their deterioration was neither deep nor irreversible. 'Nothing strikes the intelligent traveller in India more forcibly', observed a senior police official, 'than the friendly and peaceable attitude of all castes and classes towards each other'.[60] He was right. Communal friction was not ordinarily a major source of civil disturbance in the last quarter of the nineteenth century. During the quinquennium, 1889–94, there was no communal violence in Bengal, except one in Calcutta and its suburbs.[61] Such sporadic outbursts did not signify, as some writers are wont to suggest, the fragmentation of Indian society along communal lines. Intercommunity tensions and conflicts were counterposed to the quiet, commonplace routines in which Hindus and Muslims intermingled without notice or incident and could still be found involved in a range of 'religiously promiscuous' practices. In 1909, the *Imperial Gazetteer of India* stated that 'it was, until recently, the regular practice of low-class Muhammadans to join in the Durga Puja and other festivals'; it mentioned Muslim consultation of Hindu almanacs, worship of Sithala and Manasa, use of vermilion, and joint offerings to village deities before the sowing or transplanting of rice seedlings.[62] Another inspiring legitimation of the more mundane expression of peaceful coexistence came daily in the sounds of Muslim *shahnai* players joining in the *arti* at Hindu temples, including the arti at the most sacred Vishwanath temple in Banaras.[63]

Contemporary writings took note of cordial Hindu–Muslim relations, highlighting the ongoing process of social and cultural fusion.[64] The poet Mohammad Iqbal shared the vision of a united India—one that was free of both alien domination and inner dissensions. In 'Sayyid's Tomb', he called his land of birth as a garden, and the people inhabiting it as members of a *qaum* (nation), with the two circles of Islam and *watan* intersecting and at several places coalescing into a coherent whole. *Himala*, the first poem in *Bang-i Dara*, was inspired by the beauty of the land of his birth, while *Hindustani Bachhon ka Qaumi Geet* (National Anthem of Indian Children) and the *Tarana-i Hindi* (The Song of India) were refined, buoyant, and non-communal expressions of patriotic sentiments.[65] In *Naya Shiwala* (New Temple), he chided both Hindus and Muslims for their narrow mental horizon,[66] and appealed to the keepers of the temple and the mosque to foster mutual goodwill and understanding.[67] Indeed, Iqbal echoed, in large measure, the ideology of secular nationalism.

Akbar Allahabadi, a merciless satirist equipped with an irrepressible sense of humour, had similar concerns. He subjected to ridicule, to scathing criticism or damning exposure the social and political strategy of imperialism and Syed Ahmad's policy of loyal co-operation with the government.[68] And, like Iqbal, he championed Hindu–Muslim unity. Both Hindus and Muslims, he said, have to bear the blows of those who wield the rod of worldly power, but they should respond by being like water, on which the blows of a rod have only a momentary effect.[69]

Iqbal and Akbar were stating the obvious. They recognized, as indeed did others, that the direction in which patronage, economic welfare, and authority flowed in everyday life indicated the continuing importance of cross-communal networks.[70] Syed Ahmad's Aligarh project was backed by Hindus and Muslims alike.[71] He encouraged, despite his misgivings over the Nagri agitation, a Hindu–Muslim *entente* in culture and religious matters. His contemporary, Ajudhia Nath Kunzru, owed his fortunes as much to the wealthy Muslim landholders as to his extensive banking and commission agencies.[72] In east UP and Awadh generally, the dominant factor in the politics of the towns tended to be an Urdu-speaking elite connection based on landed interests. Communal matters did not always foul the path of politics.[73]

The competing units in early municipal politics were multi-factions, not antagonistic communal groups. In the composition of early municipal factions, conflicting caste and communal considerations played a secondary role to personal rivalries and connections. A Muslim lawyer, Maulvi Serajul Islam, was elected from Chittagong to the Bengal legislative council, largely on the Hindu vote. Surendranath Banerjea, on the other hand, was backed by Muslims for a seat on the prestigious Calcutta Corporation.[74] Around the same time, a similar move was afoot in UP, where the Congress backed Hamid Ali Khan for a seat in the council.

Nor did communal divisions last long after they had been politicized. Soon after the violent eruptions in 1893, tempers began to cool everywhere and there was much display of 'mutual love and affection' in the riot-torn cities of UP.[75] Public statements and newspaper editorials on national unity and the commonality of Hindu–Muslim interests were matched by strenuous efforts of local reconciliation committees to resolve and diffuse tensions.[76] When asked how the 'upper classes' of the two communities behaved when riots occur, the Assistant Magistrate of Gorakhpur replied:

By taking leading Hindus and Muslims into confidence, matters are satisfactorily arranged.... In Aligarh, we left the whole matter to leading Hindus and Muhammadans and everything went off without hitch.[77]

Such was the pattern everywhere, reinforcing the view that, by the end of the nineteenth century, there was no sign of Hindus and Muslims going their separate ways. If anything, the lines of cleavages in north India were more sharply drawn between the Sunnis and the Shias rather than Hindus and Muslims.[78] Though expressed in exaggerated terms, there is merit is the observations of W.S. Blunt and Henry Cotton that Hindu–Muslim animus was accentuated only after the government decided to pursue the principle of divide and rule with vigour.[79]

NOTES

1. There is evidence of considerable mutual antipathy between the so-called Muslim leaders. In Bengal, for example, Ameer Ali and Abdul Latif hurled mutual accusations at each other. W.S. Blunt, who was in India in 1883–4, recorded that Latif criticized Ameer Ali for having 'broken with the mass of the community by affecting English dress and ways, and posing as reformers, although they were in no way qualified in a religious sense for such a position'. W.S. Blunt, *India Under Ripon: A Private Dairy*, London, 1909, p. 97.
2. *Hindu*, 16 January 1888.
3. *Report of the Public Service Commission, 1886–7*, Calcutta, 1888, vol. 4, pp. 196, 201, 262–8. A common grudge was that Muslims had limited chances of representation on local bodies, because franchise extended only to those who fulfilled property, wealth, and educational qualifications. Thus in 1875–6, six of the 25 Indians on local bodies were Muslims. They fared still more poorly in the triennial election to the Calcutta municipality, held in 1897; there were only six Muslims as against 37 Hindus. *Administrative Report on the Municipality of the Suburbs of Calcutta 1875–6*, Calcutta, 1876, p. 6; *Statement Exibiting the Moral and Material Progress of India, 1897–8*, p. 6.
4. Ibid., p. 162.
5. *Najmul Akhbaar* (Etawah), 24 March 1890; *Jubilee Paper* (Lucknow) and *Azad* (Lucknow), 1 April 1890; *Mihir-i Nimroz* (Bijnor), 7 May 1890, Selections from the Native Newspaper Reports (hereafter SNNR), UP, 1890.
6. *Aligarh Institute Gazette*, 12 September 1896.
7. For a summary of various interpretations, C.W. Troll, *Sayyid Ahmad Khan: A Reinterpretation of Muslim Theology*, Delhi, 1978.
8. Maulvi Mohammad Imamuddin (ed.), *Mukammal Majmuah wa Speeches*, Lahore, 1901, pp. 197–8.
9. J.M.S. Baljon, *Reforms and Religious Ideas of Sir Sayyid Ahmad Khan*, Leiden, 1949, p. 36.

10. Iqbal Ali (ed.), *Sayyid Saheb ka Safarnama-i Punjab*, Lahore, 1979, pp. 140–67.

11. Hafeez Malik, *Sir Sayyid Ahmad Khan and Muslim Modernization in India and Pakistan*, New York, 1980, p. 240; and Hardy, *Muslims of British India*, London, 1972, p. 136.
    [...]

12. Anil Seal, *Emergence of Indian Nationalism*, Cambridge, 1968 p. 319; David Lelyveld, *Aligarh's First Generation Muslim Solidarity in British India*, Princeton, 1978, p. 305. Notice the following comment by a 'Muslim: A Political Observer': 'Do not his writings and his whole political conduct of the pre-Congress days show that he had himself been an advocate of what the Congress demanded later on—the full recognition of our political rights? What was his position with regard to the Ilbert Bill?... Above all, had he not written the 'Causes of the Indian Revolt' in which he traced the origin of the Mutiny to the shortsighted policy (of) the British?... Was he not in one sense the creator of the 'spirit' that found its culmination in the Congress movement?'
    'The Indian Muhammadans and the National Congress', *Kayastha Samachar*, Allahabad, November 1902, vol. 6, no.5 (New Series), p. 392.

13. S. Banerjea, *A Nation in Making*, Calcutta, 1963, reprint, p. 45.

14. It has been argued that the ideological basis of Syed Ahmad's opposition to Indian nationalism had been clearly articulated well before either Beck or the Congress had appeared on the scene. This view is based on Syed Ahmad's speech on the local self-government bill of the Central Provinces, delivered in January 1833. See Lelyveld, *Aligarh's First Generation*, p. 311, and, Francis Robinson, *Separatism among Indian Muslims*, Cambridge, 1974, p. 110.

15. Ibid., 3 May 1888. Theodore Beck letter to his mother, Beck Papers, India Office Library And Records (hereafter IOLR).

16. Ibid., 28 March and 20 September 1888.

17. Lelyveld, Aligarh's First Generation, p. 220.

18. To his mother, 24 April 1888, Beck Papers.

19. Ibid., 28 March 1888.

20. Ibid., 28 April 1888.

21. Beck to Syed Ahmad, 13 February 1890, F. No. 69/10, AMUA. To his mother, 3 June 1888, Beck papers.

22. To his mother, 28 August 1888. He also mobilized Syed Ahmad to get a petition signed by Muslims against the Braudlaugh's Bill of Indian Councils (1889). To his father, 25 February 1890, Beck Papers.

23. Beck referred to a meeting with UP's lieutenant-government at which he discussed the Congress agitation. He was 'immensely flattered' at the reception he received and 'felt myself quite a big man, discussing the affairs of state with the King of the province'. Two years later, he went up to Shimla to meet Lansdowne and discussed the 'official encouragement'

given to the Congress in some circles. To his mother, 3 June 1888, 16 June 1890, ibid.

24. Ibid., 20 September 1888.
25. Ibid., 10 April 1888.
26. Beck was alarmed to notice that the Syed was inclined to 'take matters too calmly' and that he was not keen to prosecute the anti-Congress movement. A few months later, he complained to his mother that the Syed did not attach 'sufficient importance to educate the community in sound political thought'. 24 April and 20 September 1888, ibid.
27. Ibid., 28 April 1888.
28. Ibid.
29. *Aligarh Institute Gazette*, 18 September 1897.
30. For criticism of his political views in a section of the Urdu press, Prem Narain, *Press and Politics in India, 1885–1905*, Delhi, 1970, pp. 83, 92–4. Speeches of Muslim Congressmen like Maulvi Hidayat Rasul, Nawab Reza Khan, Hamid Ali Khan, Maulvi Syed-Sharfuddin, and Shaikh Kadir Buksh are reproduced in A.M. Zaidi (ed.), *The Muslim School of Congress*, Delhi, 1987, pp. 345–50, 358–64.
31. Mushirul Hasan (ed.), *Mohamed Ali in India Politics: Select Writings*, Delhi, 1982, vol. 1, p. 32.
32. J.L. Hill, 'Congress and Representative Institutions in the United Provinces 1886–1901' (Unpublished Ph.D. thesis, Duke University, 1969).
33. Husain Ahmad Madani, *Naqsh-i Hayaat: Khudnawisht Sawaanih*, Karachi, 1979 edn, pp. 481–2; I.H. Qureshi, *Ulama in Politics*, Karachi, 1974, p. 227. Allan Octavian Hume boasted that in Punjab 'we are sweeping Sir Syed away.... The Ludhiana Maulvis have the absolute command of over 40,000 Muslims'. To Tyabji, 5 November 1888, Tyabji Papers.
34. Beck to his mother, 3 April 1888, Beck Papers.
35. Ibid., 10 February 1888.
36. Beck Papers, 5 March 1888.
37. Ibid.
38. He was at the Aligarh college from October 1889 to April 1894, where he developed a keen interest in nationalist affairs. In January 1903 he started the *Asr-i Jadeed* from Meerut, a paper with nationalist concerns. The paper ceased publication in December 1908 on account of the illness of Ghulam-us-Saqlain.
39. Wilayat Ali was born in 1887 in Masauli village in Barabanki district. He belonged to the Kidwai clan, which traced its descent to Kidwatuddin who came to India in the wake of the Ghorid invasion of north India. He was educated at the Aligarh college and was a contemporary of Syed Mahmud, Khaliquzzaman, Shuaib Qureshi, and Raja Ghulam Husain. His humorous sketches were credited with literary excellence. In July 1918, Wilayat Ali, popularly known as 'Bambooque', was stricken with cholera. Dr M.A. Ansari rushed to his bedside in Barabanki but could not save his life.

40. Margaret H. Case, 'The Aligarh Era: Muslim Politics in North India 1860–1910' (Unpublished PhD thesis, Chicago, 1970), p. 179.
41. J.L. Hill, 'Congress and Representative Institutions ...', p. 41, fn. 41.
42. MSS. EUR. E.251/3, Hallet Papers, IOLR.
43. They addressed several public meetings with Kunzru who was their senior colleague at the Allahabad bar. *Tribune*, 22 February 1888.
44. Mushirul Hasan, 'Sectarianism in Indian Islam: The Shia-Sunni Divide in the United Provinces', *The Indian Economic and Social History Review*, vol. 27, no. 2, p. 90; J.R.I. Cole. *Roots of North Indian Shiism in Iran and Iraq*; *Religion and State in Awadh, 1722–1889*, Delhi, 1989.
45. C.A. Bayly, *The Local Roots of Indian Politics—Allahabad, 1880–1920*, Oxford, 1975, p. 130. Beck noted that the Maulvi, 'a Man of great learning and piety' was drawn into the anti-Congress movement by Syed Ahmad's speeches and by the agitation against cow slaughter. Expressing satisfaction at Maulvi Mohamed Husain's presence at an anti-Congress rally in Allahabad, Beck observed: 'I think the National Congress is doing the Muslims a lot of good. These meetings are infusing spirit into the community and inducing it to shake off its fatal stagnation'. To his mother, 2 March 1888, Beck Papers.
46. Some of the important Congressmen in Punjab were: Muharram Ali Chishti, Syed Nadir Ali Shah, Hakim Ahmad Ali, and Munshi Nabi Baksh, editors of *Rafiq-i Hind, Rehbar-i Hind, Takmilul Hikmat*, and *Koh-i Noor*, respectively. Among the prominent lawyers associated with the organization were Shaikh Umar Baksh and his brother Nabi Baksh. They headed the district Congess committees of Hoshiarpur and Gurdaspur. See *Tribune*, 14 October, 25 November, and 13 December 1893. In general, however, there was not much enthusiasm for the Congress in Punjab. K.W. Jones has explained why this was so. In the case of some groups, such as the militant Arya Samajists, the Congress appeared pro-Muslim. This impression was confirmed when the Congress Subjects Committee decided to drop the discussion on the Punjab Alienation Act from the agenda as a concession to the feelings of Punjabi Muslims. Soon thereafter, plans were set afoot to organize an exclusively 'Hindu' body. According to Jones, the provincial world appeared far more real and relevant than the wider sphere of the Congress and national issues. Instead of national politics, factional struggles and communal competition commanded far greater attention. K.W. Jones, *Arya Dharm: Hindu Consciousness in 19th Century Punjab*, Berkeley, 1976; pp. 241–50, 254–5; N.G. Barrier, 'The Arya Samaj and Congress Politics in the Punjab 1894–1908', *Journal of Asian Studies*, vol. 26, May 1967.
47. Sumit Sarkar, *Swadeshi Movement in Bengal, 1903–08*, Delhi, 1973, pp. 426–35; Jayanti Maitra, *Muslim Politics in Bengal 1885–1906: Collaboration and Confrontation*, Calcutta, 1984, pp. 244–6, 249–50.
48. In London, Tyabji was among those who rallied round Dadabhai Naoroji to found the London India Society.

49. A.G. Noorani, *Badruddin Tyabji*, Delhi, 1969, p. 132.
50. Hume to Tyabji, 3 December 1887, Tyabji Papers.
51. Tyabji to Ameer Ali, 3 December 1887, ibid.
52. *Report of the Indian National Congress*, 1887, p. 72
53. Syed Ahmad to Tyabji, 24 January 1888, Tyabji Papers.
54. *Rast Goftar* and *Kaside Mumbai*, 12 August 1888; *Parsi Punch*, 19 August 1888, SNNR, Bombay.
55. Tyabji to Hume, 27 October 1888, Tyabji Papers.
56. John R. Mclane, *Indian Nationalism and the Early Congress*, Princeton, New Jersey, 1977, pp. 271–331, for an insightful account of the cow-protection movement. See Robinson, *Separatism*, pp. 66–78, for a sensitive portrayal of Hindu revivalist tendencies, including the development of the Hindi–Urdu conflict and the campaign for Hindi. The Hindi–Urdu controversy is also discussed in: Aziz Ahmad, *Islamic Culture in the Indian Environment*, Oxford, 1969, pp. 259–62; Paul Brass, *Language, Religion and Politics in North India*, London, 1974, pp. 127–38, and Jyotirindra Das Gupta, *Language Conflict and National Development: Group Politics and National Language Policy in India*, Berkeley, 1970, ch. 4.
57. Subscriptions were raised at Kanpur in aid of Turkey, prayers were offered at Jhansi and Agra for the success of the Khalifa, who was commonly described as the *Khalifat al-Muslimeen* in contemporary newspapers. An indication of the depth of Muslim feelings is reflected in the bitter criticism of Syed Ahmad's views on pan-Islamism. *Zamanah* (Kanpur), 13 May 1897, *Nasim-i Agra* (Agra), 22 May 1897, *Akhbaar-i Islam* (Agra), 23 May 1897, *Azad* (Lucknow), 4 June 1897, *Shahna-i Hind*, 1 July 1897, *Riaz al-Akhbaar*, 4 July 1897, *Naiyar-i Azam* (Moradabad), 5 February 1900, *Jami al-ulum* (Moradabad), 14 February 1900, SNNR, UP.
58. Asim Roy, The *Islamic Syncretistic Tradition in Bengal*, Princeton, 1983, p. 251, and Rafiuddin Ahmad, *The Bengal Muslims 1871–1906: A Quest for Identity*, Delhi, 1996, p. 184; S.M. Ikram, *Muslim Civilization in India*, London, 1964, pp. 282–6.
59. *Al-Waqt*, Gorakhpur, 21/26 February 1894, SNNR, UP.
60. T.C. Arthur, *Reminiscences of an Indian Police Official*, London, 1894, p. 145. English and Indian witnesses before the Public Service Commission testified to the harmonious relations between the Hindus and Muslims and took serious note of the cross-communal links. *PSC*, NWP & O Sub-commission, Calcutta, 1888, pp. 15, 23, 26.
61. Rajat Kanta Ray, *Social Conflict and Political Unrest in Bengal 1875–1927*, Delhi, 1984, p. 121. The Commissioner of Dacca noted the 'extraordinary fact' that in five years 'not a single riot of any description should have occurred'.
62. *Imperial Gazetteer of India*, pp. 48–9.
63. Judy, F. Pugh, 'Divination and Ideology in the Banaras Muslim Community', Katherine P. Ewing (ed.), *Shariat and Ambiguity in South Asian Islam*, Berkeley, 1988, p. 289.

64. For instance, Syed Ahmad Dehlavi, *Rasum-i Delhi*, Delhi, 1905, pp. 37–41, and for comments and reactions of Asaduilah Khan Ghalib, see Percival Spear, 'Ghalib's Delhi', Ralph Russell (ed.), *Ghalib: The Poet and His Age*, London, 1977, p. 49. Again, for Hindu–Muslim relations in Delhi, see C.F. Andrews, *Zakaullah of Delhi*, Cambridge, n.d., pp. 11, 15–17.

65. See the collection of essays in Hafeez Malik (ed.), *Iqbal: Poet-Philosopher of Pakistan*, Columbia University Press, 1971.

66. I' ll tell you truth, Oh Brahmin, if I may make so bold!
    Those idols in your temples—these idols have grown old;
    To hate your-mortals is all they teach you, while
    Our God too sets his preachers to scold and revile;
    Sickened, from both your temple and our shrine I have seen,
    Alike our preachers' sermons and your fond myths I shun.
    In every garden image you fancied God: I see
    In every speck of my country's poor dust, divinity.
        V.G. Kiernan, *Poems from Iqbal*, Karachi, 2004, p. 8.

67. Come, let us remove all that causes estrangement,
    Let us reconcile those that have turned away from
    each other, remove all signs of division.
    Desolation has reigned for long in the
    habitation of my heart:—
    Come, let us build a new temple in our land.
        M. Mujeeb, *The Indian Muslims*, London, 1967, p. 485.

68. Ibid., p. 477.

69. I say the same to Hindus and to Muslims:
    Be good, each as your faith would have you be.
    The world's a rod? Then *you* become as water.
    Clash like the waves, but still remain one wave.
        Ralph Russell and Khurshidul Islam, 'The Satirical verse of Akbar Illahabadi (1846–1921)', *MAS (Modern Asian Studies)*, 1974, vol. 8, no. 1, pp. 44–6.

70. D.A. Washbrook, *The Emergence of Provincial Politics. The Madras Presidency, 1870–1920*, Cambridge, 1976, pp. 143–4, 262.

71. For example, one Sita Narain, a barrister at Rajkot, donated Rs 45,000 to the Aligarh college and Rs 16,000 to the Central Hindu College at Banaras. *Al-Bashir*, 24 February 1901.SNNR, UP.

72. Henry Sender, *The Kashmiri Pandits: A Study of Cultural Choice in North India*, Delhi, 1988, p. 244.

73. Robinson, *Separatism*, p. 79.

74. Ray, *Social Conflict*, pp. 41, 131–2.

75. The years 1897 to 1900 may well be regarded as a period of exceptionally cordial Hindu–Muslim relations in most parts of the country. This was, in part, attributed to the combination of the two communities against plague measures. 'Let the people', stated the *Jami al-ulum* (Moradabad) of 21 March 1897, 'welcome the return of the plague to India a thousand

NATIONALIST MOVEMENT IN INDIA

times, were it for the purpose of effecting a union among them. The government was alarmed by the combination. Elgin's private secretary apprehended that 'if Hindus and Muslims were forced into active opposition (against the plague measures), the combination between them might be perpetuated and might assume a dangerous from'. Quoted in Ray, *Social Conflict*, p. 118.

76. For example, *Ria al-Akhbaar* (Gorakhpur), 8 January 1894; *Nagari Nirad* (Hindi weekly: Mirzapur), 8 February 1894; *Mehr-i Nimroz* (Urdu weekly: Bijnor), 7 February 1894, and *Hindustani* (Lucknow), 19 December 1894. For references to local reconciliation committees and to public meetings on Hindu–Muslim amity in UP and Punjab, see *Hindustani*, 8 June 1898, *Oudh Punch*, 9 June 1898; *Akhbaar-i Alam* (Meerut), 13 June 1898, *Raiz al-Akhbaar*, 1 November 1898, *Anis-i Hind* (Meerut), 2 November 1898, SNNR, UP.

77. *PSC*, NWP & O, Evidence, p. 158.

78. See Mushirul Hasan, 'Sectarianism in Indian Islam: The Shia-Sunni Divide in the United Provinces', *The Indian Economic and Social History Review*, vol. 27, no. 2, p. 90; J.R.I. Cole, *Roots of North Indian Shiism in Iran and Iraq; Religion and State in Awadh, 1722–1889*, Delhi, 1989.

79. Henry Cotton, *India and Home Memoirs*, London, 1911, p. 317; Blunt, *India Under Ripon*, p. 94.

13 Exploding Communalism*
The Politics of Muslim Identity in South Asia

Ayesha Jalal

Farewell O Hindustan, O autumnless garden
We your homeless guests have stayed too long

Laden though we are today with complaints
The marks of your past favors are upon us still

You treated stranger like relations
We were guests but you made us the hosts
...

You gave us wealth, government and dominion
For which of your many kindnesses should we express gratitude

But such hospitality is ultimately unsustainable
All that you gave you kept in the end

Well, one has a right to one's own property
Take it from whoever you want, give it to whoever you will

Pull out our tongues the very instant
They forgetfully utter a word of complaint about this

But the complaint is that what we brought with us
That too you took away and turned us into beggars
...

You've turned lions into lowly beings, O Hind
Those who were Afghan hunters came here to become the hunted ones

We had foreseen all these misfortunes
When we came here leaving our country and friends

* Originally published in Sugata Bose and Ayesha Jalal (eds), *Nationalism, Democracy and Development: State and Politics in India*, Delhi, Oxford University Press, 1997, pp. 76–103. In the present version some portions of the text and notes have been removed. For the entire text see the original version.

We were convinced that adversity would befall us in time
And we O Hind would be devoured by you

...

So long as O Hindustan we were not called Hindi
We had some graces which were not found in others

...

You've made our condition frightening
We were fire O Hind, you've turned us into ash.[1]

Altaf Husain Hali (1837–1914) in the inimitable way captures the dilemma of Muslim identity as perceived by segments of the *ashraf* classes in nineteenth-century northern India. Steeped in nostalgia for Islam's past glories and a wry sense of the Muslim predicament, Hali's *Shikwa-e-Hind*, or complaint to India, cannot be dismissed as simply the bigoted laments of a man who has accepted social closure on grounds of religious difference and antipathy towards non-Muslims. To challenge Hali's questionable reading of the history of Islam in the subcontinent or his spurious representations of Indian Muslims in undifferentiated terms as descendants of foreign immigrants is to concentrate on the obvious and miss out the richness of the poetic nuances. What is instructive about the poem is how a committed Muslim with more than a surfeit of airs was hard pressed to deny the decisive and irreversible impact of India on his co-religionists. As the metaphor of fire to ashes makes clear, this is an assertion of a cultural identity, once distinctive but now all too faded. Hali's grievance is precisely the loss of distinctiveness which he believes had given Muslims a measure of dignity and humanity. Bereft of any qualities of friendship or fellowship, Muslims had become selfish, inward looking, indolent, and illiterate. None of this is the fault of India. Hali instead blames *qismat* which brought Islam to the subcontinent and made certain that, unlike the Greeks, the Muslims did not turn away from its frontiers in failure.

India without Islam is an ingenious idea. It would certainly have obviated the need for endless scholarly outpouring on communalism. But however much Muslims may take Hali's lead in blaming qismat, Islam in India, united or divided, is a fact of history and an intrinsic feature of the subcontinent's future. What is less clear is whether communalism should continue to serve as a descriptive or analytical clincher in representations of the Muslim past, present, and future in the South Asian subcontinent. [...] The original sin of being communalist for the most part has been reserved for the subcontinent's Muslims. Notwith-standing the compromises of secular nationalism with Hindu commu-nalism, the burden of this negative term in the history of late colonial India has fallen on the Muslim minority. The establishment of a Muslim state at the moment of the British withdrawal added immeasurably to the weight of the burden. [...] This asymmetry has expressed itself not only in state policy but also in secular academic discourse. Muslim minority 'communalism' has occupied a critical location in academic texts orga-nized around the binary opposition between secular nationalism and religious communalism. If this neat but misleading dichotomy is to be dismantled, the entire notion of a Muslim minority 'communalism' at the subcontinental level needs to be subjected to a probing analysis.

This task has become especially urgent since such an overarching and loaded term as communalism ends up essentializing the very religiously informed identities, politics, and conflicts it purportedly aims at explaining and combating. It is not as if this danger has escaped the attention of scholars engaged, as many of them have been, in disturbing and decentering notions of monolithic religious communities and singular identities.[2] What is remarkable, however, is the continued usage of a term in a debate which widely acknowledges communalism as at best the pejorative 'other' of nationalism and at worst a borrowing from the colonialist project of essentializing Indian society and history.[3] Even those who deploy it as a matter of convention, while inveighing against its analytical utility, have to concede that as the accepted designation for religiously based cultural identities, politics, ideology, or conflict, communalism lays emphasis on the peculiarly Indian aspects of what is a global problem of negotiating and accommodating social differences. Whether this compartmentalization of one of the subcontinent's most gnawing and lingering problems–the shifting politics of religiously informed identities-is not an unwitting form of academic communalism remains an open question.

This paper is an attempt to spot the blots in the historiographical discourse on Muslim communalism. While exploring the nexus of culture and political power the argument avoids presuppositions which erroneously link a religiously informed cultural identity with the politics of cultural nationalism. By contrasting the 'inevitability' of a Muslim iden-tity, variously defined, with the 'impossibility' of a supra-regional and specifically Muslim politics in the subcontinental context, the paper aims at demonstrating the largely arbitrary, derogatory, and exclusionary nature of the term 'communal' as it has been applied to individuals and political groupings claiming to represent the interests of Indian Muslims.

Such an argument requires a new typology of Muslim political thought, one that goes beyond the facile and rigid distinctions between 'liberals' or 'traditionalists', 'modernists' or 'anti-modernists', 'communalists' or 'secular nationalists'. The chronological starting point of the argument is the late nineteenth century when many of the salient features of a Muslim political discourse began to be worked out by members of the north Indian ashraf classes smarting under the loss of sovereignty on the one hand, and the onset of Western colonialism and 'modernity' on the other. Written in an accessible 'new' Urdu, the dissemination of the discourse was facilitated by a rapidly expanding print media. Popular among Muslim middle and upper classes in Muslim-majority provinces like the Punjab and, to a lesser degree, Bengal, the prose and poetry of this era bears the marks of the regional and class identity of its Muslim-minority province exponents. [...] By both historicizing and conceptualizing the twin issues of Muslim cultural difference and a Muslim politics, the purpose is to show why exploding communalism may not be a wit too late and is perhaps the only hope of genuinely rethinking and renegotiating the perennial problem of difference and identity in South Asia as a whole.

DIFFERENCE, EXCLUSIVISM, OR COMMUNALISM: THE LATE NINETEENTH AND EARLY TWENTIETH CENTURIES

A more than common preoccupation with their distinctive religious identity has been a feature shared by upper and middle class Muslims in the subcontinent, irrespective of their 'liberal', 'modernist', 'conservative', or 'anti-modernist' leanings. This sense of distinction from non-Muslims has led to the suggestion that 'communal consciousness' is an intrinsic, indeed a normative, part of the Muslim socio-religious and political world view. The elision of religious difference with an essentialized Indian Muslim community is explained in terms of the legitimizing ideals of Islamic solidarity and the necessary subordination of the individual will to the *ijma* or consensus of the community.[4] It is extraordinary, but also revealing, that a decidedly elitist discourse should be seen as not only reflective of Indian Muslims but also their 'communal consciousness'. The politics of Muslims identity in the subcontinent cannot be reduced to a mere rationalization of normative Islamic discourse. There is much variation even within this elite discourse, not all of which focused on the knotty issue of electoral representation, and still greater evidence of Muslim willingness to differ from rather than defer to the consensus of the community, however contrasted, in the rough and tumble of practical politics.

Before the 1920s when Congress' inclusionary secular nationalist paradigm gained wider currency, the assertion of difference even when bordering on cultural exclusivism did not automatically translate into Muslim 'separatism' or minority 'communalism'. Remarkable as it may seem from vantage point of today, Hali's *Shikwa-e-Hind* did not stir a public controversy over his, or for that matter his community's, putative lake of allegiance to India. This raises the cardinal question: were concerns about the Muslim community as a distinctive religious entity destined to keep the adherents of this perception on a separate, if parallel, track with those engaged in the project of invoking an inclusionary idea of a single Indian nation? Apparently not if one considers that in 1874 Hali himself had written feelingly in his poem *Hubb-i-Watan* or love of the motherland that a patriotism which went no further than mere attachment to the community was nothing short of selfishness. A true patriot was one who regarded all the inhabitants of India, whether Muslim, Hindu, Buddhist, or Brahmosamaj, as one:[5]

> If you want your country's well being
> Don't look upon any compatriot as a stranger[6]

Granted the range of moods that are the wont of a poet, there is no evident tension or contradiction in Hali's mind between an affinity to the people of India and pride in a selectively imagined and recreated Islamic past. Less inclined to glorify Islamic history but equally conscious of his Muslimness was Hali's mentor, Sayyid Ahmed Khan. Not a religious scholar by training, his rational approach to Islamic theology and law earned him the lacerating abuse of orthodox Muslim *ulema* bunched in the theological serminaries at Deoband and, less vociferously, Farangi Mahal in Lucknow.

The ulema were not alone in opposing Sayyid Ahmed's new-fangled views. His ardent promotion of Western Knowledge and culture as well as loyalty to the Raj drew acerbic comments from Muslims attached to their societal moors and the ideal of a universal Muslim *ummah*. Among Sayyid Ahmed's fiercest critics was the Persian Islamic scholar Jamaluddin al-Afghani who lived in India between 1879 and 1882 and called for Hindu–Muslim unity as the first step to dislodging British colonialism. The contest between Muslims moved by Islamic universalism and those for whom the immediacy of the colonial context constituted the overwhelming reality was to be played out on the political stage during the first few decades of the twentieth century.

For now it was Sayyid Ahmed's policy which held sway. The Aligarh movement which he fathered became the source of modernist and rational thinking among the Muslim elite and, ironically enough, also provided the catalyst for later day Muslim political 'separatism' and 'communalism'. By contrast, his more culturally exclusive Muslim opponents, harbouring anti-colonial and Islamic universalist sentiments, immersed themselves in religious strictures at traditional educational institutions like *madrassahs* and *maktabs* only to end up squarely on the side of an inclusionary and 'secular' Indian nationalism. Identifying the twisted knots in these two contending and overlapping strands in Muslim thinking highlights the curiosity that passes for minority 'communalism' in subcontinental history.

Unabashedly elitist in his thinking, Sayyid Ahmed has been hailed as the author of the notorious 'two nation' theory by the officially subsidized historians of Pakistan and condemned for being the evil genius who helped carve out a separate niche for India's Muslims within the sphere of colonial policy and political discourse. Yet despite his resolute stance against the Indian National Congress, Sayyid Ahmed was more concerned with dissuading his fellow Muslims from the plague of religious bigotry. Like Hali's, Sayyid Ahmed's Muslimness was rarely at odds with his Indianness. Quite as much as the Hindus, Muslims too 'consider[ed] India as their homeland'. Presaging Hali's *Shikwa-e-Hind* five years earlier without the romanticism or the complaint, he confessed that by living together in India 'the blood of both have changed, the colour of both have become similar, the faces of both, having changed, have become similar.... We mixed with each other so much that we produced a new language—Urdu, which was neither our language nor theirs'.[7] The essence of Sayyid Ahmed's message to his co-religionists was to keep religion and politics on separate tracks. It was *mazhabi tahsab* or religious bigotry which was preventing Muslims from partaking of the new education.[8]

This was Sayyid Ahmed's strategy for the uplift of a demoralized, disparate and disunited 'Muslim community' which his aristocratic imaginings in combination with colonial census enumeration were in the process of giving more supra-local substance than warranted by the empirical reality. Yet Sayyid Ahmed with his arrogant belief in the superiority of ashraf culture was palpably uninterested in mobilizing the Muslim *ajlaf* classes. To confuse his ideas on electoral representation with Muslim politics in an era which required at least a partial mobilization of the subordinate social classes is unacceptable teleology. Sayyid

Ahmed's understanding of the position of Muslims in the colonial context was more relevant than the normative aspects of Islamic political theory. Since the British saw the Indian Muslim community as unified, if not united, by the common bond of religion, Sayyid Ahmed couched his appeal accordingly.

His rejection of the Congress, which he regarded as a creation of the more advanced Bengali 'nation' and not of Hindus as such, stemmed in large part from the uneven impact of colonial economic and educational policies in the different regions of India.[9] Just a year before the formation of the Congress, Sayyid Ahmed Khan had asserted unequivocally that 'Hindu and Mussalmans are words of religious significance, otherwise Hindus, Mussalmans and Christians who live in this country constitute one nation'. In his 'opinion all men are one'; he did 'not like religion, community or group to be identified with a nation'.[10] That a call for Muslim non-participation in the early Congress should have qualified Sayyid Ahmed for the role of a 'separatist' and anti-nationalist underscores the political nature of the distinction between a 'communalist' and 'non-communalist' posture in retrospectively constructed nationalist pasts.

Sayyid Ahmed may have been the most prominent spokesman of a north Indian regionally based Muslim elite. Yet his sharpest critics were also Muslim. His emphasis on *ijtihad* or independent reasoning and disapproval of *taqlid* or adherence to the four authoritative schools of Islamic jurisprudence set him apart from the ulema who saw in his modernist intellectual stance a barely disguised attack on their pre-eminent status in Muslim society. While sharing an ashraf culture, an affinity for Urdu, and a core of Islamic beliefs with Sayyid Ahmed's modernist associates at Aligarh, the guardians of the faith kept these *ladini* or irreligious Muslims at an arm's length.

If issues of religious interpretation divided Muslim from Muslim, Sayyid Ahmed's policy of subservience to the British Raj and reception of Western modernity and culture elicited contempt from a section of his co-religionists. Sayyid Akbar Husayn (1846–1921), better known as Akbar Allahabadi, in his bitingly humorous and brilliant satirical verses developed a powerful critique of modernity, mercilessly ridiculing Sayyid Ahmad Khan and his associates for their shallow imitation of Western culture:

> The venerable leaders of the nation had determined
> Not to keep scholars and worshippers at a disadvantage
> Religion will progress day by day
> Aligarh College is London's mosque[11]

Scathing and relentless in his criticism of a modernity wanting in spirituality, Akbar Allahabadi neither fits the bill of a diehard anti-modernist enamoured of obscurantist *maulvi*s nor of a religious bigot. He recalled that as a child, a maulvi tried teaching him knowledge and he in turn tried teaching the maulvi reason; the enterprise ended in tears, neither the maulvi learned reason, nor Akbar knowledge. It was the degenerate state of the community rather than threats to its existence which agitated him. He could declare with equanimity that India was neither an Islamic country nor of Lakshman and Ram. Every Indian was the pliant well-wisher of the English and Hind simply the warehouse of Europe.[12] It is a measure of Allahabadi's distinctiveness as a poet that, while enormously popular in Urdu literary circles on both sides of the 1947 divide, he forms no part of either the Indian or the Pakistani nationalist pantheon.

Maulana Shibli Numani (1857–1914) also defies categorization as a 'liberal modernist' or 'anti-modern conservation' and appropriation into mainstream Indian and Pakistani nationalist narratives. An associate of Sayyid Ahmed Khan, Shibli adopted the idioms of modernity without disavowing the basic grammar of Islamic learning. His thematics spawn a rich and varied corpus of writings on Islamic history, theology, law as well as literary criticism and poetry. Not an Islamic universalist, Shibli endorsed Sayyid Ahmed's line that Indian Muslims were British subjects and not bound by religion or Islamic history to submit to the dictates of the Ottoman Caliphate. Yet on matters closer to home, Shibli's Islamic sentiments led him to take political paths different from those charted by Sayyid Ahmed Kahn. By 1895 he was publicly opposing Sayyid Ahmed Khan's policy of Muslim non-participation in the Congress.[13] Shibli's perspectives reflect the new and competing trends in Muslim discourse at a time when Sayyid Ahmed Khan's intellectual influence, if not his legacy, had been overshadowed by events.

By the late 1880s British imperial policies in India and the Islamic world were leading more and more Muslims to eschew Sayyid Ahmed Khan's policy of non-participation in the Congress and loyalty to the Raj. Yet during the closing decades of the nineteenth-century Hindu revivalist activities, especially in northern India centring on the issue of Urdu versus Hindi in the Devanagri script and cow slaughter, seemed to lend substance to colonial and ashraf notions of an Indian Muslim 'interest' that needed articulation and representation. But while the interests of the 'majority' religious community could be subsumed under the umbrella of the emerging Indian 'nation', those of the largest religious 'minority' remained marooned in the idea of the 'community'.

Instead of stopping to challenge the formulations of majoritarianism and minoritarianism in the evolving discourse of Indian nationalism, scholars seem to have been more fascinated by the 'separatist' and 'communal' claims of a privileged and pretentious segment of the Muslim community. It would not be too far-fetched to suggest that communalism in the subcontinent has been more a function of interpretation than of the actual phenomenon in its manifold dimensions. A shared core of Islamic ideals had never prevented Muslims from taking oppositional positions in relation to one another even at the level of elite discourse. This can be made light of if one regards the strategic essentializing of religious community as more important than its utility as a point of reference for the assertion of cultural difference. To wholly concentrate on the Islamic dimensions of the discourse, as if these are unproblematically singular in meaning, is to ignore key aspects of historical change and the new contradictions and contestations within the Indian 'Muslim community'.

The partition of Bengal in 1905 may have provided the main impetus for the orchestration of the Muslim claim to separate political representation and the establishment of the self-professedly 'communal' All-India Muslim League in December 1906. But it was the Morley–Minto reforms of 1909 which institutionalized what until then had been a dominant colonial perception of the importance of religious divisions in Indian society by granting Muslims separate electorates in representative bodies at all levels of the electoral system. A momentous step, it gave Muslims the status of an all-India political category but one effectively consigned to being a perpetual minority in any scheme of constitutional reforms. The structural contradiction between communally compartmentalized electorates and the localization and provincialization of political horizons was to have large consequences for India's regionally differentiated, economically disparate, and ideologically divided Muslims and, by extension, for Congress' agendas of an inclusionary and secular nationalism. If the shared idioms of an otherwise varied discourse appear to substantiate the colonial construction of Muslims as a separate and identifiable 'communal' category, the actual politics of Muslims in the different local and regional settings uncovers how common ideas led to uncommon deeds.

After 1911, the annulment of the partition of Bengal, the crisis in the Balkans and the Kanpur mosque incident of 1913 created the conditions for major reformulations of the discourse and politics of upper and middle class Muslims. Voicing the mood in certain Muslim elite quarters, Shibli wrote a series of polemical poems against the All-India Muslim League, rejecting the very notion of a separatist and loyalist politics, and endorsing the establishment of a joint Hindu–Muslim front. Well versed in the normative aspects of Islam, Shibli refused to treat religion as a code for Muslim participation in politics.

This was a stretch removed from the stance being advocated at the time by Abul Kalam Azad through his organ *Al-Hilal*. By far the most important Muslim 'traditionalist', Azad's somersaults on religion and politics convey the paradoxes of 'communalism' in the subcontinental context. Azad is celebrated in the tomes of Indian nationalist historiography for his steadfast opposition in the forties to the Muslim League's inexorable drift towards 'separatism' and 'communalism'. This is why his early writings on religion and politics make for fascinating reading. Islam was not only the vital component in Azad's identity but also the main source of his intellectual and political orientation. In 1904 he described the Congress as a Hindu body. 'There will be nothing left with us', he wrote, 'if we separate politics from religion'.[14] Azad was crestfallen to see that his co-religionists were 'not united and organized as a community'; they had 'no *quaid* (leader)', a mere 'rabble scattered among the population of India' they were living an 'un-Islamic and irreligious life.[15] The more than explicit exclusivism and separatism, to say nothing of the implicit sense of superiority, was tempered only by Azad's consistent anti-British posture and support for the Congress.

Azad's Islamism led him to even greater excesses in the name of religion. In 1920 at the height of the Khilafat agitation Azad, backed by the newly founded Jamiat-ul-Ulema-i-Hind, issued a *fatwa* declaring that under the Shariah it was an 'Islamic obligation' for Muslims to 'quit India'.[16] According to the most prominent Muslim spokesman of Congress' secular nationalism and notion of composite culture, given the choice between country and faith, Indian Muslims could only opt for the later. These utterances for the most part have been swept under the carpet. Politically 'correct' alignments, not the integrity or substantive content of the thinking, have been the more important factors determining the allotment of titles 'nationalist' or 'communalist' to would-be spokesmen of India's Muslims.

An assessment of the political positions of that other champion of Islamic universalism and the Khilafat, Maulana Mohamed Ali, will suffice to make the point. In 1912 he castigated Congress 'nationalists' for refusing to accept that the educated Hindu 'communal patriot' had turned Hinduism into an effective symbol for political mobilization and Indian 'nationality'. The Hindu 'communal patriot' simply 'refuse[d] to give quarter to the Muslims unless the latter quietly shuffles off his individuality and becomes completely Hinduised'.[17] This was a powerful indictment of Indian 'nationalism' from a man who during the non-cooperation and Khilafat agitation of the early 1920s was closely allied with Gandhi. Nothing dissuaded Mohamed Ali from speaking freely and fearlessly as a Muslim 'communal patriot'. Not even the honour of delivering the presidential address at the Congress session in December 1923. Mohamed Ali ascribed his belated entry into the Congress in 1919 to the 'political history of the community' to which he belonged. Making political capital out of Congress's acceptance of separate electorates for Muslims in its Lucknow pact of 1916 with the Muslim League, Mohamed Ali called the Simla deputation a 'command performance'. Separate electorates were 'the consequence, and *not* the cause of the separation between Muslims and their more numerous Hindu brethren'. India's most hopeful future lay in becoming a 'federation of faiths', not in a 'misleading unity of oppositon'.[11] Stated uncategorically from the Congress pedestal, this was a command performance indeed!

Yet few historians of Indian nationalism trace Mohamed Ali's 'communal' lineage to this period. It was only after his falling out with the Congress on the issue of the Nehru report in 1928 that his communal colours begin to be spotted. So even the statements of a self-styled 'communal patriot' enunciated from within the Congress are 'nationalist'; outside its ambit they acquire the ignominious status of 'communal reaction'. For those who participated in the Khilafat agitation, the collapse of the movement amidst heightened social conflict along communitarian lines became a litmus test for their allegiance to Indian nationalism. Azad, whose political speeches during the campaign had been peppered with verses from the Quran, 'kept himself aloof from the murky communal politics of the twenties'.[19] By contrast, Mohamed Ali became a rabid 'communalist'. The assertion that he belonged to 'two circles of equal size...which are not concentric—one is Indian and the other is the Muslim world' is seen as the 'tragedy' of Mohamed Ali's life.[20] Not particularly convincing as a tragic figure, in November 1930 he made an impassioned plea for Indian freedom while strongly advocating the 'Muslim case' for separate electorates, safeguards, and majority provinces:

I have a culture, a polity, an outlook on life
—a complete synthesis which is Islam. Where God
Commands I am a Muslim first, a Muslim second, and
a Muslim last, and nothing but a Muslim.... But where

India is concerned, where India's freedom is concerned,
where the welfare of India is concerned, I am an Indian
first, an Indian second, an Indian last, and nothing but
an Indian.[21]

A respectable 'nationalist' position in an earlier period, by the 1930s
such an expression of the multiple identities of India's Muslims from
outside the Congress fold entailed being called a 'communalist'.

The arbitrariness of sifting 'nationalists' from 'communalists'
becomes a trifle more glaring once the spotlight is shifted away from the
level of discourse onto the formal political arenas. Anyone not belonging
to the Congress and articulating a politics of 'Muslim interests' is a
communalist, not a nationalist. So while the unity of religion and politics
at the level of discourse and pro-Congress 'nationalist' activity does
not make for a communal position—for instance during the Khilafat
movement—the most explicitly non-religious manoeuvrings and
machinations in the name of a 'community' are sufficient for a reputation
as a communal politician. Bickering over the loaves and fishes of office
in local and provincial councils, hardly proof of religious concerns, throws
up a colourful medley of Muslim political sinners, one more 'communal'
than the other. The main qualification for 'communalism' appears to be
pursuit of power politics, least engaged with specifically religious issues.

Different historians have examined the growth of 'communalism'
in the provinces under the Montford reforms, correctly attributing it to
the structural imperatives of the representative institutions created by
the colonial state. Yet without a consideration of the politics of Muslims
qua Muslims, these interpretations run the risk of becoming tautological.
Under separate electorates Muslims voted for Muslims; the elected
representatives worked in the interest of their constituents with the result
that the politics of Muslims were thoroughly 'communalized'. It might
be more even-handed to condemn all politics within the inadequate
representative institutions of the colonial state as reflecting the religious
divide. But that would mean abandoning the binary opposition between
secular nationalism and religious communalism. So the slanted logic ends
up insinuating that an elected Muslim had to make a real hash of
representative office to escape being a 'communalist'. No such difficulties
pin down 'nationalists' drawn from the majority community if elected
on the Swarajist or the Congress ticket.

Underplayed in analyses of the Montford reforms is the extent to
which the provincial dynamic in electoral and representative activities
countered the process of 'communalizing' Muslim politics at the all-India

level. The essentialization of religious difference implicit in 'communal-ism' has clouded any sense of maintaining an analytical distinction between levels of politics. Identifying the well-springs of 'communalism' in distinct locales and provinces does not add up to an undifferentiated political dynamic of all-India proportions. The convergence of Muslim and Punjabi or Muslim and Bengali did not mean exchanging provincial interest for a common religious identity. With their identities bounded by region and informed by religion the interests of Indian Muslims did not pour neatly into all-India 'communal' moulds. This is brought out in stark form by the conflict of interests between Muslims in the majority and the minority provinces. Supra communal alliances were forged not only in the U.P. where Muslims were in a minority but also in the Punjab and Bengal where they had bare majorities.

In the Punjab the Unionist leaders Fazl-i-Husain and Sikander Hayat Khan, and in Bengal the Krishak Praja leader Fazlul Haq, had made sure that by 1937 the provincial imperative had prevailed over a specifically Muslim communal line within the domain of representative Muslim politics. The pursuit of power, not the preservation of religious distinctiveness, tended to empty an elite political discourse of its normative and substantive content, leaving the Indian Muslim category as an unlikely vehicle for cultural nationalism. The All-India Muslim League's dismal performance in the 1937 elections reveals the complete bankruptcy of any notion of an all-India Muslim 'communalism'. It was the perceived threat from the singular and uncompromising 'nationalism' of the Congress to provincial autonomy and class interests which gave the discourse and politics of the Indian Muslims as a subcontinental category a fresh lease of life.

From Community to Nationhood: Separatism or Exclusion?

A teleological view of history would interpret the transformation of the discourse and politics of a minority religious community into a demand for nationhood as the logical culmination of the 'communal' tendencies among Indian Muslims. Those who subscribe to the 'two nation' theory are among the more notorious practitioners of this approach. But their sharpest opponents have been no less culpable. Reading 'composite culture' for 'nation', assimilation for distinctiveness, does not banish the *telos* of partition for those wedded to the convention of perceiving historical trends in the binary mode of secular nationalism and religious communalism. The subaltern thunder in South Asian historiography has certainly struck fear in the minds of historians beyond the pale of this select circle. But it has not shed much useful light on how to link 'communal consciousness' and periodic outbursts of inter-communal violence among marginal social groups in the public arenas of localities with the partition of India along ostensibly religious lines. Subaltern consciousness is shaped by too many contending identities to allow for an unquestioning privileging of the 'communal' element within it. 'Communal consciousness' itself has been subject to far greater recent and dramatic historical change than is acknowledged by these historians. Asserting the autonomy of the subaltern subject from elite manipulations in the making of history can be meaningful proposition only if based on an assessment of the inter-connections between different levels of politics. Short of holding subaltern consciousness and violence responsible for the partition of India, and that is surely not the intention, there can be no adequate explanation of the post-colonial transition which does not address the calculations and miscalculations of those located at the highest level of politics.

What such an explanation cannot afford, however, is the historio-graphical error of treating the end result of the 1947 partition as the ultimate goal of Muslim politics and also of broader historical trends subsumed under the theme of 'communalism'. If discrepancies based on class, regional, and ideological differences permeated the discourse and politics of Muslim identity in the late nineteenth and early twentieth century, the metamorphosis of a minority community into a 'nation' was designed more as a powerful rhetorical device than an accurate state-ment of the reality.

The idea of a Muslim state, albeit within India and restricted to the north-western Muslim majority provinces, had been voiced in December 1930 by Mohammad Iqbal at the All-India Muslim League's annual session. A critic of Western nationalism, Iqbal did not declare Indian Muslims a 'nation' when he initially called for a state based on the territorial amalgamation of the Punjab, the North-West Frontier Province, Sind, and Baluchistan. This was proposition that, for a change, bore the marks of Punjabi Muslim rather than Muslim minority province interests. Islam as a living cultural force in India demanded its 'centralization in a specified territory' and was the only sure 'basis of permanent communal settlement'. None of this was actuated by 'narrow communalism' or 'any feeling of ill-will towards other communities'. There were 'communalisms and communalisms' and it was not the 'low and ignoble' communalism based on antipathy towards other communities but the 'higher aspect of communalism' as culture, which even the Nehru report had endorsed, that Iqbal had in mind.[22] Yet the demand for a state within India where only a fraction of Muslims could live according to their culture and religious traditions was too obviously in the interests of the majority provinces, particularly the Punjab, to excite an All-India Muslim League council dominated by Muslims from the minority provinces. So Iqbal's ideas were dismissed as mere poetics in established Muslim political circles.

The famous resolution passed at the Muslim League's Lahore session marked the transition of the Indian Muslims from a minority to a 'nation'. One point of view which needs putting to rest is that in declaring the Indian Muslims a 'nation', the League was inspired by a normative ideal in Muslim consciousness, namely that the preservation of the religious identity of the community demanded the exercise of political power by representatives of the Faithful.[23] Given the varied uses Muslim thinkers make of the normative ideals of Islam, arguments focusing on discourse do not offer satisfactory explanations of changing historical dynamics. The statement of Muslim 'nationhood' which emanated from Lahore in March 1940 was, to quote one critic, 'an extreme step for solving communal problems'.[24] An explicit revolt against minoritarianism, it was also an implicit *coup* against the dominant binary mode which extolled Congress' 'secular nationalism' as legitimate and denigrated Muslim difference as illegitimate 'religious communalism'. Declaring the Indian Muslims a 'nation', Jinnah confessed that the idea of being a minority had been around for so long that 'we have got used to it... these settled notions sometimes are very difficult to remove'. But the time had come to unsettle the notion since 'the word "Nationalist" has now become the play of conjurers in politics'.[25]

No amateur conjurer himself, Jinnah came away from the League's session with a mixed bag of tricks. The weightiest was the demand that all future constitutional arrangements be reconsidered 'de novo' since Indian Muslims were a 'nation' entitled to equal treatment with the Hindu 'nation'. But in attempting to give territorial expression to the Muslim claim to nationhood, Jinnah and a mainly minority province based All-India Muslim League had to make large concessions to the autonomy and sovereignty of the majority provinces, not a very tidy beginning to the search for statehood. If reconciling the contradictory interests of Muslims in majority and minority provinces had thwarted the All-India Muslims League's representative pretensions in the past, the sheer impracticability of squaring the claim of nationhood with the promise of statehood required something more than an artful conjuring trick.

The historiographical debate has deliberated on the issue of Muslim 'nationhood' rather more than on the ambiguities surrounding the demand for Muslim 'statehood'. This has to do with that other telos which presumes the orchestration of separate nationhood as an inevitable overture to exclusive statehood. Recent revisionist historiography on partition, including my own,[26] has noted the uneasy fit between an assertion of Muslim 'nationhood' and the uncertainties and indeterminacies of politics in the late colonial era that led to the attainment of sovereign 'statehood'. While the insistence on national status for Indian Muslims became a non-negotiable issue after 1940, the demand for a wholly separate and sovereign state of 'Pakistan' remained open to negotiation as late as the summer of 1946. The scholarly blindness to this is a product of the double mental barrier, both against maintaining an analytical distinction between 'nation' and 'state' and expunging the telos of partition from interpretations of the historical evolution of the demand for a 'Pakistan'.

The claim that Muslims constituted a 'nation' was perfectly compatible with a federal or confederal state structure covering the whole of India. With 'nations' straddling states, the boundaries between states had to be permeable and flexible. This is why Jinnah and the League remained implacably opposed to the division of the Punjab and Bengal along religious lines. It was the veritable absence of an all-India Muslim 'communalism' which had given rise to the claim for Muslim 'nationhood'. This did not translate into a secessionist demand for a Muslim nation-state, but was intended as the building block for a confederal arrangement with the Hindu-majority provinces, or Hindustan, at the subcontinental level.

In the event the strategy went awry, resulting in the exclusion from India of the leader and the party which had staked a claim on behalf of all Indian Muslims. Communally compartmentalized electorates had helped transform the case of Muslim distinctiveness into an assertion of 'nationhood' at the level of all-India political discourse. But the emphasis on provincial and local arenas of politics pitted Muslim regional interests against those raised on behalf of a subcontinental 'community' or 'nation'. The resort to Islam was a mobilizational technique to generate momentum for a political movement seeking a substantial share of power for Muslims in an independent India. If the League's politics lent a 'communal' colouring to the demand for a 'Pakistan' at the social base, there were Muslim groups opposed to its strategy who made an even greater play of Islam as a religious ideology.

After 1940, the Muslim League did a better job manipulating the discourse than in riveting control over the politics of Muslims in the majority provinces. Yet even at the level of the discourse, the League was not the most convincing pretender in the race for the Islamic trophy. As late as the final decade of the British Raj in India, prominent Muslim thinkers, including 'Nationalist Muslims' like Maulana Azad and Maulana Husain Ahmad Madani of the Jamiat-ul-Ulema-i-Hind, promoted *muttahiddah qawmiyyat* or composite nationalism with the same passion as their belief in religious and cultural differences between Muslims and non-Muslims. With the exception of Azad, the most ardent believers in the *ummah vahidah* or one nation theory patented by the Congress were ulema who could not imagine an independent India without *shariah* rule. The irony of this of this non-secular vision co-existing harmoniously with the Congress' secular programme underscores the political motivations behind the binary opposition between secular nationalism and religious communalism. More ironic still was the enthusiastic support for the Pakistan demand by Muslim communists and socialists, especially those associated with the Progressive Writers movement.[27] The participation of ungodly socialists in the Pakistan movement fuelled charges by Islamic ideologues that the demand for 'Pakistan' was no more than a 'secular' charade. Yet having fiercely opposed Jinnah and the Muslim League, a good number of these religious ideologues and organizations adopted Pakistan as the terrain to launch their crusade for shariah rule. The rabidly religious Jamat-i-Islami, the bigoted Majlis-e-Ahrar and the idiosyncratic Khaksars are all examples of this legion.

Unable to resolve the contradictions among Muslims at the level of discourse, the League did even more miserably in the realm of actual politics. At the end of the day the singular nationalism of the Indian National Congress got the better of both the Muslim claim to 'nationhood' and the majoritarian provincialism of Muslims in the north-western and eastern extremities of the subcontinent. The Congress leadership, keen on grasping the centralized apparatus of the colonial state, was prepared neither to share power with the Muslim League at the all-India level nor accommodate Muslim majoritarian provincialism within a loose federal or confederal structure. It was ready instead to wield the partitioner's axe—in concert one might add with the Hindu Mahasabha—to exclude both the League and the Muslim-majority areas from the horizons of the secular Indian nation-state. Cast against its will into the role of the seceding state, Pakistan was left to begin its independent career with an ideology of Muslim 'nationhood' which could not plausibly be squared with the mutilated and moth-eaten territorial contours of its truncated statehood.

[...]

CONCLUSION

An exploration of the discourse and politics of Muslim identity over a period stretching more than a century reveals the grave flaws in categorizing the multiple articulation of difference as 'religious communalism' or cultural nationalism. Muslim identity as difference has been riven with too many internal contradictions to be capped by an all encompassing 'communalism'. Historicizing and conceptualizing the related issues of Muslim difference and Muslim politics has suggested the inevitability of the one and the impossibility of the other. A common source of reference in the normative ideals of Islam does not warrant the essentialiazation of Muslimness implied by 'communalism'. But by the same token, ideological and political disagreements among Muslims do not nullify the case for difference. What it indicates is that the problem of Muslim difference and in South Asia has been more complex and nuanced than permitted by the protagonists of the 'two nation' theory or the practitioners of a historiography based on a binary opposition between secular nationalism and religious communalism.

[...]

That the dominant idioms of states, and the ways in which these are reflected in elite discourse, so often fly in the face of the shifting structural contours of politics at the base is reason enough for abandoning some of their more questionable premises. Exploding 'communalism' to uncover the manifold and contradictory interests driving the politics of Muslim identity in South Asia might enable a better appreciation of difference as a lived cultural experience, one that is forever changing in response to broader historical dynamics, rather than an abstract, sterile, and essentialized category awaiting a fresh round of scholarly bandaging.

NOTES

1. Altaf Husain Hali, 'Shikwa-e-Hind', (1888) in *Jawhar-e-Hali*, compiled by Iftikhar Ahmed Siddiqui, Lahore, Kereven-e-adab, 1989, pp. 314–30.
2. For instance Romila Thapar, 'Imagined Religious Communities? Ancient History and the Modern Search for a Hindu Identity', *Modern Asian Studies*, 1989, vol. 23, no. 2, pp. 209–31.
3. See Gyanendra Pandey *The Construction of Communalism in Colonial North India*, New Delhi, Oxford University Press, 1990.

4. Farzana Shaikh, *Community and Consensus in Islam: Muslim Representation in Colonial India, 1860–1947*, Cambridge, Cambridge University Press, 1989.
5. Cited in Mushir U. Haq, *Muslim Politics in Modern India, 1857–1947*, Lahore, Book Traders, n.d., p. 35.
6. *Jawhar-e-Hali*, pp. 200–9.
7. Speech at Patna on 27 January, 1883, in Shan Mohammad (ed.), *Writings and Speeches of Sir Syed Ahmad Khan*, Bombay, Nachiketa, 1972, pp. 159–60.
8. Sayyid Ahmed Khan, 'Tahsab', in *Mazameen-e-Sir Sayeed: Muntakhab Tehzib-ul-Akhlaq*, compiled by Dr Ghulam Hussain Zulfikar, Lahore, Sange-e-Meel, 1993, pp. 44–9.
9. See his speeches at Lucknow, 28 December, 1887 and Meerut, 16 March, 1888 in Mohammed (ed.), *Writings and Speeches of Sir Syed Ahmed Khan*, pp. 180–94 and pp. 204–20.
10. Ibid., pp. 266–7.
11. *Kulliyat-e-Akbar Allahabadi*, vol. 1, Delhi, n.d., p. 95.
12. See *Intikhab-e-Kalam-e-Akbar*, compiled Dr Ghulam Hussain Zulfikar, Lahore, 1966, pp. 110, 112.
13. Mehr Afroz Murad, *Intellectual Modernism of Shibli Nu'mani: an Exposition of his Religious and Political Ideas*, Lahore, Institute of Islamic Culture, 1976, p. 100.
14. Cited in Haq, *Muslim Politics in Modern India*, p. 72.
15. Ibid., p. 108.
16. Ibid., p. 124.
17. Mohamed Ali, 'The Communal Patriot', February 1912, in Afzal Iqbal (ed.), *Writings and Speeches of Maulana Mohamed Ali*, first edition 1944, revised edition, Lahore, 1987, pp. 75–7.
18. Mohamed Ali's presidential address to the Indian National Congress at Cocanada, 26 December, 1923, in ibid., pp. 111–18.
19. B.R. Nanda, *Gandhi-Pan-Islamism, Imperialism and Nationalism*, Bombay, Oxford University Press, 1989, pp. 391–2.
20. Ibid., p. 390.
21. Mohamed Ali's speech at the fourth plenary session of the Round Table Conference in London on 19 November 1930, in Iqbal (ed.), *Select Writings and Speeches of Mohamed Ali*, p. 356.
22. Mohammad Iqbal's presidential address to the All-India Muslim League at Allahabad, December 1930 in Syed Sharifuddin Pirzada (ed.), *Foundations of Pakistan, All-India League Documents: 1906–47*, Karachi National Publishing House, 1970, vol. II, pp. 158–61, 166.
23. Shaikh, *Community and Consensus in Islam*, ch. 6.
24. Dr Radha Kumud Mookerji, *A New Approach to the Communal Problem*, Bombay, Padma Publications, 1943, p. 59.

25. Jinnah's presidential address to the All-India Muslim League, Lahore, March 1940 in Pirzada (ed.), *Foundations of Pakistan, All-India Muslim League Documents: 1906–47*, vol. II, p. 335.
26. See Ayesha Jalal, *The Sole Spokesman: Jinnah, the Muslim League and the Demand for Pakistan*, Cambridge, Cambridge University Press, 1985.
27. See Khizar Humayun Ansari, *The Emergence of Socialist Thought Among North-Indian Muslims (1917–47)*, Lahore, Book Traders, 1990, ch. 6.

PART V

NATION, REGION, AND CASTE

14 'Denationalising' the Past[*]
'Nation' in E.V. Ramasamy's Political Discourse

M.S.S. Pandian

Thus the days of magicians and fetishes will end; you will have to fight...
—Jean-Paul Sartre in preface to Fanon (1985: 26)

By now it is part of the academic common sense that nations, in their search for legitimacy, reinterpret and usurp remote past(s) as their own. As Benedict Anderson[1] puts it in his book on nationalism, 'If nation-states are widely conceded to be "new" and "historical", the nations to which they give political expression always loom out of an immemorial past...,' and 'that image of antiquity' is 'central to the subjective idea of the nation.'

Departing from such a conception which claims the 'nationalisation' of the past as a universal given of nations, the present paper argues that it has been possible at least in certain cases to imagine nations as disengaged from the past. Towards illustrating such an alternate possibility, the paper analyses the concept of the 'nation' as propagated by E.V. Ramasamy, a man who perennially carried the appellation of an 'anti-national'. Freed from the mainstream nationalist binary of nationalism vs colonialism, anchored in history and rationalism as progress, troubled all the time about citizenship, E.V. Ramasamy's concept of the nation denied its origin in the classical Indian/Tamil past and envisaged it fully in the anticipatory. Further, it constantly violated the certitude about boundaries, identities, agents of change and went beyond the territoriality of the nation.

In tracing the contours of E.V. Ramasamy's 'nation', my attempt is not only to explore the relationship between the nation and the past, but also to recover one of the marginalized discourses on the nation, which has been fossilized in the Indian nationalist historiography as

* Originally published in *Economic and Political Weekly*, vol. 28, no. 42, 16 October 1993, pp. 2282–7. In the present version some portions of the text and notes have been removed. For the complete text see the original version.

belonging to the 'other' of the national, that is, 'anti-national'. Such attempts at recovering alternate concepts of the nation seem pertinent and urgent as the official 'nation' has become one of the most important sources of legitimacy for the state in India as well as for a range of political formations varying from the Hindu communalists to the leftists.

I

Citizenship, Colonialism, and Nation

E.V. Ramasamy's sojourn in the Indian National Congress was brief, a mere five years in an active political career spanning over half a century. Joining the organization in 1920 during the non-cooperation movement, he not only spent considerable time, energy, and money for such nationalist causes as 'khadder' and prohibition, but also engaged himself spiritedly in taking up a series of issues which had a direct bearing on the question of citizenship in the nation-in-the-making: he obdurately staged 'satyagrahas' in front of the Mahadevar temple in Vaikkom, which earned him two jail terms and the honorific 'Vaikkom Veerar' ('Hero of Vaikkom'), seeking rights for the lower castes to enter the temple streets; opposed bitterly the practice of having separate dining arrangements for brahmin and non-brahmin students in Shermadevi Gurukulam, a traditional school funded partly by the Tamil Nadu Congress committee and run by a former 'revolutionary terrorist' V.V.S. Iyer with the objective to impart 'high ideals of national education': and repeatedly argued for 'communal representation' (or what has come to be called today as 'reservations') for the non-brahmins in public services and representative bodies such as the legislature—a demand which was marginalized and dismissed by the mainstream nationalists as 'detrimental to national unity'. E.V. Ramasamy's conception of free and equal citizenship as the key constitutive element of the nation did not evoke the kind of response he had hoped for from the Tamil Nadu Congress, the leadership of which was dominated by brahmin elite. After a series of experiments within the Congress, which may be termed as experiments on the question of citizenship in the nation, he finally broke ranks with the organization in November 1925 when two of his resolutions favouring 'communal representation' were disallowed in the Kancheepuram conference of the Tamil Nadu Congress.[2] Thereafter he declared his political agenda to be: 'no god; no religion; no Gandhi; no Congress; and no brahmins'.[3]

E.V. Ramasamy's doubts about the place of the subordinate classes in the Congressite nation and his resolve to fight the Congress, Gandhi, and brahminical Hinduism were strengthened by Gandhi's utterances in Tamil Nadu during 1927. In the highly charged Tamil political environment, Gandhi not only said, 'Varnashrama Dharma is not an unmitigated evil but it is one of the foundations on which Hinduism is built [and] defines man's mission on earth',[4] but also described the brahmins as the 'finest flower of Hinduism and humanity'. He added: 'I will do nothing to wither it. I know that it is well able to take care of itself. It has weathered many a storm before now. Only let it not be said of nonbrahmans that they attempted to rob the flower of its fragrance and lustre...'[5]

Importantly, the identity that E.V. Ramasamy established between god, religion, Gandhi, the Congress, and the brahmins was based on his understanding that all of them stood in the way of different subordinate social groups such as the sudras, the dalits, and women, attaining free and equal citizenship in the nation-in-the-making. His political career then onwards was more or less an unwavering journey through the Self Respect Movement (founded in 1926) and the Dravidar Kazhagam (founded in 1944) in search of substantive, as opposed to formal, citizenship for the subordinate groups. The centrality that he assigned to citizenship as constitutive of the nation is more than evident from the way he assessed and combated the nationalist concept of 'swaraj' and the manner in which he responded to the British raj.

'Swaraj'

At one level, he viewed the nationalist demand for swaraj or self-rule as a conspiracy by the local elite (who, for him, were as varied as the brahmins as opposed to the sudras, the Marwaris as opposed to the Tamils, men as opposed to women...depending on differing relational contexts) to hegemonize the subordinate classes, and as a process which would eventually affirm rather than erase their unequal status. At another level, he viewed it as an impossible project given the innumerable crisscrossing of hierarchies and relations of authority and subordination. Writing in 1928 about the condition of untouchables and women, he noted:

> [We] have been telling that unless the above two oppressions [i e, of untouchables and women] are destroyed, asking for freedom to India, or claiming that Indians themselves will take care of India's administration and security, or telling that India does not need even a little association with outsiders...is utterly foolish or dishonesty involving selfish conspiracy...

...we are keeping sections of our people enslaved, oppressed and degraded—without thinking that they are of our society, our brothers; without any compassion; without giving them the freedom we so desire; without thinking that they are human beings. So handing over the welfare and freedom of these oppressed people to us is nothing other than handing over sheep to a butcher....[6]

In 1948, his dream of a separate Dravida Nadu already in shambles, he queried, 'Is the brahmin's rule swarajya for the Parayan [untouchable]? Is the cat's rule swarajya for the rat? [Is] landlord's rule [swarajya] for the peasant? Is owner's rule swarajya for the worker?...'[7] He argued that India was not a nation but a mere museum of castes, religions, languages, and gods.[8]

In short, with citizenship being invested with singular primacy in E.V. Ramasamy's discourse on the nation, it was, for him, the moment of equality of the subordinate social groups with the rest of the nation alone which could signify the arrival of the nation. For instance, referring to the position of Indian women—an issue which engaged him all through his political career[9]—he interpreted their freedom and equality as real swaraj:

> The concept of husband-wife relationship has been one of master-slave relationship. The essential philosophy of marriage has been to insist on women's slavery.... Until women are liberated from such marriages and from men, our nation cannot attain freedom.[10]

He treated this lack of equality for women in the indigenous society as the proof of Indians not having the 'spirit of freedom' and they being 'children of slaves'.[11] Thus, 1947 did not signal the nation for him and he declared 15 August as a day of mourning.

British Raj

Let us now turn to his attitude towards the British raj. He, as a Congress-man 'fanatically' committed to Gandhi, condemned the raj unequivo-cally: 'The Britishers love to repeat that we Indians are brutes. Maybe; you are and I am too. And it is up to us to demonstrate to them that we are brutish enough to drive them out to wrest our national freedom.'[12] Following his disenchantment with the Congress, he re-evaluated his stance on the raj and found several things of the raj worthy of support. He argued, 'The "Hindu India" which believed that people should abide by the authority of the king and the king is the god was taught only by the "English India", that the king should abide by the people and the king is the servant of the people.'[13] According to him, 'Though we have lost much from being the slaves of the British, we have profited at least a little and understood ourselves as human beings. If we had remained the slaves of north Indians, we would have remained "sudran", "rakshashan", "chandalan", "asuran", "kundakan", "kolakan", "pratilokan", "narakan"...'[14] He, time and again, claimed that substituting the British rule with swaraj would be equivalent to the 'suicide of the common people'—unless one could be confident of a new rule based not on Manu Dharma, Varnashrama Dharma, and brahmin hegemony, that is institutions which, according to him legitimized inequality across castes, gender, and forms of labour, and thus invalidated the possibility of overarching equality.[15]

However, E.V. Ramasamy's approval of the raj was not unqualified and was often only a grudging approval. He was disappointed that the British, unlike in their own nation, did not attempt sufficiently to establish a full-fledged rule of Manitha [Human] Dharma in India, but also followed Manu Dharma in large measure. He offered two sets of reasons for such differential politics practised by the British–one in their own nation and the other in the colony.

Indigenous Elite

According to him, the first set of reasons which disabled the British raj from going all the way in affirming Manitha Dharma in the colony could be located in the resistance to such dharma by the Indian national elites themselves. He repeatedly cited instances of sustained Indian opposition to such initiatives as the Devadasi Abolition Act, the Child Marriage Restraint Act, and the Hindu Religious Endowment Act, which were represented as the excesses of the British rule. We may bear in mind here that such nationalist opposition to 'social legislations' was rather intense in the Tamil-speaking areas [...].[16] E.V. Ramasamy reminded the nationalists that it was due to the efforts of '"sarkar dasas" and "traitors of the nation" and the [British] government' that these acts were passed.[17] The other event which he used as an illustration of native elite opposition to the efforts of the raj to establish a rule of equality was that of 1857. He argued that '...there [was] no scope to treat the events of 1857 as the first event of national freedom struggle. [It was] an attempt to protect Vedic ideas, obscurantism and religion',[18] and congratulated the British for suppressing it.[19] He viewed the sepoys who participated in the events of 1857 as being used by the conservative Indian elites to regain power.

While the first set of reasons offered by E.V. Ramasamy for the British reluctance to establish Manitha Dharma in India placed the blame squarely on the indigenous elite, his other set of reasons implicated both the British and the local elite. Here, he claimed, the British reluctance was a result of their need to have local collaborators so as 'to carry on their rule in this country [India] for ever and to generously loot and transfer the wealth of this country to their own'.[20] In identifying such collaborators as the indigenous elite, he implicated both colonialism and the indigenous elite as upholders of Manu Dharma instead of full-fledged Manitha Dharma.

[...]

II

'DENATIONALISING' THE PAST

Such foregrounding of substantive citizenship of the subordinate social groups as the principle constitutive element of the nation placed E.V. Ramasamy outside the mainstream Indian nationalism as well as the incomplete modernity of the British in the colonial context. In other words, he was free from the need to set the nation in opposition to the colonizer. From this relatively 'unencumbered' political location, he could view the national past as an unmitigated narrative of victimhood which prefigured and resulted in current hierarchies of power and powerlessness within the indigenous society. Through such a narrative of victimhood, at one level, he marked out his discourse on the nation as distinct from the discourse of the elite mainstream nationalism which searched for the authentic national self in a classical Indian past. At another level, his narrative refused to be a mere appropriation of the colonialist construction of the Indian past as uncivilized since he, in his search for citizenship, implicated the British as unwilling modernists. In this context, his engagement with the past may be characterized as a project of 'denationalising' the past in the name of the nation.

In analysing how E.V. Ramasamy 'denationalised' the past, we shall first take a look at his construction of the pan-Indian past and then move on to his engagement with the Tamil past. The need to analyse his engagement with the Tamil past acquires certain urgency given the widespread academic and popular belief that he uncritically privileged a Tamil past and placed it in opposition to the Indian past.[21]

Past in the Present

E.V. Ramasamy was fully aware of the mainstream nationalists' use of the so-called classical Indian past in their public discourse.[22] For him, this classical Indian past, which was privileged by the mainstream nationalists, was a continuous and uninterrupted story of the hegemony exercised by the iniquitous brahminical Hinduism and Varnashrama Dharma. [...]

[...]

Given this reading of the Indian past as a narrative of victimhood, he treated religious texts such as *Manusmriti, Puranas, Mahabharata,* and *Ramayana* as fantastic and crafty instruments invented by the upper castes to perpetuate their hegemony.

If such a history of oppression and inequity could have an uninterrupted career for over thousands of years, it was because the superordinate social groups violently put down any challenge to their hegemony, and when violence failed, they co-opted their opponents. He illustrated his claim with the example of Buddhism and argued that the Buddhists, because of their opposition to the hierarchies legitimized by Hinduism, were 'beaten up, kicked and tortured on stakes' by upper caste Hindu zealots; and when such violence failed to erase the influence and fame of Buddha, they incorporated Buddha within Hinduism as the 'tenth incarnation of Maha Vishnu' and Buddhism as a sect, similar to Saivism and Vaishnavism.[23] Likewise, he pointed out, the brahminical Hinduism co-opted those lower caste opponents who used violence by conferring Kshatriya status on them.[24]

This diachronic narrative of the past continuously established its links with the present and argued that the continuation of the past into the present was the source of the continuing subjugation of the subordinate social groups. Tracing the link between his version of the past and the current devaluation of physical labour, for instance, he argued: '...you should realise that if all of you are workers, it is because you were all made into sudras according to Varnashrama Dharma of Hindu religion. Let that pass. If workers are thought of as lowly people, it is because they [sudras] were thought of as lowly people in Hindu religious dharma'.[25] Similarly, referring to the current status of women, he noted:

> What Hindu religion tells about women is that god created women at birth itself as prostitutes; so they should not be allowed to be free at anytime; they should be controlled by the father at childhood [and] by their sons during old age...

There is more such evidence in religious shastras. Their intention is nothing other than making women slaves of men.[26]

Thus the past was not at a remove: it was here and now, feeding into the present, legitimizing hierarchies, and denying free and equal status to all. It had to be combated if substantive citizenship was to constitute the nation.

Qualified Approval

Let us now turn to E.V. Ramasamy's engagement with the Tamil past. During the course of the anti-Hindi agitation which contested the compulsory introduction of Hindi in schools by the Congress government in 1937, E.V. Ramasamy began airing his demand for a separate Tamil Nadu, which evolved over time into a demand for a separate Dravida Nadu. Till the end of his life, he, more or less steadfastly, denied legitimacy to India as one nation and kept his demand alive.

In this context, he did differentiate the Tamil past as more equitous compared to the pan-Indian past. Basing his arguments on ancient Tamil literary texts, he claimed that both the caste system which degraded the non-brahmins and the current marriage customs which emphasized women's subordination were alien to the Tamil past. What is important here is that he used this difference primarily as a heuristic device to deny legitimacy to the Hindu north India to exercise hegemony over other regions and people who had a better record on matters relating to equality. Beyond that, his position on the Tamil past was not different from that on the Indian past, that is, he 'denationalised' the Tamil past too. Interestingly, even in contexts where he favourably referred to the equitous Tamil past, he simultaneously discounted it and claimed that one would not benefit by harping back to the past.[27]

In 1943, when separate Dravida Nadu was very much on the agenda of E.V. Ramasamy, he wrote: 'The unnecessary ancient principles of the Tamils...have become useful [only] for deceiving outsiders and plunging [oneself] into foolishness: It has become a duty of the rationalist that such talk [about ancient Tamil ideas] should not be evoked for any reform from now on'.[28] He proceeded further: 'If several of our "Pandits" do not have rational thinking, it is because of the obscurantism of the ancient Tamil principles. *There is nothing at present to be achieved by the talk of ancient Tamils.* Therefore it is an important duty of the people not to give any place for [such] fraudulent speech...' (emphasis mine). A striking illustration of E.V. Ramasamy's contempt for the Tamil past could be his reaction to the glorification of ancient Tamil women by the women leaders of the anti-Hindi agitation. He intervened to tell them: 'It will be worth-while if you discuss the present status of women and what can be done about achieving women's liberation, instead of glorifying our grandmothers like Allirani, Kannagi and Madhavi'.[29]

His overarching denouncement of the Tamil past spared neither the classical Tamil literature nor the ancient Tamil rulers: the Cheras, the Cholas, and the Pandyas. *Thirukural* and *Silapathikaram*, which along with *Purananuru* constitute the three so-called glorious texts of the Tamils, came in for barbed criticism in the hands of E.V. Ramasamy—for they, in his opinion, degraded women and denied them equality with men. He characterized *Silapathikaram* as a text 'which began in prostitution, grew in "chastity" and ended up in foolishness and superstition'.[30] We may note here that chastity, for him, signified women's unfreedom. He wrote:

> The manner in which women are oppressed in Kovalan Kathai *Silapathikaram* is extremely bad...
> On the marriage dais itself Kovalan desired a *dasi* and goes with her. Till Kovalan returns, Kannagi didn't decorate herself...didn't eat any good food, ate only food without salt and remained worried. Why should one do all these? Imagine a man in that place [of Kannagi]. What would happen? If the wife had left with another man, would the husband eat food without salt? Would he remain worried without why physical comfort till god brought the wife back? In it *Silapathikaram*, a separate moral is given for woman and [a separate one] for men...[it was] written so badly as to degrade women.[31]

Similarly, despite his qualified approval of *Thirukural*, he subjected it to severe criticism for emphasizing the subordination of women by glorifying chastity. Referring to the couplet, which claims that a woman who does not worship god but her husband can make rain to shower at her instant command, he wrote: 'Would Thiruvalluvar have written these...if he were a woman instead of a man?'.[32] He viewed *Kamba Ramayanam* as a text which degraded the Dravidians and posed to those who defended it on its literary merits: 'They say [*Kamba*] *Ramayanam* is a rare literature. What is the use? However starved one is, would one pickup food from shit...How can anyone who desires self-respect read *Ramayanam*?...'[33]

As much as the Tamil literature of the past, Tamil historical personages such as the Chera, the Chola, and the Pandya kings too were scrutinized from the point of whether they upheld or denied equality to their subjects. According to him, the Tamil kings lacked intelligence and self-respect, and but for them, the Tamils would not have remained the lowest of the castes and as degraded people for the past 2,000 to 3,000 years. They were unworthy of emulation as they impaled the Buddhists and the Jains, who tried to inculcate better sense among the people, on stakes; patronized and promoted temple culture which helped the idle and foolish to cheat the people; and kept the common people illiterate. He referred to their rules as 'malevolent and barbaric'.[34]

E.V. Ramasamy reserved the most scathing of his criticisms for the Tamil pundits who constructed and propagated a glorious version of the Tamil past through their readings of classical Tamil literature. He derisively characterized their skills as the mere ability to 'memorise "literature", give several meanings to one word, confuse the people and collect money...' The Tamil pundits for him were liars, propagandists of obscurantism, and lacking in reasoning powers'.[35]

The past, thus, was bereft of anything worth appropriating for the national agenda. The nation could arrive only as a break from it. In short, the past stood 'denationalised' in E.V. Ramasamy's discourse on the nation.

III

META-NARRATIVES OF THE 'MODERN'

A politically unusable and 'denationalised' past and an iniquitous present did not lead E.V. Ramasamy into a politics of despair. Instead, he located the notion of equal and free citizenship in the anticipatory. What needs to be underscored here is 'that this future was denied, as we have just seen, the facility of being a recovered past. He framed the journey to this future in what may broadly be termed as the meta-narratives of the 'modern'[36] rationality and science, faith in human emancipation and progress through struggle, and history.

Though he thought of the past as a continuous story of inequality and unfreedom, he insisted that 'change is inevitable: nobody can stop it'.[37]

> Aryan-Dravidian conflict is a conflict which had been going on since the Puranic age. Though we do not know enough about the Puranic age, [we know that] the Buddhists had struggled to destroy the Aryan culture. Mughals, who had the Islamic culture which was opposed to the Hindu, i.e, Aryan, culture, also tried to destroy Aryanisin. But they didn't succeed.

That is why the brahmins ridicule us. 'When they [the Buddhists and the Mughals] could not succeed, how can the Dravidar Kazhagam succeed!' Let them ridicule [us]! We are not bothered!

I strongly believe that our efforts will succeed... Two hundred years of British rule and 25 years of our rationalist propaganda have reduced the hegemony of Aryan culture.[38]

Similarly, he, in one of his innumerable public speeches, illustrated his faith in history through the changes witnessed by the institution of kingship in India: 'Our kings were venerated as gods: [they were] thought of as the incarnation of gods; [people] did to the king whatever they did to god. But what has happened to all those kings? They were turned into kings who [now] receive their salary from the government'.[39]

Recovery of Self-worth

But such change through history would not take place on its own; it needed concerted human intervention, and therefore the victims of the past should become active subjects. Here E.V. Ramasamy elaborated and energetically propagated the concept of 'Suyamariathai' or self-respect—the foremost thing an active political subject required was the realization of his/her self-worth. He privileged the concept of Suyamariathai over everything else. He claimed: 'If we attain self-respect, swaraj will arrive within a bat of the eyelid...' He similarly asserted: 'Self-respect is the only means to attain true swaraj [and] that is man's birth right...'[40]

Extending this concept of self-worth to the sphere of political intervention, he argued that it was the victims of inequity and unfreedom alone, who, through their active intervention in history, could ensure self-emancipation. In contrast to the mainstream nationalist thought, he believed that no one could speak for and represent the victims of the past, but themselves. For instance, he discounted men's participation in the movement for women's freedom and argued that only women, by appropriating political agency to themselves, could attain independence and equality: 'Can rats ever get freedom because of cats? [Can] sheep and fowl ever get freedom because of foxes? [Can] Indians' wealth ever increase because of the white men? [Can] non-brahmins ever get equality because of brahmins?...'[41] He repeated the same line of argument to different subordinate social groups such as the sudras, the dalits, workers, and villagers, whom he continually addressed throughout his life as a political propagandist. Thus, his discourse on the nation proliferated with innumerable oppressors and oppressed, each changing into the other contextually and relationally: a sudra male was the oppressed in relation to the brahmin, but simultaneously he was an oppressor in relation to women. The following quote from Annapurna, one of the women activists of the movement led by him, may capture this well: 'Generally our country is colonised by the British; the north Indians have colonized our economy; the brahmins have hegemonised our society; but the most important of all these, men have colonised and oppressed women'.[42] If Annapurna privileged women's oppression over the rest in her political agenda, it is because of her gender location; and in other relational contexts, other oppressions might have got privileged. In short, the struggle for the nation through history was multiple, with porous boundaries, shifting identities, and numerous agents of change. Its resolution lay beyond the simple binary of national versus colonial.

As we have seen above, in E.V. Ramasamy's discourse on the nation, self-respect or the recovery of self-worth was the only means to arrive at the nation. What was the modality for the subordinate social groups to recover their self-worth? He thought that it was reason/rationality/science alone that could restore their self-worth and in turn their political agency: 'Man today does not have self-confidence. He doesn't think that [it is] he [who] conducts himself. [He] doesn't believe that he is responsible for what he does. He has made a confusion of god, god's commands, god's philosophy, all of which were invented by man himself'. Explicating further, he noted: 'God and fate are the direct enemies of reason. Because, the person who is enslaved by god and fate has nothing for himself. He is a [mere] piece of wood, floating on water'.[43]

Reason/Rationality/Science

He applied his positivist rationality to religious mythologies, read them literally to show how they were impossible tales of fantasy and craft meant to degrade the sudras, the dalits, women, and so on. In 1924 he described the idol at the Vaikkom temple as 'a mere stone fit only to wash dirty linen with', and such criticism continued all through his career: 'Had it not been for the rationalist urge of the modern days, the milestones on the highways would have been converted into gods. It does not take much time for a Hindu to stand a mortar stone in the house and convert it into a great god by smearing red and yellow powders on it...'[44] (English translation in the original). For him self-respect and rationality could only go together. 'I have...broken the idols of Pillayar or Vinayakar and burnt pictures of Rama. If in spite of these words and acts of mine, thousands of people throng to my meetings, it only indicates that self-respect and wisdom have dawned on the people'.[45]

E.V. Ramasamy's rational critique, in the very name of the nation, repeatedly violated the cultural certitudes of the nation. The best example here would be his attitude towards language. In his opinion, for a language to be acceptable to the nation, it should be accessible to rational thought, and should enunciate equality and freedom. His attack on Hindi was premised on the argument that it would help people only to read such irrational texts as Tulsi Ramayana and puranas, and contained nothing rational: 'Hindi can help only in reaching the heaven; but heaven itself will disappear soon'.[46] On the same count, he thought Tamil was better; yet it was greatly lacking. He criticized it for, among other things, being derogatory to women, not having words for the male counterpart of adulteress and widow. And he invented the neologism vidavan for widower and vibacharan for those men who went to prostitutes, and sought their popular use.[47] He argued: 'If Tamil has to progress and join the ranks of the world languages, Tamil and religion should be separated'.[48] He often expressed in public that English was better than Tamil. He even needed a different Tamil for his Tamil Nadu!

Equally important is his view that the teleology of rationality was interminable, continuously invalidating the past, and disclosing newer avenues of freedom all through. He told his followers that the march of rationality would invalidate his own legacy:

> What is known as rationality will keep changing. What we think today as fit for reason, may be rejected tomorrow as superstition. We ourselves will reject several things—even the sayings of those who are praised as great men. Similarly, the future generation may at a time say about me, 'There was a [man] of irrational thinking called Ramasamy'. That is natural; a sign of change; a sign of the times.[49]

Thus the course of rationality, for E.V. Ramasamy, is such that it does not offer a fixed goal, a fixed Utopia—the search for freedom can only be an ever-continuing endless search.

IV

HISTORY AND RATIONALITY

Let us now turn to the implication of E.V. Ramasamy's concepts of history and rationality for the career of the nation, for these were the concepts

which framed the nation's course. The interminable teleology of rationality which constantly invalidated cultural certitudes and progress
through struggle as a process with volatile boundaries, identities, and
agents, rendered his nation a nation without a 'moment of arrival'. It
was ever-fluid, remorselessly struggling for citizenship, informed by ever-
changing contours of rationalism, and continuously violating boundaries—both in the sense of territory and otherwise. He could thus, while
talking about Dravida Nadu, accommodate the whole of the sudras of
the north India in his nation: '... [People] who suffer from this [Aryan]
degradation are not only those who speak Tamil... [They are] also there
in other states, i e. states like Bengal, Bihar, Bombay, Maharashtra where
they speak different languages. The degraded comrades there are calling
themselves Dravidians; In fact, they are Dravidians'.[50] And, similarly, he
could denounce Tamil, while opposing the imposition of Hindi in schools:
in 1939, when Hindi was a burning issue in Tamil Nadu, he said in the
course of a public-address:

> I do not have any attachment to the Tamil language for [the reason] that it
> is my mother tongue or the tongue of the *nation*.
>   I am not attached to it for [the reason] that it is a separate language,
> ancient language, language spoken by Shiva [or] language created by
> Agastiyar. I do not have attachment for anything in itself. That will be foolish
> attachment, foolish adulation. I may have attachment [for something] for
> its qualities and the benefits such qualities will result in. I don't praise
> something because it is my language, my nation, my religion...
>   If I think my nation is unhelpful for my ideal and cannot [also] be
> made helpful, I will abandon [it] immediately. Likewise, if I think my
> language will not benefit my ideals or [will not help] my people to progress
> [and] live in honour, I will abandon it...[51] (emphasis mine).

In short, E.V. Ramasamy's nation, freed from the past, located in the
anticipatory and framed by notions of 'modernity from below' was a
metaphor, a metaphor which stood for ever-fluid, free, and equal
citizenship. Its success can never be assessed in terms of its arrival, but
perhaps only in terms of its continuing ability to inspire diverse
subordinate social groups in the present-day Tamil Nadu to question the
Indian nation-state for its failings, and to imagine nations of equity and
freedom lying in future

NOTES

† An earlier version of this paper was presented at a workshop on
'Nationalising the Past', held in Goa on 21–3 May 1993. The workshop

was sponsored by the Social Science Research Council, New York. The paper draws liberally from the ongoing joint work on the history of the Dravidian Movement by A.R. Venkatachalapathy, Anandhi, S., and myself. I am grateful to Padmini Swaminathan and J. Jeyaranjan for their extremely useful comments on an earlier version.

1. Benedict Anderson, *Imagined Communities: Reflections on the Origin and Spread of Nationalism*, London, 1983, pp. 19, 47.
2. For details of E.V. Ramasamy's role in the Indian National Congress, see Eugene F. Irschick, *Politics and Social Conflict in South India: The Non-Brahmin Movement and Tamil Separatism, 1916–26*, Berkeley and Los Angeles, 1969, pp. 268–74; Nambi Arooran, *Tamil Renaissance and Dravidian Nationalism, 1905–44*, Madurai, 1980, pp. 152–9, and E.Sa. Visswanathan, *Political Career of E.V. Ramasamy Naicker*, Madras, 1983, pp. 38–65.
3. *Kudi Arasu*, 2 May 1925; see also Pnratchi, 24 December 1933.
4. Irschick, *Politics and Social Conflict in South India*, pp. 337–8
5. Saroja Sundararajan, *March to Freedom in Madras Presidency, 1916–47*, Madras, 1989, p. 457. On how Gandhi tried to solve the question of varna on a moral plane—by idealizing hierarchies as differences—rather than on a political plane, see Parekh, Bhikhu: *Colonialism, Tradition and Reform: An Analysis of Gandhi's Political Discourse*, New Delhi, 1989, pp. 207–46.
6. E.V. Ramasamy Periyar, *Penn Yean*, Adimaiyaanaal, Madras, 1984, p. 71.
7. *Viduthalai*, January 19, 1948, in Aanaimuthu, V. 1974: *Periyar Ee Ve Ka Sinthaikal*, Tiruchirapalli, vol. II, p. 673.
8. *Kudi Arasu*, 1 June 1930, in Aanaimuthu, *Periyar Ee Ve Ka Sinthaikal*, vol. II, p. 649.
9. An obituary of E.V. Ramasamy published in the *Economic and Political Weekly*, 12 January 1974, summed up his engagement with women's issues thus: 'He championed the cause of widow remarriage, of marriage based on consent, and of women's right to divorce and abortion. Pointing out that there was no Tamil word for the counterpart of an adulteress, he fumed, ...the word adulteress implies man's conception of. woman as a slave, a commodity to be sold and hired'. Periyar's demand at a conference two years ago that no odium should be attached to a woman who desired a man other than her husband (which the press so avidly vulgarized), as well as Periyar's advocacy of the abolition of marriage as the only way of freeing woman from enslavement, were about as radical as the views of any women liberationist'.—For a detailed account of E.V. Ramasamy's position on women's issues, see Anandhi, S. (1991): 'Women's Question in the Dravidian Movement, 1925–48'. *Social Scientist*, May–June.
10. *Viduthalai*, 11 October 1948.
11. Periyar, *Penn Yean*, Adimaiyaanaal, p. 73.
12. Visswanathan, *Political Career of E.V. Ramasamy Naicker*, p. 38.

13. Speech in Kollampalayam on 19 September 1937, in Aanaimuthu, *Periyar Ee Ve Ka Sinthaikal*, vol. II, p. 682.
14. *Kudi Arasu*, 25 November 1944, in Aanaimuthu, *Periyar Ee Ve Ka Sinthaikal*, vol. II, p. 703.
15. *Kudi Arasu*, 17 May 1931, in Aanaimuthu, *Periyar Ee Ve Ka Sinthaikal*, vol. II, p. 777.
16. R. Parthasarathy, *S. Satyamurthi*, Delhi, 1979, p. 116; Saroja Sundararajan, *S. Sathyamurthy: A Political Biography*. New Delhi, 1983, pp. 54–5 and 136: and Anandhi 'Women's Question in the Dravidian Movement, 1925–48', pp. 37–8.
17. *Kudi Arasu*, 17 May 1931, in Aanaimuthu, *Periyar Ee Ve Ka Sinthaikal*, vol. II, p. 777.
18. *Viduthalai*, 15 August 1957, in Aanaimuthu, *Periyar Ee Ve Ka Sinthaikal*, vol. II, p. 691.
19. *Viduthalai*, 16 October 1966, in Aanaimuthu, *Periyar Ee Ve Ka Sinthaikal*, vol. II, p. 846.
20. *Kudi Arasu*, 17 May 1931, in Aanaimuthu, *Periyar Ee Ve Ka Sinthaikal*, vol. II, p. 777.
21. Viswanathan *Political Career of E.V. Ramasamy Naicker*, p. 75; and C.S. Lakshmi, 'Mother, Mother Community, Mother-Politics in Tamil Nadu', *Economic and Political Weekly*, 20–27 October 1990. For a critique of Lakshmi 'Mother, Mother Community, Mother-Politics in Tamil Nadu', see M.S.S. Pandian, S. Anandhi, and A.R. Venkatachalapathy, 'Of Moltova Mothers and Other Stories', *Economic and Political Weekly*, 20 April 1991.
22. For instance, see *Kudi Arasu*, 19 March 1933, in Aanaimuthu *Periyar Ee Ve Ka Sinthaikal*, vol. I, p. 376.
23. Speech in 1954, in Aanaimuthu, *Periyar Ee Ve Ka Sinthaikal*, vol. I, p. 312.
24. *Kudi Arasu*, 15 August 1926, in Aanaimuthu, *Periyar Ee Ve Ka Sinthaikal*, vol. I, p. 11.
25. *Viduthalai*, 20 January 1948, in Aanaimuthu, *Periyar Ee Ve Ka Sinthaikal*, vol. II, p. 786.
26. Periyar, *Penn Yean*, Adimaiyaanaal, pp. 84–5.
27. For instance, see Aanaimuthu, *Periyar Ee Ve Ka Sinthaikal*, vol. I, pp. 23, 215.
28. *Kudi Arasu*, 10 January 1943, in Aanaimuthu, *Periyar Ee Ve Ka Sinthaikal*, vol. II, pp. 1251–2.
29. *Kudi Arasu*, 27 November 1938.
30. Periyar, *Penn Yean Adimaiyaanaal*, p. 28.
31. Periyar, *Suyamariathai Thirumanam Yean*, Madras, 1986, pp. 13–14.
32. Periyar *Penn Yean Adimaiyaanaal*, p. 15; see also, Aanaimuthu, *Periyar Ee Ve Ka Sinthaikal*, vol. II, pp. 1039, 1229, 1257, 1259–66.
33. *Kudi Arasu*, 26 January 1936, in Aanaimuthu, *Periyar Ee Ve Ka Sinthaikal*, vol. II, p. 977.
34. *Viduthalai*, 15 August 1957, in Aanaimuthu, *Periyar Ee Ve Ka Sinthaikal*, vol. II, p. 692.

35. *Viduthalai*, 16 March 1967, in Aanaimuthu, *Periyar Ee Ve Ka Sinthaikal*, vol. II, p. 984.

36. As the paper proceeds, we shall see that E.V. Ramasamy's engagement with modernity was rather opposed to the mainstream nationalists' engagement with the same. While the mainstream nationalists, through a discourse of modernity, turned the state into the sole spokesperson for the nation [Chatterjee, Partha (1986): *Nationalist Thought and the Colonial World—A Derivative Discourse*, London, Chapter 5], Ramasamy's modernity perennially remained contestatory. One may differentiate his version of modernity as 'modernity from below' as opposed to 'modernity from above'. Such distinction seems important as scholars ranging from Ashis Nandy to Dipesh Chakrabarty to Ramachandra Guha, in the Indian context, represent modernity only as an elite agenda, and arrive at conclusions like 'caste is eco-friendly' [Madhav Gadgil and Ramachandra Guha, *This Fissured Land: An Ecological History of India*, Delhi, 1992]. In fact, the need for such distinctions about modernity is repeatedly emphasized in the feminist criticism of the current wave of post-modernism [for instance, see Lovibond, Sabina, 'Feminism and Postmodernism', *New Left Review*, November–December, 1989.

37. Aanaimuthu, *Periyar Ee Ve Ka Sinthaikal*, vol. II, p. 1120

38. *Viduthalai*, 27 January 1950, in Aanaimuthu, *Periyar Ee Ve Ka Sinthaikal*, vol. II, p. 683. See also, Periyar, *Penn Yean Adimaiyaanaal*, p. 73.

39. *Viduthalai*, 23 December 1954, in Aanaimuthu, *Periyar Ee Ve Ka Sinthaikal*, vol. I, p. 337.

40. E.V. Ramasamy Periyar, *Thanthai Periyar Arivurai-100*, Madras, 1978, p. 13.

41. Periyar, *Penn Yean Adimaiyaanaal*, pp. 83–4.

42. *Kudi Arasu*, 29 November 1947.

43. *Kudi Arasu*, 25 May 1935, in Aanaimuthu, *Periyar Ee Ve Ka Sinthaikal*, vol. II, p. 1117.

44. Aanaimuthu, *Periyar Ee Ve Ka Sinthaikal*, vol. I, p. xxix.

45. Ibid: xxviii.

46. Speech on 19 September 1937, in Aanaimuthu, *Periyar Ee Ve Ka Sinthaikal*, vol. II, p. 655.

47. Anandhi, 'Women's Question in the Dravidian Movement, 1925–48', p. 26.

48. *Kudi Arasu*, 26 January 1936, in Aanaimuthu, *Periyar Ee Ve Ka Sinthaikal*, vol. II, 976.

49. Aanaimuthu, *Periyar Ee Ve Ka Sinthaikal*, vol. II, 1120

50. *Viduthalai*, 27 January 1950, in Aanaimuthu, *Periyar Ee Ve Ka Sinthaikal*, vol. II, 683.

51. Sami Chidamparanar, *Tamilar Talaivar: Periyar Ee Ve Ra Vazhkai Varalaru*, Madras, 1983, (first published in 1939), p. 214.

REFERENCES

Fanon, Frantz (1985): *The Wretched of the Earth*, Middlessex.

Jaggar, Alison, M. (1990): 'Sexual Difference and Sexual Equality' in Deborah L. Rhode (ed.), *Theoretical Perspectives on Sexual Difference*, New Haven and London.

15 Congress and the Untouchables, 1917–50*

Eleanor Zelliot

In the early days of Independence, India enacted legislation forbidding the practice of Untouchability, made any discrimination against ex-Untouchables a penal offence, and instituted the most comprehensive system of 'compensatory discrimination' in the world to redress the age-old disabilities of the lowest castes.[1] The record of Congress in dealing with a socially disadvantaged minority at the same time that it was attempting to gain independence from Great Britain is a study in the politics of nationalism as well as the politics of social reform.

From its birth in 1885 until 1917, the India National Congress deliberately avoided social issues. Even its most reform minded leadership agreed with Dadabhai Naoroji's statement at the second annual Congress meeting that Congress was a political body 'to represent to our rulers our political aspirations, not to discuss social reforms'.[2] Indian nationalist reformers met at the rise of Congress, in the Congress pavilion, from 1887 until 1895, but even that link threatened to divide Congress membership. At the eleventh Congress meeting in 1895 in Bal Gangadhar Tilak's stronghold of Poona, the objections of Tilak and other extremists were so strong that the Social Conference was forced to disassociate itself completely from the Congress venue. Unity on political matters was difficult enough; issues of social reform, at that time chiefly affecting the status of women, would have been impossible.

The situation in 1917 was very different: the extremists and the moderates had merged the year before, the Muslim League and Congress agreed on a common platform, and Congress met in the atmosphere of a British promise of eventual self-government. The need now was for mass support and politicization of the masses, and by 1917 one-seventh of the Indian population that was Untouchable had come to be recognized as socially deprived but politically important 'Depressed Classes'.[3] As Congress met in December 1917, Secretary of State of India Edwin

* Originally published in R. Sisson and S. Wolpert (eds), *Congress and Indian Nationalism*, Berkeley, University of California Press, 1988, pp. 182–97.

Montagu and Viceroy Lord Chelmsford had begun their cold weather tour to gather responses to the proposed idea of political reforms. They were deluged with petitions and pleas from various groups, including at least ten from groups that can be identified as Depressed Classes, all asking for representation in the forthcoming legislative bodies.[4]

In Bombay and Madras Provinces some of these groups of Untouchables were identified with non-Brahman movements that opposed the Indian National Congress fearing that the high-caste Congress elite would dominate any Indian representative body.[5] In Bombay, conferences of Depressed Classes were called alternatively by Congress reformers and non-Brahman reformers, bringing the issue of Untouchability before Congress in 1917 in such a way that it could hardly be ignored. A Depressed Classes Conference, attended by 2,500 people, met on 11 November 1917, in Bombay under the chairmanship of Justice Sir Narayan Ganesh Chandavarkar (1855–1923), President of Congress in 1900, General Secretary of the Indian National Social Conference, and President of the Depressed Classes Mission Society.[6]

Resolutions called for Depressed Class rights to elect their own representatives to the Legislative Councils in proportion to their numbers, for compulsory free education, and for higher-caste Hindus to 'remove the blot of degradation from the Depressed Classes'. The Conference also resolved to support the 1916 Congress–League agreement on self-government and as if in return for its allegiance asked the Congress:

> to pass at its forthcoming session a distinct and independent resolution declaring to the people of India at large *The necessity, justice, and righteousness of removing all* the *disabilities imposed by* religion and *custom upon the Depressed Classes, Those disabilities being of a most vexatious and oppressive character, subjecting those classes to considerable hardship and inconvenience* by prohibiting them from admission into public schools, hospitals, courts of justice and public offices, and the use of public wells, etc. Those disabilities, social in origin, amount in law and practice to political disabilities and as such fall legitimately within the political mission and propaganda of the India National Congress.[7]

The portion of the resolution reproduced exactly in the Indian National Congress resolution of December 1917 has been underlined in the present quotation.

A week after the Chandavarkar-led conference in November 1917, a conference of 2,000 Untouchables chaired by Bapuji Namdeo Bagade, a leader of the Non-Brahman party denied support to the Congress–Muslim League scheme but also asked for representation according to

numbers for Depressed Classes. Another non-Brahman took two
politically active Untouchables to visit the secretary of state for India in
December following these conferences, and although one did not speak
English, Montagu was struck by 'their extraordinary intelligence'.[8] The
conference continued in the early months of 1918. The Depressed Classes
Mission sponsored a second conference, this one chaired by the reform-
minded Gaikwad of Baroda, to which Bal Gangadhar Tilak came and
said: 'If a God were to tolerate untouchability, I would not recognise
him as God at all'.[9] A little later yet another conference was held in
Bombay under the leadership of Subhedar Ganpatrao Govind Rokde,
probably of the Untouchable Mahar caste. This group demanded not
only representation but also separate electorates (analogous to those
granted to Muslims) in which only the Depressed Classes would be
permitted to vote for their representatives[10]—a demand that would
become a serious issue by 1932.

The British response to all this petitioning was to nominate one or
two Depressed Class members as members of the Legislative Council in
each province. Congress' response was to issue continued statements
urging the removal of disabilities from 'Untouchables'. With the rise of
Mohandas K. Gandhi to Congress power in 1919, social reform became
a legitimate cause for Congress concern. Gandhi's leadership introduced
a major change in the approach toward Untouchability, however, for
under Gandhi, the issue of Untouchability was more religious than social.

RELIGIOUS CONSCIENCE AND SOCIAL REFORM:
THE GANDHIAN APPROACH TO UNTOUCHABILITY

The resolutions of Congress in the 1920s, its subcommittees on
Untouchability and its efforts to deal with the work of the Untouchable
caste that most directly affected its sessions—the santitation work of the
Bhangis—all reflect the basic Gandhian approach to the problem that
dominated Congress from 1920 until Independence.

The first resolution on Untouchability in the Gandhian Congress
appeared in the last paragraph of the lengthy, historic 1920 Resolution
on Non-Cooperation, stating:

> Inasmuch as the movement of non-co-operation can only succeed by
> complete co-operation amongst the people themselves, this Congress calls
> upon public associations to advance Hindu—Muslim unity and the Hindu
> delegates of this Congress call upon the leading Hindus to settle all disputes
> between Brahmins and Non-Brahmins, wherever they may be existing,

and to make a special effort to rid Hinduism of the reproach of untouchability, and respectfully urges the religious heads to help the growing desire to reform Hinduism in the matter of its treatment of the suppressed classses.[11]

The Untouchable problem was now a 'reproach to Hinduism' rather than a 'hardship' to Untouchables. The request to religious heads to help reform Hinduism is a Gandhian touch not found in earlier reform literature, and as if to indicate that this appeal was valid, the resolution was supported at the Congress session by the Sankaracharya of Sarada, who claimed his own Guru had taught that the uplift of the Depressed Classes was in accordance with the Shastras.[12]

In the excitement of the Non-Cooperation campaign, all this urging rather naturally was secondary to the action of the campaign itself. Nevertheless, the Congress Report of 1921 indicates two new tactics— the elevation of the Untouchable Bhangi caste's sanitation work to respectability and the attempt to agree on a policy regarding Untouchable children's entrance into nationalist schools. A third tactic that was tried for the first and only time was a pledge, a required statement of belief. Article 5 of the pledge for the National Volunteer Corps read: 'As a Hindu I believe in the justice and necessity of removing the evil of untouchability and shall, on all possible occasions, seek personal contact with and endeavour to render service to the submerged classes'. Such a pledge was never required for Congress membership, but Congress trusted 'that every person of the age of 18 and over will immediately join the volunteer organisations'.[13]

The innovation of the 1921 Congress that continued the longest was the stress on sanitation as honourable work. In the large temporary cities that were the homes of the Annual Congress sessions, sanitation had to be as carefully planned as any other part of the programme. At Khadi Nagar, the Congress camp near Ahmedabad, trench privies were maintained by a 'devoted band of volunteers who had, of their own free choice, undertaken to supervise the sanitation of the privies'.[14] Gandhi reported shortly after the Congress in *Young India* on 5 January 1922: 'The work of attending to the trenches was done not by paid Bhangis but by unpaid volunteers belonging to all castes and religions'.[15] The Untouchable as Bhangi had long been a concept in Gandhi's mind.[16] His approach was to make Bhangi work acceptable rather than remove the Bhangi from sanitation work. Gandhi was well aware that not all Untouchables were Bhangis, and that myriad sorts of work, from shoemaking to village watchmen, were traditional to other Untouchable castes. Nevertheless, he stressed the symbol of Bhangi, the remover of pollution, all his life, he held that 'a Brahmin and a bhangi should be regarded as equals', according to the *Gita*,[17] and in his last days 'I would rejoice to think that we had a sweeper girl of a stout heart, incorruptible and of crystal purity to be our first President...assisted in the discharge of her duties by a person like Pandit Nehru'.[18]

Congress itself adopted the idea of Bhangi work as noble with sporadic enthusiasm. The 1923 Cocanada Congress passed a resolution thanking the municipality sanitary staff for keeping latrines and urinals clean, but at the Belgaum Congress of 1924 there were 'nearly seventy-five volunteers, mostly Brahmans, who were engaged in conservancy work in the Congress camp. The Municipal Bhangis were, indeed, taken, but it was thought necessary to have the volunteers also...Indeed sanitary work must be regarded as the foundation of all volunteer training'.[19] Again at Haripura in 1938, 'at all Congress sessions, the work of scavenging is not done through paid workers, but is done by volunteers'.[20]

The matter of Untouchables and education brought up at the 1921 Congress was more complex than that of the sanitation work. In his welcome address as chairman of the Reception Committee, Vallabhbhai Patel said, 'We have perhaps made the greatest advance in the matter of untouchability'—as against boycott, national education, Khadi production, and the picketing of liquor shops!—but he adds, 'The national schools are open to them in theory for which the Senate had to fight a tough battle. In practice, however, there is not yet the insistent canvass to bring the children of these countrymen to our schools and make them feel that they are in no way inferior to our own'. He then notes that separate schools may have to be maintained for Untouchable children for some time to come.[21]

When the matter of education comes up again in 1924, a real division in Congress can be seen. The Working Committee recommended to the Subjects' Committee that 'Congress does not regard any such institution to be national which does not actively encourage Hindu–Muslim unity and which *excludes untouchables*, which does not make handspinning and carding compulsory, and in which students and teachers do not habitually wear khaddar'.[22] In the Resolution on National Educational Institutions that was passed that year at the Belgaum sessions, the requirement of the teaching of an Indian language was added, all the specifics on spinning and khaddar were kept, but the stricture on the exclusion of Untouchables was softened to 'the Congress does not regard any such institution to be national which does not...actively *encourage*

Hindi–Muslim unity, education among untouchables and *removal of untouchability*.[23] No debate on this is recorded in the 1924 Congress report. One wonders who required this telling change. Much as some urged it, *requiring* national schools to accept Untouchable children was beyond the acceptable boundaries for others.

In 1922 the Working Committee had appointed a very thoughtful and serious group of four to formulate schemes to better the condition of the Untouchables and allotted them five lakh rupees. In keeping with Gandhi's 'religious head' idea, Swami Shradhanada, was made chairman; Sarojini Naidu and two important regional Congressmen, Indulal Yagnik of Gujarat and G. B. Deshpande of the Karnatak, were appointed members.[24] It came to nothing. The Swami resigned from the committee and later from Congress in protest over the failure of Congress to heed his recommendations.[25] After several vain attempts to help the committee function without its Swami, the 1923 Working Committee asked the more orthodox and conservative Hindi Mahasabha to consider the matter.

The next subcommittee on Untouchability was formed in 1929, this one with Pandit Malaviya of the Hindu Mahasabha as president and millionaire Marwari businessman Jamnalal Bajaj as secretary. Malaviya appears to have done very little; Bajaj, however, toured many parts of India. In 1928 he had opened his own temple in Wardha, the Lakshminarayan Temple, which all described as 'magnificent', and his tour was chiefly to persuade other temple owners and trustees to admit Untouchables. Temple entry was now an issue taken up by Congress in subcommittees and pursued over the next decade, always on a voluntary basis of persuasion. There were temple entry movements in the 1920s, which probably influenced Congress's stress on this issue, with Vaikom and Parvati standing for early efforts of the Depressed Classes themselves to claim religious rights.

The Vaikom satyagraha was launched in Kerala in the spring of 1924 by members of the Ezhava caste, Syrian Orthodox Christians, and some high-caste Hindus. The issue was the use of public roads on all four sides of the temple at Vaikom in Travancore. Gandhi came to Travancore for a month in March 1925 and spent much time in fruitless discussion with temple priests on the problem of Untouchables and their *karma*— their status as the result of previous action.[26] The satyagraha did not end until the fall of 1925, and the results were 'flimsy', according to Gandhi, though use of some of the roads was finally allowed.

This is the only instance in which Gandhi associated himself with a satyagraha against a Hindu institution. One wonders what set of circumstances caused him to eschew it so totally after Vaikom. When Untouchables and others began a nonviolent satyagraha at the holy hill of Parvati in Poona 1929, a Gandhian Committee visited the site and talked to the trustees but found that the satyagraha had created an atmosphere of 'bitterness and distruct'.[27] Neither the Parvati satyagraha nor one begun at Nasik in 1930 met with Congress approval. At an All-India Suppressed Classes Conference held in Lahore in the Congress pavilion on 25 December 1929, Gandhi made his position clear: 'Those temples where you are excluded from, because of your low birth, have no gods in them and those who enter them forcibly have no godliness within them'.[28] Although Gandhi and Congress came to the position that all temple entry should be completely without coercion or demonstration, the *idea* of temple entry for all had been firmly established as a legitimate concern of Congress. The Anti-Untouchability Committee had been charged with a number of concerns,[29] but temple entry became the overriding field of action for the next decade.

The issue that was at the core of the 1917 petition to Congress from the Depressed Classes Conference—admission to public office, public schools, and public wells—seems to have been largely bypassed by the Gandhian religious approach. There is an interesting note from the 1924 Belgaum Congress, of which Gandhi was president: the Hindu members of the Provincial Congress Committee were to ascertain the wants to the Depressed Classes in regard to wells, places of worship, facilities for education, and so on and make 'provision for meeting such wants'.[30] This seems almost in direct response to a resolution passed in 1923 by the Bombay Legislative Council allowing Untouchables the use of all public watering places, wells, schools, dispensaries, and other facilities.[31] The Bombay resolution had no teeth; in fact, district collectors were to advise local bodies to consider accepting the recommendation. Both actions bore little fruit, but that of the Bombay Legislative Council seems much bolder.

SECULAR NATIONALISM, AMBEDKAR, AND THE GOVERNMENT OF INDIA

What thinking other than Gandhi's prevailed in Congress concerning this issue? In *The Depressed Classes*, a collection of essays published in 1912 by G.A. Natesan, proposer of the 1917 resolution on Untouchability,

Ambica Charan Mazumdar, former Congress president, wrote: 'The question about the Depressed classes...is now happily engaging the attention of our public men in almost every province'.[32] Lala Lajpat Rai and V.M. Mahajani as well as N.G. Chandavarkar show in their essays considerable knowledge of Untouchable conditions and the history of various proposals for changing them.

There seems to be little new thought on the issue in the next decade, however, either within or without the Congress. The flavour as well as the direction of the 1920s Congress position on Untouchability comes through remarks on the 1924 resolution on Untouchability. L.B. Bhopatkar, an orthodox Hindu of Poona and one of the founders of the Law College in that city, moved the resolution, with noted progress, urging the members of Provincial Committees to devote greater attention to the issue, and congratulating the Satyagrahis of Vaikom. The resolution was seconded by Babu Sailes Nath Bisi, High Court Vakil, Calcutta, who announced that he was speaking only to Hindus:

> Think of the injustice when you deny a Bhangi to enter a temple! Is he not a Hindu? Has he not a right to worship his God and enter his Creator's temple? Isn't it inhuman? How can we expect to talk of Swaraj when we have not given Swaraj to those who are below us, viz., the so-called lower caste?
>
> If you are not going to relax the rigour now, I tell you they will snatch away their rights from us and remember, the sins of your fore-fathers shall be visited in the next generation.... This resolution is a sort of compromise between the orthodox and the modern. So my earnest appeal to you who are young (I do not think of the old, because they will die soon) who feel that this is inhuman is to do something practicable for them which will touch their hearts. Allow them to enter your temple, allow their children to sit with your children in the same school and above all allow them to draw water from your wells.[33]

Three other developments must be noted at this time: the platform of secular socialist nationalists within Congress, the work of the Untouchable leader B.R. Ambedkar outside Congress, and the slow response of the government, particularly in Bombay, to demands of the Depressed Classes.

The remarkable Karachi resolution of 1931 helps to explain the position on untouchability—or rather the lack of such a position—among the secular nationalists. This document of human rights simply assumes that the state *must* guarantee equality to all citizens—that in the process of modernization, democratization, and the development of socialism, full rights for all will emerge naturally. Untouchability was not a 'problem' for Jawaharlal Nehru, one of the chief authors of the 1931 Karachi resolution. Untouchability was not mentioned, since the faith of the secular nationalists was in the modernization of Indian life, economic improvement, adult suffrage, and free primary education for all.

For one nationalist Untouchable, however, the matter of Untouchable disabilities and rights *was* a problem. Dr B.R. Ambedkar, who held a PhD from Columbia and a DSc from London University, testified from 1919 all throughout the 1920s before official commissions, published newspapers, organized conferences, served in the Bombay Legislature, taught at Government Law College, supported three temple satyagrahas, and achieved a considerable following among politicized Untouchables and enlightened high-caste reformers. In 1930 he spoke at a Depressed Classes conference in Nagpur, calling for independence for India and speaking of Untouchables as only 'slaves of the slaves'. In the same year, he was appointed to attend the Round Table Conference in London, where the issues of further devolution of power to Indians were to be discussed.

Gandhi did not attend the first Round Table Conference, since his famous Salt Satyagraha of 1930 had ended in a jail sentence. He came to the second Round Table Conference in 1931, and here a clash of beliefs about the solution for the problem of untouchability led to long-lasting differences between Gandhi and Ambedkar.[34] The Round Table Conference found Muslims, Sikhs, Anglo-Indians, and Indian Christians all demanding separate electorates to guarantee their political rights. In this context, Ambedkar demanded a separate electorate for Untouchables while Gandhi pleaded that Untouchables should not be considered a separate group. In 1932 the British Government awarded the Depressed Classes a separate electorate for seventy-eight representatives in the provincial legislative assemblies. Gandhi, again imprisoned, responded by launching a 'fast unto death',[35] and Ambedkar was forced to contemplate Gandhi's death if he continued to press for a separate electorate.

Pandit Mohan Madan Malaviya, president of the 1929 Congress Sub-Committee on Untouchability and leader of the Hindu Mahasabha, called a conference on 19 September 1932, which sought a compromise solution as the Mahatma weakened in his Yeravada Prison cell. More than one hundred caste Hindus and Untouchables attended the conference, held between Bombay and Poona. The Poona Pact, which resulted after five days of negotiations, bound together a wide spectrum of political leaders from Malaviya to Ambedkar. Although lost on the issue of separate electorates, he won 148 reserved seats in the provincial legislatures, rather than the seventy-eight allowed under the Communal Award.

Signed by ninety-seven caste Hindus and Untouchables, including such Congress stalwarts as Rajendra Prasad and C. Rajagopalachari, the Poona Pact was not viewed as a victory by either side. Ambedkar regretted th: loss of separate electorates. Many Congress leaders, particularly from Punjab and Bengal, felt that the number of seats reserved for Untouchables far outweighed the actual problem of Untouchability in those provinces.[36] Government, however drew up a Schedule of those castes considered to be Untouchable in each province, and the term 'Scheduled Castes' was henceforth used for the some 600 different 'Untouchable' groups who qualified for the reserved seats in legislatures.

Gandhi devoted himself with greater passion to the removal of Untouchability after he was released from jail. He coined the name 'Harijan' (people of God), to which both orthodox Hindus and Ambedkar took offence. He renamed his newspaper *Harijan*, went on a Harijan tour, and established a Committee on the Removal of Untouchability that became the Harijan Sevak Sangh. That Committee operated, however, without reference to Congress. Indeed, Nehru attached 'little importance to the *swadeshi* and Harijan movements',[37] and 'Gandhi made it clear that only those Congressmen who were too weak to court arrest or had lost faith in civil disobedience should join the Harijan movement, and forbad its use to strengthen the political activities of the Congress or its hold on the people'.[38]

One Congressman took a tack different from either Nehru or Gandhi's approaches. Rajendra Prasad of Bihar, who was to become India's first President, began to groom an Untouchable for the sharing of political power. Prasad met Jagjivan Ram, young, well-educated Chamar in 1933. By the time Congress assumed power in the Bihar Legislative Assembly in 1937, Jagjivan Ram was ready for a position in the Bihar Congress ministry. Ram soon became the best known, often the only, nationally famed Scheduled Caste Congressman.

Congress came to power in eight of India's provinces in 1937 without a programme for the problem of Untouchability beyond Gandhian concern and the previous steps of provincial legislatures. During its two-year period of working within the structure set by the Government of India Act of 1935, Congress performance was disappointing to secular socialists such as Nehru and to Untouchable leaders such as Ambedkar. There were Scheduled Caste cabinet members in Assam, Bihar, and Madras, although they do not seem to have much impact on reforms. In Bihar, Jagjivan Ram became a Parliamentary secretary. In all provinces but Bombay, where Ambedkar's Independent Labour party captured most of the reserved seats, representatives of the Scheduled Caste were associated primarily with Congress.

Given the Gandhian emphasis on temple entry and on the change of attitude and 'heart' among caste Hindus, Congress could hardly be expected to enact compulsory legislation on Untouchables' rights. The two provinces which dealt most seriously with the Untouchable problem were Madras and Bombay.

In Bombay, Ambedkar's Independent Labour Party was second in numbers, as an opposition to Congress, only to the Muslim League. Its various proposals before the legislature involved new labour laws, the removal of the agricultural systems of *watan* and *khoti*, and the provision of education and drinking water for all. All its proposals were ignored. The Bombay Harijan Temple Worship (Removal of Disabilities Act, XI of 1939), which enabled trustees of any Hindu temple to declare it open, was passed with silence from Ambedkar and objections from the orthodox gathered outside the chamber.[39]

In Madras, Chief Minister Rajagopalachari guided four bills through the legislature. Three related to temple entry, making it possible for temples to be opened if the majority of caste Hindus in a taluk agreed (The Malabar Temple Entry Act, XX of 1938) or if the trustees so wished the provincial government approved (Madras Temple Entry Authorization and Indemnity Act, XXII of 1939). The third bill indemnified reformist officials and trustees. The Removal of Civil Disabilities Act, XXI of 1938, provided that no Harijan could be denied access to public office or public facilities and that no court or public authority should recognize customary civil disabilities.[40]

Reginald Coupland reported that the policy of admitting Scheduled Caste children into ordinary schools, the provisions of scholarships, free textbooks, and other 'methods of dealing with the problem were maintained and in some cases expanded under the Congress regime. The number of Harijan pupils in the schools rose by some thousands each year in all the Congress Provinces except Madras and Orissa'; however, Coupland started that 'In general...it cannot be said that the Congress Governments showed a great deal more courage than their predecessors in their handling of the thorny question of the Harijan'.[41]

Congress resigned from provincial governments in 1939, and from then until Independence, any initative on the matter of Untouchability was taken by the British government and Ambedkar. In 1942, the year of the Quit India movement, Ambedkar established a Scheduled Castes Federation to fight once more for a separate electorate. He also became

Labour Minister in the viceroy's cabinet. In 1943 the affirmative action policy of establishing a percentage of vacancies in government service to be filled only by Scheduled Castes was adopted. The initial percentage of 8.33 was raised to 12 in 1946.[42] In 1944 the Ministry of Education adopted a scheme of post-Matriculation scholarships for Scheduled Caste students, an innovation that went far beyond the recognition of the need for simple literacy.

TOWARD INDEPENDENCE AND EQUALITY

As World War II ended and the question of Indian independence again surfaced, Ambedkar unleashed an attack on the thirty-year record of Gandhi and the Congress in *What Congress and Gandhi Have Done to the Untouchables*, published in 1945 and reprinted in 1946. Ambedkar found the 1947 Resolution on Untouchability a purely political 'device,' criticized the lack of compulsion in matters of anti-Untouchability in the 1920s (in contrast to compulsory Khaddar), found the Poona Pact 'a mean deal' and the Harijan Sevak Sangh a 'Congress plan to kill by kindness' and then, in the bulk of the book, pleaded for separate electorates as a way for Scheduled Castes to attain political safeguards. It is a bitter book but more than a polemic. There is lengthy documentation, and the basic case is made for removal of caste disabilities as political matters, not one to be left for religious leaders alone to resolve. 'Under Gandhism the Untouchables are to be eternal scavengers', Dr Ambedkar argued, ending his book 'Good God! Is this man Gandhi our savior?'[43]

Congress' answer to Ambedkar was left to C. Rajagopalachari, who claimed for twenty years that prohibition and the removal of Untouchability were his chief interests. In tones more restrained but equally emotional, C.R.'s *Ambedkar Refuted* based the case of Congress primarily on the idea that 'the progress of conditions respecting the Scheduled Castes in India does not compare ill with what has been done in America for Negroes or in the South African republic for the natives of Africa, or for the Jews in civilized Europe'.[44] Rajaji did not realize that such arguments reinforced the minority status idea of Ambedkar rather than the integrative image posed by Gandhi. Rajaji defined his record in Madras during the 1937–9 Congress-dominated provincial legislature, finding 'What is at present going on peacefully in the temples of Madura and Palani...a great and remarkable achievement'.[45]

The Scheduled Caste Federation of Ambedkar did not do well in the 1946 elections; although it secured many Scheduled Caste votes, it returned no candidates in Bombay and only one each in the Bengal and

Central Province legislatures. The Cabinet mission could not consider Ambedkar's plea for separate electorates in view of the failure of his party. Ambedkar was deprived of his place on the Executive Council at the centre when the Interim Ministry, with Jagjivan Ram as the Scheduled Caste minister, was formed in August 1946, and his protests that one Scheduled Caste minister was not enough were undercut when Jogendranath Mandal, a Namashudra from Bengal and a member of Ambedkar's Scheduled Castes Federation, was selected by the Muslim League as a Minister in October 1946. As Independence neared, Ambedkar's power and his programme for the Scheduled Castes seemed defeated.

The inclusion of Ambedkar in Independent India's first Cabinet in 1947, within two years of his scathing attack on Congress and Gandhi, is a tribute to all concerned. No one's memoirs indicate just how this remarkable act of political generosity came about. Ambedkar had been first elected to the Constituent Assembly from the Bengal Legislature Assembly by the grace of Jogendranath Mandal and the Muslim League. Then on 22 July 1947, the Bombay Legislature's Congress Party nominated Ambedkar to the Constituent Assembly in a by-election. S.K. Patil, a Congress activist since 1920 and a modernist in economic policy, claimed later that he secured Ambedkar's place in the Assembly.[46]

The selection of Ambedkar as chairman of the Drafting Committee of India's Constitution was a tribute to Ambedkar's ability as well as a reflection of the euphoria of India's first days of Independence. All the varying strains of the Gandhi–Congress–Untouchable situation seemed to come together: Gandhi's passionate conviction that Untouchability must go before India could be free; Prasad's encouragement of Scheduled Castes in political positions, Ambedkar's demands for political solutions and the rights of the Scheduled Castes, and Nehru's belief that a secular democracy would eliminate the problems of caste. Religious, social, and political approaches to the problem of Untouchability were in harmony for a brief moment. Untouchability was abolished in a Constituent Assembly in which Ambedkar brought each drafted segment to the general body—and Gandhi's name was cheered. Nehru, whom Ambedkar had criticized as a Brahman who never in all his writings even mentioned Untouchability, appointed Ambedkar Law Minister in his first cabinet. In the countryside, temples flew open: Pandharpur temple in Maharashtra which had stayed shut in spite of the fasting of a highly respected Gandhian writer, Sane Guruji; and the Guruvayur temple in Kerala, where K. Kalappan had lain in the hot sun in 1932 until Gandhi

asked him to stop. India's Independence began with a new openness
for radical change, both at the centre and in the hinterland.

The Indian Constitution, with all its declarations, directives, rights,
and privileges concerning Untouchables—or ex-Untouchables, once
untouchability had been abolished—is clearly a document of the national
mood of the time. The simple, bold statement adopted by Independent
India reflected a genuine commitment:

'Untouchability' is abolished and its practice in any form is forbidden.
(Article 17, The Constitution of India, 1950.)

This statement stands as a triumph—of Congress, for Gandhi, for
Ambedkar, and for India—however imperfectly the idea of complete
equality and justice has been realized. India intertwined nationalism and
social concerns in a way most unusual in the modern world and the
result is a system of rights and benefits as unusual as the history of
Congress itself.

NOTES

1. For discussions of all the provisions regarding law and Untouchability,
   see Marc Galanter, 'Law and Caste in Modern India', *Asian Survey*,
   November 1963, pp. 544–59; 'Compensatory Discrimination in Political
   Representation: A preliminary assessment of India's thirty-year experience
   with reserved seats in legislatures', *Economic and Political Weekly*,
   vol. 14, February 1979, pp. 437–54. See also Marc Galanter's *Competing
   Equalities: Law and the Backward Classes in India*, Berkeley, Los Angeles,
   London, University of California Press, 1984, and his 'The Abolition of
   Disabilities—Untouchability and the Law'. See also Lelah Dushkin's
   'Scheduled Caste Politics', in J. Michael Mahar (ed.), *The Untouchables
   in Contemporary India*, Tucson, University of Arizona Press, 1972.
2. P.C. Ghosh, *The Development of the Indian National Congress, 1892–
   1909*, Calcutta, Firma K.L. Mukhopadhyay, 1960, p. 73.
3. *The Depressed Classes—An Enquiry into Their Condition and Suggestions
   for Their Uplift*, Madras, G.A. Natesan, *c.* 1912, (articles originally published
   in *The Indian Review*, 1909–11) is the first full-scale work on the problem.
   The Gaikwad of Baroda and N.G. Chandavarkar, both involved in
   encouraging the 1917 Congress resolution on untouchability, are
   represented in the book. The publisher, G.A. Natesan, was the mover of
   the 1917 resolution on Untouchability.
4. Among the *Addresses Presented in India to His Excellency the Viceroy
   and the Rt. Hon., The Secretary of State for India*, London, Her Majesty's
   Stationery Office, 1918; (Cmd. 9178 Parl. Paper 1918: XVIII) are pleas for
   representation from Panchamas, Oppressed Classes, Adi Andhras,
   Ezhavas, Buddhists in South India, Dheds, the Depressed Classes Mission

CONGRESS AND THE UNTOUCHABLES, 1917–50   233

Society, the Depressed India Association, the Namashudras of Bengal, and the Adi-Dravida Jane Sabha. Scholarly work is available only on the Ezhavas (also called *Irava* and *Illuvan*).

5. See Eugene Irschick, *Politics and Social Conflict in South India: The Non-Brahman Movement and Tamil Separation, 1916–29,* Berkeley and Los Angeles, University of California Press, 1969. Gail Omvedt covers 'The Non-Brahman Movement in Western India, 1893 to 1930' in *Cultural Revolt in a Colonial Society,* Bombay, Scientific Socialist Education Trust, 1976. See Rosalind O'Hanlon, *Caste, Conflict and Ideology,* Cambridge, Cambridge University Press, 1985. For a detailed study of Jotirao Phule's low caste protest in the nineteenth century. Further study is badly needed on politics in the Marathi-speaking area from 1930 to Independence, a period that witnessed the slow but thorough takeover of Congress by non-Brahmans.

6. A new biography in English of the founder of the Depressed Classes Mission Society is Shivaprabha Ghugare, *Renaissance in Western India: Karmaveer V.R. Shinde* (Bombay: Himalaya Publishing House, 1983), which details Shinde's work with the Untouchables and his efforts to bring the non-Brahmans into Congress.

7. The full text of the Depressed Classes Conference resolutions appears in B.R. Ambedkar's *What Congress and Gandhi Have Done to the Untouchables,* vol. 2, 2nd edn, Bombay, Thacker & Co., 1946, pp. 14–15.

8. Edwin S. Montagu, in Venetia Montagu, ed., *An Indian Dairy,* London, Heinemann, 1930, p. 306. The Untouchables were G.A. Gawai and Kisan Fago Bansode, who were Mahars of the Marathi-speaking area, both active in social work and education from the turn of the century.

9. Quoted in G.P. Pradhan and A.K. Bhagwat, *Lokamanya Tilak: A Biography,* Bombay, Jaico Publishing House, 1959, p. 306.

10. C.A. Kairmode, *Dr Bhimrao Ramji Ambedkar,* vol. I, Bombay, Y.B. Ambedkar, 1952, pp. 266–7 (in Marathi).

11. *Report of the Thirty-Fifth Session of the Indian National Congress, on the 26th, 28th, 30th and 31st of December, 1920,* Nagpur: B.S. Moonje, part 2 of appendix F.

12. Ibid., pp. 77–80.

13. *Report of the 36th Indian National Congress, Ahmedabad, 1921,* Ahmedabad, Vallabhbhai J. Patel, 1922, p. 32.

14. Ibid., p. 3.

15. Ibid., p. 6.

16. Gandhi records in *Young India,* 27 April 1921, his distress over not being able to touch Uka, the family bathroom cleaner, when he was a child.

17. D.G. Tendulkar, *Mahatma: Life of Mohandas Karamchand Gandhi,* vol. II, pp. 1920–9, New Delhi, Publications Division, Government of India, (rev. edn 1961), p. 253.

18. Pyaralal, *Mahatma Gandhi: The Last Phase,* Ahmedabad, Navajivan Publishing House, 1958, p. 228.

19. 'Belgaum Impressions' by Mahatma Gandhi, *Young India*, 1 January 1925, reprinted in *Report of the Thirty-Ninth Indian National Congress held at Belgaum, 1924*, p. ix.

20. *Report of the 51st Indian National Congress, Haripura, 1938*, p. 24.

21. *Report of 36th Indian National Congress*, p. 12. Patel also notes with pride 'Our suppressed countrymen freely attend meetings'. I am unable to evaluate the importance of this remark in terms of the numbers of Untouchable participants.

22. *The Indian National Congress, 1924, Being the Resolutions of the Congress and of the All-India Congress Committee and of the Working Committee...*, Allahabad, The Allahabad Law Journal Press, 1925, p. 36. *Khaddar or khadi* is handspun, handwoven cloth. The wearing of khaddar was a symbolic rejection of both British cloth imports and modern machine-made cloth and in its early days was seen as a return to the 'golden age' of Indian dominance in the production of fabric.

23. Ibid., p. 43.

24. *The Indian National Congress, 1920-23, Being a Collection of the Resolutions of the Congress and of the All-India Congress Committee and of the Working Committee...*, Allahabad, Allahabad Law Journal Press, 1924, p. 162.

25. J.T.F. Jordens, *Swami Shraddhananda: His Life and Causes* (New Delhi: Oxford University Press, 1981), pp. 130-67, tells the long, complex story of the Swami's work on the question of Untouchability. The letters of the Swami to Patel and Motilal Nehru on the committee's work appear in Ambedkar, *What Congress and Gandhi Have Done to the Untouchables*, pp. 309-14 (appendix 1).

26. D.G. Tendulkar, *Mahatma*, p. 182. Mahadev Desai, *The Epic of Travancore* (Ahmedabad: Navajivan Publishing House, 1937) contains the most complete report of Gandhi at Vaikom.

27. Indian National Congress, *Report of the Work Done by the Anti-Untouchability Sub-Committee*, April-December, 1929.

28. N.N. Mitra (ed.), *Indian Quarterly Register*, 1929, vol. II, pp. 326-7.

29. *Navajivan*, 2 June 1929, reported the main objects of the Committee for the Removal of Untouchability were to (1) get public temples thrown open to the *Antyajas* (the lastborn), (2) secure for the Antyajas the use of public wells, (3) remove the restrictions that face Antyaja Children in public schools, (4) improve the Antyajas' condition in respect to cleanliness, and (5) induce the Antyajas to give up their habit of eating carrion and taking liquor. See *Collected Works of Mahatma Gandhi*, vol. XLI, June-October 1929, New Delhi, Publications Division, Government of India, 1970, p. 3.

30. *Report of the Thirty-Ninth Indian National Congress*, p. 7.

31. Dhananjay Keer, *Dr Ambedkar: Life and Mission* (2nd edn), Bombay, Popular Prakashan, 1962.

32. *The Depressed Classes* (cited in note 3 above), p. 24.

33. *Report of the Thirty-Ninth Indian National Congress*, pp. 95–6.
34. See Eleanor Zelliot, 'Gandhi and Ambedkar—A Study in Leadership', in Mahar, *Untouchable in Contemporary India*, for a study of Ambedkar in direct comparison with Gandhi.
35. Pyaralal, *The Epic Past* (Ahmedabad: Mohanlal Maganlal Bhatt, 1932) is the fullest account of Gandhi's fast from a Gandhian perspective. B.R. Ambedkar's speeches and memorandums for the Round Table Conferences as well as all the subcommittee interchanges have been reprinted in Vasant Moon (ed.), *Dr Babasaheb Ambedkar: Writings and Speeches*, vol. 2, Bombay, Education Department, Government of Maharashtra, 1982.
36. Discussion on the Poona Pact before the Joint Committee on Indian Constitution Reform has been republished in Moon, *Dr Babasaheb Ambedkar*.
37. Sarvepalli Gopal, in *Jawaharlal Nehru*, vol. 1, Cambridge, Harvard University Press, 1976, p. 178.
38. Ibid., p. 184.
39. *Indian Annual Register*, 1938, vol. I, pp. 143.
40. Reginald Coupland, *The Indian Problem*. Part II, 'Indian Politics, 1936–42', New York, Oxford University Press, 1944, p. 144.
41. Ibid., p. 145.
42. *Scheduled Castes, Scheduled Tribes, Backward Classes Through Official Documents*, Bangalore, I.S.I. documentation; mimeographed report, n.d..
43. Ambedkar, *What Congress and Gandhi Have Done to the Untouchables*, p. 308.
44. C. Rajagopalachari, *Ambedkar Refuted*, Bombay, Hind Kitab, 1946, p. 14.
45. Ibid., p. 33.
46. *Times of India*, 27 November 1951, reprinted in B.G. Kunte (ed.), *Source Material on Dr Babasaheb Ambedakr and the Movement of Untouchables*, vol. 1, Bombay, Government of Maharashtra, 1982, p. 388. The report quotes Dr Ambedkar saying that it was one of the greatest surprises of his life that he got into the Cabinet, particularly 'when the Congress was determined...not to permit him to enter even the portals of the Constituent Assembly'. There had been a rumour in 1938, however, that Congress had wanted a 'suitable Harijan candidate' in each provincial cabinet, that Gandhi had approved, and that Ambedkar was being considered for the Bombay Cabinet. See *The Bombay Chronicle*, 8 October 1938. There is some contemporary opinion that Gandhi was behind the choice of Ambedkar in the 1947 Cabinet.

Part VI

Women in the
Nationalist Movement

16 Gandhi and Women's Role in the Struggle for Swaraj*

Madhu Kishwar

[...]

In the first non-cooperation movement of 1921, Gandhi consciously involved women in the attempt to link their struggle with the struggle for national independence. But the programme for women was devised in a way that they could remain at home and still contribute to the movement. As a part of non-cooperation, Congressmen were asked to boycott government educational institutions, law courts and legislatures, and to defy the government and its unjust laws in a peaceful manner. But the constructive programme of Swadeshi hinged around boycott of British goods, and the spinning and wearing of khadi. Both these were eminently suited to the limitations imposed upon the contribution of women by their roles in the household with which Gandhi had no serious quarrel. His programme for women in fact complemented their household role and yet seemed to give them a sense of mission within their prosaic existence.

> The restoration of spinning to its central place in India's peaceful campaign for deliverance from the imperial yoke gives her women a special status. In spinning they have a natural advantage over men...Spinning is essentially a slow and comparatively silent process. Woman is the embodiment of sacrifice and therefore, non-violence. Her occupations must therefore be, as they are, more conducive to peace than war.[1]

It was with a remarkable insight that Gandhi, without challenging their traditional role in society; could make women an important social base for the movement. As with the other important groups such as the students and the peasantry, he told them they had to take the responsibility not just for changing their own situation, but that of the society at large, 'The economic and the moral salvation of India thus rests mainly with you!'[2] Because khadi was seen as a symbol of self-reliance and regeneration, it

---

* Originally published in *Economic and Political Weekly*, vol. 20, no. 40, 5 October 1985, pp. 1695–1702. In the present version some portions of the text and notes have been removed. For the complete text see the original version.

seemed to provide solutions to various problems. 'I swear by this form of Swadeshi, because through it I can provide work to the semi-starved, semi-employed women of India. My idea is to get these women to spin yarn, and to clothe the people of India with khadi woven out of it'[3] With the destruction of India's village crafts, especially the textile industry, due to the impact of colonialism, millions of women lost their means of subsistence. They responded to Gandhi's appeal: 'Today, the Charkha Sangha covers over one hundred thousand women against less than 10,000 men'.[4]

[...]

Gandhi's relentless propaganda in favour of charkha spinning and wearing of khadi was designed to bring the spirit of nationalism and freedom into every home, even in the remotest village. In this way, abstract political ideas, such as struggle against colonial rule assumed concrete form for ordinary people. [...] To wear khadi came to mean many things—opposition to colonial rule, identification with the poor and the exploited, and an assertion of the spirit of self-reliance, of freedom.[5] [...]

[...]

WOMEN IN THE VANGUARD

The salt satyagraha marked a new high watermark of women's participation in the movement. Gandhi's choice of salt as a symbol of protest had amused many. The British had laughed while the Congress intellectuals were bewildered by the strange idea. This, once again, proved Gandhi's genius for seizing the significance of the seemingly trivial but essential details of daily living which are relegated to the woman's sphere. Salt is one of the cheapest of commodities which every woman buys and uses as a matter of routine, almost without thought.

In the past, people could pan their own salt or pick it up out of natural deposits. The Britishers tried to acquire a monopoly over this item of everyday consumption. The only legal salt was government salt from guarded depots. The price had a built-in levy. Thus the government was able to tax everyone, even the poorest of the poor.

To manufacture salt in defiance of British laws prohibiting such manufacture, became a way of declaring one's independence in one's own daily life and also of revolutionizing one's perception of the kitchen as linked to the nation, the personal as linked to the political. This was another campaign in which women in large numbers were galvanized into action, precisely because the action, though simple, appealed to the imagination. Its symbolic value was such as to touch the everyday life of women.

On the famous Dandi march through the villages of Gujarat, Gandhi originally started off with 79 satyagrahis. People from the villages on route and around spontaneously joined the march. When the procession neared Dandi, there were thousand of people walking with Gandhi. Among them were many women. Some of them were wealthy women from cities but a majority were ordinary village women.

Kasturba initiated women's participation by leading 37 women volunteers from the ashram at Sabarmati to offer satyagraha and to demand abolition of the salt tax. Sarojini Naidu, with Manilal Gandhi, led the raid on Dharasana Salt Works in the course of which the police force went berserk trying to crush the non-violent satyagrahis.[6] Kamaladevi led a procession of 15,000 to 'raid' the Wadala Salt Works.[7] Women's associations played an active role in violating the salt laws. Women volunteers carried *lota*s of water from the Chowpatty beach to make salt at home, and many others went out onto the streets selling this contraband salt at fancy prices.

While the salt satyagraha and the civil disobedience movement encouraged and brought about greater participation of women, they also clearly brought out the fact that Gandhi, for the time being, could only envisage a supportive role for women in the movement. By now, some women were getting impatient of playing an auxiliary role, and they urged Gandhi to let them join the famous Dandi march, as volunteers in the core group that was selected to accompany Gandhi all the way. They wanted to fight for freedom like men, and not extend the traditional division of labour between men and women to the movement as well. Up to this point, women had been mainly assigned tasks which they could do while remaining at home such as practising Swadeshi and spinning, and men were primarily responsible for political organizing and public protest actions. Now they were demanding a more active political role. Gandhi saw this impatience as 'healthy sign' but refused to allow them to join the salt march on the plea that they had a 'greater' role to play than merely breaking salt laws. Although women were not permitted to join the march, it was clear that every man and woman was expected to break the salt laws all over the country.

However, according to Gandhi, the job even more suited to women's genius was the picketing of liquor and foreign cloth shops. 'Who can make a more effective appeal to the heart than women?' He chose women for this job because of their 'inherent' capacity for non-violence. He felt that the non-cooperation movement of 1921 had partially failed because men had been entrusted with picketing and violence had crept in. 'Drink and drugs sap the moral well-being of those who are given to the habit. Foreign cloth undermines the economic foundations of the nation and throws millions out of employment. The distress in each case is felt in the home and therefore by the women'.[8] Again, their personal lives and problems were shown to them as being linked with the national cause. Moreover, this agitation of picketing was to be 'initiated and controlled exclusively by women. They may take and should get as much assistance as they need from men, but, the men should be in strict subordination to them'.[9]

Gandhi was not very wrong when he said that if women would 'take up these two activities, specialize in them; they would contribute more than man to national freedom. They would have an access of power and self-confidence to which they have hitherto been strangers'.[10] Nor could the government 'long remain supine to an agitation so peaceful and so resistless'.[11] This was an agitation likely to hit as much the Indian traders and merchants who dealt in foreign goods. The use of women as pickets would help prevent uncalled-for provocation from both sides. It was a brilliant tactical move on the part of Gandhi inasmuch as it prevented the blatant hostility of this trading class from splitting the ranks of Indians. In fact, there is hardly any evidence of their having resisted women pickets.

Further, the merit of the movement lay in the fact that 'In this agitation thousands of women, literate and illiterate can take part'. Highly educated women had an 'opportunity of actively identifying themselves with the masses and helping them both morally and materially'. The job was no less an 'adventure' for being non-violent, Gandhi warned them. 'They might even find themselves in prison...be insulted and even injured bodily' but 'to suffer such insult and injury would be their pride'.[12]

This programme of picketing did manage to fire the imagination of women participants for some time, at least. Hansa Mehta saw it as an effort towards 'Purna Swaraj'. From mere spinning to picketing marked a definite transition. The market now became the sphere of women's activity. For instance, the Provincial Committee for Prevention of Liquor Consumption issued an appeal for 2,500 volunteers in Bombay. Women dressed in orange khadi saris picketed shops. Hundreds went to prison. '...and always more women emerged from seclusion to take their places'.[13]

[...] [T]his movement too petered out in the wake of the general disenchantment with the civil disobedience movement [...]. Women from extremely traditional and conservative families, who had never been out of parda, 'faced the barefacedness of walking unveiled in public processions and all that was afterwards involved in prison life'.[14] They gave up their religious and caste prejudices in the process. 'The cause of Swaraj swept all taboos and old customs before it'.[15] They willingly accepted food from untouchables in the prison. [...] In all, about 3,000 women served prison sentences. As Brailsford observes, the movement would have been worthwhile even 'if it had done nothing more than emancipating women'.[16] From this point on, there was no going back.

Gandhi succeeded in galvanizing the traditional housebound woman as a powerful instrument of political action. The incidental impact of this phenomenon was no less significant for not being immediately visible. By opening the gates to women's political participation, Gandhi facilitated the acceptance of the women's cause by the Nationalists.

Sarojini Naidu was Gandhi's choice for Congress presidentship in 1925, much before the emergence of a women's lobby within the party. Even more significant was the way women came to be represented in legislatures in the 1920s. When Montague and Chelmsford came to India in 1917 to work out some reforms towards self-government, Sarojini Naidu and Annie Besant led a small delegation of women to demand that the same rights of representation in legislatures be granted to women as well. The British government tried to evade the issue by suggesting that the new legislatures they were creating, which included Indian representatives, should be allowed to decide for themselves on this issue. This was said on the assumption that Indians, being more 'backward', would never be able to accept the idea of equal political rights for women. But within a few years of Gandhi's entry into politics and his attempts to integrate women's issues into the movement, there had developed an unusual kind of sympathetic awareness within large sections of the Congress towards the idea of equal rights for women. Thus, beginning with the Madras legislature, between 1924 and 1928, each one of the legislatures voted to make it possible for women to be represented in them.

The sudden and massive entry of women into salt satyagraha in 1930 opened up for women further opportunities which could not be denied again. Participation in public and political life brought with it a new prestige and status vis-à-vis their male counterparts. This was a major reason why as early as 1931, the Congress party passed a resolution at its Karachi annual session committing itself to the political equality of women, regardless of their status and qualifications. It is significant that at that time, women in most European countries had not yet won the right to vote, despite a much longer history of struggle on this issue.

However, as independence drew nearer, Gandhi kept emphasizing with more vigour: 'Women must have votes and an equal legal status. But the problem does not end there. It only commences at the point where women begin to affect the political deliberations of the nation'.[17]

NON-VIOLENCE AND WOMEN'S LEADERSHIP

The participation of women in the movement should not be seen as one of the peripheral gains of the movement. Gandhi had designed his strategy and chosen his particular forms of struggle very consciously and deliberately so as to encourage this:

> My contribution to the great problem [of Women's role in society] lies in my presenting for acceptance of truth and ahimsa in every walk of life, whether for individuals or nations. I have hugged the hope that in this woman will be the unquestioned leader and, having thus found her place in human evolution, will shed her inferiority complex.[18]

[...]

Gandhi's insistence on non-violence as a revolutionary weapon contributed to creating favourable conditions for mass participation of people, especially women. More and more people felt encouraged to come out of their homes, instead of hiding in fear, as they tend to do when movements encourage the use of violence. The programmes of action undertaken as part of nonviolent satyagraha were such that women would not feel limited or unequal to men; as they inevitably do when sheer muscle power or capacity for inflicting violence are to determine the outcome of a struggle. Thus women's traditional qualities, such as their lesser capacity for organized violence, were not downgraded but were held up as models of superior courage. When used consciously and collectively, this form of non-violence could put the mightiest weapons to shame.

[...]

It is significant that Gandhi admitted to having learnt the technique of non-violent passive resistance from women, especially from his wife and his mother. He tells us that even when he managed to bulldoze his way with Kasturba, her passive resistance to what she saw as his unreasonable actions and attitudes, compelled him to change his bearing

from that of a dominating husband to that of a person who believed in the spirit of equality and acted on the principle of mutual consideration.
    [...]

WOMEN IN THE FREEDOM MOVEMENT:
SOME CONTRADICTIONS

[...]

Gandhi continually emphasized that if Swaraj was to be more meaningful than a mere transfer of power, Congress members must go and work for a radical reconstruction of the economy and polity in villages. He laid particular stress on the duty of educated urban women to work with their rural sisters. While he himself travelled widely in rural areas, establishing independent and direct communication with the people, not enough Congressmen followed his example. Few dedicated themselves to consistent work in villages. Of these few, very few were women.

Most of the urban women activists, and leaders came to be involved through the involvement of their male relatives. When a household was mobilized, the extent of women's involvement was likely to be decided by that of the men. And the fervour of even leading nationalist leaders did not go so far as to encourage wives, mothers, daughters to abandon hearth and home, and go off to work in villages. To respond to Gandhi's call could well mean a break with one's family, and a very few women did make that break. But the large majority of even the middle-class women could not have taken such a step forward in defiance of the wishes of their families. A major cause for this inability was that women were not likely to have independent means of their own, either by way of jobs or property. The small handful of women, like Kamaladevi, who made efforts to live and work in villages, remained individual exceptions, so their efforts yielded limited results. Apart from this paucity of urban women activists going to work in rural areas, there was also a dearth of rural women who could develop into full time workers. Many rural young men who went to nearby towns to study, would get exposed to, and drawn into nationalist activity, and would then return to their villages, motivated to spread the message there. Rural women had relatively much less access to education, much less mobility and contact with urban areas. Thus, existing differences in the social possibilities open to men and to women inevitably led by a chain reaction to the development of fewer women activists and consequently, lesser mobilization of women.

Even for the mass of middle-class women in cities, participation remained at a very rudimentary level such as picketing during certain phases, distributing nationalist literature, attempting meetings, and occasionally joining demonstrations. The activity of women was even more sporadic and fitful than the movement as a whole. Active involvement in Congress activities was confined to a few outstanding women such as Sarojini Naidu, Kamaladevi, and Hansa Mehta. The debates within the National Congress and the different points of view of different groups were not reflected in the discussions of the women's associations. The policy programme of the All India Women's Conference for the 1930s spells out this policy of maintaining a certain apolitical stance.

> The All India Women's Conference shall not belong to any political organization nor take an active part in party politics, but shall be free to discuss and contribute to all questions and matters that affect the welfare of the people of India, with particular reference to women and children.[19]

Women's activity and discussion focused on spinning, hawking khadi, fund raising, enrolling new members, picketing, and fitfully working for removal of untouchability and for promotion of Hindu–Muslim unity. The role of the women in the national movement thus remained auxiliary and supportive. They did not come out for direct action as women had in South Africa. This despite the fact that Gandhi thought satyagraha, as a new weapon of agitation, was eminently suited to the non-violent temperament of women. Gandhi's tribute to 'a woman's sacrifice' puts forward clearly the role that women came to play, which had much in common with the role played by women in many other movements. Gandhi quotes the letter of a young Congressman who had been staying for a while in the home of a woman whose son, also a Congress worker, had just been imprisoned:

> During the great awakening that took place last year amongst women there were heroines whose mute work the nation will never know. How and then however one gets information of such village work. Here is one such sample...when our Congress camp was declared illegal and locked up by the police we shifted to the hut of a poor Mahishya woman—Habu's mother of Baradongal. We have read of Gorki's mother. We saw her incarnate in Habu's mother.[20]

Night and day, she used to cook for them, nurse the sick among them, and look after all of them out of her meagre resources with great sacrifice and devotion. Here was the ideal 'mother' in the service of the motherland. But unlike Gorki's mother, women, by and large, could not emerge as important political leaders in the movement. They continued to play a supportive and nurturant role for the men in the movement.

Women and harijans were rightly seen by Gandhi as the two most depressed groups in Indian society since their disabilities had certain specificities which needed special attention. Yet neither women as a body nor the mass of harijans have lost their disabilities. Neither group had won an equal place in the national mainstream. What Gandhi ensured for both these groups by the manner in which he took up their cause was a two-fold achievement. First, he contributed greatly to loosening the traditional biases to such an extent that the rare exceptions among these groups could indeed stand on an equal footing vis-à-vis the rest of society, and could reach high positions. Sarojini Naidu, Gandhi's choice for Congress presidentship, in 1925 is a case in point. Speaking after the resolution on fundamental rights and economic policy, drafted by Nehru in consultation with Gandhi in 1931, had been passed, Gandhi said:

> Then there is the abolition of all disabilities attaching to the women, in regard to the public employment, office of power or honour, etc. The moment this is done, many of the disabilities to which the women are subjected will cease. So far as the Congress is concerned, we have admitted no such disability. We have had Mrs Annie Besant and Sarojini Devi as our residents, and in the future free state of India it will open to us to have the women presidents.[21]

However, Gandhi realized that this kind of advanced legislation could benefit only the exceptional woman who had the means to make use of these opportunities.˘

Second, even though Gandhi failed to evolve a concrete programme for materially altering the socio-economic condition of the mass of women, he succeeded in raising the question of their depressed condition as a moral question for society to reckon with. He made a major contribution towards creating a general climate of sympathetic awareness of women's situation. Though he had a personal predilection for idealizing certain roles played by women, yet he did not shrink from accepting the logical consequences of his insistence on absolute equality between men and women. For instance, when someone suggested that if women, were given equal property rights, it would lead to 'immorality' amongst them, Gandhi's reply was categorically in favour of women having such rights [...].[22]

However, the necessity for independent control over economic resources was not integrated into the struggle for womens rights. Gandhi did advocate spinning of khadi as a means of livelihood for women and a way of combating the declining employment of women, especially in rural areas where such decline followed the destruction of traditional crafts and occupations. However, spinning on the charkha could not, at that juncture, become a viable means of livelihood for most women. Khadi was not and could not be a real alternative to mill-made cloth for the mass of people, because khadi works out to be more expensive and far less durable than most mill-made cloth. The disappearance of British textiles from the Indian market did not mean a victory for khadi but a victory for Indian-owned textile mills.

Thus Gandhi cannot be said to have evolved a concrete programme to tackle one of the basic causes of women's powerlessness—their total economic dependence and lack of control over the resources of the family. In the absence of a programme for the economic empowerment of women or the material betterment of their condition, the moral concern for them soon degenerated in the post-Gandhian era into the payment of lip service to the cause of women on public platforms and in party manifestos, while the life condition of most women continued to deteriorate unchecked, and everyday attitudes towards women remain obscurantist and insulting.

One of the limitations of Gandhi's thinking, then, was that he sought to change not so much the material condition of women as their 'moral' condition. [...] Gandhi failed to realize that, among other things, oppression is not an abstract moral condition, but a social and historical experience related to production relations. He tried changing women's position without either transforming their relation to the outer world of production or the inner world of family, sexuality, and reproduction.

For Gandhi, equality of the sexes did not mean equality of occupations nor did it mean equality in the time of work and power. He was in favour of maintaining a 'harmonious' division of labour between men and women which had been operative since the time of Adam and persists to the present day. 'Adam wove and Eve span'.[23] He did not believe in women working for wages or undertaking commercial enterprises. Gandhi did not envisage any fundamental change in the traditional role-relationship of women. Whilst both men and women were seen as fundamentally one, at some point there was a vital difference between the two. Hence the vocations of the two must also be different. Gandhi could go on dogmatically asserting this in spite of the fact that in several other contexts, he challenged the idea of a rigid division of labour between the sexes. For instance, in reply to a professor's charge that he was wasting the energies of the nation by asking 'able-bodied men to sit for spinning like women' instead of letting them fight for freedom with 'manlier weapons', Gandhi put forward in defence of his spinning programme the following arguments:

> It is contrary to experience to say that any vocation is exclusively reserved for one sex only... Whilst women *naturally* (emphasis mine) cook for the household, organized cooking on a large scale is universally done by men throughout the world. Fighting is predominantly men's occupation, but Arab women fought like heroines side-by-side with their husbands in the early struggles of Islam... And today in Europe we find women shining as lawyers, doctors and administrators.[24]

Even the fact that in rural India, women among the agricultural labourers and small peasants are equally, if not more, involved in the actual production process could not shake Gandhi's belief that the woman might 'supplement the meagre resources of the family, but man remains the main breadwinner'. This he saw as 'the most natural division of spheres of work.'[25] The duty of motherhood was seen as requiring qualities which men need not possess. 'She is passive, he is active. She is essentially mistress of the house. He is the bread winner, he is the keeper and distributor of the bread!'[26] In his opinion, it was 'degrading both for men and woman that women should be called upon or induced to foresake the hearth and shoulder the rifle for the protection of that hearth. It is a reversion to barbarity'.[27]

Thus he saw male and female in terms of the 'active-passive' complementary which has been an important ideological device for denying women any chance to acquire power and decision-making ability in the family and in society. The unjust domination of woman by man that Gandhi thought he opposed is something inherent in the very role relationship that he envisaged for her—that of being a 'complement' to man. He felt that since man is supreme in the outward life, therefore, it is appropriate that he should have a greater knowledge of that world. On the other hand, home life is entirely the sphere of woman and, therefore, in domestic affairs women ought to have more control. 'True they are equals in life, but their functions differ'.[28]

Furthermore 'as Nature has made men and women different, it is necessary to maintain a difference between the education of the two'.[29] So, he concluded, 'it is a woman's right to rule the home. Man is master outside it'.[30] In his view, 'The woman who knows and fulfils her duty realizes her dignified status. She is the queen, not the slave, of the household over which she presides'.[31]

Gandhi could not envisage 'the wife, as a rule, following an avocation independently of her husband. The care of the children and the upkeep of the household are quite enough to fully engage all her energy'.[32] He felt that 'In a well-ordered society the additional burden of maintaining the family ought not to fall on her. The man should look to the maintenance of the family, the woman to household management; the two thus supplementing and complementing each other's labours'.[33] 'In trying to ride the horse that man rides, she brings herself and him down'.[34] In the new order of Gandhi's imagination, 'all will work according to their capacity for an adequate return for their labour'. But where women's capacity is concerned, he has already arbitrarily drawn the limit: 'Women in the new order will be part-time workers, their primary function being to look after the home'.[35]

When Gandhi was asked whether the wheel was to be a revolutionary weapon in the hands of women as he said it was in the hands of a Jawarharlal, he said: 'How could it be such in the hands of an ignorant woman? But if every woman in India span, then a silent revolution would certainly be created of which a Jawaharlal could make full use':[36]

What Gandhi opposed was the 'excessive subordination of the wife to the husband', not the fact of women generally playing a subordinate role. For instance, Gandhi always dismissed as 'hysterical exaggeration' any outright attack on the institution of the family. From many instances, I quote one. In response to an angry letter from a young man, narrating the pathetic plight of his sister who was married to a pervert and a debauch, and describing her helplessness as 'one of the most shameful aspects of Hinduism, where woman is left entirely at the mercy of man', Gandhi insisted that this kind of rabid condemnation was 'based on a hysterical generalization from an isolated instance. For millions of Hindu wives live in perfect peace and are queens in their own homes. They exercise an authority over their husbands which any woman would envy'.[37]

He could envisage women being 'free' even while playing a socially subordinate role. This contradiction is related to the entire Gandhian world-view and his concept of 'trusteeship' in society, which represents his dual attitude of simultaneous acquiescence in and revolt against authority. As a good patriarch, the maximum he could bring himself to do was to rationalize authority, make it 'just' and 'humane'. He would not acknowledge the inherent interconnection between most forms of authority and injustice, or between the enslavement of women and the denial of economic independence to them by keeping them confined to the household as their main sphere of activity. He advocated 'harmony' and 'tyranny' in the social division of labour.[38] [...]

Gandhi's dual attitude of obedience to and rebellion against authority is evident in every single movement or campaign he led, and in the very philosophy of non-violent satyagraha. The attempt of the satyagrahi was not only to try to transform and win over the oppressor into being more 'just', but also meticulously to accept the general jurisdiction of the authority and its laws, even while protesting against the 'unjust' aspect of those laws. The line was each time arbitrarily drawn by Gandhi. Therefore, it was not only the women's movement that he tried to contain and fit into a supplementary role vis-à-vis the national movement. He did likewise with the independent self-activity of all other oppressed groups—the poor peasants, the landless labourers, the industrial workers, and the harijans. It was partly a matter of political farsightedness in anticipating the threat of movements parallel or rival to the national-movement. It was also partly due to his deep-rooted, never successfully implemented, conception that authority could be made to act in benevolent 'trust'—whether it was the authority of husband over wife or that of millowner over labour.

While Gandhi could see that the self-view imposed on women with regard to their inferiority was part of the 'self-interested teaching of man' and the age-old 'subordination of women', he failed to revise his concept of the 'natural division of labour', between the sexes, nor could he see this division as part of the same 'self-interested teaching of man' which had resulted in the confinement and subordination of woman. While he could be critical of women who 'delight in being ladies this and what not, simply for the fact of being the wives of particular lords'[39] servilely cling to the privileges bestowed on them by their husband's status, he could not go on to see that the very division of labour he upheld made a vicarious existence inevitable for women.

The dichotomy does not end here. He laments that 'a vast majority of girls disappear from public life' as soon as they leave school and college because they are married off.[40] Therefore, 'it is high time that Hindu girls produce or reproduce...a glorified edition, of Parvati and Sita'.[41] In other words, though he might insist that every girl 'is not born to marry', the symbols put forward to draw them into public life are those of ideal wives whose chief qualification was that they spent their lives in selfless service of and unending devotion to husbands. These women had followed their husbands to the end of the world, and helped them to fulfil 'their' duty.

CREATING A FAVOURABLE ATMOSPHERE

Gandhi helped ensure the entry of women into public life without their having to assume a competitive posture vis-à-vis men. The way of their participation in these initial years was patronized by participation of urban, middle-class women in the political life of the country. It is due partly to the Gandhian legacy that every political party tends to reserve a few seats for women in each election without women having to organize themselves as a pressure group to make such a demand. Thus women's entry into social and political life came not only without sufficient pressure from below, but was also characterized by the marked absence of the kind of hostility from men that women's movements in some other parts of the world had to face. This perhaps accounts for the lack of sufficient militancy in the women's movement on women's own issues in India, and the fact that the movement constantly tried to accommodate its demands within a male-dominated power structure. The same pattern characterizes most of the movement today.

Gandhi realized that even if Congressmen manifested no blatant hostility, they tended to shelve this issue, so he kept reminding them: 'It is the privilege of Congressmen to give the women of India a lifting hand' because 'women are in the position somewhat of the slave of old, who did not know that he could or ever had to be free. And when freedom came, for the moment, he felt helpless...It is upto Congressmen to see that they enable the women to realise their full status and play their part as equals of men'.[42]

This attitude helped create an atmosphere of benevolent patronage which has left a deep mark on the political climate of India. The testimony of Margaret Cousins, an Irish feminist who played a major role in women's organizations in India as well as in Britain, brings out this feature very well:

> Perhaps only women like myself who had suffered from the cruelties, the injustices of the men politicians, the man-controlled Press, the man in the street, in England and Ireland while we waged our militant campaign for eight years there after all peaceful and constitutional means had been tried for fifty previous years, could fully appreciate the wisdom, nobility and the passing of fundamental tests in self-government of these Indian legislators...between the Madras Legislature Council in 1921 and Bihar Council in 1929 all the legislative areas of India had conferred the symbol and instrument of equal citizenship with men on women who possessed equal qualifications—a certain amount of literacy, property, age, payment of taxes, length of residence'.[43]

However, Gandhi constantly warned women against depending on patronage. For example, he did not favour reservations for women of the kind that dalits were beginning to demand. 'Merit should be the only test... It would be a dangerous thing to insist on membership on the ground merely of sex. Women and for that matter any group should disdain patronage. They should seek justice, never favours'.[44] Yet even while he thought women's primary work ought to be care of the home, he vigorously asserted the need to give a special weightage to women: 'Seeing however that it has been the custom to decry women, the contrary custom should be to prefer women, merit being equal, to men even if the preference should result in men being entirely displaced by women'.[45]

Gandhi envisioned women entering public life as selfless, devoted social workers. As he began to see more and more clearly that many Congressmen inclined towards self-seeking and power-grabbing, he saw in women the potential force that would selflessly undertake the task of social reconstruction that was to be hallmark of Swaraj. 'The work before them was to make women 'fit to take their, place in society'.[46]

In 1946, a woman wrote to Gandhi complaining that Congress did not put up enough women as candidates for elections nor did they select enough women for official posts. She asked how the interests of women would be safeguarded in a situation where considerations of caste, community, and province outweighed those of merit. Gandhi replied:

So long as considerations of caste and community continue to weigh with us and rule our choice, women will be well-advised to remain aloof and thereby build up their prestige. The question is as to how best this can be done. Today few women take part in politics and most of these do not do independent thinking. They are content to carry out their parents' or their husband's behests. Realising their dependence they cry out for women's rights... Women workers should enrol women as voters, impart or have imparted to them practical education, teach them to think independently, release them from the chains of caste that bind them so as to bring about a change in them which will compel men to realize women's strength and capacity for sacrifice and give her places of honour. If they will do this, they will purify the present unclean atmosphere'.[47]

[...]

Gandhi saw 'women [as] the embodiment of sacrifice and suffering' and felt that 'her advent to public life should therefore result in purifying it, in restraining unbridled ambition and accumulation of property'.[48] It. was given to women to 'teach the art of peace to the warring world thirsting for that nectar'.[49] But politics and professions were to be, by and large, exclusively male domains: 'And you sisters, what would you do by going to Parliament? Do you aspire after the collectorships, commissionerships or even the viceroyalty?... I know that you would not care to, for the Viceroy has got to order executions and hangings, a thing that you would heartily detest'.[50] Gandhi's long suffering, selfless and self-effacing woman was the product of a culture. The capacity for silent suffering which Gandhi idealized was the fact one of the key symptoms of her subordination. But Gandhi made some of these symptoms of subordination a glorified cult of eternal womanhood.

The kind of activity the Kasturba Memorial Trust was involved in was Gandhi's ideal of women in public life. His comments, at the time of the Educational Conference in 1937, on Basic Education, throw further light on this:

> Here is, no doubt, an opportunity for patriotic women with leisure to offer their services to a cause which ranks amongst the noblest of all causes. But, if they come forward, they will have to go through a sound preliminary training. Needy women in search of a living will serve no useful purpose by thinking of joining the movement as a career. If they approach the scheme, they should do so in a spirit of pure service and make it a life mission. They will fail and will be severely disappointed if they approach it in a selfish spirit. If the cultured women of India will make common cause with the villagers, and that too through their children, they will produce a silent and grand revolution in the village life of India.[51]

In other words, the role of the educated, middle-class woman in public life was to be an extension of her domestic role of selfless service. Women were to enter public life as 'sisters' and 'mothers' in the same garb of pseudo-veneration which had hitherto masked their exploitation in the family where their relation to social and public life was strictly mediated through men. Gandhi's very vocabulary, in its exaggerated idealization of women as 'sisters of mercy' and 'mothers of entire humanity' reveals the bias of a benevolent patriarch.

Gandhi wanted women to act as moral guardians of society, as social workers and do-gooders without competing with men in the sphere of power and politics because that would be a 'reversion to barbarity'.[52] Was this a wilful attempt to put the clock back? Or was it that even though actively patronizing such leading women politicians and professionals as Sarojini Naidu, Sucheta Kripalani, and Sushila Nayyar, Gandhi could not thoroughly reconstruct and renovate his ideas? He is one of those few leaders whose practice was at times far ahead of his theory and his stated ideas. Just as in his early years he kept insisting that he was a loyal

citizen of the British Empire even while objectively cutting at the roots
of British imperialism, so also he could keep in harping on women's
real sphere of activity being the home even while actively creating
conditions which could help her break the shackles of domesticity.

[...]

NOTES

1. *Harijan*, 2 December 1939. *Collected Works of Mahatma Gandhi*, Navjivan
   Trust, Ahmedabad, 1982 (henceforth *CW*), vol. LXX, p. 381.
2. *Young India*, 11 August 1921. *CW*, vol. XX, p. 497.
3. M.K. Gandhi, 'Autobiography', p. 413.
4. 'To the Women', Gandhi series, vol. II (ed.) A. Hingorani, Karachi,
   (2nd edn), 1943, p. 37.
5. *Bombay Chronicle*, 27 March 1925. *CW*, vol. XXVI, pp. 419–20.
6. Geoffrey Ashe, 'Gandhi: A Study in Revolution', Asia Publishing House,
   1968, pp. 290–2.
7. Ibid., p. 292.
8. *Young India*, 10 April 1930. *CW*, vol. XLIII, p. 220.
9. Ibid., p. 220.
10. Ibid., p. 220.
11. Ibid., p. 220.
12. *Young India*, 10 April 1930. *CW*, vol. XLIII, pp. 220–1.
13. Geoffrey Ashe, 'Gandhi: A Study in Revolution', p. 295.
14. Margaret, E. Cousins, 'Indian Womanhood Today', Kitabistan, Series No. 5,
    1937, Allahabad, p. 64.
15. Ibid., p. 63.
16. Geoffrey Ashe, 'Gandhi: A Study in Revolution', p. 298.
17. *Young India*, 21 July 1921. *CW*, vol. XX, p. 410.
18. *Harijan*, 24 February 1940. *CW*, vol. LXXI, p. 208.
19. Cited in Margaret, E. Cousins, 'Indian Womanhood Today', pp. 41–2.
20. *Young India*, 21 May 1931. *CW*, vol. XLVI, p. 189
21. Cited,in Tendulkar *Mahatma*, Publications Division, vol. III, p. 89.
22. *CW*, vol. LXXII, p. 137
23. *CW*, vol. LXX, p. 381, *Harijan*, 2 December 1939.
24. *Young India*, 11 June 1925. *CW*, vol. XXVII, pp. 219–20.
25. *Harijan*, 24 February 1940. *CW*, vol. LXXI, p. 208.
26. Ibid., p. 207.
27. Ibid., pp. 207–8.
28. *CW*, vol. XIV, p. 31.
29. 20 October 1917. *CW*, vol. XIV, p. 31.
30. Ibid., p. 31.
31. *CW*, vol. LIX, p. 147.
32. *Harijan*, 12 October 1934. *CW*, vol. LIX, p. 147.

33. Ibid., p. 147.
34. *Harijan*, 24 February 1940. *CW*, vol. LXXI, p. 208.
35. *Harijan*, 16 March 1940. *CW*, vol. LXXI, p. 324.
36. Cited in Tendulkar, *Mahatma*, vol. VII, p. 87.
37. *Young India*, 3 October 1929. *CW*, vol. XLI, pp. 493–4.
38. Geoffrey Ashe, 'Gandhi: A Study in Revolution', p. 242.
39. *CW*, vol. LXII, p. 5.
40. *CW*, vol. XXXV, p. 346.
41. Ibid., p. 346.
42. Cited in Tendulkar, *Mahatma*, vol. VI, p. 24.
43. Margaret, E. Cousins, 'Indian Womanhood Today', pp. 32–3.
44. *Harijan*, vol. X, no. 9, April 7; 1946, p. 67.
45. Ibid., p. 67.
46. *CW*, vol. LXXXIII, pp. 331–2.
47. *Harijan*, 21 April 1946, 'What About Women?', *CW*, vol. LXXXIII, p. 398.
48. *Young India*, 17 October 1929. *CW*, vol. XLII, p. 5.
49. *Harijan*, 24 February 1940. *CW*, vol. LXXI, p. 209.
50. Cited in Tendulkar, *Mahatma*, vol. III, p. 61.
51. Tendulkar, *Mahatma*, vol. IV, p. 200.
52. *Harijan*, 24 February 1940. *CW*, vol. LXXI, pp. 207–8.

17 Politics and Women in Bengal*
The Conditions and Meaning of Participation

Tanika Sarkar

In the literature on women's movements politicization and general emancipation seem to be terms that are used almost interchangeably.[†] Political activity of any kind either appears to stem from a high degree of social freedom that already prevails or the very act of participation is taken to bring about an instant liberation, a permanent revolution in wider social status. An exploration of this widely held assumption within the context of a specific period of the national movement may be useful to test the validity of several such generalizations about women and politicization.

The late 1920s and early 1930s saw the growth of a rich and highly complex spectrum of political experience in Bengal: resurgence of the Congress-led nationalist movement from 1928, revival of revolutionary terrorism, and a wide variety of peasant and working class action. Instead of just ticking off the fields where women 'also ran', it might perhaps be more relevant to focus on the specific form and content of such politics: to avoid treating women as an undifferentiated, homogenized mass and to try to identify, rather, the connection between the nature of a particular movement and the social composition of its women participants. An interesting problem about these political struggles is what perceptions their male participants had about the place of women in Indian society and whether any new dimensions were added through the association of women comrades. Finally, we have to explore the wider effect of politicization: what impact it had on the immediate domestic milieu and ethos and whether it led to a radicalization in other aspects of women's life and status. The starting point of any analysis of women's political behaviour has to be a recognition of the fact that political involvement is very rarely an act of totally independent choice for women but may quite often be a matter of pressures and pulls within the entire household.

* Originally published in *The Indian Economic and Social History Review*, vol. 21, no. 1, 1984, pp. 91–101.

Women, particularly in India, are often a sum and product of diverse relationships within the family and kinship nexus. How exactly political consciousness and activity grow out of or grew in reaction to this context is, however, the matter for a different and a more interesting study.

The late twenties constituted a formative period for working class agitation and association and women workers were particularly active in the Calcutta and Howrah municipal scavengers' strike of 1928 and in the jute mill strikes in 1928 and 1929. These strikes give us some idea about the mode of existence, the forms of protest, and the capacity for political organization and leadership of working class women. Their main form of political action seemed to have been sudden, sporadic and frequently violent outbursts in the course of an ongoing struggle. During the Howrah Municipality scavengers' strike of April 1928 there was a major clash between Anglo-Indian police sergeants and women scavengers who threw pots of excreta at them—a symbolic demonstration of how their very degradation, related to impure caste and lowly tasks, might be turned into a weapon of strength. The sergeants fled, tearing off their uniforms and vowing never to return until they were permitted to fire.[1] Official reports[2] as well as contemporary accounts[3] commented frequently on women's militancy in the jute mill strikes at Bauria and Chengail in 1929. On 6 June, for instance, women strikers of the Ludlow mill at Chengail looted the local bazar, clashed with the police, and stoned an European mill assistant.[4] It seems that local traditions of militancy remained extremely tenacious for we find Bauria women in a very similar action as late as 1949.[5]

Some women leaders and organizers joined the working class movement from outside as well. In the mid-twenties Santosh Kumari Gupta encountered considerable social ostracism in a few abortive attempts to organize jute mill workers and her example was more successfully emulated by Prabhabati Das Gupta, a young student freshly returned from the United States. A prominent leader of the 1928 scavengers' strike, she earned the epithet 'Dhangarma' (mother of scavengers), used with affection by workers and scorn by her middle-class compatriots.[6] Prabhabati tried to build up a base, single-handed, among Corporation scavengers who were ritually and socially at the bottom of the city hierarchy. She began to visit them at their slums regularly and startled them by eating at their 'dhabas'.[7] This act of sharing food violated deeply-ingrained caste as well as sexist taboos for the ritual transgression was doubly odious for women who in any case had no business to organize workers for political action. Regarded at first with amused tolerance, such fraternization soon led to her acceptance by the scavengers. In November 1927 the Workers and Peasants Party set up a Scavengers Union of Bengal with Muzaffar Ahmad as President and Prabhabati as Secretary.[8] Since women formed an important section of the unskilled labour force, both among scavengers and jute workers, the demand charters in the strikes regularly reflected some of their special issues—for example maternity leave and benefits.[9]

The context to such militancy is provided by the acute and peculiar problems of largely migrant women workers[10] in an urban and industrial milieu that imposed baffling conditions of living and working. The management chose to ignore them as the ratio of women workers was declining, and in a chronic labour surplus situation that had persisted unbroken since 1914 problems of a weakening minority carried no urgency.[11] The mills operated at a relatively low technological level[12] where a largely unskilled workforce was quite adequate and the management had no interest in improving family conditions which would have ensured a stable labour force and skill formation.

Referring to work hours under the double-shift system in jute mills Babuniyah, a woman jute worker, wanted paid maternity leave and crèche facilities since:

> I leave my house at 5 in the morning to come to work at the mill and go home at 9.30. I come again to work at 11. I do not get sufficient time for proper cooking. If I am a little late in coming to work the baboos reprimand me. I feed my children after 9.30.

Muthialu, a woman from the same factory, confirmed and filled out the picture: 'I cook my food at dawn and to the mill at 5.30 in the morning, work till 6.30, return home, take my food, and go back at 8 o'clock. I then work till 1 o'clock, then go home, cook my food and eat it'. She once took her pregnant daughter (working at the same place) to a doctor attached to the mill. 'The lady doctor wrote something and told us to go to the Sahib at the mill. He read this paper and tore it. We did not know what to do. My daughter went back to work. She subsequently lost her child.[13] Managers, however, stuck to their comforting piece of traditionalism, insisting against all evidence that even if crèches were provided, working mothers would never use them.[14]

Another set of problems confronted the unmarried woman worker more particularly. Caste prejudice combined with the complete lack of privacy in accommodation prevented most migrant workers from bringing their wives into their place of work, thus creating an acute sex-imbalance in the mill *bustee*s and a good deal of blatant prostitution. This was a vicious circle as the prevalence of prostitution stiffened the resolve to leave women behind in home villages. Prostitution was very difficult to disentangle from the common state of the single woman worker who was given no separate housing arrangement. Living unprotected among a numerically overwhelming male population, she was forced to seek the protection of a single man at a time: 'There are women who come with men from outside Bengal, who are not their wives and who live very often with these men and work under their protection at the mill'.[15]

These problems help to explain the ready participation by women in strikes and the propensity for sporadic violence. What is remarkable, however, is that there was no corresponding extension of such militancy in union building or strike organizing activities which remained the preserve of men and middle-class women leaders from outside. Despite a clear will and ability to fight, women workers thus failed to throw up their own leaders. The problem cannot be explained away by the fact that leaders and male workers knew and represented their grievances adequately. Their specific demands were routinely placed towards the bottom of any charter of demands but strikes did not begin and end around these issues. In speeches of leaders we find practically no appeals directed at women particularly, no moves to debate and discuss their grievances for consciousness-raising purposes.[16] Subsuming the special problems of the woman worker within a general list set the pattern for a similar use of the these issues in labour and other political movements in general; there would always be a steamrollering of complexities, a certain failure of perception which marginalized the specific implications of her existence.

Whereas the pace of labour unrest slackened somewhat from the early thirties, a multiplicity of peasant movements characterized the whole of our period. Women, however, remained conspicuous by their absence in the entire range of open protest. They might, indeed, have cooperated from behind the scenes especially with moral approval but open, active protest seemed to have taken place without any direct participation from them. Since newspaper accounts and police and administrative reports were particularly sensitive to this theme and usually went out of their way to report on them, complete silence in this case does seem to constitute quite convincing negative evidence. A partial explanation may be found in the connection between the structure of the female workforce and women's capacity for politicization. An exploration of the 1931 census data confirms two very interesting facts. Except for domestic service, the agricultural labour sector and a few organized industries, very few other occupations in Bengal had any significant proportion of women workers. Also, wherever such employment occurred, it was almost universally caste-based. The proportion of female earners per 1,000 males in different castes was estimated as: Brahmin, 7; Kayastha, 8; Baidya, 8; Mahisya, 5; Namasudra, 7.[17] In contracts when we look at the most impure and depressed castes or untouchables, we find much higher figures: Bagdi, 29; Bauri, 52; Chamar, 17; Dom, 33.[18] The figures reveal an inverse relationship between the ritual ranking of a caste and the proportion of its women earners. If some degree of flexibility was possible in cities, in villages a stricter correlation between women earners and caste position was usually preserved.

To combine social respectability with growing economic prosperity, dominant peasant castes like Mahisyas tended to emulate the behaviour pattern of the higher castes which almost inevitably involved a distancing from manual labour. The first step in this process of distancing was to remove women from all physical labour outside the family kitchen or nursery. In Punjab, where a direct participation in the production process by men was glorified in the dominant peasant ethos, women, even when they did work on their family plots wanted to be classified in the census as dependents.[19] Poorer peasants, like the Namasudras, would in fact go even further, for to them an absolute adherence to orthodox norms would be the only way of demarcating themselves from de-peasantized labourers or untouchable communities existing on the periphery of village society. It would be rather interesting to investigate whether rising socio-economic status carried with it a changing style of dress among women— a more elaborate way of wearing the sari, a larger number of articles of clothing, cumbrous jewellery, and hairstyle—all designed to restrict free movement as external manifestations of a growing distance from manual labour, like the bound feet of Chinese women which had spread from the Manchu court to ambitious peasant families.

There seems to be then a definite equivalence between the potential for politicization and a direct involvement with the production process. This is further borne out by the tribal share-cropper women's militancy in the Tebhaga movement:[20] tribal women in North Bengal were active earning members as well as important political agitators. Since much of the peasant action in our period tended to concern stable peasant categories, women who were not involved in the production process, tended to stay out of class struggles as well.

This brings us to an interesting paradox: if women were conspicuous by their absence in peasant protest, what then explains the very active role of groups of peasant women in the Civil Disobedience movement? In several south-western and eastern districts of Bengal the cooperation of entire families was essential for the conduct of certain types of agitations. In the course of the no-chowkidari tax movement[21] all adult members of a participant family might be arrested, crops burnt down, granaries and houses looted, and all moveable property distrained, affecting the income of peasants often previously close to the substance margin. Such a large-scale risk would have been impossible to take without the full consent of all family members.[22] Rural women signified their consent in a more active manner too. In order to evade tax payment men and women would flee to nearby forests, feeding their standing crops to the cattle so that these did not fall into police hands. In the Arambagh sub-division of Hooghly, peasant women collectively resisted tax collection by the police. At Indas in Bankura, hundreds of women lay down on the road and successfully barred the exit of distrained goods from the village for three whole days.[23] After the first wave of arrests had put all adult males in a disturbed area behind the bars, women were put into positions of local leadership. Towards the end of the first phase of Civil Disobedience, we find Mahisya women like Nityabala Gole or Kaminibala Adhikary conducting the movement at Midnapur villages as local 'Dictators'. This militancy was sustained in the face of a brutal police counter-offensive; insults, molestation, lathi charges, and even firing were their daily fare.[24] Urmilabala Paria, a young Mahisya girl, was the first woman martyr from Midnapur.[25]

A similar pattern is noticeable in the highly public role assumed by women from extremely orthodox urban sections. Women from Marwari and Gujarati business families courted arrest, occupied official buildings, organized demonstrations and assumed charge of picketing, flag hoisting, and processions. In the towns of Comilla and Noakhali in Eastern Bengal, women from upper class conservative Muslim families played a similar role. Bose activized Nari Satyagraha samitis in Burrabazar, the business heart of Calcutta, and organized special wings for girl students within the Bengal Provincial Students' Association.[26] In fact, deployment of women in certain categories of agitation seemed to have been a deliberate part of Congress strategy, as this was expected to reduce the intensity of police repression, especially in the case of respectable middle-class urban women.

The apparently smooth, painless politicization of women belonging to a milieu which had traditionally restricted their role within well-defined domestic confines was a process that met with applause rather than resistance from their male guardians. This was for most women the first instance when they were allowed to share in an activity outside the household. There can be no denying that this step must have been preceded by an acute, indeed revolutionary, struggle with their own sensibilities and inhibitions, but even that must have been facilitated by the sure knowledge of social approval. What, then, explains the sanction behind women in nationalist politics to whom other forms of politicization, indeed other means of public activity, were strictly denied?

Obviously, participation in the Gandhian movement was perceived by even socially conservative nationalist families as not something antithetical to social respectability or the Sanskritization process, but, on the contrary, as an essential component of it. An important precedent was set by the example of immediate social superiors. Locally dominant peasants, like Jhareswar Majhi of Pichhaboni (in Contai sub-division, Midnapur) or zamindars like Lakshmikanta Pramanik of Mahishbathan in the 24 Parganas[27] would set the pattern by bringing out their women in nationalist action which encouraged lesser peasant nationalists. This, however, simply begs the question at a different social level: how could such peasant and zamindar families take this step?

A more fundamental exploration would be related to the nature of the Gandhian movement itself and its implications for the socially-accepted or traditionally presented role of women. Participation was intended for non-violent modes of action and therefore would not entail too drastic a violation of the feminine image that a violent struggle would have involved. Again, gradually in certain Congress strongholds like Midnapur, the Congress became something like a parallel authority, an overarching hegemony, executing police, judicial, and administrative functions and creating an alternative concept of legality.[28] Participation in the Congress movement then by extension became obedience to the properly constituted authority and not its defiance, and this too was more consonant with womanly attributes.

The most crucial element in dovetailing the feminine role with nationalist politics was perhaps the image of Gandhi as a saint or even a religious deity and the perception of the patriotic struggle as an essentially religious duty. According to this perception, joining the Congress agitation would not really be politicization, a novel and doubtful role for the woman, but sharing a religious mission—a role deeply embedded in a tradition sanctified by the example of Meera Bai and the 'sanyasinis'. The stress on the personal saintliness of Gandhi, a subtle symbiosis between the religious and the political in the nationalist message under his leadership, enabled nationalism to transcend the realm of politics and elevate itself to a religious domain. This was no innovation of Gandhi, however, who actually strengthened and continued and inherited tradition which started with Bankimchandra's Bande Mataram—his hymn to the Motherland—and was further consolidated with the Extremist discourse on nationalism. Patriotism was subsumed within religion, the country became a vivid new deity added to the Hindu pantheon and, by a sleigh of hand, became at once the highest deity from the moment of her deification: 'it is your image that we worship in the temples'.[29] The idiom of nationalist culture found its most creative fulfilment in the Swadeshi literature of Rabindranath Tagore who forged a deeply religion-oriented vocabulary steeped in the imagery of Durga, the demon-slayer and protector of the innocent: 'in your right hand shines the sword while the left hand takes away fear; both eyes smile tenderly while the third eye on the forehead glows with fire'.[30]

The Motherland has become the Mother Goddess, dominating the world of Gods and demanding the highest sacrifice from all. The special implication of all this for women, held to be aspects of Shakti herself, were not left unexploited. Mobilization of women in the nationalist movement was made repeatedly on these lines: unless the vital principle of Shakti imprisoned in women is released, the great act of sacrifice will not be complete.[31] After C.R. Das' death, Subhas Bose asked Das' wife Basanti Devi to assume leadership of the movement, 'The spiritual quest of Bengal has always been voiced through the cult of the Mother'.[32] This mode of appeal, however, had a fundamental problem: it seemed to be an evocation of the latent strength, even violence, in the woman's nature, which tradition strives to contain. The Gandhian movement resolved the tension beautifully by retaining the religious content of nationalism while turning the movement non-violent and imparting to it a gentle, patient, long-suffering, sacrificial ambience particularly appropriate for the women. If the movement itself is non-violent then no dangerous, aggressive note is imparted to the feminine personality through participation.

Patriotic action and sacrifice on an equal scale assumed new proportions within revolutionary terrorism. Women's association with the cult of individual terror had been a long-standing one and women sympathizers had often acted as couriers and organizers of logistics support. This role was widely celebrated in patriotic literature like *Chalar Pathey*, a collection of short stories on this theme which came to be extremely popular with young terrorists.[33] Saratchandra Chattopadhyaya's

Pather Dabi gave a more activist role to certain special categories of women, installing them even in positions of second-level leadership and widened the circle of potential recruits who were inspired by his Sumitra.[34] Such association with violent action, however, could still be accommodated within the traditional role of nurture, enriching rather than contradicting feminine morality.

A sharp break occurs in 1931 when two teenaged schoolgirls assassinated the District Magistrate of Comilla. Form this date women crowded into unprecedented roles and actions in quick succession. Pritilata Waddedar led the attack on the Chittagong European Club, Kalpana Dutta jumped bail and disappeared underground with Surya Sen's band of absconders, Bina Das fired on the Bengal Governor Anderson at a Calcutta University convocation function.[35] The woman terrorist was no longer the mother or sister sheltering the fugitive but a full-fledged comrade-in-arms, revolutionizing all precedents and norms for political action.

Almost simultaneously we find a swift and decisive reaction in the same patriotic literature that had enshrined her earlier role. Saratchandra's *Bipradas* appeared in 1935, ridiculing not only the political woman but also the educated, Westernized, emancipated woman who seeks a role outside her home.[36] The most powerful expression of this new attitude appeared in *Char Adhyaya* (1934), Tagore's virulent and furious attack against the creed of individual terror which he described in the novel as 'nightmarism' (*Biblishikapantha*).[37] More powerful than his disgust with terrorism appears to be his distaste for the women in politics and from this point he moves on to a horrified and explicit rejection of the emancipated woman herself—sentiments that never appeared with such force or clarity in any of his other works. When the revolutionary heroine Ela confesses her mistake in associating with politics, the hero Atin declares triumphantly:

> At last I see the real girl...you reign at the heart of home with a fan in your hand and preside over the serving of milk, rice and fish. When you appear with wild hair and angry eyes on the arena where politics has the whip hand, you are not your normal self but are unbalanced, unnatural.

'I am a serving woman', declares the reformed Ela: 'It is my duty to serve you men'. And finally: 'up to now women have served while men have provided the means of livelihood. Anything to the contrary is shameful'.[38] The reaction to the unprecedented association of violence with women thus delineated the socially-accepted limits to the image and role of the political woman and revealed deeply-rooted notions about her place in society as a whole. The most interesting aspect about Tagore's absolute critique of the political woman is the nature of the chain-reaction that in one stride encompasses all manner of non-traditional activity even beyond politics.

How did the terrorist woman come to terms with the transgression of femininity implicit in her action? Strikingly enough, having once taken this revolutionary step she then freezes her revolution at this point and hastens to fit it into an accepted and traditional model: that of sacrifice. Pritilata Waddedar left behind a last testament before committing suicide where she had tried to justify her involvement in violent action. Unlike the late nineteenth century Russian populist woman[39] or the pre-1911 terrorist women and the liberated political activists of the May Fourth generation in China,[40] the woman terrorist in Bengal seemed to claim equality in an act of sacrifice at an extraordinary crisis point, but did not extend this to a claim for equality in political choice and action. Neither did she explicitly link up her action with any corresponding leap in domestic or family relations or with a change in her lifestyle and role outside politics.[41] So even apart from the Gandhian restraint on non-violence, other forms of controls existed to pull back women from building any further on the prospects of politicization. Gandhian radical nationalist and terrorist leaders alike consistently harped on the supreme relevance of traditional roles and values for modern Indians and the basic irrelevance of alien Western 'isms' for the freedom movement.[42] At the height of the Civil Disobedience movement, a radical nationalist paper with strong connections with Subhas Bose bemoaned lyrically the degeneration of the Indian woman as a major consequence of the evils of foreign rule:

Wives used to be the Goddess Shakti to us,
But now she is just a 'dear',
Where are the 'Vrats' of Punyipukur and Gokal,
Where are the Ramayan and Gita?
Shall we ever recover our Savitri and Sita?
The household is the supreme field of religion for the woman,
Through that alone can she acquire her highest knowledge.[43]

So whether in Gandhian movements or in more militant alternatives to it, nationalists rarely sought a permanent reversal of the customary role of woman in and outside political action. Politicization was internalized as a special form of sacrifice in an essentially religious process. The language, imagery, and idiom of the entire nationalist protest remained steeped in tradition and religion as self-conscious alternatives to alien

Western norms. And herein lay the paradox: such strong traditionalist moorings alone permitted the sudden political involvement of thousands of women. But that in its turn inhibited the extension of radicalism to other spheres of life.

NOTES

† This article is a revised and enlarged version of a paper read at a seminar on Women and Culture at Indraprastha College for Women in 1981.

1. Muzaffar Ahmad, *Amar Jiban O Bharater Communist Party*, vol. 2, Calcutta, undated, pp. 33–4.

2. Government of India, Home Poll 1-2/28/1928, *Fortnightly Report on the Situation in Bengal*, 2nd half of June 1928.

3. Abdul Momin, 'Chatkal Sramiker Pratham Sadharan Dharmaghat', in *Dainik Kalantar*, 10–12 August 1970.

4. *Annual Report on the Administration of Bengal, 1927–8*, Calcutta, 1929, p. 23.

5. Renu Chakravarty, *Communists in Indian Women's Movement*, New Delhi, 1980, p. 118.

6. I am grateful to Shri Chinmohan Sehanobis for this detail.

7. *Interview with Miss Das Gupta*, recorded by Nehru Memorial Museum and Library, 24. 4. 1968.

8. Ahmad, *Amar Jiban*, p. 22.

9. *Meerut Conspiracy Case Proceedings*, P 1938 T. Speech by Ahmad, 4 March 1928. See also Abdul Momin, 'Chatkal Sramiker Pratham Sadharan Dharmaghat'.

10. Ranajit Das Gupta, 'Factory Labour in Eastern India: Sources of Supply, 1855–1946. Some Preliminary Findings, *Indian Economic and Social History Review*, vol. 8, no. 3, 1976, p. 298.

11. Evidence of I.J.M.A. representatives, *Royal Commission on Labour in India, 1930–Evidence*, vol. 5, part II, pp. 140–76. There had been a 28 per cent decline in the number of women in organized industries between 1921 and 1931. See *Census of India*, 1931, vol. 5, p. 281.

12. See Dipesh Chakrabarty, *The Working Class in a Pre-Capitalist Culture: A Study of the Jute Workers of Calcutta, 1890–1940*, ch. 2. Unpublished PhD thesis from Canberra National University, 1983, p. 13.

13. Evidence of Babuniyah and Muthialu, *Royal Commission on Labour*, pp. 77–80.

14. Evidence of IJMA representatives, *Royal Commission on Labour*.

15. Evidence of representatives of the Bengal Presidency Council of Women, *Royal Commission on Labour*, pp. 5–6.

16. An exploration of speeches by labour leaders in the *Meerut Conspiracy Case Proceedings*, confirms this.

17. Mahisyas and especially Namasudras would be ritually in an extremely low position in the cast hierarchy but within the agricultural community the Mahisyas had a rather elevated and privileged position and Namasudras were a rising peasant group.

18. *Census of India*, 1931, vol. 5, pp. 281, 300.

19. Neeladri Bhattacharya, *Agricultural Labour in Production (Central and South Eastern Punjab; 1870–1940)*, unpublished paper.

20. Renu Chakravarty, *Communists in Indian Women's Movement.*

21. The no-chowkidari tax agitation was an important part of the Civil Disobedience movement in Bengal. In Order to paralyse the functioning of union boards at the village level, villagers were instructed to withhold the payment of the chowkidari tax. It was a form of political protest rather than the expression of an economic grievance against a tax imposition since participation in the movement frequently entailed the erosion of a lifetime's saving for the non-payment of a tax which amounted to a few rupees a year.

22. Tanika Sarkar, *National Movement and Popular Protest in Bengal, 1928–34*, unpublished doctoral thesis, University of Delhi, 1980.

23. 'Laban Satyagraha', in *Ananda Bazar Patrika*, Annual Number, 1930.

24. *Law and Order in Midnapur: Report of the Non-official Enquiry Committee*, Calcutta, 1930, Proscribed Book, P 1 B 9/32 (B.M.). See also *Amrita Bazar Patrika*, 14 June 1932.

25. Gopinandan Goswami, *Medini-purer Shahid Parichay*, Calcutta, 1977, p. 1.

26. *Ananda Bazar Patrika*, Annual Number, 1930; see also, *Home Confidential, GOB, Poll 599 (Sl No. 1–14) of 1930*. Letter 387 C of 24/5/1930 from District Magistrate, Comilla; *GOB Home Confidential. Poll 441 (Sl No. 1) of 1929–Lowman's Note on Youth Association in Bengal.*

27. *Ananda Bazar Patrika*, Annual No. 1930. Also interview with Saibal Gupta (then SDO, Contai), 20 July 1978.

28. Government reports confirmed nationalist claims that in many areas in south-western Bengal Congress parallel courts had eclipsed the regular legal courts and were dispensing justice according to their own norms. Large-scale and highly organized social boycott of loyalist families by a rebellious village community or by nationalist neighbours would be another device for the implementation of Congress discipline and instructions within the household. See Tanika Sarkar, *National Movement.*

29. Bankimchandra Chattopadhyaya, *Anandamath, Bankim Rachanabali*, vol. 1, Calcutta, 1960, p. 726.

30. Rabindranath Tagore, *Gitabitan*, Vishwa Bharati, 1973, p. 25.

31. See, for instance, appeals to women in a collection of articles by radical nationalists *Yanbaner Dak*, Calcutta, 1929, Proscribed Book, PP Ben B (68), IOL.

32. Letter from Shillong, 17/7/27, Subhas Chandra Bose, *Correspondence, 1924–32*, (ed.) Sisir Bose, Calcutta, 1967.

33. Bhupendra Kishore Rakshit Ray, *Chalar Pathey*, Calcutta, 1931.
34. *Pather Dabi, Sarat Sahitya Sangraha*, vol. 13, Calcutta, 1960.
35. D.M. Lanshey, *Bengal Terrorism and Marxist Left*, Calcutta, 1975, ch. 4.
36. *Bipradas, Sarat Sahitya Sangraha*, vol. 6, Calcutta, 1960.
37. Rabindranath Tagore, *Char Adhyay*, Calcutta, 1934, Introduction.
38. Ibid., pp. 8, 9, 68, 70.
39. Barbara Engel, 'Women as Revolutionaries: The Case of the Russian Populists', in Brindenthal and Koonz (eds), *Becoming Visible: Women in European History*, Boston, 1977.
40. Mary Backus Rankin, 'The Emergence of Women at the End of the Ching: The Case of Chiu Chin, and Yi Tsi Feuerwerker, 'Women as Writers in the 1920s and 1930s,' in Wolfe and Wilke (eds), *Women in Chinese Society*, Stanford, 1975.
41. Waddedar, 'Long Live Revolution', in Sachindranath Guha (ed.), *Chattogram Biplaber Bahnishikha*, Calcutta, 1974.
42. Articles by Subhas Bose, Surendramohan Ghose, and Trailokyanath Chakravarti in *Yanbaner Dak, op. cit.*
43. *Shiksha Bipad*, a poem in *Bangabani*, 10 April 1930.

PART VII

CAPITALISTS, WORKING CLASSES, AND NATIONALISM

18 Congress and the Industrialists (1885–1947)*

Dwijendra Tripathi

[...]

The Indian industrialists found Gandhi's charm irresistible, as did other sections of the Indian population. His stress on truth, non-violence, peace, and self-reliance appealed to them immensely as these virtues seemed to conform to their own cultural orientation. His saintly demeanour created the kind of aura around him which has always made a deep impression on the Indian people in general and business in particular. He symbolized the general urge among Indians for self-rule, but his determination not to deviate from peaceful means under any circumstances fitted in admirably with the businessman's abhorrence of conflict. Gandhi's doctrine of trusteeship was particularly appealing to them, for it held no immediate threat to the capitalist system which was experiencing increasingly severe strains after the success of the Bolshevik Revolution.[1] There was much in the Gandhian scheme of things with which the industrialists could have little sympathy—his emphasis on *gram swarajya* or village self-sufficiency, his advocacy of cottage and small-scale industries, and his stress on the abrogation of wealth[2]—but as long as coercion was ruled out as a means, these planks in Gandhi's programme were of no immediate relevance. Never in the history of the Congress organization did any of its leaders succeed in establishing such an intimate bond with the Indian industrialists as Gandhi did. While their relationship with the organization during the first thirty years of its history was purely institutional, it become intimately personal after 1915, thanks to the spell that Gandhi cast on them.

The Ahmedabad millowners, most of whom were Jains and Vaishnava banias, were the first to come under his influence, partly because of their physical proximity—he had settled down in the textile town after returning from South Africa—and partly because he seemed

---

* Originally published in Dwijendra Tripathi (ed.), *Business and Politics in India: A Historical Perspective*, New Delhi, Manohar, 1991, pp. 86–123. In the present version some portions of text and notes have been removed. For the complete text see the original version.

to personify and articulate the Vaishnav–Jain ethos. They met him frequently, attended his prayer meetings, and treated him and his advice with utmost deference. Not only persons with a traditional outlook, such as Mangaldas Girdhardas and Kasturbhai Lalbhai, but also more westernized individuals, like Ambalal Sarabhai, were irresistibly drawn towards him. As the saint of Sabarmati grew in stature and influence, industrialists belonging to other parts of the country joined the growing herd of his disciples. Among the most important and useful discoveries were Ghanshyam Das Birla, a Calcutta-based industrialist who was fast emerging as the principle spokesman of Indian business interests, and his fellow Marwari in Bombay, Jamnalal Bajaj.[3] A large number of traders and merchants of lesser standing were attracted to him in the Bombay presidency—the 'keep of Gandhism',[4] in the words of a British official. This is not to suggest that all business leaders flocked to Gandhi's banner. Many, including some of the most influential once such as Purshotamadas Thakurdas of Bombay, remained sceptical of his aims and methods. But there is no doubt that Gandhi's leadership won for the Congress a much wider base of support and sympathy among the Indian businessmen than ever before. More that anything else, his charisma, his precepts, and his personal lifestyle served to politicize the Indian business class beyond measure.

It must be stressed, however, that the industrialist admirers of Gandhi did not always see eye to eye with him or submit to his judgement. Far from it. Ambala Sarabhai, for example, whose anonymous donation is reported to have saved the Sabarmati Ashram from premature closure gave, in his capacity as the President of the Ahmedabad Millowners Association, a determined fight to the politician-saint when the latter led a protracted labour strike in Ahemdabad in 1918.[5] Kasturbhai Lalbhai's 'great respect for Mahatmaji' did not prevent him from castigating the 'outsider' for meddling in an industrial dispute; the fast undertaken by Gandhi to force the millowners into an amicable settlement was, in the eyes of this Ahmedabad millowner, a coercive measure.[6] Even Birla who looked upon himself as one of Gandhi's 'pet children' acted against his advice on several occasions.[7] Gandhi was, however, too clever or too catholic a leader to permit minor frictions to interfere with enduring relationships. After all, his industrialist followers were not the only ones who disagreed with him; some of his closest political disciples and coworkers, including Jawaharlal Nehru, had even more violent differences with him.[8] But there was something in the nature of the man which helped him discriminate between the community of intrinsic interests and the grounds of extrinsic divergence and, shape his strategies accordingly. He needed the support of the industrialists to build a national consensus against the alien rule, and their money to finance his numerous constructive programmes. And the industrialists, in their turn, had no doubt whatsoever that if there was one man who could restrain the Congress from adopting a rabid anti-capitalist posture, it was Gandhi, and that their economic demands could not be secured without the help of the Congress.[9]

Even the most ardent supporters of Gandhi and most vocal sympathizers of the Congress among the Indian industrialists, however, were not prepared to alienate the government of the day. This can be explained in the context of the growing clash of interest between the Indian and British business classes. As the former became increasingly more conscious of their distinct identity and destiny, the European interests began to experience a mounting threat to their position of superiority which they had no intention of giving up. The process of estrangement was somewhat subtle in the beginning, but the gulf between the two groups became unbridgeably wide because of post-war developments. The prospect of an increasing role for Indians in the governance of the country, as promised in the Montagu Declaration of 1917, made the Europeans exceedingly uneasy and the Indians could not view with equanimity the determined efforts of manufacturers in England to regain their position in Indian markets which they had nearly lost during the war. The growing rift between two the groups was reflected in the formation, first, of the Associated Chambers of Commerce (ASSOCHAM) in 1921, and later, and as a reaction to it, of the Federation of Indian Chambers of Commerce and Industry (FICCI) in 1927. The former was a coalition of all European trade organizations in the country and the latter was an apex body of the Indian chambers.[10] The 1920s thus witnessed for the first time a clear polarization between the two groups of businessmen—now much more suspicious of each other than ever before—and a hostile administration could tilt the delicate balance unduly against the Indians.

Fortunately, the government was as keen to retain the goodwill of Indian big business. In an era of mounting mass political activity, which Gandhi's leadership had ushered in, the landed gentry and industrial mercantile interests were perhaps the only groups whom the alien rulers could hope to prevent from gravitating towards the Congress. The basis of representation as provided in the Reform Act of 1919 was a clear pointer to the government strategy. The legislatures created under the act were to comprise, among others, the representatives of various interest groups including labour and capital, and capital was further subdivided into various categories as millowners, merchants, Indian business, European business, and the like. The system of interest representation was expected to preclude the domination of nationalist elements over the legislatures and prevent them from developing into a united forum against the government. Another indicator of the government anxiety not to alienate Indian business interests was its flat refusal to lower the duty on Manchester goods in 1920 in spite of severe pressure. The duty had been raised as a revenue measure during the war, when English producers, unable to export goods to India, could not have been overly exercised over the decision.[11] Admittedly, 'the mystic bond of racial affinity'[12] with the rulers of the land, to Bagchi's picturesque phrase, was a factor in favour of the British business interest in India. The government, nevertheless, was keen to project an unbiased image of itself and, thus, its support for European interest could not be taken for granted. Any move on the part of the Indian big business to align itself unequivocally with the Indian National Congress under these conditions would have been counter-productive.

Consequently, the visible affiliation of Indian industrialists with the Congress, a characteristic feature of national politics before the First World War, declined as the organization set off on an agitational course under Gandhi. Not a single important leader of Indian business was actively associated with the Congress after 1919. A policy of equidistance from the government and the Congress was considered to be more appropriate. Even a man like Birla, whose personal loyalty to the Mahatma was beyond question, assumed the role of 'having' to defend Bapu before Englishmen and Englishmen before Bapu.[13] With free access to the Congress leaders and the ruling authorities alike, he could act as unofficial mediator between the two parties and, thus, enjoy considerable leverage with both. Behind these factors of equidistance, however, we can detect a four-pronged strategy: (a) keep aloof from the confrontational-agitational aspects of the freedom struggle, (b) support with funds such constructive activities which were indirectly linked with the Congress organization, (c) influence policy formulation by the Congress to ensure that its thinking on major issues affecting business interests was in tune with their own, and, (d) act in unison with the nationalist minded elements in the legislatures to press the demands of Indian industry.

The strategy unfolded itself only gradually; various elements of it emerged in response to the exigencies of the situation rather than as part of a pre-planned grand design. Also the Indian business class as a whole did not support this strategy. For, there was a very strong section of Bombay-based industrialists, including Dorabji Tata, Ibrahim Rahimtoola, and Cowasji Jehangir, who differed from this approach which seemed to be heavily weighted in favour of the Congress.[14] Socially closer to the ruling race, these elements remained suspicious of the Congress leadership and leaned more towards the government. Further, there were groups within groups. For instance, those who sympathized with the Congress were divided between the moderate and militant nationalists. There were divisions within the loyalist group as well. Some were more vocal in their support for the government, others were more subdued, and a few found it difficult to take an unequivocal position.

None perhaps personified the loyalist dilemma more than Purshotamdas Thakurdas who was intimately connected with the house of Tatas. Sometimes he sided with the Tatas, and on other occasions with the Birlas. In 1920, when the loyalists decided under Dorabji Tata's inspiration to form an anti-non-cooperation society in Bombay to counter the agitational plan of the Congress, Purshotamdas cooperated with them. But later in 1929, when Tata and some other pro-government industrialists attempted to form a capitalist association in the legislative assembly in cooperation with European interests, the cotton king of Bombay reacted sharply against the move. Pointing to the inherent clash of interests between indigenous and foreign business, he added that 'Indian commerce and industry are only an integral phase of Indian nationalism and that deprived of its inspiration in Indian nationalism, Indian commerce and Indian history stand reduced to mere exploitation'.[15] These words could as well have been spoken by G.D. Birla whose nationalist bias was more pronounced. Again, while the Tatas remained aloof from the FICCI, Purshotamdas was one of its founder members.[16]

The Bombay cotton merchant was not the only one to alternate between the two positions; innumerable groups and individuals shifted their sympathy from one side to the other depending on the issues, or adopted postures entirely independent of the two. To view the Indian business class as a cohesive entity or divide it neatly into various groups with reference to its attitude to the Congress would be misleading indeed. And yet it can be safely maintained that those who generally sympathized with the nationalist cause and subscribed, consciously or unconsciously, to the four-pronged strategy outlined above represented the more dominant coalition.

[...]

A brief discussion on the reaction of the Indian business class to specific issues and developments would support the conclusion reached at the end of the preceding section. The first major event that unfolded the Gandhian technique of political action and marked a break from the earlier period was the non-cooperation movement of 1921. Whatever their private sympathies, the public posture of big industrialists and merchants, by and large, was one of utter indifference, and some like Purshotamdas Thakurdas, were downright hostile. While deprecating the 'listlessness' of the government in attending to 'genuine and apparent grievances' he chastised the Congress for having given to 'the masses the dreary and dangerous satisfaction of resting content with destructive work'.[17] Birla, Ambalal Sarabhai, Kasturbhai Lalbhai, or other industrialist disciples of Gandhi remained silent; we at least have no record of their views. In fact the major part of the financial support for the agitation came from traders and speculators in Bombay rather than big industrialists, even though the boycott of foreign goods benefited the millowners. After the withdrawal of the movement, however, when Gandhi decided to devote his time and energy to constructive programmes, industrialists of all hues favoured the legislative route to reform even though the Mahatma was unequivocally opposed to entry into the assembly. Instead of accepting the ticket of the Swaraj party which had captured the leadership of the Congress, those representing Indian business interests came to the assembly either as independents or as nominees of the less militant Nationalist Party, led by Lajpat Rai and Madan Mohan Malaviya, with whom Gandhi had a 'fundamental difference of opinion'.[18]

Within the assembly, however, the industrial members worked closely with the Swarajists. Kasturbhai, elected at the initiative and with the support of Vallabhbhai Patel to represent the Ahemdabad Millowners Association, had a close liaison with Motilal Nehru and Vithalbhai Patel whose candidacy for the speakership he actively supported. Though he avoided joining any faction, he attended most of the private meetings of the Swarajists and invariably voted with them. Motilal Nehru, in fact, regarded him as a better Swarajist than any of the regular members of his party. Purshotamdas Thakurdas, who represented the Indian Merchants Chamber, had no particular sympathy for the Swarajists and yet his positions on major issues were often similar to those of Kasturbhai, one of his closest friends. So was the case with G.D. Birla who had a brief stint as a legislator in 1926–7 on the ticket of the Nationalist Party. Not the party label or the lack of it but the community of interests bound these somewhat disparate elements together.

[...]

Whatever their minor differences, the representatives of Indian business and political factions in the assembly, thus, made common cause against the government on matters affecting Indian economic interests. If the hidden agenda behind the concept of interest representation was to wean the burgeoning industrial class from the rising wave of nationalism, the strategy failed conspicuously. In fact, it produced just the opposite result. The schism between Indian business and the British expatriates, visible in the beginning of the 1920s, widened further as a result of frequent clashes between their respective representatives in the legislature, and repeated attack on the British imperial policy by the business leaders in the course of debates on various issues gladdened the nationalist politicians. The latter's support, in turn, for various concessions for which the industrial leaders were clamouring softened the attitude of even those who, like Purshotamdas Thakurdas, had been sceptical of nationalist intentions earlier. Whatever might have been Gandhi's calculations in opposing the entry into the legislatures, there is no doubt that no other forum could have provided a better opportunity to the spokesmen of economic nationalism on the one hand and those of political emancipation on the other to appreciate each other's respective positions and the basic community of their interests and objectives.

While flouting Gandhi's advice against legislative involvement, a section of Indian business leadership had kept open the line of communication with him. G.D. Birla never failed to take the Mahatma into confidence about his moves and activities through a regular exchange of letters and occasional meetings. The leaders of the Gujarati millowning class—Ambalal Sarabhai, Kasturbhai Lalbhai, and others—did not write as many letters, but they met Gandhi frequently. Another method through which they ingratiated themselves with the saint-politician was by donating liberally for his innumerable constructive activities which, though technically unconnected with the Congress, served to expand its mass base. In virtually every alternate letter, Gandhi asked Birla for some amount or other and the Marwari magnate never refused—be it for the khadi programme, Harijan uplift, or publication of journals and magazines. In fact, during the 1920s, Birla emerged as the most important single financier of Gandhi who, in his characteristic humility, regarded the Marwari as one of his 'mentors'. The Mahatma did not need money for himself but other Congressmen, whose material requirements were more pressing, did. By helping them tide over their financial difficulties on several occasions, Birla established a claim on their gratitude and a right to be heard and taken seriously in the corridors of the Congress conclave. At the same time he scrupulously avoided giving any donation to the Congress directly. The Gujarati millowners were less generous with their money but a sense of cultural affinity bound them with Gandhi and Vallabhbhai Patel, his principal lieutenant in the Gujarat region.[19]

Another factor that influenced the attitude of an important section of the Indian business class towards the Congress in the 1920s was the rising tempo of the left-dominated labour movement. Particularly affected were the Bombay mills which witnessed a series of strikes in 1928 and 1929. Cotton manufacturers of the city had faced labour unrest several times before but what they experienced during the closing years of the 1920s was something very different. The leadership of the Girni Kamgar Union, which spearheaded the movement, was now in the hands of 'a group of firebrands who were firm believers in the Communist ideology'. Never before had such a ferocious propaganda been unleashed, not only against the Bombay millowners but also against the capitalist order itself. Never before had the Indian cotton manufacturer experienced such perpetual fear of disruption. Strikes caused dislocation in the Tata Steel Works also around the same time. Dorabji Tata's ill-fated move to form a party of the capitalists was provoked by these events. The more practical among the industrialist leaders, however, concluded that the Congress was a lesser evil under the prevailing conditions, although the Congress was no less active on the labour front. Its pro-labour posture was not always to the liking of the capitalists, but the irritating propaganda of the Congress-controlled All India Trade Union Congress (AITUC) was much less biting than the fear generated by the activities of the leftist unions. Business leaders had no doubt that as long as Gandhi had the commanding voice in the Congress organization, conciliation rather than confrontation would be the guiding principle for the AITUC. The effectiveness of the Gandhian approach to labour-management relations was there for all to see in Ahmedabad. The principal manufacturing centre in Gujarat was not quite free from the symptoms of labour unrest in the closing years of the 1920s, but the arbitration machinery created under Gandhi's inspiration, following the strike of 1918, helped resolve differences between the textile workers and their employers. Industrial relations in Ahmedabad, consequently, continued to be peaceful while Bombay reeled under prolonged strike.[20]

[...]

The 1920s, thus, witnessed a growing congruence of purpose between the Congress and the Indian capitalist class. Despite all their sympathy for the nationalist cause and protests against the discriminatory policies of the government, however, the industrial leaders had no intention of losing whatever leverage they still enjoyed with the authorities. These contradictory pressures were reflected in their approach to the civil disobedience movement of 1930. Fearing that an open confrontation between the government and the Congress would further hurt their interests at a time when economic prospects were none too bright, they tried to dissuade Gandhi from throwing down the gauntlet. The best way to do this was to convince the Mahatma, who had once again regained his position as the undisputed leader of the Congress, of the usefulness of attending the first Round Table Conference to be convened in November 1930 to resolve the Indian political question. [...]

Gandhi, however, ignored the plea. Instead of going to London, he decided to march to Dandi. This was the beginning of the second major agitation Gandhi launched against the British rule. Nothing he or any other political leader had done before had ignited the masses to such an extent as Gandhi's trek to this little known place on the Gujarat coast. Every section of society heeded the call of the Mahatma; no part of the country remained unaffected by the nationalist upsurge. The peasants in the rural areas broke the salt law and challenged the British authority in various other ways; the urban centres witnessed powerful campaigns in support of the boycott of foreign goods.

While the masses gave the fullest possible support to Gandhi, the response of big business was not very different from what it had been to the non-cooperation movement. Little concrete support came from the industrialists. Birla, who continued to remain in close touch with the Mahatma, provided no financial support and his father was a known opponent of the movement.[21] Purshotmadas Thakurdas remained sceptical of Gandhi's methods. Civil disobedience, in his opinion, was 'a very dangerous weapon in the hands of a population, the majority of whom are illiterate'. Distrustful of mass politics in general, he felt that the movement would 'teach the people an extremely dagerous lesson which may greatly inconvenience even a Swaraj Government'. With all his sympathy for Gandhi, Ambalal Sarabhai remained too preoccupied with his doubt about the constitutionality or otherwise of the movement to do anything tangible.[22] Kasturbhai Lalbhai was among a small group of industrialists who risked a more viable support to the agitation. On the suggestion of G.V. Mavlankar, a prominent nationalist lawyer of Ahmedabad, he had agreed to be the custodian of the funds of a trust associated with Gandhi, out of which the families of the Dandi marchers were being supported. This aroused the ire of the government. His name had 'come into such prominence with the government that they raided our office at Pankore Naka and I had a telephonic message from my friend Lala Shri Ram from Delhi that I was likely to be arrested'. Since the police search revealed nothing incriminating, the Ahmedabad industrialist was left alone.[23]

As on the occasion of the non-cooperation movement, commercial interests—merchants and traders—supported the agitation more enthusiastically than the industrialists. Throughout the 1930s, the latter were repeatedly condemned for their aloofness by the radical elements. Attempts have been made to explain this cleavage in the Indian business classes with reference to their differing perception of the economic distress caused by the depression.[24] It is true that there was much in the boycott movement which seemed to threaten the interest of the industrialists who abhorred violence and the hatred that went with it. It is also undeniable that the Congress propaganda that the economic distress was solely due to the government's fiscal policies made a greater impact on the trading classes. But to explain their respective attitudes to the agitation in the context of their immediate economic interest alone will be misleading for, boycott was no unmixed evil to either group. The industrialists' fear of disrupted production would have been more than counterbalanced by the hope that a depressed demand for foreign goods would augment indigenous production at least at the initial stages when the adverse consequences of the boycott were yet to manifest themselves. And whatever might have been his other calculations, the trader could not have seen a direct and immediate benefit to himself in the disruption of the market for imported goods. Almost up to the onset of the civil disobedience movement, some captains of the Indian industry were expressing their faith in Gandhi's judgement and stressing on self-government as the only solution of India's economic ills.[25] If they became more cautious in their professions and actions after the movement gained momentum and the government adopted a tough attitude, it could not have been due to their immediate economic difficulties caused by Gandhi's call to boycott foreign goods.

The fact of the matter is that the industrial leaders' response to civil disobedience conformed to the set pattern of their behaviour during periods of open confrontation between the government and the nationalist movement. During quieter times, they could shout support for the Congress position on major issues without burning their bridges with the authorities, but when the battle lines were clearly drawn, a more discreet behaviour was called for. [...]

In view of the congruence of purpose that had developed between the Congress and the industrialists by this time, however, it was not possible for their leaders to remain as indifferent to the civil disobedience movement as they had been to the non-cooperation movement. A complete neutrality would have indirectly helped the government and thus alienated the Congress. What is worse, this would have caused a division among the industrialists themselves for, quite a few of their leaders, particularly Birla and Gujarati millowners whose personal loyalty to Gandhi remained intact, would have certainly resented a do-nothing stance. By way of compromise, as it were, they decided to support the causes for which the Congress was fighting without supporting its agitational tactics. [...]

The apex organization of Indian business [FICCI] also condemned the police brutalities and refused to participate in the proposed Round Table Conference or even permit any member to participate in his individual capacity. Even Purshotamdas Thakurdas was constrained to resign his seat in the central legislative assembly because of the growing pressure from the 'vast Indian commercial community'.[26] And yet the farthest that the FICCI went in its tangible support for the civil disobedience movement was to recommend the setting up of swadeshi *sabha*s in different regions. [...]

Even these steps, signifying only token support for the movement, were not to the liking of a section of big business. [...] Notwithstanding these difficulties, the FICCI resolutions, coupled with the rapport that some of its prominent leaders had established with the Congress during peace-time, enabled them to retain their position as honest brokers between the government and the leaders of the movement—particularly Gandhi, who was its supreme arbiter. The following letter written by Birla at the height of the agitation is probably the most clear exposition of both the dilemma and the mission of the Indian industrial class:

> Regarding the present agitation and the result of the Round Table Conference, I agree that we should try our best to get the country out of the present political turmoil. [...] *We should, therefore, have two objects in view: one is that we should jump in at the most opportune time for a reconciliation and the other is that we should not do anything which might weaken the hands of those through whose efforts we have arrived at this stage*[27] [emphasis added].

This strategy was no more effective in persuading Gandhi to come to terms with the government than it had been in dissuading him from launching the agitation. Birla and others of his line of thinking knew the

Mahatma too well to believe that he would easily retrace his steps once he had taken the plunge. [...] They began to see some hope in the closing months of 1930 when there were definite signs that the movement was sagging even though it was still quite potent in some pockets.[28] No less a supporter of the agitation than Jawaharlal Nehru, who was to fret and fume when Gandhi reached an understanding with the viceroy only a few months later, felt in October that 'civil disobedience activities, though still flourishing everywhere, were getting a bit stale. ... the cities and middle classes were a bit tired of hartal, and processions'.[29] Official reports told the same story to the government, and Thakurdas, no enthusiastic supporter of the agitation but an uncanny judge of the situation, felt likewise.[30]

This perhaps was the time for the mediation to succeed. But the Mahatma, still in jail, was perhaps unaware of the change in the mood of the people. [...] It was only after he was released in January 1931, as a gesture of goodwill on the part of the viceroy, that he could have realistically sensed the situation. [...] Gandhi [...] agreed to meet Lord Irwin because he could 'no longer resist the advice' from 'friends whose advice I value'.[31] This paved the way for the Gandhi-Irwin Pact which led to the suspension of civil disobedience. To suggest, however, that 'business pressure played a crucial role' in bringing about this reconciliation[32] or that the Mahatma was won over by the viceroy's charm is to ignore the totality of compulsions impinging on Gandhi's thinking. Neither view does justice to the intelligence of a remarkably astute political strategist.

[...]

When a frustrated Gandhi abandoned the conference and resumed civil disobedience in January 1932, resulting in his reincarceration, Birla and his associates once again reverted to their mediatory role. Though the Marwari industrialist himself refused to participate in the negotiations any further, he persuaded the FICCI to continue to cooperate with the government 'in the framing of a suitable constitution for India' even though a faction led by Lala Shri Ram favoured complete non-cooperation.[33] While the FICCI resolution permitted Purshotamdas to participate in the discussion, Birla himself continued his efforts to bridge the gulf between the Mahatma and the government through his letters to Sir Samuel Hoare, Secretary of State for India, Lord Lothian, Parliamentary Under Secretary of the India Office, and other officers of the government as well as to the leaders of Indian liberals, particularly Tej Bahadur Sapru, and the captains of European business in India. Through these negotiations he kept his lines of communication open and retained his position as a well-meaning mediator acceptable to both parties.[34] [...]

It must have been clear to Birla, however, that his mediation bid had little chance of success until the Indians were willing to water down their demand. One of the issues on which business leaders and the Congress were in complete agreement was the control over Indian finance—'the crux of the full demand' according to Birla.[35] The government conceded the point in principle, but what it was willing to offer was hedged by so many safeguards that Birla thought that, in practice, ninety-nine per cent of the financial control was going to be vested in the hands of the governor-general.[36] A few other events also indicated to the industrialists that their business interests were not quite safe in an imperial order. For example, the Imperial Economic Conference held at Ottawa in 1932, which was supposed to adopt a tariff agreement 'for the benefit of the trade of both the countries' resulted in the imperial preference system which indirectly offered protection to British industries in the preserved market of the empire. The commercial interests and nationalists alike condemned the agreement as an example of colonial exploitation and found it detrimental to Indian trade and industry. [...]

Another incident which incensed an influential section of the industrial community was the Mody-Lees Pact of 1933. This resulted from a tripartite conference which discussed ways and means to check the rising imports of Japanese textile goods into India. The British side led by Sir William Clare-Lees conceded that Indian industry was entitled to a 'measure of protection against the imports of United Kingdom yarn and piece-goods', and the Indians were willing to accept the principle of a lower level of protection against the United Kingdom as compared to other countries. Disagreement, however, arose on specific terms. The English products on which the import duty was sought to be lowered were in direct competition with the Ahmedabad mills which had a greater stake in the production of finer counts. To minimize the danger, therefore, Kasturbhai Lalbhai, one of the FICCI representatives, insisted on fixing a ceiling on imports from the United Kingdom and, when this was rejected, walked out of the conference. Sir Homi Mody, who represented the Bombay Millowners Association, signed the pact on behalf of the Indian cotton manufactures, splitting the Indian millowning class as no other event had ever done before. Unconcerned, however, the government ratified the agreement.[37]

Coming as they did on the heels of the decision to fix the rupee-sterling ratio at 18d and tie the Indian currency to the British pound, these two events reinforced the doubts of the nationalist-minded industrialists about the intentions of the government. Industrialists, at the same time, did not fail to notice the rising tempo of economic radicalism in a section of the Congress. Ever since the Lahore Congress, Jawaharlal Nehru, the rising star on the Indian political firmament, was veering towards socialist doctrine and was even willing to 'honour and respect the red flag'[38] which was anathema to the Indian capitalist class. Largely because of his influence on the counsels of the Congress the Karachi session, meeting in the last week of March 1931, adopted the famous resolution on the 'fundamental rights and economic programme' which emphasized, among other things, that 'political freedom must included real economic freedom of the starving millions' and 'safeguard the interests of industrial workers'. The resolution also advocated state control of 'key industries and services, mineral resources, railways, waterways, shipping and other means of transport'.[39]

While Nehru's concept of socialism was still rather vague, a band of young enthusiasts, openly wedded to Marxian doctrines, was becoming very vocal in the Congress. The capitalists, however, believed that Gandhi's overarching presence was a foolproof shield against radical propaganda. And the Mahatma was quick to allay their fears at the annual convention of the FICCI which met barely a week after the Karachi session. Reacting to the complaint of the president, Lala Shri Ram, that the Karachi declaration was issued without consulting the business community on their 'vital interests' concerning economic matters, Gandhi declared in his inaugural address that the Congress 'would always be glad to avail of your advice and help'. To assure his listeners still further he added: 'The Congress stands for the industrial prosperity and progress of India. I cannot forget the services rendered by the commercial classes, But I want to go a step further. I want you to make the Congress your own and we would willingly surrender the reins to you. The work can be better done by you'.[40]

[...] Not all capitalists belittled the radical sceptre and a section of them was to raise a hue and cry against the socialist proclivities of Nehru a couple of years later, but for the time being the rise of the leftist tide did not have much impact on the Congress-industry ties. In fact, Birla never lost hope that even if the Congress as an organization was captured by the radical elements, Gandhi would still carry the country with him and isolate them. He always made a subtle distinction between the Congress and its patron saint.[41]

These were the calculations which guided the endeavours of Birla and his associates, after the break-up of the second Round Table

Conference, to bring about a rapprochement between Gandhi and the government. [...] Birla had not wholly succeeded in removing the distrust between the two parties when the British Parliament passed the Government of India Act of 1935, creating a federal structure for India. Based on the principles of a white paper published earlier, the act gave little satisfaction to the Congress or the business interests, and was denounced by both.[42] Gandhi, however, privately felt that the act was capable of producing good results if worked in the right spirit. Birla, with his uncanny business instinct, concluded that it contained the 'seeds which were to germinate, blossom and bear fruit' in full independence for the country.[43] He therefore, did not want to let this opportunity slip. With Gandhi's blessing, he proceeded to London immediately after the act was passed and established very useful contacts with the principal leaders of both the major political parties in England [...].

Birla returned to India in September 1935 with the impression that the imperial authorities were serious about the new constitutional arrangement and that the safeguards provided in the act would not be misused to meddle with the Indian administration, once the Indian ministers joined the government. Without losing a moment, he went straight to Wardha to give his mentor 'a first hand report of my impressions'. Gandhi still remained very sceptical because of his feeling that the friendliness that Birla 'experienced in England did not yet prevail in government circles in India', but he agreed to advise the Congress 'to make no new commitment about the reforms' before the arrival of the new viceroy, and 'promised to use his influence to that end'.[44] If the Congress eventually agreed to give a fair trial to the reform act, Birla's behind-the scene role—to 'interpret Bapu to Britishers and the Britishers to Bapu'—must be given due credit.

[...]

The adoption of the new scheme for the governance of the country provided a sort of respite from confrontational politics, even though the Congress continued to be sceptical about the motives of the British government. The ensuing phase of relative tranquility, particularly after the formation of the Congress ministries in most of the provinces, witnessed once again a growing nexus between the Congress and the industrialists, as had been the case during the mid-1920s, occasional irritants notwithstanding. It was so because the big business depended on the new governments for all sort of concessions and the Congress ministries demonstrated little of that rabid leftism some had feared.[45] The resignation of the Congress governments did not herald a period of real confrontation. The government did not feel unduly threatened by the individual civil disobedience movement launched by Gandhi in November 1940, and did little to suppress it except arresting the individual satyagrahis. And the Mahatma took pains to explain to the authorities that he had no intention to hinder war efforts; his policy was 'to live and let live' and that he could not at once 'swear by non-violence and embarrass England in the hour of her difficulty'.[46]

It was no surprise under these conditions that during the initial phase of the Second World War, the Indian industrialists did not see any contradiction between supporting the war efforts on the one hand and expressing sympathies for the national movement on the other. [...]

There was a subtle but significant change in this position as Gandhi drew closer to the confrontation of 1942. Just before the adoption of the 'Quit India' resolution by the Congress, Purshotamdas Thakurdas—according to his biographer, he never hesitated 'to throw the full weight of his support' for the British—joined a group of industrialists including G.D. Birla and J.R.D. Tata, the leaders of the two opposite camps, to assure the viceroy of their opposition to a politics of open conflict. 'We are all businessmen', they wrote in their memorandum, 'and therefore we need hardly point out that our interest lies in peace, harmony, good will and order throughout the country'.[47] And during the holocaust that engulfed the country following the arrest of the Congress leaders, they lived up to this assurance. We have no evidence of any material support from the industrial bourgeoisies to the agitators. A few, however, acquiesced in the strikes of the workers in their factories. It is difficult to fathom their motives in the absence of full records [...].

[...]

As the British government's anxiety to placate the Congress became increasingly clear despite the apparent failure of the agitation, the industrialists returned to their dual policy—of benefiting by support to the war efforts and extracting maximum gain from the government on the one hand, and re-establishing a claim on the gratitude of the Congress leadership on the other. They continued to fulfil their obligations under the military contracts and their apex body FICCI agreed to associate itself with the Department of Planning and Reconstruction set up by the government in 1944. At the same time some of them resumed their financial contribution to the Congress. Their political attitude during the days following the 1942 rebellion was best summed by the correspondent of the *New York Times* who after a visit to Ahmedabad in March 1943 wrote: The local millionaires deplored what had been happening in the country and pointed out that their object in life being to make money, like most Indian businessmen, they were keeping one foot in the Congress camp, which they expected to see running the country, and another in the British camp which is running it now and gives them fat orders.[48]

As the possibility that the transfer of power might take place sooner rather than later became more and more distinct, the industrialists' anxiety to draw closer to the Congress became more pronounced. Nothing illustrates it better than their conversion to the concept of economic planning. While it is true that a FICCI president had advised as early as 1934 that 'it would be exceedingly unwise to offer opposition to planning' his organization took no more than 'passing interest in industrial planning and in the work of the National Planning Committee' (NPC)[49] constituted by the Congress in 1938 under Nehru's chairmanship. Despite the fact that some prominent leaders of the FICCI were connected with the committee, the federation refused to contribute even a paltry sum of one thousand rupees, citing budgetary constraints. The NPC could not achieve much in concrete terms, but it was clear to perceptive observers that planning would be an essential component of the economic policy under a future Congress government. It was no surprise therefore that seven prominent businessmen—Purshotamdas Thakurdas, J.R.D. Tata, G.D. Birla, Lala Shri Ram, Ardeshir Dalal, A.D. Shroff, and Kasturbhai Lalbhai—representing all sections of Indian bourgeoisie assisted by John Matthai, a well-known economist close to the Tatas, produced in 1944 what is popularly known as the Bombay Plan.[50] [...]

[...]

[T]he Bombay Plan anticipated in many ways the fundamentals that guided the formulation of the industrial policy of the national government, formed after the transfer of power, and the Five-Year Plans.[51] The authors of the document recognized the need for planned development, emphasized state ownership and control of key industries, and concurred with the idea of a central directing authority to ensure successful implementation. Although they assigned a legitimate role to the private sector in the future economic setup, they candidly conceded that it would have to function under tight state direction. They went to the extent of saying that 'practically every aspect of economic life will have to be so rigorously controlled by government that individual liberty and freedom of enterprise will suffer a temporary eclipse'.[52] [...] Obviously, on the eve of India's independence, the Indian industrialists were anxious to wake up in the new era with as much demonstrated cordiality for the new rulers as possible—a vague reminder of the attitude of the Indian commercial class towards the colonial government before the emergence of Gandhi.

What were the underlying forces that shaped the industrialists' response to the Congress? To say that they were motivated by their class interest is to repeat a truism, but other factors such as their personal equations with the leaders of the national movement as well as the government and the rising tide of patriotism engulfing segments of society cannot be ignored in our analysis. Eschewing too rigid adherence to consistency, they adopted a pragmatic approach to various issues and developments as they arose from time to time and avoided too pronounced a tilt to any one side—colonial government or the Congress—for fear of alienating the other. With the wisdom of hindsight we may discover a common thread in their response to political developments, but to think that their actions were informed by a well-conceived grand strategy would be an overstatement. A weak and fragmented collectivity, as the Indian industrialists were, can seldom afford such dangerous luxuries.

NOTES

1. For a concise account of some aspects of Gandhian philosophy see B.S. Andholia and D. Tripathi (eds), *Gleanings from Gandhian Thought*, Jabalpur, 1959.
2. G.D. Birla, *In the Shadow of the Mahatma*, Bombay, 1968, Introduction, p. xv.
3. While Birla was more active on the political front, Bajaj helped Gandhi in his constructive programme. See Kaka Kalelkar (ed.), *To a Gandhian Capitalist: Correspondence between Mahatma Gandhi and Jamnalal Bajaj*, Wardha, 1951; also B.R. Nanda, *In Gandhi's Footsteps: The Life and Times of Jamnalal Bajaj*, Delhi, 1990.
4. A.D.D. Gordon, *Business and Politics: Rising Nationalism and Modernizing Economy in Bombay, 1915–33*, New Delhi, 1978, p. 238.
5. No documentary evidence for Sarabhai's donation is available as it was made anonymously, but his geneorus gesture to Gandhi is common knowledge in Ahmedabad.
6. Dwijendra Tripathi, *Dynamics of a Tradition: Kasturbhai Lalbhai and His Entrepreneurship*, New Delhi, 1981, pp. 171–3.
7. Birla, *In the Shadow* [...] pp. 8–9, 16–17, 52.
8. Among the bitterest attacks on Gandhian economic philosophy is Jawaharlal Nehru's chapter entitled 'Paradoxes' in his *Autobiography*, London, 1936.
9. G.D. Birla quoted in *Sunday*, 26 June–2 July 1983, p. 24.

10. Stanley Kochanck, *Business and Politics in India*, Berkeley, 1974, pp. 108–30, 156–96; II. Venkatasubbiah *Enterprise and Economic Chang: 50 Years of FICCI*, New Delhi, 1977, 1–2; Rajat K. Ray, *Industrialization in India*, Delhi, 1979, pp. 297–309.

11. B.R. Tomlinson, *The Indian National Congress and the Raj*, London, 1976, ch. I; S.D. Mehta, *Cotton Mills[of India, 1854–1954*, Bombay, 1954, p. 153.

12. Amiya Kumar Bagchi, *Private Investment in India, 1900–1939*, Cambridge, 1972, p. 166.

13. G.D. Birla quoted in *Sunday* (n. 29), p. 24.

14. S. Bhattacharya, 'Cotton Mills and Spinning Wheels: Swadeshi and the Indian Capitalist Class, 1920–22, *Economic and Political Weekly*, II–47, 20 November 1976, pp. 1828–34.

15. Purshotamdas Thakurdas to N.M. Mazumdar, 7 June 1929. Purshotamdas Thakurdas Collection (hereafter cited as PT collection), Nehru Memorial Museum and Library, New Delhi, file no. 23/II; also see G.D. Birla to Purshotamdas Thakurdas, ibid., 19 June 1929. file no. 42/II; Purshotamdas Thakurdas to G.D. Birla, 30 July 1929, ibid., file no. 42/V. File nos 24/I and 24/III contain several letters written by businessmen to Purshotamdas Thakurdas against the non-cooperation movement. Also see Jamnadas Dwarkadas, 'Non-Cooperation: A Cry for Halt', *Bombay Chronicle*, 7 June 1920.

16. Kochanek, *Business and Politics in India*, p. 159.

17. Thakurdas to Sir Henry Craik, 14 September 1920, PT collection, file no. 24/III; Thakurdas to Birla, 11 December 1923, PT collection, file no. 42/III.

18. Gandhi to Birla, *In the Shadow*, p. 586; Birla's speech is reproduced in G.D. Birla, *Path to Prosperity*, Allahabad, 1950, pp. 146–53; for the support of others see, *Legislative Assembly Debates*, 14 February 1927, IX–16, Delhi, 1927, pp. 746–85.

19. The correspondence between Birla and Gandhi contained in Birla, *In the Shadow* and Birla, *Bapu: A Unique Association*, Bombay, 1977, 4 vols, provides a good idea of Gandhi's financial demands on the Marwari industrialist. Also see, *Sunday* (n. 29), p. 25. For the attitude of the Gujarati and Bombay industrialists see Tripathi, *Dynamics of a Tradition*, pp. 170–90: and Gordon, *Business and Politics*, pp. 238–9.

20. The Bombay Millowners Association, *Report of 1928*, Bombay, 1929, pp. ii–iv; Ambalal Sarabhai to Thakurdas, 5 November 1929 and reply; Naoroji to Thakurdas, 28 March 1930; Birla to Thakurdas, 3 November 1929, PT collection, file no. 91; Mazumdar to Thakurdas, 22 May 1929 and Thakurdas to Mazumdar, 7 June 1929; Birla to Thakurdas, 26 April 1929, ibid., file no. 42/II; Mehta, *Cotton Mills*, p. 167.

21. Sumit Sarkar, 'The Logic of Gandhian Nationalism: The Civil Disobedience and the Gandhi-Irwin Pact (1930–31)', *Indian Historical Review*, vol. III, 1976, p. 121; Gordon, *Businessmen and Politics*, pp. 229–33.

22. Sarabhai to Thakurdas, 17 November 1930, and reply, PT collection, file no. 42/II.
23. Niranjan Bhagat et al. (eds), *Tribute to Ethics: Remembering Kasturbhai Lalbhai*, Ahmedabad, 1983, p. 68.
24. For this interpretation see Gordon, *Businessmen and Politics*, pp. 200–1. On the possible gain to the mill industry, see Birla to Gandhi, 28 April 1930 in Birla, *Bapu*, vol. I, pp. 140–2.
25. See, for instance, D.P. Khaitan's Address to the Indian Chamber of Commerce, Calcutta, 5 March 1930, *Annual Report for 1930*, Calcutta 1931. Also see Sumit Sarkar, 'The Logic of Gandhian Nationalism', pp. 122–3.
26. Thakurdas to Irwin, 31 May 1930, PT collection, file no. 99/II.
27. Birla to Thakurdas, 16 January 1931, PT collection, file no. 42/VII.
28. Sumit Sarkar, 'The Logic of Gandhian Nationalism' has given a brief account of the official reports, pp. 133–4; Thakurdas to Mody (undated but appears to have been written in August 1930). PT collection, file no. 100.
29. Jawaharlal Nehru, *Autobiography*, p. 232.
30. Thakurdas to Motilal Nehru, 22 September 1930, PT collection, file no. 104; Thakurdas to D.P. Khaitan, 8 October 1930, PT collection, file no. 99/II.
31. Gandhi to Irwin, 14 February 1931, *Collected Works[of Mahatma Gandhi*, Ahmedabad, 1971, vol. XLV, pp. 175–6.
32. Sumit Sarkar, 'The Logic of Gandhian Nationalism', p. 141.
33. Birla to Samuel Hoare, 14 February 1932, *In the Shadow*, p. 49; Rajat K. Ray, *Industrialization in India*, p. 322.
34. For a feel of the nature of Birla's correspondence with some of the key persons see Birla, *In the Shadow*, pp. 41–67.
35. Birla to Thakurdas, 28 November 1930, PT collection, file no. 42/VII.
36. Birla to Tej Bahadur Sapru, 31 October 1931, in Birla, *In the Shadow*, pp. 42–5.
37. S.D. Mehta, *Cotton Mills*, p. 182; also Tripathi, *Dynamics of a Tradition*, pp. 179–80.
38. Nehru's statement on 28 January 1930, Jawaharlal Nehru Memorial Fund, *Selected Works*, New Delhi, 1973, vol. IV, p. 232; Bipan Chandra, *Nationalism and Colonialism in Modern India*, New Delhi, 1979, pp. 172–3.
39. Indian National Congress, *Resolutions on Economic Policy and Allied Matters*, New Delhi, 1969, pp. 3, 6–9.
40. Arun Joshi, *Lala Shri Ram* [(New Dehli 1978)], pp. 226–7.
41. Birla to Samuel Hoare, 14 March 1932, in Birla, *In the Shadow*, p. 51; also see Birla's record of an interview with Sir Henry Craik on 30 June 1935, ibid., p. 145.
42. Venkatasubbiah, *Enterprise and Economic Change*, p. 18.
43. Birla, *In the Shadow*, p. 130.

44. Ibid., p. 181.
45. Claude Markovits, *Indian Business and Nationalist Politics, 1931–9,* London, 1985, pp. 150–78.
46. Birla, *Bapu,* vol. IV, p. 136; P. Sitaramayya, *The History of the Indian National Congress,* Bombay, 1957, vol. I. p. 278.
47. Frank Moraes, *Sir Purshotamdas Thakurdas,* pp. 213, 219.
48. Venkatasubbiah, *Enterprise and Economic Change,* p. 42. A note on 'Congress and Big Business' prepared by the Intelligence Bureau of the Home Department, Government of India in 1944 referred to the industrialists' financial help to the Congress. The *New York Times* quotation is from the same source. See Suniti Kumar Ghosh, *The Indian Big Bourgeoisie,* Calcutta, 1985, pp. 228–9.
49. Venkatasubbiah, *Enterprise and Economic Change,* p. 22.
50. P. Thakurdas et al., *A Brief Memorandum Outlining a Plan of Economic Development for India,* Bombay, 1944.
51. This was ably demonstrated by H.V.R. Iyengar in his A.D. Shroff Memorial Lecture delivered in 1967. See, Forum of Free Enterprise, *The Bombay Plan and Other Essays,* Bombay, 1968, pp. 1–17.
52. Thakurdas et al., *Plan of Economic Development,* p. 48.

19 Attitude of the Indian National Congress Towards the Working Class Struggle in India, 1918–47*

Vinay Bahl

Industrialists had no doubt whatsoever that if there was one man who could restrain the Congress from adopting a rabid anti-capitalist position, it was Gandhi, and that their common demands could not be secured without the help of the Congress.

—G.D. Birla, *Sunday,* 21 June 1983

This study deals with a hitherto glossed over aspect of the labour history of India, that is, the role of the Indian National Congress in the working class movement and its politics in this regard. Existing studies[1] have not sufficiently highlighted this aspect, though they do give us an idea of the way the Congress gave a particular direction to the workers' movement. The purpose of this study is to closely examine the contribution of the Congress in the development or otherwise of the workers' movement. Our task is facilitated by the availability of a few case studies[2] recently attempted in relation to such major industrial centres or sectors before independence as Bengal, Bombay, Kanpur, Jamshedpur, and the Railways. Concentrating on the period between the emergence of the Congress as a mass party till the attainment of independence, our study seeks to indicate the broad trends within the relationship of the Congress with the native and foreign capitalists as also with that between the nationalist movement and the workers' movement.

I

R.P. Dutt correctly commented:[3]

> While the workers were ready for the struggle the facilities for office organisation were inevitably in other hands hence arose the contradiction

* Originally published in K. Kumar (ed.), *Congress and Classes: Nationalism, Workers and Peasants,* New Delhi, Manohar, 1988, pp. 1–33. In the present version some portions of text and notes have been removed. For the complete text see the original version.

of the early labour movement. There was not yet any political movement on the basis of socialism, of the conceptions of the working class and the class elements who came forward, for varying reasons...brought with them the conceptions of middle class politics.

This made the workers' movement a movement for and not by them. Much before the Congress took the official decision to organize the working class, the earlier nationalists had set the pattern for the later trend. We find them opposing the Factory legislation aimed at shortening the working day and providing for better working conditions on the basis of such reasons as the absence of complaint from the workers, their willingness for work as well as the richness and health of the working class. This betrayed a lack of active sympathy for the working class and the nationalists' 'undivided devotion to industrialisation'.[4] In 1905 a sharp rise in prices coincided with the Swadeshi movement. Nationalist leaders started taking interest in setting up unions and organizing meetings. But whenever the struggle began to take a radical turn, as during the Jamalpur strike, they withdrew from the scene. Soon even this little interest vanished and they returned to 'petitioning'.

The nationalist [...] attitude was in tune with the Congress spirit of devotion to the native industry at the cost of the working class. This was reflected when they opposed the Mines Bill for protection of women and children while supporting the Assam Labour and Emigration Bill as it was against the British-owned plantations. For the same reason they supported the GIP Railway strike and condemned the textile workers' strike against the reduction in wages. The motive behind bringing the working class struggle under Congress control, as explained by C.R. Das in 1922, was the realization that failure to do so or if the Congress delays this matter, India might face a people's revolution on the basis of class struggle. [...][5]

This warning came in 1922. But the Congress organizers had already taken the first step in 1919 to pass a resolution of this nature at Amritsar:[6]

This Congress urges its provincial Committees and other affiliated associations to promote labour unions throughout the country with the view of improving social, economic and political condition of the labouring class for securing for them a fair standard of living and a proper place in the body politics of India.

Resolutions to the same effect were passed by the Congress in 1920, 1922, 1924, and 1930 as well.[7]

The clearest expression of policy in this regard, however, came only in 1936.[8] This time the Congress asked for the appointment of a committee which would suggest possible methods of establishing closer contacts between the Congress and labour/peasant organizations. The Congress had two clearly defined aims: it should remain a party of all classes; and the workers' struggle should be so handled and areas of influence so extended as to restrain labour and develop the labour movement under the Congress umbrella. The Congress did more than formulate its own policies. It went beyond the imperialist government in formulating laws to restrain the independent growth of the working class movement. The government had passed in 1926 the Trade Union Act in which the clauses relating to membership and recognition, as well as the use of funds, were intended to contain trade unionism within clearly defined limits and within purely economic issues. This attempt to channelize and control was extended further by the Bombay Industrial Disputes Act 1939 which, significantly, was passed by the provincial Congress government.

The year 1938 witnessed the peak of strike waves before independence, which had begun in the twenties. These strikes were effective in demanding wages and union recognition and reducing intensification of work. Most of the strikes were over union recognition and inspired by the conscious use of the strike weapon as a protest against the infringement of civil liberties and the emergence of working class solidarity not only locally but on a national scale.[9] The Bombay Industrial Disputers Act was initiated in response to this wave of strikes with the aim to prevent strike and lock-outs as far as possible.[10] This was to be achieved by making arbitration a necessary condition for union recognition. This opened the way for employer-sponsored unions and long drawn out legal procedures. The Trade Disputes Act of 1929 prevented lightning strikes by prescribing a month's notice in public utility services. The Bombay Trade Disputes Act 1938 not only demanded a notice of strike but made illegal every strike which took place before the conciliatory proceedings were over. The notice provision together with inordinate prolongation of conciliatory proceedings were calculated to minimize, if not obviate, to paralyse strikes.

During the war years further laws enfeebling unionism were passed. The main aim of the Essential Services Ordinance of 1941 was to prevent workers in any establishment, which had been declared essential by the government, from disobeying orders, leaving their employment, or absenting themselves.

The incorporation of the Defence of India Act into Rule 81 A of the Trade Disputes Act of 1929 further restricted the right to strike. All these restrictions culminated in the Industrial Disputes Act of 1947. Legislative attempts at channelling the working class movement rested on ideological appeals to 'national interest'.

Thus right from the beginning of the labour movement in India, the Congress sought to check its growth on independent lines, betraying greater keenness than did the imperialist government to keep the labour under strict legislative control. What manifested in the post-independence days was a logical and a harsher confirmation of the policies pursued by the Congress during the pre-independence period.

[...]

The broad spectrum of the Congress policy towards the labour movement comprised three strands of thought. Sharing the same ideological orientation, these strands differed from one another in terms of tactics for handling the labour. They believed in restraining the workers' movement from growing militant and to keep it under the Congress control.

The first of these strands was represented by Gandhi who, with his faith in class harmony, did not support any type of coercion either by the millowners or by the workers. Another set of leaders—those who formed the All India Trade Union Congress (AITUC)—believed in class harmony. But they did not agree with Gandhi's methods. Mostly reformists, like N.M. Joshi, V.V. Giri, and Diwan Chamanlal, theses leaders did not eschew cooperation with the British government as is clear from their association with various conferences and commissions. Supporting forcible and repressive methods of control over the working class activity, the second strand was represented by leaders like Sardar Patel, Rajendra Prasad, and C. Rajagopalachari. Capitalists like Birla and Tata, naturally, had great faith in them and strengthened their hands to safeguard vested interests.[11] A section of Congressmen was affected by socialist ideas. They were mainly led by Jawaharlal Nehru and Subhash Bose. In spite of their 'socialist' sympathies, they never deviated from the Congress policies vis-à-vis the working class. Later on some radicals inside the Congress, who realized how antagonistic the party was towards the working class, broke off and joined the Communist Party of India.

II

[...]

CONGRESS AND LABOUR 1918–20

After the First World War prices had gone up and the workers were getting restive all over the country. The Royal Commission on Labour observed:[12]

Prior to the winter of 1918–19, a strike was a rare occurrence in Indian industry. Strikes took place occasionally on the Railways and in other branches of industry, but to the majority of industrial workers the use of strike was probably unknown. Lacking leadership and organisation and deeply imbued with a passive outlook of life, the vast majority of industrial workers regarded the return to the village as the only alternative to the endurance of hard conditions in industry. The end of the war saw an immediate change.

The condition of the worker deteriorated.

But this period was dominated by Gandhian ideology. An isolated incident like the formation of the Madras Labour Union, under B.P. Wadia in 1918, was away from the mainstream, though this was the first effort to formally organize the workers under a modern trade union. However, being a liberal constitutionalist who sincerely believed in the British sense of 'justice'[13] Wadia could not lead the workers on an independent path of struggle. The same year the workers of Ahmedabad Textile Mills went on strike. The reason of the strike was that the 'plague bonus' was being withdrawn by the millowners after the end of the war and the epidemic. The latter were offering a 20 per cent wage increase, whereas the workers wanted the increase to be 50 per cent to neutralize the hardship of price rise. When the situation was about to get out of control, Gandhi intervened. With his new ideology and calculations, he advised the workers to demand 35 per cent increase and stick to that. At the same time he told the workers 'not to indulge in mischief, quarrelling, robbing...but behave peacefully'.[14] Gandhi felt obliged to resort to his method of 'fasting' in order to bring moral pressure on the millowners. He was ultimately 'successful' and an agreement was reached. The provisions of the agreement will explain the extent of Gandhi's 'success'. According to the agreement[15] on the first day of the settlement the workers would be given 35 per cent increase (to keep the prestige of Gandhi), on the second day they would get 20 per cent as was earlier offered by the millowners so that the millowners should not feel that they had lost their prestige. There after the half of the remaining 15 per cent would be given to the workers until the decision of the arbitrators. If the decision was 35 per cent, the millowners would pay the balance; if the decision was 20 per cent, the worker would refund the balance.

Gandhi, it is clear from the agreement, had checked the growth of a militant workers' movement and put it on the path of arbitration. This, as we shall notice in the subsequent discussion, became the main goal of the Congress. The Ahmedabad Textile Union, formed under Gandhi's guardianship, remained loyal to him and his ideology; except in 1934 when even these workers could not remain passive under the mass wage cut and retrenchment policy of the millowners. Gandhi again used the threat to 'fast' and persuaded the workers to accept the wage cut 'cheerfully'.[16] [...]

After the end of the First World War the decline in real wages led to mass unrest among the working class in 1920. This coincided with the Non-Cooperation Movement and the formation of the All India Trade Union Congress. There was no link between these two movements. The workers were not yet penetrated by the Congress party. Going by their own experience of capital, they had learnt to oppose it, in this period, by going on spontaneous strikes. But soon under Congress leadership this independent expression of labour unrest came to be controlled by the bourgeoisie. For several years the potential militancy of labour remained dormant.

Various case studies show that the Congress did not organize any strike in this period. Indeed, whenever one occurred, it tried to take charge of it, lest it should turn into an independent movement. The Ahmedabad Textile Union provides the only instance of consistent labour participation in the nationalist movement. This was due to the Union's loyalty to Gandhi. The other possible example is that of Railway workers whose support of the Non-Cooperation Movement may be attributed to 'the racial division in the work force'. But their support to the Congress-led nationalist movement began to wane after 1930.[17]

In the Kharagpur Bengal Nagpur Railways strike of 1927, which was brutally repressed by the British-owned Company, the Tatas helped the Railway authorities. The Tatas, it may be noted, were supported by the nationalist leadership when the TISCO workers went on strike during the period under study. On the other hand, when in 1920 the workers of A.B. Railways at Chandpur went on strike in sympathy with the tea plantation labourers of Assam who were fighting against the oppression of the British-owned planters, reformist leaders like C.R. Das rushed to take charge of this strike to prevent it developing into a more class conscious militant struggle. Gandhi, Andrews, and Hardayal simply condemned the strike in the name of public 'inconveniences'[18] although the public of Bengal was fully supporting the strike. Naturally the strike collapsed for want of financial and other help. Support to this strike could have advanced the cause of the working class and sharpened their class consciousness. It could also have enlisted labour to the nationalist movement. But the Congress found such support inconsonant with its own class interests.

In Kanpur and Jamshedpur the Congress leadership were busy trying to implement Gandhi's ideology of 'class harmony'. Interestingly there is a striking similarity in these two places regarding the approach of the Congress. In Kanpur workers started their strike in 1919. Soon certain Congressmen got associated with the Union called Mazdoor Sabha and expressed their concern for the working class. Initially they played the role of mediators to help settle the strike. But soon after they tried to restructure the Mazdoor Sabha. Some of them like G.S. Vidyarthi, Murari Lal, and N.P. Nigam became important office bearers of the Sabha. All these leaders were closely associated with the Home Rule League, Khilafat, and Non-Cooperation Movement. They emphasized the principle of maintaining goodwill and harmony between the workers and employers and showed a Gandhian faith in the benevolence of the millowner. A belief in an abstract and undefined principle of 'justice' and 'reciprocity' seems to have prevailed in their ideas just as it did in Gandhi's conception of working class struggle.[19] Leaders like G.S. Vidyarthi felt that the employers could be made aware of their duties toward the workers and with the methods of persuasion the hearts of the millowners could be changed. They went to the extent of calling the recurrent strike after the 1919 settlement as 'unjustified' because according to them the millowners were generally 'fair' in their dealings with the labour. This opinion of the local Congress leadership in Kanpur was formed at a time when the strikes were mostly in protest against the non-fulfilment of the settlement and promises made earlier. Without bothering about the workers, problems these leaders went on emphasizing the principle of arbitration and conciliation and also got them incorporated in the Mazdoor Sabha constitution so that they could prevent 'violent' strikes and 'destructive tendencies' among the workers.[20]

Almost the same type of behaviour is noticed when Congressmen from Calcutta went to Jamshedpur in 1920 to take charge and guide the workers' strike at TISCO. We may say that the Congress attitude in the case of TISCO was more cautious because it was considered a 'national industry' which had the largest number of workers under one roof. Though Tata claims to be the most 'benevolent capitalist' in India, there was no system of increment in wages in TISCO. Jamshedpur, where TISCO was located, suffered the highest price hike after the War. The workers of TISCO were not organized under any union till 1920. But their unbearable situation made them go on strike on their own. Later they sent two of their educated workers to Calcutta to find a leader to guide their strike. These workers contacted Byomkesh Chakrovorty and

S.N. Haldar, two advocates who were also members of the Congress. Interestingly one millowner, Mr Jain, who was a member of the Congress also joined the other leaders in their visit to Jamshedpur.[21]

These leaders immediately formed a union of the workers and started negotiating with the management. These leaders undermined the seriousness of the situation and on their own tried to compromise for lesser percentage of wage increase. In spite of being inexperienced, the workers were very clear about their needs. They would not allow the leaders to compromise. Mr Jain found the workers so adamant that he told the Superintendent of Police that 'if the men now decline to behave let them go to hell'.[22] He soon left Jamshedpur. The other two leaders also were not very successful in persuading the workers to agree to their compromise. They tried to weaken the struggle by demanding a settlement for those who wished to go to their villages. The tactics of the Congress leaders did not bring anything to the workers of TISCO, and in the end they had to join back the works. In the course of the struggle they lost five of their comrades in a shooting spree by the Company's honorary magistrate and twenty of them were injured. Soon after, Teja Singh, a local leader of the workers who claimed to be in touch with Gandhi, informed them that Gandhi had sent a message asking the workers to 'suffer in silence for the national industry'.[23]

Subsequent to this strike the local Congress leadership publicly eulogized the General Manager of the Company and said that he had been misled by the advice of wrong people and so workers should forget and forgive these actions. This appears to have been a calculated move, because the Congress led JLA was more interested in getting recognition from the TISCO management in order to control the workers through their union. They knew that to get recognition they must cooperate with the management which was under the control of an Indian capitalist—a person who was in the good books of nationalist leaders like Gandhi and Motilal Nehru. These calculations were made clear when the workers were told that the Calcutta leaders were busy revising the rules of JLA, and the main principles would be: (1) to cooperate with the Company, increase its output and promote its interests; and (2) to safeguard the interests of the employees.[24]

Incidentally after the tragic end of the 1920 strike Tata management passed a resolution thanking the government authorities for helping in the termination of the strike. These new developments were well analysed by the Deputy Commissioner of Jamshedpur. He wrote that the first principle with the Congress was that since the Company was

Indian and financed by Indian capital it was incumbent on the workers, as Indians, to look after the interest of the Company. The second principle seems to have been that since a hungry man could not do a full day's work, the Association should see that he was well fed and so should assist the Company in turning out more work.[25]

In the next phase of the workers' struggle, we find a shift in the Congress policy, that is, to check the workers' militancy not only in the native industry but also in the foreign-owned industries.

[...]

III

1921–7: There was no amelioration in sight of the workers' unbearable plight. Their exploitation was increasing even after the strike wave of 1920. Consequently there was a shift towards greater militancy. 'The shortened amicable and successful strikes of 1919–20 had become less frequent, industrial unrest was reaching new heights and the working class struggles had become more bitter in their character and duration'.[26] The Congress was persisting in its policy of checking strikes, irrespective of whether they occurred in foreign- or native-owned industries. The issues of Kanpur workers' protest in 1923 against ill treatment by the European officials in foreign-owned mills, like Elgin Mill and Victoria Mill[27] could have been employed for its anti-imperialist dimension. Instead the Congress worked hard to check the workers' struggle from taking a militant turn.

In Jamshedpur the JLA leadership decided that it would not initiate any strike, but if one occurred it would take charge of it. Since the JLA was not helping the workers of TISCO to realize their demands, the workers on their own once again went on strike in 1922.[28] The JLA tried to take charge of it, but in vain. Thereupon the workers invited Dewan Chamanlal, President of AITUC, to negotiate with the management. He proved no better than the Congress-led JLA. He made a verbal agreement with the Company, the contents of which no one knew, and told the workers to join back work. Naively the workers believed the nationalist leader and joined back. All they got was the dismissal of 1,000 workers; many of them were put on jobs lower paid than the ones they had held before the strike.[29]

It may be mentioned here that although the JLA tried hard to cooperate with the Company and sabotage the workers' strike, it was not recognized by the owner of the 'national industry'. When all efforts of JLA failed to get recognition, it tried to influence the passing of Protection

Bill for steel by issuing a pamphlet highlighting the workers' grievances in TISCO. Soon Tata met Motilal Nehru, convinced him, and got the Protection Bill passed. Motilal Nehru came to Jamshedpur and told the workers: 'They should carry...the instructions peacefully and cooperate with the proprietors as guided by the leaders who had taken up their cause along with the cause of *Swaraj*. Everything would be settled when the question of *Swaraj* was settled'.[30] C.R. Das, who also had come with Motilal stressed that 'by the recognition of Association your responsibilities will increase because you will have to do everything very carefully and mutually in cooperation with the company and it is an Indian concern and you will have to see it is not failed'.[31] In spite of all these big words the JLA was not recognized by Tata. Not surprisingly the workers of TISCO believed the rumour that the Tariff Act has cost the Company a contribution of 4–1/2 lakhs of rupees to Swarajists' party funds. The Deputy Commissioner of Jamshedpur significantly noted that the visit of Motilal and Das marked 'an epoch in the history of labour in Jamshedpur'. He felt that the labour leaders would realize that the Swarajist leaders were not concerned with the workers' grievances.[32]

Similarly, in Bombay the Gandhian leader N.M. Joshi, who was the chairman of the workers' union, did nothing to organize a successful struggle against the capitalists who were forcing a strike on the workers. The millowners of Bombay announced a 20 per cent cut in DA in 1925. The workers were forced to go on strike. All that Joshi did was to ask for a settlement for the workers so that they could leave the town and go to their villages. He could not see that the millowners were using this strike to pressurize the Government to give levy exemptions. The strike could be brought to an end only when the Bombay Government suspended the levy of excise duty which helped the millowners to withdraw the wage cut.[33] Joshi was only interested in avoiding tension between the labour and capital and not concerned with the suffering and needs of the workers.

In the late twenties there was once again a shift in the policy of the Congress. This was mainly due to the emerging force of communist ideology among the working class as well as the intelligentsia.

1928–30: Congress leaders like Jawaharlal Nehru were greatly attracted towards the socialist ideology. The same was true of certain local Congress leaders in some of the industrial centres. But this should not be confused with the communist involvement. Sometimes the local Congressmen had to take a more millitant stance in order to neutralize the communist hold, more so in areas like Kanpur, Bombay, and Bengal.

For example, in Kanpur where in 1929 the Mazdoor Sabha was more influenced by the Congress-socialists like H.N. Shastri and Raja Ram Shastri, these leaders were even talking in terms of class war and destruction of capitalism. They were distinguishing their conception of *Swaraj* from that of Congress: 'The Swaraj of the Congress cannot meet the wishes of labourers and peasants in as much as it will be under the control of Indian capitalists who are naturally opposed to them'.[34] Local Congressmen had thus to come to terms with the new militant philosophy of workers' struggle introduced by the communists.

In Bengal the Congress was similarly motivated to support the jute workers' strike in 1929. Intelligence reports were quick to note this.[35] Jawaharlal Nehru rushed to Calcutta in order to observe the situation personally. This became imperative because at the time of the 1928 Congress session in Calcutta, workers numbering 30,000 had demonstrated in front of the Congress *pandal*. They had taken over the session for two hours, passing resolution for the complete independence of India and a welfare scheme for the working class. This historic demonstration of the growth of class consciousness among workers had shaken the Congress.

In contrast to Bengal there was no communist influence in Jamshedpur. Consequently Congressmen adopted a very different attitude there. The TISCO workers had only a Congress-led union in which they had no faith and which was described by them as 'Company *Ka Dalal*' (the broker of the Company). Since this union was more keen on helping the management than the workers' cause, the workers went on strike again on their own in 1928 against the traditionally low wages and bad living and working conditions. In spite of being much influenced by socialist or communist ideas, the workers refused to listen to any counsel that bade them to cooperate with the Company. JLA tried to capture the leadership of these strikers by inviting N.M. Joshi and V.V. Giri to address the workers. But the workers hooted them away. Joshi had to escape in a car. The JLA eventually invited Subhash Bose. The workers believed him due to his national image and the strike became more severe. Soon the initial militancy of Bose faded away at the promptings of Motilal Nehru who in turn was approached by the Tatas. Bose also started talking of saving the 'national industry'. Very soon the workers realized that Bose was no better than other nationalist leaders; so they broke away from the JLA and formed their own Federation and chose a local advocate as their president.[36] Bose tried to regain his image at Jamshedpur, but he had to give up his efforts after 1930 as the workers refused to believe any nationalist leader. This was also the period when the Government came down with an iron hand upon the communists. Towards the end of 1929 the Congress hesitatingly declared *purna swarajya* as its goal. Consequent upon it Gandhi launched his Civil Disobedience Movement. But there was no mention of purna swarajya; there were only demands for more reforms.[37]

1931–4: With the onset of the world economic crisis labour struggle intensified. Recession in the textiles and jute industries led to massive wage cuts and retrenchment. In the Bombay textile industry, out of 140,000 workers approximately 10,000 workers were thrown out of employment.[38] In spite of considerable organizational disunity, the working class waged economic struggles in the face of this crisis. But largely due to lack of unity, the struggles could not be very extensive and effective. The most significant of these struggles was the general strike of 1934. An action committee was formed on behalf of all the unions in Bombay, Nagpur, and Sholapur. The characteristic features of the strike, visible from the very beginning, were mass picketing of the mills, daily meetings, and mass demonstrations. In the beginning N.M. Joshi, R.R. Bakhale, and other reformist leaders were against the strike. Subsequently the militant mood of the workers obliged them to support the strike. But they did so on certain conditions. When these conditions were not accepted by the united strike committee, a rival committee was formed at the initiative of M.S. Kandalker, Alve, Maniben Kara, and other reformist leaders.[39] These developments gave a blow to the united struggle of workers. At the same time split in the AITUC and formation of a rival union led to the calling off of the strike. Soon the government showed its teeth by suspending the use of conciliation machinery, banning the Communist Party and arresting the union leaders.

Significantly, during this economic crisis the Ahmedabad Millowners Association proposed a 25 per cent cut in the workers wages. The cumbersome machinery of compulsory arbitration, introduced in Ahmedabad by Gandhi, led to a prolonged negotiation between the Millowners' Association and the Majdoor Mahajan on the issue of wage cut. Meanwhile the workers were growing impatient for a general strike in the textile industry. An agreement was ultimately signed in 1935 which actually admitted wage cuts. Gandhi hastened to send a personal letter to the workers, advising them to accept the cut 'cheerfully'. Thus the Congress leaders managed to keep the Ahmedabad workers under control.

When the Congress decided to fight the elections under the Government of India Act (1935), it realized the need to win over the working class. Consequently, it included in its election manifesto promises for the welfare of the workers. These promises generated a new hope among the workers and they thought that the coming of the Congress in power would mean no more repression for them. A different experience was in store for them.

1935–8: The Congress, having formed ministries in seven out of nine provinces, pursued towards the labour a policy, during the two-and-a-half years of its rule, that was symptomatic of what was to follow during Congress rule in independent India. Assumption of office, Nehru had hoped in 1937, would not mean becoming partners in the repression and exploitation of our own people.[40] That is what the Congress ministries actually became. They turned out to be the direct instruments of repression and exploitation of the Indian working class.

The hope of the working class having been aroused by the Congress manifesto, a sharp increase in industrial disputes occurred in 1938–9. This led to a sharper definition of the Congress attitude towards different classes. In the process of defining its attitude it became a repressive force in the areas where it was in power; but it performed a militant role in a non-Congress province like Bengal.

In Bombay the Congress ministry introduced the notorious Industrial Disputes Bill which was strongly opposed by the workers. The aim of the Bill was 'the prevention of strikes and lock-outs as far as possible'. The Congress made it clear that it was opposed to 'loose talks' along the lines of confiscation of property and class war which was declared to be 'contrary to the Congress creed of non-violence'. Interestingly, in Bombay which was then the most industrialized place in India, this ban on 'strike and lock-out' actually meant a ban on 'strike only' [...].[41] This restriction of the right of the workers and the emphasis on compulsory and comprehensive arbitration of industrial disputes also heralded an era in which industrial grievances would be settled through state machinery rather than through collective bargaining of the parties involved.

The snatching away of the workers', right to strike and rendering it punishable stringently revealed the nakedly anti-labour attitude of the Congress Ministry. The workers of Bombay struck work in protest against this anti-labour Bill and the Congress Ministry deployed police who mercilessly fired upon and lathi-charged them resulting in the death of twenty workers.[42] Gulzarilal Nanda, a stalwart of the Ahmedabad Association and a trusted disciple of Gandhi, was appointed the Parliamentary Secretary of Labour in the Bombay Congress Ministry. He played an active role in the prosecution of the anti-labour policies of the Congress government.

The situation in UP was no better. In Kanpur in August 1937 about 24,000 workers were on strike and almost all the mills were affected. Both G.B. Pant, the Premier, and Katju, the Minister of Industries, resented the outbreak of these strikes and called these 'untimely' and 'uncalled for'. The Congress made it clear that it would not tolerate any 'spontaneous' activity by the workers without the sanction of the KMS, or any 'violent', 'aggressive' activity. Soon the Congress sanctioned the use of repressive measures to control the striking workers who, it was felt, were becoming 'violent' and 'unruly'. Over 1,000 armed and civil policemen patrolled the mill area, prohibiting orders under Section 144 were imposed, and a number of lathi charges were made on the strikers. Repression reached its height on 6 August when the police opened fire on the picketeers. These actions, it may be emphasized, were appreciated and supported by the imperialist government as these were in tune with its own policy. It was reported that because of 'the outstanding support given by U.P. Congress Committee to the action of the local officials at Kanpur with the approval of the Government in order to maintain peace and as a result of vigorous measures taken [that is, the repression] Kanpur is quiet at present'.[43] Nehru was very much concerned about the welfare of the mills in Kanpur and he stressed:[44]

> If violence is resorted to, it cannot be expected that the government will not interfere and the army or police will not be called. The workers should remember that the government is very powerful and will put down violence by violence and that the workers will be subdued in no time.

However, the same Congress and Nehru whole-heartedly supported the strike of jute workers in Bengal in 1937, because it was a non-Congress Province under the Haq Ministry. The Bengal Pradesh Congress Committee passed a resolution condemning the repression of the jute workers' strike.[45] Subhash Bose made appeals to help the workers with funds. Nehru said:[46]

> The mere fact this strike has gone on for this long period shows the determination of the workers and their belief in the justness of their cause. I trust that Congressmen will draw attention of the public to this great struggle for freedom.

It is not clear what Nehru meant here by word 'freedom'. Was it the freedom from Haq Ministry, or India's freedom, or freedom from the capitalist? Certainly he did not mean freedom from the capitalists as is clear from the views expressed by him at other places. If he meant 'freedom for India', how is it that the struggle of Bengal workers sym- bolized the struggle for India's freedom whereas similar struggles in Bombay and Kanpur were mercilessly crushed by the Congress Govern- ment? Interestingly, Gandhi remained non-committal during the strike in Bengal while the whole of the Congress was supporting it.[47]

There was another case of industrial tension in a major 'national industry' during this period which was resolved in a very different way by the Congress leaders. It would be interesting to examine this case in order to understand the pattern of behaviour of the Congress in dealing with the working class struggle during the period of Provincial Autonomy. TISCO, as mentioned earlier, could never be used as the hold of the Congress-led JLA and the workers suspected the leadership of being in league with the Company. However, since TISCO employed the largest working force, the Congress was very keen to win over these workers for its election purpose. Professor Bari was chosen for the task. Bari (a true Congressman) used all possible filthy words to abuse the Tatas in public meetings and promised economic gains for the workers. These tactics convinced the TISCO workers that Bari was their friend. But it could not be so simple. The Tatas objected to these methods and complained to higher authorities in the Congress. The Congress leaders were in a dilemma. They did not wish too lose their hold over the working class. At the same time they wished to retain the support of the Tatas and check Bari from using abusive language and opposing the management. The situation worsened when Bari refused to give up the working class leadership and almost gave a call for strike in 1937–8 at the time of the 'Founder's day' celebration in TISCO. Ultimately Nehru and Rajendra Prasad became arbitrators between the Tatas and the TISCO workers led by Bari. The Award givers condemned Bari and asked the workers to behave with dignity. The Congress did not hesitate to condemn one of its own important and respected leaders when it came to saving the 'national industry' and containing the working class struggle.

It is important to note in this case that Bari owed his popularity among TISCO workers not to his affiliation with the Congress but to his demonstration, at least in his speeches, of a determined anti-capitalist attitude. Not surprisingly, Bari was soon called back by the Congress. The field was now left open to local Congressmen like Michael John and Moni Ghosh who were more Gandhian and faithful to the Company than Bari. These leaders could not prove very effective in face of other workers like the Communists and Congress Socialists who had started taking interest in TISCO workers by this time.

The Congress realized that the only way to keep the TISCO workers under its influence was to send back Bari. He came in 1943–4 and made two very important agreements with the Tatas on behalf of the workers. These set the trend for industrial relations in Jamshedpur along lines of collective bargaining. Soon after Bari was murdered, supposedly in a dialogue with a security guard on the border of Bihar.[48]

It may not be possible to establish conclusively the reasons for Bari's murder. But circumstantial evidence suggests some clues. Bari had become very popular in TISCO. He was becoming difficult to handle even by his own party. The local Congressmen especially felt left out due to the arbitrary methods of Bari. Moreover, as is suggested by interviews with some living workers of that period, he was maintaining relations with local Communist leaders like Kedar Das.[49] These circumstances explain the background in which this murder took place, and indicate that political motives for the murder cannot be ruled out.

1939–47: The working class movement suffered a setback during the War years. The AITUC was dominated by the Communists who decided to support Allied War effort following the German invasion of Soviet Russia. The Defence of India Rules also kept in check the occurrence of any strike, the only instances being the strikes in Ahmedabad and Jamshedpur during the 'Quit India' movement. Ahmedabad took part in this movement due to its devotion to Gandhi. But the case of TISCO was different as it is alleged that the Tatas were behind this strike. The speeches made by the General Manager, Sir A. Dalal, are quoted in this regard.[50] However, a close look at the TISCO records reveals that the supervisory staff—sympathetic to the Congress—spread the rumour that it was the management's order to strike. As the supervisory staff was telling them so, the workers believed it. But it was mainly the former who went on this political strike.[51] The management was all set to seek help from the Government's Amunition Factory, if the said strike of supervisors and foremen continued.[52] However, going by the outwardly posture of the Tatas, M.N. Roy sued the Tata management for their involvement in this strike. The case dragged on till 1947 when Roy realized that, if pursued further, would enhance the image of the Tatas in the eyes of the Congress.[53]

Immediately after the War violent industrial unrest broke out. The Congress government used this as a pretext to pass the Industrial Disputes Act, 1947. The Act embodied many of the restrictive features of the Defence of India Rules. Even leaders like N.M. Joshi felt that the government was doing the workers great harm by prohibiting the right to strike.[54] Dissatisfied with the AITUC, as it was captured by the Communists, the Congress recommended that Congressmen should work with the Hindustan Mazdoor Sevak Sangh (labour advisory body sponsored by leaders associated with the Ahmedabad TLA). Two months later the HMSS adopted a resolution, directing its members to affiliate their unions with the AITUC and promote through AITUC the policies of HMSS and change its constitution. Clearly the intention was to capture the AITUC. But the Congress soon got frustrated and in May 1947 a high level conference was held. Attended by Jawaharlal Nehru, Sardar Patel, and other members of the Congress high command, the conference decided to form a new labour organization called INTUC (Indian National Trade Union Congress). In 1948 the Congress government declared INTUC to be the most representative working class Union in India; which meant that the INTUC alone could represent the workers in ILO meetings.[55] Overnight a new labour federation was ushered in to control the labour on behalf of the ruling party.

[...]

IV

The Congress claim of being an 'all class' party is thus discredited by the above account which demonstrates two aspects of the Congress policies and action vis-à-vis the working class. First, it did not allow or help the development of an independent working class movement. The Congress was keen on channelizing the workers' struggle along the path of 'arbitration' in its bid to neutralize the ideology of 'class war'. In the process the Congress became as harsh and merciless (if not more) as the imperialist government. The Trade Union Act of 1947 thus incorporated all the repressive provisions of the colonial labour laws, the Defence of India Act, and the notorious Bombay Trade Dispute Act of 1937.

Secondly the Congress tried to protect all the 'native and national' industries (sometimes the foreign owned also) against the workers' struggle, in spite of the fact that these 'national industries' firmly believing in crushing the workers' movement, bothered not a bit about the Gandhian principles of 'class harmony'. This was the essence of the professed Congress policy of promoting the interest of 'all classes' of the Indian society. It is not without significance that Gandhi found the Tatas very 'generous' capitalists when they gave him a red carpet treatment and a 'silver' casket with money. In 1934, as we have seen, he advised the workers of Ahmedabad to cheerfully accept the 'wage cut' imposed by the employers. That was his way of effecting industrial peace.

If this is what the Mahatma did, it is not surprising that top leaders like Motilal, Jawaharlal, and Bose showed towards the poor labour the kind of solicitude we have seen they did.

Different ideological trends may have emerged within the Congress. But so far as the workers' struggle was concerned in effect and in practice the party seems to have shown astonishing consistency in following the path of so-called 'class harmony' and in curbing the growth of an independent and militant working class movement. The Bengal Jute strike of 1937 was an exception. But the exception became possible because of political and ideological considerations in that support to this strike which offered a chance to discredit the Haq ministry and weaken the Communists. In fact, what the Congress did in the name of class harmony was to further strengthen the position of the capitalists by subordinating the struggle of the working class to the logic of a nationalism that was little more than the rationalization of dominant vested interests.

NOTES

1. V.B. Karnik, *Indian Trade Unions: A Survey*, New Delhi, 1977; J. Mathur, *Indian Working Class Movement*, Lucknow, 1964; C. Meyers, *Industrial Labour in India*, Bombay, 1958; R.K. Mukherjee, *Indian Working Class*, Bombay, 1954; C. Reveri, *The Indian Trade Union Movement*, New Delhi, 1972; Sukomal Sen, *Working Class of India*, Calcutta, 1977; G.K. Sharma, *Labour Movement in India*, Delhi, 1963; and V.B. Singh, *Industrial Relations in India*, Bombay, 1958.

2. Vinay Bahl, 'Labour in TISCO, 1920–28' (unpublished MPhil thesis, Jawaharlal Nehru University); 'Labour, Capital and Leadership—A Case Study of Tata Iron and Steel Co. 1918–47 (unpublished ms); Rakhahari Chatterjee, *Working Class and the National Movement in India: The Critical Years*, New Delhi, 1984; William Dawson, 'Trade Union Development in Western Indian Textile Industry' (unpublished PhD thesis, Wisconsin University 1971); V. Gupta, *Labour Movement in Bombay—Origin and Growth into Independence*, Bombay, 1981; Lajpat Jagga, 'Formation of an Industrial Labour Force and Forms of Labour Protest in India—A Case Study of the Railways 1919–37' (unpublished PhD Thesis, JNU, 1983); Chitra Joshi, 'Kanpur Textile Labour: Some structural characterists of the Labour Force and aspects of the Labour Movement 1919–39' (unpublished PhD thesis, JNU, 1981); Amrita Chachi, 'Towards a Theory of the Labour Movement—A Critical Review of the Studies on the Indian Working Class' (unpublished MPhil, thesis, JNU, 1978). Sujata Patel, *The Making of Industrial Relations*, New Delhi, 1987.

3. R.P. Dutt, *India To-day*, London, 1940, p. 368.

4. B. Chandra, *The Rise and Growth of Economic Nationalism in India*, Calcutta, 1970, p. 332.

5. *Indian Annual Register*, 1923, vol. I, pp. 843–4; Chatterjee, *Working Class*.

6. All India Congress Committee Papers, F. No. 1/1919, NMML.

7. Ibid.

8. Ibid., F. No. G. 309/1937.

9. C. Reveri, *The Indian Trade Union Movement*, p. 228.

10. Ibid., p. 230.

11. Birla wrote: '...we who represent healthy capitalists should help Gandhi as far as possible and work with a common objective', P.T. Das Papers, NMML, F. 42 VI.

12. *Report of the Royal Commission on Labour 1931*, p. 333.

13. R.P. Dutt, *India To-day*, p. 369.

14. V.B. Karnik, *Indian Trade Unions*, pp. 105–6.

15. Ibid. The recent work on this is, Sujata Patel, *The Making*.

16. Sukomal Sen, *Working Class*, p. 332; Sujata Patel, *The Making*, p. 122.

17. Lajpat Jagga, 'Formation of an Industrial Labour Force'.

18. Ibid.

19. P. Saha, *History of the Working Class*, pp. 53–4. (History of the Working Class Movement in Bengal, New Delhi, 1978.)

20. For discussion on Kanpur in detail, see Chitra Joshi, 'Kanpur Textile Labour'.

21. For detailed study on Jamshedpur, see Vinay Bahl, 'Labour in TISCO, 1920–28'.

22. Bihar State Archives (hereafter BSA), Political (special) F. No. 176/1920.

23. Ibid.

24. Ibid.

25. Ibid.

26. R. Kumar, 'The Bombay Textile Strike 1919', *Indian Economic and Social History Review*, March 1971.

27. See Chitra Joshi, 'Kanpur Textile Labour'.

28. *Amrita Bazar Patrika*, 21 September 1922.

29. V. Bahl, unpublished Ms, 'Labour in TISCO, 1920–28'.

30. BSA, Political (special), File No. 51/1924.

31. Ibid.

32. Ibid.

33. V. Gupta, *Labour Movement in Bombay*, p. 49.

34. Chitra Joshi, 'Kanpur Textile Labour'.

35. Quoted in P. Saha, *History of the Working Class*.

36. V. Bahl, 'Tata Workers Struggle', *Social Scientist*, August 1982.

37. Sukomal Sen, *The Making*, pp. 294–5.

38. Reveri, C., *The Indian Trade Union Movement*, p. 175.

39. Sukomal Sen, *The Making*, p. 333.

40. Ibid., p. 357.

41. Ibid., pp. 365–6.
42. Ibid.
43. Chitra Joshi, 'Kanpur Textil Labour'.
44. Ibid.
45. P. Saha, *History of the Working Class*, p. 160.
46. *Amrita Bazar Patrika*, 22 April 1937.
47. *Indian Annual Register*, vol. I, 1937, p. 185.
48. Vinay Bahl, unpublished ms, 'Labour in TISCO, 1920–28'.
49. Interview by the author with Kedar Das in 1976 at Patna. Interview with Jamshedpur AITUC branch leaders, 1981.
50. TISCO, Personnel Department, 28 August 1942, Radio Relay Station, Jamshedpur, Speech by Mr A. Dalal.
51. Home Political, F. No. 146/1942 (National Archives of India). Also Superintendent of Police Report, Jamshedpur (S.P. Archives, Jamshedpur). Interview with the TISCO workers and officers, 1981.
52. General Manager, TISCO to Russel, 3 September 1941, TISCO Papers. JRD Tata told the board on 27 August 1942, that 'If the Situation does not improve by Monday, Dalal proposes that he and I should go to Delhi and discuss with Government of India the steps to be taken'. ibid. It is interesting that after independence the 1942 strike was cited by Tatas to promote their patriotic image. *Hindustan Times*, 2 November 1979.
53. M.N. Roy Correspondence Roll No. 27, NMML.
54. Quoted by C. Meyers, *Industrial Labour in India*, p. 63.
55. INTUC, Proceedings of the Inaugural Conference, New Delhi, 1947.

PART VIII

THE RESTLESS FORTIES

20 Popular Movements and National Leadership, 1945–47[*]

Sumit Sarkar

[...]

The last two years of British rule have been both well-served and ill-served by historians. Thanks to the *Transfer of Power* series edited by Mansergh, certain types of official documents are more easily available for the 1940s now than for any other period of Indian history, and a mass of historical literature exists on the tortuous negotiations between British, Congress, and League politicians which culminated in a freedom which was also a tragic Partition.[1] [...]

It is the central argument of this paper, however, that in this as well as in other periods of modern Indian history, the decisions and actions of leaders, British or Indian, cannot really be understood without the counterpoint provided by pressures from below. Certain obvious world developments apart, it was popular action, above all, which made continuance of British rule impossible. Fear of popular 'excesses' made Congress leaders cling to the path of negotiation and compromise, and eventually even accept Partition as a necessary price—while the limits of popular anti-imperialist movements made the truncated settlement of August 1947 unavoidable. [...]

[...]

The framework for post-War developments was set by the aftermath of the 1942 revolt, together with the socio-economic impact of the last three years of the War.

The total confrontation of August 1942, paradoxically enough, ultimately strengthened forces preferring a compromise on both sides. The British had required no less than 57 army battalions to suppress what Linlithgow privately described as 'by far the most serious rebellion since that of 1857, the gravity and extent of which we have so far concealed from the world for reasons of military security'.[2] British policy during

* Originally published in *Economic and Political Weekly*, Annual Number, April, 1982, pp. 677–89. In the present version some portions of the text and notes have been removed. For the complete text see the original version.

the early years of the War[...] had often been deliberately provocative. From 1940 onwards, the bureaucracy had been planning a wholesale crackdown on the Congress on the pattern of 1942, compromise efforts had been repeatedly spurned, and Linlithgow, Wavell, and Churchill had successfully torpedoed the Cripps initiative at the last moment.[3] After Quit India, the British would never again risk such a confrontation, and that the decision in 1945–6 to try for a negotiated settlement was not just a gift of the new Labour Government is indicated by the attitude of Wavell, the by no means ultra-liberal army commander who succeeded Linlithgow in October 1943. In a letter to Churchill dated 24 October 1944, Wavell pointed out that it would be impossible to hold India by force after the War, given the likely state of world opinion and British popular or even army attitudes (as well as the economic exhaustion of Britain, he might have added). [...] [I]t would be wise to start negotiations before the end of the War brought prisoners' release, demobilization, and unemployment, creating 'a fertile field for agitation, unless we have previously diverted their [Congress] energies into some more profitable channel, that is, into dealing with the administrative problems of India and into trying to solve the constitutional problem'.[4] Churchill's pig-headedness [...] delayed the process somewhat, but this was precisely what the British were able to persuade the Congress leadership to do after 1945.
          [...]

The complex interactions between British policies, Congress attitudes, and popular outbursts during 1945–7 can best be grasped through a firm chronological framework. Four phases can be distinguished here: (i) from the surrender of Germany and Japan (in May and August 1945) to February 1946 (the RIN [Royal Indian Navy] revolt, coinciding with the announcement of the Cabinet Mission); (ii) February–August 1946 (from Cabinet mission to the Calcutta riots); (iii) August 1946–February 1947 (when Wavell was replaced by Mountbatten and Attlee fixed a deadline for British withdrawal); and (iv) February–August 1947, the working-out of the Mountbatten Plan.

          Till the autumn and winter of 1945–6, British policy on the whole was marked by continuity rather than change. Though in June 1945 (with Germany defeated and British elections just a month ahead) Churchill at last permitted Wavell to release Congress leaders and start negotiations, the Simla Conference (June 25–July 14) was allowed to be wrecked on the rock of Jinnah's insistence that only the League had the right to choose the Muslim members of the proposed new Executive Council (which would be entirely Indian but for the Viceroy and the Commander-in-Chief, but would still be within the 1935 structure of a central executive not responsible to the Assembly. This, it needs to be emphasized, was a fantastic demand in mid-1945, for the League then ruled (and that largely on Congress sufferance) only in Sind and Assam. The Punjab Unionist ministry under Khizar Hyat Khan had openly broken with Jinnah in mid-1944, NWFP once again had a Congress government once its MLAs had been released, and even the Nazimuddin ministry in Bengal had fallen in March 1945. So far (till August 1946, in fact) there was little evidence that the League would be able to organize real mass sanctions behind its Pakistan demand. Yet by dissolving the Conference, Wavell in effect gave Jinnah the veto he was asking for—in sharp contrast to British attitudes a year later, when the Congress would be invited, however reluctantly, to form an Interim government on its own.[5]

The massive Labour victory of July 1945 initially did not bring about any major change, even though the new Prime Minister (along with Cripps) had been party to the informal Filkins agreement with Nehru in June 1938 by which Labour leaders had promised a complete transfer of power to a constituent assembly based on universal suffrage when they came into power.[6] Wavell's private fears that with 'too big' a majority, Labour might try to hand over 'India to their Congress friends as soon as possible' were soon revealed as exaggerated. By December 1946, he would realize that most Labour leaders—like Foreign Secretary Bevin, for instance—were 'in reality imperialists' who 'like everyone else hate(s) the idea of our leaving India but like everyone else...(have)... no alternative to suggest'.[7] The announcement of new central and provincial elections (last held in 1934 and 1937) made on 21 August 1945 was inevitable now that war had ended. It was welcomed by bureaucrats like the UP Governor Hallet as the 'first step' towards providing 'constitutional activities for the agitators'.[8] After consultations with the new Labour government, Wavell on 19 September merely reiterated the promise of 'early realization of full self-government' (the term 'independence' was still being avoided). Post-election talks were promised with MLAs and Indian states for setting-up a 'constitution-making body' (a step back, this, from the Filkins acceptance of a constituent assembly based on universal franchise), and efforts would be made again to set up an Executive Council 'which will have the support of the main Indian parties'.[9] How little British policies had changed as yet was indicated by the initial decision to put on trial no less than 600 of the 20,000 INA [Indian National Army] prisoners, while another 7,000 would be dismissed from service and detained without trial.[10] Indian troops were sent out to help restore French and Dutch colonial rule in Vietnam and Indonesia, though about this Wavell did express some nervousness.[11]

The decisive shift in British policies during the ensuing months obviously had an international dimension in the world-wide weakening of imperialist forces. Fascism had been routed, socially, radical regimes with Communist leadership or participation were emerging throughout Eastern Europe and seemed on the point of doing so even in France and Italy, the Chinese Revolution was forging ahead, and a tremendous anti-imperialist wave was sweeping through South-East Asia, with Vietnam and Indonesia in the vanguard. A war-weary, economically-ravaged, Britain no longer had the resources to hold on to an entire subcontinent by force. That the British came to realize this, however, at this specific moment was above all due to mass pressure—and not due to anything done by the top national leadership, Congress or League.

The autumn and winter months of 1945–6 have been perceptively described by Penderel Moon as 'The Edge of a Volcano'. The very foolish decision to put the INA men on trial, and that in the Red Fort and with a Hindu, a Muslim, and a Sikh (P.K. Sehgal, Shah Nawaz, Gurbaksh Singh Dhillon) together in the first batch, unleashed a countrywide wave of protest. Nehru, Bhulabhai Desai, and Tejbahadur Sapru appeared for the defence, the Muslim League also condemned the trials, and on 20 November an Intelligence Bureau note admitted that 'there has seldom been a matter which has attracted so much Indian public interest and, it is safe to say, sympathy—this particular brand of sympathy cuts across communal barriers'. A journalist (B. Shiva Rao) visiting the Red Fort prisoners on the same day reported that 'There is not the slightest feeling among them of Hindu and Muslim...A majority of the men now awaiting trial in the Red Fort is Muslim. Some of these men are bitter that Mr Jinnah is keeping alive a controversy about Pakistan'.[12] The British were extremely nervous about the INA spirit spreading to the Indian army, and in January the Punjab Governor reported that a Lahore reception for released INA prisoners had been attended by Indian soldiers in uniform.[13] A second issue was provided by the use of the Indian army in Vietnam and Indonesia; the impact this had on popular (at least urban) sentiments as well as on sections of the army bore vivid testimony to the tremendous advance in anti-imperialist consciousness brought about by the War. Meanwhile the usual post-war problems of high prices and retrenchment were being sharply aggravated by a major food crisis, with Wavell in January 1946 estimating a deficit of three million tons. A drastic cut in rations in February reduced the calorie value to 1,200 per head, while even wartime London in 1943 had got over 2,800 calories.[14]

What the officials feared in the autumn of 1945 was another Congress revolt, a revival of 1942 made much more dangerous this time by the likely combination of attacks on communications with widespread agrarian revolt, labour trouble, army disaffection, and the presence of INA men with military expertise.[15] Violent speeches by Congress leaders (Nehru above all, but also at first Patel and regional leaders in Bihar, CP, UP and elsewhere) initially aroused acute alarm, with their glorification of the heroes and martyrs of 1942, demands for stern punishment for official atrocities, and calls for immediate release of INA prisoners. The British began to realize fairly quickly, however, that this sabre-rattling was essentially election propaganda combined with the need to accommodate the popular mood. 1942 after all was the electoral trump-card of the Congress, and as for the INA, Asaf Ali in a private conversation in October was reported to have explained that his party 'would lose much ground in the country' unless it took up their cause, but if the Congress came to power it would certainly remove the INA men from the army and might even put 'some of them on trial'.[16] Another indication was the bitter campaign against the Communists, in which for the first time Nehru played a very active role, culminating in the expulsion of Communist AICC members in December. That much more was involved here than legitimate anger about the CPI's wartime role is indicated by the fact that there was no such concerted campaign against the Hindu Mahasabha, some of whose leaders had actually been in ministries in August 1942[17] while Rajagopalachari, whose attitude on the Quit India and Pakistan issues had been very similar to that of the Communists, remained a top Congress leader. In UP election meetings, reported an official source in November 1945, Congress speakers, 'while condemning the invocation of religious issues by their Muslim rivals, concentrate upon the alleged atheist tenets of the Communists in their appeals to their audiences not to support them'.[18]

The crucial shifts, alike in British policies and Congress attitudes, came in the wave of three major popular explosions—in Calcutta on 21–3 November 1945 and again on 11–13 February 1946, and in Bombay with the RIN revolt of 18–23 February 1946. In Calcutta on 21 November 1945 a Forward Bloc student procession on Dharmtala street demanding release of INA prisoners was joined by Communist Students Federation cadres (so long considered their bitterest enemies) as well as by Islamia College students carrying the green flag of the League, and spontaneously the Congress, League, and Red Flags were tied together, as symbol of all-in anti-imperialist unity. Police firing which killed a Hindu and a Muslim student was followed on 22 and 23 November by trouble all over the city: strikes by Communist-led tram workers, Sikh taxi-drivers, and in many factories, burning of police and army vehicles (150 were destroyed), crowds blocking trains; and veritable street fighting and barricades—'the crowds when fired on largely stood their ground or at most only receded a little, to return again to the attack'.[19] Order could be restored only after 14 cases of firing, which killed 33 and injured about 200. Calcutta erupted again between 11 and 13 February 1946 in protest against the 7-year rigorous imprisonment sentence passed on Abdul Rashid of the INA. This time the League student wing had given the initial strike call, and at least the appearance of total political unity was achieved by a mammoth Wellington Square rally on 12 February addressed by League leader Suhrawardy, Gandhian Congressman Satish Dasgupta, and the Communist Somnath Lahiri. But the real initiative in the strikes and street fighting, as in November, came from below, and to some extent from the Communists, described in an official account as 'without doubt the most disruptive organization concerned in the disturbances'.[20] The situation was 'worse than that in November 1945', with a Communist-led general strike paralysing industrial Calcutta, all jute mills in the city and suburbs closed for two days, train services disrupted upto Chinsura and Najhati and bitter street clashes with the police and the army (two British and a Gurkha battalion had been deployed) which left 84 dead and 300 injured.[21] As in November, the striking features were the total unity on the streets of Hindus and Muslims, students and workers, and violent anti-white feelings, with numerous attacks on *sahib*s, and attempts 'to boycott everything European, to disaffect servants of Europeans and to prevent the sale of food to Europeans'.[22]

The greatest explosion of all was the naval mutiny in Bombay and the accompanying mass upsurge from 18 to 23 February 1946—one of the most truly heroic, if also largely forgotten, episodes in our freedom struggle. The RIN ratings' strike began on 18 February in the signals training establishment *Talwar* as a protest against bad food and racist insults from white officers. It spread, rapidly to Castle and Fort Barracks on shore and 22 ships in Bombay harbour, and, as in Calcutta in November, the tricolour, crescent, and hammer-and-sickle were raised jointly on the mastheads of the rebel fleet. The demands, as formulated by the elected Naval Central Strike Committee, combined service grievances with national political slogans: release of INA and other political prisoners, withdrawal of Indian troops from Indonesia, acceptance of Indian officers alone as superiors. Desperately seeking advice and help from national leaders but getting little or nothing[23] the ratings hesitated fatally on the borderline of peaceful strike and determined mutiny, and obeyed orders on the afternoon of 20 February to return to their respective ships and barracks only to find themselves surrounded by army guards. Fighting broke out next morning at Castle Barracks when the ratings tried to break out of their encirclement, and there were remarkable scenes of fraternization that afternoon as crowds thronged the Gateway of India with food for the sailors and shopkeepers invited them to take whatever they needed. The pattern of events in fact unconsciously echoed the course of the mutiny on the Black Sea Fleet during the first Russian Revolution of 1905: that, too, had begun over inedible food, and fraternizing crowds had been shot down in a scene immortalized later on in the 'Odessa steps' sequence of Eisenstein's film classic *Battleship Potemkin*. On 22 February, the Bombay working-class, already restive over a recent ration-cut (three mills in Parel had gone on strike on this issue on 21 February), responded massively to a Communist call for a general strike, closing down all textile mills, railway workshops, and city transport. There was bitter street fighting throughout the 22nd and 23rd, with crowds 'erecting road blocks and covering them from nearby buildings', particularly in the proletarian districts of Parel and Delisle Road. Armoured cars and four military columns were needed to restore order, and official casualty figures were 228 civilians killed and 1,046 injured (plus 3 police deaths and 91 wounded); 10 police outposts, 9 banks, 10 post offices, and 64 government grain shops had been attacked.[24] The strike spread to naval bases all over the country, there were serious clashes also in Karachi, and throughout February there was considerable unrest in the air force and army too. The Bombay ratings, however, surrendered on 23 February, not so much in face of British threats (though Admiral Godfrey had flown in bombers and warned that he was prepared to destroy the navy), but because Patel and Jinnah in a rare display of unanimity advised them to do so, giving an assurance that the national parties would prevent any victimization—a promise soon quietly forgotten.

The RIN ratings, in sharp contrast to the men of the Azad Hind Fauj, have never been given the status of national heroes—though their action involved much greater risk in some ways than joining the INA as alternative to an arduous life in Japanese POW camps. As in the Calcutta explosions, a striking feature was total submergence of communal divisions—the Naval Central Strike Committee, incidentally, was headed by a Muslim, M.S. Khan. The last message of the Committee deserves to be remembered far better than it is: 'Our strike has been a historic event in the life of our nation. For the first time the blood of men in the services and in the streets flowed together in a common cause. We in the Services will never forget this. We know also that you, our brothers and sisters, will not forget. Long live our great people! Jai Hind!'[25]

Even apart from the massive political strikes in Calcutta and Bombay, the winter of 1945–6 marked the beginning of an unprecedented wave of countrywide labour unrest as prices shot up and rations were cut. A glance through Wavell's Journal and the Mansergh documents immediately reveals how worried British officials had become, particularly in the context of repeated strike threats by all-India organizations of railway workers, postal employees, and government clerical associations. The development of effective countrywide labour organizations in strategic sectors gave a new muscle-power to the Indian trade union movement; strikes in the 1920s and 1930s had been mainly confined to single industrial centres, primarily Bombay or Calcutta textiles.

In the context of the present paper, the main significance of the Calcutta and Bombay explosions and labour militancy lies in their impact on British and Congress attitudes. On 30 November 1945, a week after the Calcutta outburst, New Delhi informed London that while the original INA trials policy would have involved at least 200–300 accused and possibly 40 to 50 death sentences, it had to be recognized now that 'abstract justice must to some extent give way to expediency'. Future trials, it was announced on 1 December, would be 'limited to cases of brutality and murder', instead of the sweeping charge of 'waging war against the King' used in the first case,[26] and imprisonment sentences passed against the first batch were remitted in January. By February 1946, Indian soldiers were being withdrawn from Vietnam and Indonesia. On 28 November the British Cabinet sub-committee on India decided on a Parliamentary delegation; on 22 January the much more significant decision was taken to send a Cabinet mission in March to negotiate with Indian leaders. Wavell meanwhile had started preparing a 'breakdown plan'. As presented to the Cabinet Mission on 30 May 1946, this visualized a withdrawal of the British army and officials to the Muslim provinces of NW and NE India, handing over the rest of the country to the Congress.[27] While evidently reflecting a desire in some high official circles to make of Pakistan an Indian Northern Ireland, the 'plan' is still interesting evidence of the British recognition that it would be impossible to suppress any future Congress-led rebellion.

On the Congress side, there were indications from November 1945 onwards that the forces which had restrained militancy in the past were at work again, while Wavell on 31 December, would recognize the Calcutta disturbances of 21–23 November as the 'turning-point', which 'caused at least a temporary detente'.[28] The point requires much further research, but it does seem that, as on some earlier occasions, business pressures played an important role here.[29] The Governor of Sind on 3 November, Finance Minister Rowlands on 17 November, and Secretary of State Pethick-Lawrence on 30 November independently referred to G.D. Birla as getting 'alarmed at the virulence of Congress speeches'.[30] '[T]he strong capitalist element behind Congress... is becoming nervous about the security of its property', Wavell informed Pethick-Lawrence on 5 December. 'There have recently been indications that the Congress leaders want to reduce the political tension by making it clear that there must be no mass movement until after the elections'.[31] [...]

In Calcutta on 21 November, Sarat Bose, so long adored as the brother of Subhas, refused to come to address the students squatting on Dharamtala Street and later blamed the Communists for instigating violence.[32] Patel at a Bombay election rally on 24 November condemned the 'frittering away' of energies in 'trifling quarrels' with the police.[33] Gandhi began a fairly friendly dialogue with the Bengal Governor, and the Calcutta AICC Working Committee session of 7–11 December strongly reaffirmed its faith in non-violence[34]—in significant contrast to the September AICC session where many members had glorified every aspect of the by-no-means non-violent 1942 struggle. During the February days in Calcutta, 'the Indian National Congress, whatever individual members may have done, took no part...in the disturbance', while Suhrawardy's appearance at the Wellington Square meeting and the subsequent procession on 12 February was explained by the Police Commissioner in terms of his 'intention of not committing the error of Sarat Bose who lost much popularity by not showing himself at Dhurrumtolla on the 21st November'.[35] An official Situation Report on 13 February noted that there were 'reassuring signs that the more well-to-do Indians are definitely annoyed by the riots and will bring pressure to bear to stop them. Congressmen are patrolling with loudspeakers telling the people to get off the streets....[36]

In Bombay during the RIN upsurge, the Governor reported to Wavell that 'the Congress leaders had decried any share in the mutiny, and had advised people to preserve order. I received a message from Vallabhbhai Patel to this effect on Thursday' (21 February). Next day messages came from Chundrigar and S.K. Patil, heads of the provincial League and Congress units, 'offering the help of volunteers to assist the police'.[37] An official telephone message from Bombay on 22 February reported that 'Congress were against today's hartal, and Vallabhbhai Patel was emphatic about this, but the Communists' call for sympathy with the RIN ratings has won the day and the Congress Labour Union has been totally ineffective'.[38] Patel explained his attitude clearly in a letter to Andhra Congress leader Viswanathan on 1 March 1946: '...discipline in the army cannot be tampered with.... We will want Army even in free India'.[39] Against Patel's advice, Nehru accepted Aruna Asaf Ali's invitation to come to Bombay, but quickly allowed himself to be 'restrained from inflaming the situation, as on arriving here he had been impressed by the necessity for curbing the wild outburst of violence'[40]—though he did later on hail the RIN strike for breaking down the 'iron wall' between army and people.[41] Gandhi, it has to be noted was as unequivocally hostile as Patel. On 22 February he condemned the ratings for setting 'a bad and unbecoming example for India', advised them to peacefully resign their jobs if they had any grievances, and made the very interesting statement that 'a combination between Hindus and Muslims and others for the purpose of violent action is unholy...'. Aruna Asaf Ali made the pertinent comment in reply that 'It simply does not lie in the mouth of Congressmen who were themselves going to the legislatures to ask the ratings to give up their jobs.' She also made a tragically accurate prophecy that it would be far easier to 'unite the Hindus and Muslims at the barricade than on the constitutional front'.[42] It is tempting to set beside Gandhi's statement of 22 February Wavell's private comment of May 30, 1946: 'We must at all costs avoid becoming embroiled with both Hindu and Muslim at once.'[43]

The Congress rationale behind firmly rejecting mass confrontations was the need to concentrate energies on fighting the elections. The Congress did win a massive victory, polling 91.3 per cent of votes in the Central Assembly general constituencies, and winning majorities in every province except Bengal, Punjab, and Sind. The Hindu Mahasabha and other right-wing groups were routed, while Communists could capture only eight provincial assembly seats, all but one of them in constituencies reserved for labour (here they did put up a fairly tough fight, winning 112, 736 votes against 321, 607 of the Congress).[44] The most significant feature of the elections, however, was the prevalence of communal voting, in sharp contrast to the sporadic but quite remarkable anti-British unity forged so often in these very same months in the streets of Calcutta, Bombay, or even Karachi. The League swept all the 30 Muslim seats in the Centre, and won 442 out of 509 provincial Muslim constituencies— a very major advance as compared to 1937, though it still narrowly missed a majority in the Punjab, and was defeated in the NWFP.

Apart from the logic of separate electorates, it is possible that the extremely limited franchise (about 10 per cent of the population in the provinces, less than one per cent for the Central Assembly) may have had something to do with this stark contrast between united mass action and communal voting. The NWFP Governor reported to Wavell in February 1946 that Muslim officials and the 'bigger Khans' or landlords were all for the League, but the Congress was still getting the support of the 'less well-to-do' Muslims due to its promises of economic reforms[45] —promises however which Congress ministries did little to implement either after 1937 or in 1946–7. In this context, the tacit (and little noticed) surrender by the Congress of its central slogan of the late-1930s—a Constituent Assembly elected on universal franchise—acquires crucial significance in understanding the course of events. Of all Indian political groups, only the Communists pressed this demand seriously in 1945–6, in their election manifests, *For the Final Bid For Power*, (1945), for instance, or in P.C. Joshi's meeting with the Cabinet Mission on 17 April 1946.[46] Congress leaders, in contrast, quietly accepted the Cabinet Mission decision to have the Constituent Assembly elected by existing provincial legislatures based on limited voting rights. Much more was involved here than a mere question of abstract democratic principle. The League next year would win its demand for Pakistan without its claims to represent the majority of Muslims being really tested, either in fully democratic elections or (as Congress claims had been) in sustained mass movements in the face of official repression (as distinct from occasional communal riots not unaccompanied often by official complicity). It may not be irrelevant to recall here that the Congress after 1947 would go on winning all-India elections for 30 years, while the League was routed in East Pakistan in the very first vote held on the basis of universal franchise (1954), and would fail to provide political stability even in West Pakistan.

In the long and tortuous negotiations which went on from 24 March to 29 June 1946, the Cabinet Mission at times seemed to lean marginally towards the Congress, arousing grave suspicions in the mind of the Viceroy, who once even accused its members—and particularly Nehru's old friend Cripps—of 'living in the pocket of Congress'.[47] Yet this was

due basically not to Labour pro-nationalist sympathies, but because, as
Wavell himself pointed out in a note to the Mission on 29 March, the
British had 'an extremely difficult hand to play, owing to the necessity
to avoid the mass movement or revolution which it is in the power of
the Congress to start, and which we are certain that we can control'.[48] It
is difficult to avoid the conclusion that the Congress leadership once
again spiked its own guns in its eagerness for quick and easy power and
desire at all costs to preserve social order. The spring and summer of
1946 marked the height of the 'greatest strike wave in the history of
colonial India, and there is ample evidence that apart from-disaffection
in the armed forces, it was urban labour unrest which alarmed British
officials most. Strikes in 1946 totalled 1,629, involving 1,941,948 workers
and a loss of 12,717,762 mandays; in no previous year had stoppages
exceeded 1,000, or the workers involved 8 lakhs.[49] There were
widespread police strikes in April (in Malabar, Andamans, Dacca, Bihar,
and Delhi), threats of an all-India railway stoppage throughout the
summer, a postal strike in July, and on 29 July, less than three weeks
before the Great Calcutta Killing of 16 August, a total, absolutely peaceful,
and remarkably united *bundh* in Calcutta under Communist leadership
in sympathy with postal employees. The Home Member pointed out in
a note dated 5 April that in the case of a break with the League, 'even if
they fight, they would be beaten', but 'On the whole, I doubt whether a
Congress rebellion could be suppressed'. In such a situation, 'by no
means all units [of the army] could be relied on', 'police over a large
area would be likely to crack', and 'a call to a general strike would be
widely obeyed...labour in (sic) amenable mostly to Communist and
Congress leadership'.[50]

The Congress High Command, however, had already opted for a
different policy. Congress President Azad on 3 March publicly welcomed
the ration-cut (a major labour grievance) as 'far-sighted', and declared
that strikes were 'out of place today', as the British were 'now acting as
caretakers'.[51] Patel's correspondence reveals desperate efforts, by local
Congress labour leaders in May 1946 to prevent a strike ballot in the
railways 'since if a ballot is taken it will be in favour of the strike'.[52] In
August, the Working Committee meeting in Wardha condemned 'hasty
or ill-conceived stoppages' and the 'growing lack of discipline and
disregard of obligations on the part of the workers'.[53]

There is some interesting evidence that fear of labour militancy,
combined with a growing awareness of essential Congress moderation
played a crucial part in bringing about the next major shift in official

policy: the decision to allow Nehru to form a purely Congress Interim Government on 2 September 1946. The brief agreement, always more apparent than real, between the Congress and the League in accepting the Cabinet Mission's long-term three-tier plan had broken down by the end of July, and Wavell had also failed in his efforts to set up a short-term coalition government in the centre. On 31 July, with the postal strike still on and two days, after the Calcutta bundh, the Viceroy wrote to Pethick-Lawrence: 'I dislike intensely the idea of having an Interim Government dominated by one party but I feel that I must try to get the Congress in as soon as possible....If Congress will take responsibility they will realize that firm control of unruly elements is necessary and they may put down the Communists and try to curb their own Left wing. Also I should hope to keep them so busy with administration that they had much less time for politics.[54] [...]

From 16 August 1946 onwards, the whole Indian scene was rapidly transformed by communal riots on an unprecedented scale: starting with Calcutta on 16–19 August, touching Bombay from 1 September, spreading to Noakhali in East Bengal (10 October), Bihar (25 October); Garmukteswar in UP (November), and engulfing the Punjab from March 1947 onwards. The British, who as late as June 1946 had been making plans to bring five army divisions to India in the context of a possible Congress movement,[55] made no such move while presiding over this awesome human tragedy. [...]

The Interim Government of Nehru found itself presiding helplessly over this growing communal inferno. Collective functioning became all but impossible after Wavell had persuaded Jinnah to join the government on 26 October without the League giving up its Direct Action programme, its Projection of the Cabinet Mission long-term plan, or its boycott of the Constituent Assembly. [...]

Confronted by Calcutta, Noakhali, Bihar, and Punjab, the secular ideals of many within the Congress ranks and leadership tended to evaporate. If Nehru, consistently denounced Hindu communalism in Bihar and elsewhere, and Azad blamed Wavell for not calling out troops promptly in Calcutta to suppress 'the hooligans of Calcutta's underworld' unleashed by Suhrawardy,[56] Patel sympathized with hostile Hindu reactions to Nehru's condemnation of Bihar.[57] Communal riots, combined with the evident unworkability of the Congress–League coalition at the Centre, compelled many by early 1947 to think in terms of accepting what had been unthinkable so far—Partition—and these came to include Nehru as well as Patel. [...]

To one man, however, the idea of a high-level bargain by which the Congress would attain quick power in the major part of the country at the cost of a partition on religious lines still seemed unimaginably shocking and unacceptable. Gandhi had taken little part in the tortuous negotations since 1945, while he had also condemned the united anti-imperialist outbursts in 1945–6 as tainted with violence. Increasingly isolated from the Congress leadership, as well as from business leaders like Birla who had now developed closer ties with Patel,[58] the old man of 77 with undiminished courage now shaped his all in a bid to vindicate his life-long principles of change of heart and non-violence, in the village of Noakhali, followed by Bihar and then the riot-torn slums of Calcutta and Delhi. Gandhi's unique personal qualities and true greatness were never more evident than in the last months of his life: courage to stand against the tide, total disdain for all conventional forms of political power which could have been his for the asking now that—India was becoming free, and a passionate anti-communalism which made him declare to a League leader a month after Partition, while riots were ravaging the Punjab: 'I want to fight it out with my life. I would not allow the Muslims to crawl on the streets in India. They must walk with self-respect'.[59] [...]

Intensely moving and heroic, the Gandhian way in 1946–7 could be no more than an isolated personal effort with a local—and often rather shortlived impact. It is futile and dangerous to speculate on what might have been, but one might still argue that the only real alternative lay along the path of united militant mass struggles against imperialism and its Indian allies—the one thing which, as we have seen, the British really dreaded. Despite the obvious and major disruption caused by the riots, this possibility was by no means entirely blocked even in the winter of 1946–7.

Three months after the Calcutta riots, villages in many parts of Bengal (particularly Thakurgaon sub-division in Dinajpur and adjoining areas of Jalpaiguri, Rangpur and Malda in North Bengal, as well as pockets in Mymensingh, Midnapur, and 24 Parganas) resounded to the slogans of *Tebhaga chai* and *nijkhamara dhan tolo,* as sharecroppers responded to the call of the Communist-led Kisan Sabha to fight against the *jotedar*s for the two-thirds share of the harvest promised by the Floud Commission (1940) but never implemented. Though Muslim-majority South-East Bengal was largely untouched by *tebhaga,* and its strongest base was among low-caste semi-tribal groups like the Rajbansis, many Muslims did participate in the strongholds of the movement, producing leaders like Haji Muhammad Danesh, Niamat Ali, and even some *maulvi*s who quoted the Koran to condemn jotedar oppression.[60]

A second major outburst was in the Shertalai–Alleppey–Ambalapuzha area of Travancore state where the close proximity of small-town industries with agricultural occupations made the formula of worker-peasant alliance more of a reality than in most areas, and where Communist-led coir-factory, fishermen, toddy-tapper, and agricultural labourer unions had become powerful enough to control recruitment, establish arbitration courts, and even win the right to run their own ration shops. Economic grievances, sharpened by acute food scarcity, coincided in the autumn of 1946 with national opposition, spearheaded by the Communists, to Dewan C.P. Ramaswami Iyer's plans for an independent Travancore under an 'American-model' constitution which would have perpatuated his own power. Intense repression led to violent clashes and attacks on police camps in Punnapra and Vayalar on 24–7 October 1946, which left about 800 killed and ultimately vastly enhanced the prestige of the Communists in Kerala. The massacre prevented the alliance with the totally discredited Dewan towards which some right-wing Congress leaders had been moving and Ramaswami Iyer next year accepted integration with India fairly easily, no doubt because he had realized that the alternative might well be a violent revolution. In this sense it was Punnapra-Vayalar which really brought about the integration of Travancore with India, blocking the road towards Balkanization.[61]

Where *Tebhaga* and Punnapra–Vayalor had gone to the brink of armed struggle, but failed to cross it, Telengana in Hyderabad State between July 1946 and October 1951 saw the biggest peasant guerilla war so far of modern Indian history, affecting at its height about 3,000 villages spread over 16,000 square miles and with a population of 3 million. The beginning of the uprising is traditionally dated from 4 July 1946, when thugs employed by the *deskmukh* of Visunur (one of the biggest and most oppressive of Telengana's landlords, with 40,000 acres) murdered a village militant, Doddi Komarayya, who had been defending a poor washer-woman's mite of land. Unlike tebhaga and to a much greater extent than in Tranvancore, the Communist-led agrarian revolt in Telengana against particularly gross forms of feudal oppression retained, till the entry of the Indian army in September 1948, the broader dimensions of a national-liberation struggle to overthrow the Nizam and his Razakar bands and unite Hyderabad with India. [...]

[...]

The socially radical movements of which Telengana was the climax never coalesced into an organized and effective countrywide political alternative. The fear they undoubtedly inspired, however, helped to bring about the final compromise by which a 'peaceful' transfer of power was purchased at the cost of partition and a communal holocaust. [...]

[...]

NOTES

†   Paper presented at a seminar on Aspects of the Economy, Society, and Politics in Modern India, 1900–1950, at the Nehru Memorial Museum and Library, New Delhi, December 1980.

1. The published first-hand sources include N. Mansergh (ed.), *Transfer of Power* (henceforth *Mansergh*), Volumes VI–VIII, London, various dates, Wavell (ed. Moon) , *The Viceroy's Journal*, Oxford 1973; Durga Das edition of *Sardar Patel's Correspondence*, Ahmedabad, 1971; and the contemporary writings of Gandhi and Nehru. Among the well-known secondary works may be mentioned V.P. Menon, *Transfer of Power in India*, London, 1957; and *Story of Integration of Indian States*, Bombay 1956; A. Campball Johnson, *Mission with Mountbatten*, London, 1951; Penderal Moon, *Divide and Quit*, London, 1961; H.V. Hodson, *The Great Divide*, London, 1969; Maulana Azad, *India Wins Freedom*, Bombay 1959; Pyarelal, *The Mahatma: The Last Phase*, Two Volumes, Ahmedabad, 1956, 1958; C. Khaliquzzaman, *Pathway to Pakistan*, Lahore, 1961; S. Ghosh, *Gandhi's Emissary*, London, 1967 as well as Collins and Lapierre's journalistic bestseller, *Freedom at Midnight*, Delhi, 1976.

2. Linlithgow's telegram to Churchill, 31 August 1942; Government of India (Home) to Secretary of State, 12 September 1942, Mansergh, vol. II, pp. 843, 952–3.

3. R.J. Moore, *Churchill, Crips and India 1939–45*, Oxford, 1979, and *Mansergh*, vol. I.

4. Wavell, *The Viceroy's Journal*, pp. 97–8.

5. For details of the Simla Conference, see Mansergh, vol. V; and Wavell, *Viceroy's Journal*, pp. 141–58.

6. Subject only to an Indo.British treaty safeguarding British interests in India for a transitional period. See P.S. Gupta, *Imperialism and British Labour*, Macmillan, 1975, pp. 257–9.

7. *Viceroy's Journal*, pp. 159, 169–171, 399, (entries for 26 July and 4 September 1945 and 24 December 1946).

8. Hallet to Wavell, 14 August 1945, *Mansergh*, vol. VI, p. 68.

9. *Viceroy's Journal*, pp. 170–1.

10. GOI (Government of India) (War Department) to Secretary of State, 11 August 1945, *Mansergh*, vol. VI, pp. 49–51.

11. Wavell to Secretary of State, 1 October, 17 October, ibid., pp. 305–6, 360.

12. Ibid., pp. 514, 564.
13. Glancy (Governor of Punjab) to Wavell, 16 January 1946, ibid., p. 807.
14. Wavell to Secretary of State, 29 January, 18 February 1946, ibid., pp. 868–9, 1006.
15. C.P. Governor Twynham to Wavell, 10 November 1945. On 24 November 1945. Commander-in-Chief Auchinleck in an appreciation of the internal situation expressed fears about a 'well-organised revolution next Spring—if and when trouble comes it may be on a greater scale than in August 1942...'. Ibid., pp. 468, 577–83.
16. Jenkins to Turnbull, reporting a talk of a returned POW, Captain Badhwar (whose name was 'not to be disclosed') with Asaf Ali, 23 October 1945, ibid., p. 387.
17. Golwalkar's RSS had kept strictly aloof from the August Rebellion; Savarkar on 4 September 1942 had urged Mahasabha members of local bodies, legislatures, and services to 'stick to their posts and continue to perform their regular duties', (Indian Annual Register, Chronicle of Events, 1942) while Shyamprasad Mukherji was actually a minister in Bengal while Midnapur was being ruthlessly suppressed.
18. Fortnightly Report, UP, 2nd half of November, 1945; Government of India, Home Political (Internal), 18/11/45. (Hence Forward Home Poll (1)).
19. Bengal Governor Casey to Wavell, 2 January 1946, summarizing the enquiry report of the Calcutta Police Commissioner, Mansergh, vol. VI, pp. 724–7.
20. Calcutta Police Commissioner's Report on Political Aspects of Calcutta disturbances of February 1946, 3 April 1946; Home Poll (I), 5/22/46.
21. Situation Report, February 12, 1946, ibid. See also Gautam Chattopadhyay, 'The Almost Revolution', in Essays in Honour of S.C. Sarkar, New Delhi, 1976.
22. Situation Report, 13 February 1946, (3.30 PM), Home Poll (I), 5/22/46.
23. The ratings contacted Aruna Asaf Ali at her house in Dadar who expressed sympathy and issued an appeal for 'moral support' on 20 February. 'She consulted Vallabhbhai Patel who snubbed her saying—that it was no business of his or hers to interfere when the ratings did not abide by discipline. Mrs Aruna Asaf Ali left Bombay for Poona on the morning of February 20, 1946'. Bombay Police Commissioner's Office (Special Branch) to Government of Bombay Home (Special), 20 February 1946, Home Poll (1), 5/21/46.
24. Bombay Governor Colville to Wavell, 27 February 1946, Mansergh, vol. VI, pp. 1081–84.
25. Subrata Banerjee, The RIN Strike (by a group of victimized ratings), New Delhi, 1954, p. 75.
26. Governor-General (War Department) to Secretary of State, 30 November 1945, Mansergh, vol. VI, p. 572.
27. Viceroy's Journal, Appendix IV, pp. 485–6.
28. Wavell to George VI, 31 December 1945, Mansergh, vol. VI, p. 713.

29. For the role of business groups in the making of the Gandhi–Irwin Pact of 1931 and in the 'taming' of Nehru in 1936, see Sumit Sarkar, 'Logic of Gandhian Nationalism: Civil Disobedience and the Gandhi–Irwin Pact 1930–31', *Indian Historical Review*, July 1976; and Bipan Chandra, 'Jawaharlal Nehru and the Capitalist Class', (reprinted in 'Nationalism and Colonialism in Modern India', Delhi, 1979).

30. Rowlands, as reported in *Viceroy's Journal*, p. 185. H. Dow (Governor of Sind) wrote to Wavell on 3 November that 'Birla...is getting a little frightened of the Frankenstein's monster he has helped so much to create', *Mansergh*, vol. VI, p. 438. The Secretary of State commented on 30 November: 'I am glad to hear that Birla has told *Hindustan Times* to lower its tone. It rather looks as if the richer supporters of Congress may be beginning to wonder where the caravan is going.' Ibid., p. 572.

31. Ibid., pp. 602–3.

32. Fortnightly Report from Bengal, 2nd half of November 1945, Home Poll (1) 18/11/45. Wavell to Secretary of State, 5 December 1945, *Mansergh*, vol. VI, p. 602.

33. *Indian Annual Register*, July–December 1945.

34. Ibid.

35. The Commissioner added that Suhrawardy's foreknowledge (as a member of the League ministry) that the 12 February procession would not be stopped by the police 'enabled him to pose with safety as a hero of liberty...'. Calcutta Police Commissioner's Report, 3 April 1946, Home Poll (1), 5/22/46.

36. Situation Report No. 7, 13 February 1946, ibid.

37. Colville to Wavell, 27 February 1946, *Mansergh*, vol. VI, p. 1081–2.

38. Home Poll (I), 5/21/46.

39. *Sardar's Letters*, vol. IV, Ahmedabad, 1977, p. 165.

40. Colville to Wavell, 27 February 1946, *Mansergh*, vol. VI, p. 1084.

41. Wavell to Secretary of State, March 5, 1946, quoting from the *Statesman*, 4 March, ibid., p. 1118.

42. *Sardar's Letters*, vol. IV, Ahmedabad, pp. 162–63.

43. *Viceroy's Journal*, p. 485.

44. Statistics in *AICC FN G26/1946*.

45. Cunningham to Wavell, February 27, 1946, *Mansergh*, vol. VI, p. 1085.

46. *Mansergh*, vol. VII, pp. 291–93.

47. *Viceroy's Journal*, pp. 324–5.

48. Ibid., p. 232.

49. J.B. Kriplani's analysis of post-war labour unrest, *AICC FNG 26/1946*; V.B. Singh, 'Trade Union Movement', in Singh (ed.), *Economic History of India 1857–1956*, Bombay, 1965, p. 600.

50. Note by J.A. Thorne, 5 April 1946, *Mansergh*, vol. VII, pp. 150–1.

51. Wavell to Secretary of State, 5 March 1946, enclosing extract from *Hindustan Times*, 3 March, *Mansergh*, vol. VI, p. 1116.

52. Shantilal Shah to Patel, 7 May 1946, Durga Das (ed.), *Sardar Patel's Correspondence*, Ahmedabad, 1971, vol. III, pp. (sic) 64–5.
53. J.B. Kriplani's note, *AICC FN G26/1946*.
54. *Mansergh*, vol. VII, pp. 154–5.
55. *Mansergh*, vol. VIII, pp. 13–15.
56. Interview with Wavell, 19 August 1946, *Mansergh*, vol. VIII, p. 261.
57. 'We would be committing a grave mistake if we expose the people of Bihar and their ministry to the violent and vulgar attacks of the League leaders'. Patel to Rajendra Prasad, 11 November 1946, Durga Das (ed.), *Sardar Patel's Correspondence*, vol. III, p. 171.
58. Patel 'had now taken the place of Bapu in my correspondence'. G.D. Birla, 'In the Shadow of the Mahatma' Longmens, 1953, p. 328. Gandhi's letter to Birla on 6 December 1946 complained that Birla's letter to him of 2 December (unfortunately not included) revealed 'a lack of genuine feeling of resentment of improper conduct' about the Bihar riots. G.D. Birla, *Bapu–Correspondence 1940–47*, Bombay, 1977, p. 421.
59. C. Khaliquzzaman, *Pathway to Pakistan*, Lahore, 1961, p. 404.
60. Sunil Sen, *Agrarian Struggle in Bengal 1946–47*, New Delhi, 1972.
61. K.C. George, *Immortal Punnapra-Vayalar*, New Delhi, 1975; Robin Jeffrey, 'A Sanctified Label—Congress in Travancore Politics, 1938–48', in D.A. Low (ed.), *Congress and the Raj*, New Delhi, 1977.

21 Sailors and the Crowd
Popular Protest in Karachi, 1946*

Anirudh Deshpande

[...]

I

Everything has been overshadowed by the R.I.N. [Royal Indian Navy] Mutiny and its results.[1]

In Karachi, months before the uprising occurred, ratings, mostly from Bengal and Travancore–Cochin, had a Sailors' Association. A number of youths, affiliated to the All India Students Federation during their student days, took the lead in forming this organization whose main tasks included raising money for the INA [Indian National Army] relief funds[2] and conducting variety programmes for Durga Puja. Anil Roy, a leading member of these ventures and later the mutiny, explicitly mentions that the Sailors' Association 'never tried for [a] mutiny in Karachi though its aim was naturally .... only to spread anti-British feeling among the ratings'.[3]

The news of the strike on His Majesty's India Ship (HMIS) *Talwar* in Bombay reached the ratings in the shore establishments of Karachi through newspapers on 19 February and was received with 'tremendous excitement' and 'suppressed jubilation'. However the geographical location of Manora where these establishments were situated, induced in the authorities some confidence for they 'did not show any sign of nervousness'.[4] According to another version the commanding officer (CO) of HMIS *Chamak*, Lieutenant Commander Chatterjee, upon hearing the news from Bombay, called a meeting of all the ratings and told them that they had nothing to do with the *Talwar* strike.[5] Nevertheless, the restive ratings of the Sailors' Association called a meeting of ratings from *Himalaya, Bahadur,* and *Monze* (the shore establishments of Karachi) on the beach at Manora in the afternoon. This general body then decided

* Originally published in *The Indian Economic and Social History Review*, vol. 26, no. 1, 1989, pp. 1–27. In the present version some portions of the text and notes have been removed. For the complete text see the original version.

unanimously to launch a mutiny and concluded that action against the British would commence on the 21 February. The programme of protest they chalked out was as follows: gathering at Keamari jetty, procession and demonstration through Karachi, invitation to dock workers of Keamari to join the protest, shouting of slogans denouncing the British imperialists and urging the Congress and the Muslim League to unite, complete abstention from work and finally the attainment of Karachi-wide unity of ratings.[6]

But HMIS *Chamak* was not destined to lead the uprising for on Wednesday, 20 February, Indian sailors on board HMIS *Hindustan*, an old sloop anchored off Keamari jetty, rose in revolt.[7] Protesting against the insulting behaviour of the Captain and the executive officers, a dozen rebels disembarked, entered the city, and refused to return till the indicated officers were transferred.[8] During the day rating from HMIS *Himalaya*[9] joined these men and together they visited hotels in Keamari asking the owners to down shutters, and raised the slogans *Jai Hind* and *Inquilab Zindabad*. Later they traversed Jackson Bazar in Keamari shouting similar slogans. Then with cries of *Hindustan Azad* and *Jai Hind* around 150 mutineers marched towards the railway station, proclaiming on the way that they were marching upon Delhi.[10] Thus they publicized their inspiration and intention. In the dense bazaar and harbour areas they infused excitement among crowds which already possessed perceptions of the INA and *Delhi Chalo*.[11] News of these incidents spread rapidly in such circumstances.

The news from *Hindustan* led to another meeting of the Sailors' Association which decided to forge a Karachi-wide unity of ratings and to write slogans on the walls and posters. 'Hindustan Zindabad', 'Down with British Imperialism', 'Shed blood to get freedom', 'We shall live as a free nation', and 'Tyrants your days are over', were decided by the meeting as slogans needed for the hour.[12]

Next morning the usually placid atmosphere of Manora was rent with slogans shouted by hundreds of young sailors:

> Although (*sic*) the streets the shouting of slogans continued. The small inhabitants of Manora never saw a scene like that before. They cheered us by clapping. Some even joined us...We were now at the Manora jetty. The most heartening job was done by the local boatmen who not only made a number of trips to ferry the ratings but refused to take any money from us. Their only request was 'Zalimo ko mar dalo'—kill the tyrants.[13]

When the ratings landed at Keamari, they were faced with the option of breaking through a well-armed cordon of British troops. In the meantime incidents swiftly occurred on sea. A batch of ratings crossing to Keamari from the *Himalaya* jetty on Manora in local and motor launches, ran into a British patrol boat. The latter ordered the ratings to go back and when the order was not heeded, opened fire—killing two ratings instantaneously and wounding some. Luckily for the *Himalaya* ratings, HMIS *Hindustan* from nearby opened up with its twelve-pounders driving away the patrol boat. After the patrol fled about three to four hundred ratings with their dead and wounded boarded the *Hindustan*.[14]

The State, however, was well prepared for an emergency. A strong military and police cordon was placed across the bridge connecting Keamari with Karachi and all boats were brought across to the Karachi side of the harbour. This was successful in preventing the 'mutineers from entering the city'.[15] The government moved according to warnings received from Bombay where a close contact of the ratings with civilians had brought about an undesirable state of affairs for them. According to Governor Francis Mudie:

> If Bombay had not blown up a day or two earlier we would have been taken completely by surprise and I have no doubt that the ratings would have marched through Karachi and that, due allowance being made for the difference in size and turbulence of the two cities, the events in Bombay might have been reflected here.[16]

Anyway, since it was impossible to break through the army cordon, hundreds of ratings armed with hockey sticks demonstrated by shouting 'revolutionary slogans' throughout the afternoon. They were joined by the dock workers [imbued with and] displaying similar enthusiasm. On the other side of the cordon, an assembly of civilians watched the proceedings keenly. Towards evening the rebels decided to return to their establishments to decide fresh programmes. Finally they fixed a rendezvous with the enthusiastic dock workers, exchanged *lal salam* with them, and returned to Manora.[17] The night at Manora meetings were held, speeches made and Urdu couplets were recited. The ratings kept chanting slogans late into the night. Around eleven at night on 21 February ratings from *Himalaya* brought disturbing news to *Chamak*: the authorities had issued an ultimatum to *Hindustan*, which stood sovereign off the coast of Karachi, to surrender by 10 next morning.[18]

The military high command had calculated well. They knew that during the ebb tide before noon the *Hindustan* would sink to a lower and strategically disadvantageous position. In answer the ratings manned the ship's guns. But they were no match for the well-placed enemy who concentrated heavy fire upon a single helpless target. Thus after a brief spell of heavy, largely one-sided, firing the Indians surrendered. During this small battle, the rebels, for fear of hitting civilians, could not make full use of the fire power at their disposal.

In the meantime ratings from Manora were trying to cross over to Keamari. Very few of them managed because the British army, 'had scared away all the boatman (by) threatening to kill anybody who would come within a mile of *Hindustan*'. Some boatman did ferry a number of ratings to Keamari but at that moment everyone heard the firing between the *Hindustan* and the British troops: 'Three or four shells were fired in quick succession. We knew these were from Hindustan. We shouted "death to the tyrants". The boatmen joined us. There was no trace of fear on their faces.' When these ratings reached Keamari they were amazed to learn that everything was over:

> The British troops were standing like a wall with fixed bayonets pointing at us. In choked voices we started shouting slogans. Some screamed in utter despair, while others went on striking their chests with both of (sic) their palms.[19]

When the ratings returned to Manora they found it occupied by the Black Watch Regiment. By then the revolt was over. The next day, on 23 February 1946, Roy, Kurian, Musa, and Harjinder, in far away cremation and burial grounds, performed the last rites of their comrades killed in action. Roy calculated the number of dead as fourteen and admitted that he did not know how many of the wounded died later.[20] Official reports gave varying figures of the dead and wounded. IB1 claimed 8 killed and 37 wounded. IB2 claimed 12 killed and 30 injured. The Governor himself claimed that 5 ratings were killed and 36 wounded.[21]

At Manora on 23 February, ratings observed a complete hunger-strike protesting against the presence of British troops. Soon thereafter many ratings, including the leaders, were arrested and transported to the Malir Camp outside Karachi. The Bombay rebels also surrendered on the same day. Thus a memorable event of the Indian struggle against imperialism passed into history.

II

[...]

KARACHI IN THE NATIONAL MOVEMENT, 1942–46

In Sindh, the Muslims constituted an overwhelming majority. During the 1942 upsurge it followed the pattern of Punjab and the NWFP [North

West Frontier Province] rather than that of Maharashtra, UP, and Bihar.[22] Sindhi Muslim response to the Quit India was similar to that of Muslims elsewhere in India:

> The remarkable thing about Hindu–Muslim relations during the Quit India movement is that nothing remarkable happened, the predictions of Congressmen, Muslim Leaguers, and British officials were all belied. Hindus, did not terrorize Muslims; but neither did the Muslims join in the struggle. Most Muslims kept aloof, offering support neither to the nationalist uprising nor to their supposed British benefactors.[23]

Furthermore Karachi was dominated by the Sindhi community which had historically developed a syncretic culture.[24] But after the war when Pakistan loomed nearby and elections were round the corner communal passions became active in Sindh. The Muslim League Ministry of Sindh was deeply resented by the Congress and the Hindu Mahasabha[25] and already in October 1945 communal bitterness was rising in Sindh: 'There are signs that the approach of the elections is being accompanied by increased bitterness in communal feeling. Inflammatory communal literature is coming to notice in Karachi, Hyderabad and Sukkur.'[26]

Although Karachi was also swept by the INA wave which was being directed by the Congress,[27] the League lent its own interpretation to the INA trials. Jinnah, in *Dawn* launched a crusade against the victimization of Abdul Rashid and constantly referred to the Muslims as a community endangered on one hand by the Raj and on the other by Hindu Raj. Thus even this pinnacle of anti-imperialism in the last of the climatic years of the Raj was not free of the contradictions characterizing the Indian National Movement. Karachi was no exception in this process, albeit the event under study contained a popular exposition of remarkable Hindu–Muslim unity reminiscent of earlier united anti-imperialist struggles.

The Crowd

The population of Karachi, concentrated around the harbour, became involved in the incidents happening on the RIN front on the day the revolt broke out at Manora. This passive but keen involvement was activized on Friday 22 February when firing between British troops and *Hindustan* occurred. On the same day the harbour areas teemed with military vehicles, ambulances, and lorries. Rumours appeared and spread quickly; 'crowds collected along the route taken by service vehicles and stoned military trucks, dispatch riders, and troops. Indian military police were hooted and jeered at and a number of British troops were hit by stones....'[28] The army sealed the harbour and the dock allowing nobody to proceed beyond the port trust buildings which were four miles away from Keamari.[29] Furthermore from Thursday onwards the army, afraid of the ratings infiltrating into Karachi, began checking every vehicle which returned from Keamari.[30] Apprehension in the city began to rise and on Thursday itself, 'exaggerated accounts of these happenings quickly reached the town and the people became very excited. Crowds gathered at various points and stones were thrown at military vehicles'.[31] Spontaneous protest began on Thursday as the army sealed off the Keamari overbridge[32] from the harbour areas and prevented slogan shouting ratings from entering the town. The same day the authorities confiscated all local dhows (boats) and brought them to the Karachi side of the harbour.[33] On Thursday evening and on Friday, the excitement in the city was in large measure derived from the interpretations of events given out to the general populace by the expropriated boatmen and fishermen. An Associated Press of India (API) correspondent, touring the area within three hours of the action found Keamari village deserted with only frequent patrolling of British troops in jeeps and the nearby area strewn with stray bullets.[34] Had the army forcibly driven away the villagers or did they take to their heels at the sight of the former or the sound of action? British troops, with force and alarm moved into Keamari on Thursday and stayed on till Sunday. This dislocated life and fishing, ferrying, loading, and unloading was suspended for at least three days.[35] This leaves no doubt as to why Karachi was most turbulent on Friday and Saturday.

Initially the popular protest was spontaneous but on Friday as students and leaders stepped in, it gained a wider legitimacy and a semblance of organization. On Friday, as flashes of firing were seen[36] and sounds of heavy gunfire heard,[37] 'in great excitement ... most colleges shut at once, and processions of students were taken out in the town'.[38] Crowds attacked military vehicles in the port areas and along the routes taken by army lorries, ambulances, and jeeps carrying British paratroopers even before the students reacted. Almost simultaneously the Sindh Students' Congress, assisted by prominent local Congress leaders, took out a well attended procession which was followed by a meeting in which INA and abusive anti-British slogans were raised.[39] The speakers who addressed the mass meeting were Swami Krihsnanda, Kishan Lulla, Sital Devanathan, Ali Mohammed Makrani, and R.K. Sindhwa. Resolutions sympathetic to the RIN, critical of army action, and demanding an impartial enquiry into the whole affair were passed and anti-British speeches marked with an 'anti-racist strain' were made. Another well-attended students meeting was held outside the Law College and addressed by local leaders like Kirat Babani, Kishan Lulla, Ali Mohammed, Makrani and Mohd Hafiz Qureshi.[40]

In the evening, CPI held a meeting at the Id Gah which was attended by about a thousand people. Sobho T. Gianchandani presided and local CPI notables Asafjab Karwani, Kazi Mohd. Mutaba, Avtar Kishan Angle, S.K. Dharmani, Govind Mali, and P.H. Ghawali were present. In this assembly 'provocative and dangerous anti-British' speeches were made. For instance Mujtaba 'sarcastically' said that the British who could not face Germans could only shoot down Indians and Karwani in a 'most objectionable' way asserted that for a single rating's life Indians would take a thousand British ones. According to Gianchandani, Indians were proud of the ratings who were facing bullets to uphold national pride. It was maintained that the ratings had shown how the arms given to them could be really utilized whereas the civilians were helpless, by and large, because they were unarmed and because of their inability to contact the ratings.[41]

This rhetoric 'had a visible effect on the audience'[42] the nature of which became obvious in the actions which followed. The meeting called on all communities to organize a complete hartal and for the labourers to go on strike the next day.[43] The leaders decided to take out a procession next morning to tour the factory areas and persuade workers to strike work.[44] Finally the gathering dissolved with a resolution calling a mass meeting at noon next day at the Id Gah maidan. At this stage, the local CPI leadership was taking a radical step compared to the Congress and their speeches were violent compared to the milder tones set by the Congress.[45] The CPI leaders also calculated pragmatically and shrewdly and,

> ... appealed to all sections of the community, and the mass procession and meeting to have been held on the Id Gah maidan was scarcely likely to have passed off without any incident. *By deciding to hold their meeting at this place, they were obviously attempting to enlist Muslim sympathy.*[46] (emphasis added)

These developments together with the news from Bombay alarmed the government and generated a resolute official will to prevent disturbances.[47] In those tense moments, after having 'horrified' 'ordinary Indian opinion',[48] by its use of force against *Hindustan*, the Government retaliated swiftly. The District Magistrate issued an order under section 144 prohibiting meetings and processions on Saturday and had three prominent communist leaders arrested.[49] But these measures were unsuccessful in stemming the popular tide.

Rioting began on Saturday morning (when the RIN rebels in Bombay had already surrendered). Workers from workshops, presumably mechanics, artificers, fitters, and printers, observed a complete hartal and students from schools and colleges collected in small processions and groups. Then these groups moved around the town obstructing traffic and persuading, peacefully or otherwise, shopkeepers to close their shops.[50] The CPI took out a procession of around 30,000 people[51] and the whole city was brought to a pitch of great excitement. These activities continued while section 144 (according to which more than 4 persons could not assemble anywhere in the city) was in force which suggests police abstention or collusion. This was highly probable because during the war the police had to contend with *rising crime* and rebellion almost all over India despite being undermanned and at a considerable cost to morale. Police inertia in the initially crucial hours of Saturday can also be explained by a marginal note in a partisan source suggesting that, 'police behaviour during the disturbances was excellent, even though there had just previously been some discontent among them about scales of pay.'[52] It seems the police was not above postwar social discontent.[53] We will come back to the police later but here it suffices to state that police indifference at the outset of the riot helped it gain momentum. Consequently British troops were deployed to save the day for the government.

By noon a crowd of thousands gathered at the Id Gah maidan.[54] Congress League and Communist flags were prominent and soon the crowd was swelled by the entry of a fresh communist procession. When the police (and now it acted!) tried dispersing the crowd it retaliated by pelting the police.[55] At this stage, sensing the prevalent popular temperament, the party leaders began to waver. Even earlier many communist leaders, heeding the alarm raised by the authorities, had backed out of the situation. On Saturday many communist leaders decided against holding the meeting at Id Gah but the crowd refused dispersal and instead attacked the police.[56] The crowd fuelled by the speeches of Friday, was willing to burst through what had become the fetter of organization, for 'all efforts to disperse them peacefully failed ... and the *crowd increased* and resorted to violent stoning at every opportunity and *without provocation .... leaders had no control over the mob*, and ultimately the police were forced to open fire.'[57] (emphasis added)
[...]
The crowd symbolically destroying British power and asserting its own identity was in no mood to attend to the passivity now being

preached by its erstwhile teachers.[58] The leaders, lacking any programme of struggle beyond rhetoric and confronted with a phenomenon they helped create but could not control, performed a *volte-face* on Saturday:

> During the disturbances ... repeated attempts were made by party leaders, collectively and individually, to pacify and disperse the mob. *They met however, with no success whatsoever. A number of them including Sir Ghulam Hussain Hidayatullah, were stoned by the crowd.* These party leaders included some of the more peacefully inclined communists. A joint meeting was held of Communist, Congress and Muslim League leaders at the Swaraj Bhawan on Saturday afternoon to decide on measures to restore peace in the city. It is reported that they were unable to decide on methods to be used and no joint action was taken.[59] (emphasis added)

In the afternoon British troops occupied the Id Gah which had been transformed by the crowd into a centre of resistance.[60] 'The riotous crowds ... composed mostly of youths, both Hindu and Musalman, and hooligans',[61] now facing an enemy more formidable than the police, broke up into several groups, left the locality, and directed its attentions elsewhere. These smaller crowds attacked isolated police chowkies, post offices, other governmental buildings, and a European bank. Stray government servants were beaten up and letter boxes, and in one case a sub-post office, were set on fire. The armed forces opened fire on several occasions killing 4 and injuring more than 22—and in crowd attacks on the police 53 policemen were injured, few of them seriously.[62] According to Mudie, 8 persons were killed and 18 injured when the police fired in self-defence and 'in defence of the police outposts, post offices, one revenue department building and the Grindlay's Bank....[63] Communist leader S.K. Dharmani and 10 Hindu youths were arrested under the Police Act for hooliganism.[64] The latter were arrested while they were trying to occupy the municipal department building.[65]

Communications in the city were paralysed for the day and the tramway workers observed a complete strike, much to the relief of authorities.[66] By nightfall the crowds disintegrated and vanished as students returned home and the workers too retired to their quarters. State control became absolute as the British army clamped down a successful curfew.[67]

A perusal of the rapidly occurring events of Friday and Saturday reveals that popular protest began spontaneously with the stoning of troops near the harbour on Friday. Then students and party leaders intruded and political rhetoric became successful exhortation. Saturday was carried by the crowd with the political leaders backing out. By

Sunday, after two turbulent days, quiet began to prevail and finally by Monday troops were withdrawn and Karachi became normal.

Our survey clarifies that the crowd comprised school and college students, disaffected boatmen and fishermen (who by attire were singled out in reports as hooligans), workers from striking workshops and most probably the day-labourers from the harbour areas. In 1961, the total number of college students in Karachi was 1747, of whom hundreds became students due to expanded opportunities after 1947.[68] This would mean that in 1946 at least hundreds of students, if not thousands, protested and of these presumably the older ones stayed on longer. Most probably a few hundred college students played the most active leading part and the thousands mentioned in the reports belonged to the lower orders of Karachi.[69] Trade unions, with the probable exception of the tramway union, played no role in the upsurge. No report mentions them and even *People's Age* of the period is silent on them.

The newspapers, generally sympathetic to the RIN rebels, spoke hesitantly of the Karachi proletarians who so heroically rose to the occasion. The press, with few exceptions,[70] echoed the perspective of the national leaders. It condemned such disorderly conduct in police terminology and called it the product of a conspiracy by anti-social elements to establish goonda raj in contradistinction to the desired Swaraj.[71]

In passing we noticed police chowkies, a foreign (Grindlay's) bank, a revenue department building, and persons in western attire as the targets of popular fury. Against the historical background of nationalist struggle in India, the Karachi crowd by attacking these symbols of alien rule was, in effect, destroying the Raj of its own perceptions. Far from being meaningless, false, or incorrect this act was the outcome of mental aggregates formed in the life, and consciousness [thereby implied], of the participants. Popular violence was selective, not arbitrary, and though unplanned, signified the evolution of consciousness. And this is why a foreign bank, *not others*, was chosen for attack. Behind this may have lain the common nationalist discourse saying that the country was plundered by the British and the loot lay in their coffers.

The attacks on policemen, who embodied state power, and the snatching and burning of hats and ties, took place in a continuum within which the formation of a 'collective frame of mind had already taken place'.[72] The postwar upsurges remind us of the Quit India movement in their sharp demonstration of popular bitterness against the police. Such attacks can convey more meaning if the history of the urban/rural poor-police interaction is unearthed. Similarly the scenario of wartime and postwar black-markets brought about by soaring inflation and famine-like conditions awaits unfolding.[73]

Arson, including the snatching the burning of hats and ties, was common of Karachi and Bombay. But does this indicate something more than a cultural symbolic cremation of the Raj? Arson appears in riotous situations everywhere but its role [and analysis] varies with context. In our case the crowds of the postwar upsurge were not guided by criminal instincts. Nor did they conform to the communal type which took over completely from August 1946. In Karachi those arrested for rioting were students and reports nowhere attest the participation of identifiable criminals. In the reports of general cover term 'hooligan' sufficed when, in fact, no hooligans, that is, those known to the police as bad characters, were either identified or arrested. Thus official and much of non-official characterization of the crowd was prejudiced. So if mischief or 'malicious' intention was really absent why did the rioters resort to arson? Burning was not criminal madness. It was the manifestation of the popular desire to punish the enemy by destroying those goods which were dear to him and which formed the 'symbol and basis of his power'.[74]

Arson in this case was both an act of cultural incantation and liberation. In unsettled times when opportunity arose, crowds, composed generally of the losers, gathered to settle scores with those perceived as their tormentors. In the hour of expected apocalypse, they, if only ephemerally turned the world upside down. As the crowds stripped and burnt ties and hats in small bonfires it was as if they were celebrating. They created a moment such as would be talked about for long at tea-shop gatherings, a moment when out of their usual dark backstage they appeared under the glare and a moment immortalized in the tale each participant would carry of the event. And the event itself would signify historical victory, if only fleetingly.[75]

Our evidence does not substantiate the views aired by most, including Gandhi and Nehru, that during the days under study, anti-social elements were conspiring to subvert the *normal* course of attaining freedom. Without discounting the participation of criminals in these upsurges it seems clear that these 'anti-socials' were subsumed under the prevalent collective mentality of the riotous heterogeneous crowds.[76] This collective mentality was not that of a usual group but of an unusual social aggregate formed under specific circumstances.

The state and propertied classes have their own definition of crime but crime characteristic of communal carnages or riots perpetrated in the name of religion and often with the involvement of well-known leaders was absent from Karachi and Bombay during these days. In fact these crowds did not conform to the image of crowds carried in those days by the press, state, and leaders.[77] Not a single report from Karachi or Bombay mentions participation in abominable acts usually classified as heinous crime.[78] Indian factories and homes were not broken into, middle class security was not threatened. The protest was political as far as the identification of enemies was concerned and anti-imperialist.[79]

Earlier we noticed the moment in which the crowds were transformed into a 'state of crowd'.[80] That moment was the product of a specific historical conjuncture and one of the motives underlying its creation was rumour.

III

Rumour is the process by which a collective historical consciousness is built. The collective interpretations resulting from massive rumours lead to commonly accepted interpretations of events, non-events, or acts of events. Hence ... rumour tells us more about the mentality of the time of the happening than about the events themselves.

Jan Vansina[81]

Rumour has played a significant role at various times in Indian history.[82] The context of rumours in the case of the Karachi riots comprised:

1. The connection rumour had with the state.
2. The generation of collective consciousness in the short term.
3. The relation rumour had with the specific topography of Karachi.

Reports mention numerous rumours and for this we must be thankful to the alarm raised by the popular upheaval which rocked the Indian subcontinent during 1945–6. In crisis and especially during popular disturbances the Raj functionaries became acutely sensitive to bazaar gossip and premonition of impending turbulence led the more careful of them to record rumour.

[...]

List of rumours circulating in Karachi on Friday, 22 and Saturday, 23 February 1946.[83]

1. Indian troops in the embarkation buildings had refused food and were in sympathy with the RIN ratings.
2. *Hindustan* had been sunk with 300 ratings on board.

3. *Hindustan's* captain was an Irishman in sympathy with the
   strikers.
4. The military had tired on the ratings first.
5. In Keamari Baluch troops had refused to fire on the ratings and
   as a result had been disarmed and shelled in their lines by the
   British.
6. Police had fired on peaceful crowds.
7. Police firing had been indiscriminate and it had been bought
   over by increased rates of pay.
8. British soldiers had treacherously fired at the naval ratings under
   cover of a white flag (Newspaper news).
9. Indian soldiers had refused to fire on the ratings (Newspaper
   news).
10. *Hindustan* had been set on fire by incendiary bombs (special
    bulletin issued by the *Hindu*).[84]

[...]

[T]he INA trial and the postwar economic conditions coupled with
political and the strikes in the Allied and Royal Indian Air Force (RIAF)[85]
lent the emergent milieu in 1946 an aura of general collapse. The RIN
uprising, with the postures adopted towards it by the British, made a
decisive confrontation seem imminent and this raised hopes for change
in the minds of millions. The economic and political situations, obtained
after the war, thus met in a powerful conjuncture which instantaneously
attracted the growing militancy of the ordinary people. In the lives of
millions of working people such were the moments when a choice
between subjection and rebellion was made for: 'Even those who accept
exploitation oppression and subjection as the norm of human life dream
of world without them: a world of equality, brotherhood and freedom, a
totally *new* world without evil.'[86]

Due to the postwar posture of the Congress and later of the other
parties, regarding the INA trials it may well have appeared to the masses
that another mass nationalist upsurge was about to take place.[87] Here,
especially in the younger elements of the crowds, the memory of 1942
must have played its role.

Such were the constituents of the context within which the Karachi
riot and the rumours informing it made an appearance. Let us now try to
grasp the consciousness these rumours reflected.

It was widely believed in Karachi that troops in the embarkation
building had refused food and were in sympathy with the rebellious
ratings. Although official sources claim that during the RIN revolt the

Indian Army remained loyal, sources sympathetic to the rebels assert otherwise. According to Banerjee the embarkation unit, a heterogeneous body, was the first to be affected by the uprising. On 21 February none of these men reported for duty. Later they were arrested, put under guard, and this information was relayed to the newspaper officers by a brave Pathan private.[88] But these men were not on a hunger strike. They struck work in the morning and were removed to a camp in the afternoon. In fact at Drigh Road the RIAF men went on a hunger strike in favour of the RIN and at Mauripur too, 450 RIAF men did the same on 22 February.[89] In popular perception all these actions became merged and the attribute of one element was taken over by another. Thus rumour distorted information to make it conform to collective mentality. Further, partially substantiated newspaper reports helped this process by lending social authority to popular belief.[90] Hence news and rumour become inextricably intertwined.

Another accepted belief maintained that Indian soldiers had refused to fire on the ratings and that Baluch soldiers had been punished for disbedience. It is difficult to say what *actually* happened during those days. But from our point of view the validity of the moment for popular mentality is important. It is immaterial whether Indian troops refused to fire or not for the significant factor in our analysis is the fact that collective mentality believed it to have been so. The overwhelming presence of British troops in the harbour area and the blockade erected by them seems to have given rise to mass speculation that white soldiers were being used *because* Indian troops had become unreliable. Soon this speculation became news because of the readiness to interpret generated by collective mentality already prepared by other incidents. The army by sealing off the ratings from the general civilian assembly created fertile grounds for common apprehension. Thus heavy troop deployment involving large contingents of British troops along with heavy and medium artillery generated panic around the dock. Similarly the confiscation of boats by the authorities and the desertion of Keamari village added, in a large measure, to the general state of panic created by the situation and as a consequence popular imagination was fired into believing numerous instant stories.[91]

The Baluch troops case can be interpreted in two ways. The Baluch, a recognized 'martial race', were well known in Karachi for a variety of reasons,[92] and it is likely that the rumour mentioning the disarming and shelling of Baluch troops emanated from the large Baluchi component of the crowds. Crowd studies indicate that often crowds in action invent allies when actually none exist. Thus hope of victory is generated from the feeling dominating the moment. In Karachi too the pre-formed mentality of the rioters produced enough scope for wishful thinking.

Why Baluch and not Gurkhas or others?[93] Precisely because the Baluch troops were locally known and perhaps some even had their kin in the crowd. They were familiar and since they were ethnically Baluch it was generally believed that they would throw in their lot with the crowd. Hence ethnic loyalties guiding popular perceptions and actions during crowd mobilization and action cannot be ruled out in our analysis. However in identifying the Baluch troops with the crowd the rumour was explicit in formulation. It maintained that the Baluch troops were disarmed, taken to their lines shelled by the British. If analysed symbolically, this rumour unfolds an interesting process. First the troops disobeyed orders, thus becoming identified with the crowd. They were then disarmed, that is, alienated from their means of defence, and finally were slaughtered like goats. This theme of rebellion—expropriation—punishment was generated rapidly to suit the moment and the mood. In a flash the crowd identified the Baluch with the RIN who too were being similarly punished. Thus the imperative to defend their countrymen, being killed by the British, underpinned the creation of group solidarity in the crowd—what was happening to the RIN was also happening to the Baluchis and would happen to anyone opposing the British. In certain instances this idea could discourage rebellion and yet in others it could and it did lead to riot. The latter was decided by the development of collective sensibilities upto the point when such moments came. This explains why Karachi, sedate in 1942, exploded in 1946.

But were the Baluchis actually shelled? From where did the rumour derive legitimacy? During the hostilities between *Hindustan* and the military some 4 inch shells fired from the ship fell in the Baluch lines but did practically no damage.[94] The crowd surmised that shells had fallen into the Baluch lines and since in its view the RIN could never have shelled their brethren it must have been the British who did it. And so in a tense moment when accidentally some stray shells fell in the Baluch lines, they like the pieces of puzzle falling into place, acquired a meaning and instantly a story was born and believed. It was believed because the crowd, guided by pre-formed collective perception—in which the INA, RIAF, and RIN issues played important roles—*expected* the troops to support the RIN uprising and the rumours were *simultaneously* the products as well as the propellers of this mentality.

Somewhat similar in content was the rumour regarding the police. The crowd said the police had been bought over by increased rates of pay. The fact that it believed the police could be 'bought' emerged from its *general characterization* of the police force as an easily corruptible body. This conception emanated from everyday popular experience. The police undoubtedly must have treated Karachi as a lucrative proposition! But the rumour had a notion of betrayal attached to it. The previous section observed that the Karachi police, prior to this riot, had been restive regarding pay. It is likely that by way of casual conversation of press reports this unrest was made known to the commoners of Karachi. Such casual information went into the pool of popular memory. Further we noticed that during the initial part of the upsurge, despite Section 144 being in force, the police *did not* act against the rioters. This probably generated an impression in the crowd that the police was sympathetic. Ultimately when the police, under pressure, did act albeit ineffectively, its 'true nature' was exposed to the crowd. This ambiguity in police behaviour was thus construed as a betrayal by the crowd. Believing this the crowd proceeded to attack police stations and chowkies.

Among rumours current, three were about *Hindustan*. One mentioned that the ship had been sunk with 300 ratings on board. Another claimed that its captain, an Irishman, was in sympathy with the rebels. The third stated that the ship had been set aflame by incendiary bombs. Let us recapitulate the incidents of Friday, 22 February to analyse these rumours. In the first place the harbour area was occupied by British troops who disallowed anyone within 4 miles of the dock. Secondly from 10 in the morning citizens heard and saw heavy firing in the harbour. Thirdly after the firing ambulances and lorries carrying the wounded and other ratings left the area. The battle became a military secret and to date we do not have a single non-official eye witness account from the *Hindustan*. Nobody in fact knew what happened to the *Hindustan* during the exchange of fire

This situation, facilitated by the topography of the area, created apprehension in the crowd assembled far away from the actual battlefield. Further, as British troops kept vigil, till Sunday nobody was allowed near the quayside. This enhanced popular suspicion regarding the situation. Thus the state itself was instrumental in the emergence of rumours. Deployment of artillery, including a field gun, mortars, and heavy machine guns had a tremendous visual impact upon the crowds.[95]

Panic was enhanced by the entry, into the crowd, of boatmen and fishermen from Keamari. Their boats too had been seized and hence, in their view, the only possible means of escape for the ratings had vanished. And when in these circumstances heavy firing began everyone was convinced that *Hindustan* was being sunk.

The second rumour reflected a knowledge of the historical Irish-British rivalry. It most probably came from students aware of British history or from general perceptions of the Irish struggle handed down to popular levels by the nationalist ideology. In either case the appearance of this exceptional rumour displays the mechanism of allies at work during crowd upsurges.

The third rumour also appeared in a special bulletin issued by the *Hindu* on 22 February.[96] Studies in crowd behaviour suggest that often the belief of the crowd in itself becomes rejuvenated by a feedback, into its information pool of knowledge commanding social sanction and authority. In most literate societies the newspaper is considered an authentic source of news. Furthermore, the role of the Indian press during the anti-imperialist struggle lends basis to this idea. Hence the news from the *Hindu,* which most probably arose from popular perception of matters and then went back to the crowd greatly strengthened the collective resolve of the crowd.

In this respect certainly more important was the AIR broadcast made by the Flag Officer Commanding RIN *Godfrey* on the afternoon of 21 February in which he categorically stated that the RIN would be destroyed if the mutiny continued. The whole country heard this 'submit or perish' speech.[97] These words immediately preceding the battle in Karachi deepened the sense of gloom prevalent and heightened popular fears regarding British intentions in dealing with the RIN. Thus rumours mentioning the sinking and damaging of *Hindustan* were not without substance, as shown in the public actions of the state during those dramatic incidents of February 1946.

The consciousness generated in the Karachi crowd and brought to the fore due to its interaction with an external stimulus led to an unorganized momentary upsurge. The spontaneous outburst converted the street into a temporary battlefield but for various reasons could not be channelled into a wider movement. Another crowd which began to collect on Sunday, 24 February was homogeneous and hence motivated by a different group solidarity.

On Sunday afternoon some 'Hindus' (?) attacked Sayed Haroom, the brother of Yusuf Haroon, a member of the Central Legislative Assembly, and tried to snatch away his tie and hat.[98] That evening 'a crowd of Makranis were collecting to take revenge on Hindus, but they were persuaded to disperse.[99] According to Mudie, after the assault on Haroon, the 'Muslims who had gathered to avenge Haroon' were however persuaded to disperse 'with the assistance of Sir Ghulam Hussain.'[100] This was the same leader who was stoned by the crowds only a day before!

The Sunday crowds, under control of *their* leader, was different from that of the Saturday crowd and similar actions on Sunday provoked the crystallizing of a distinctly different collective mentality from that of a day before. Even if we do not believe that the crowd on Sunday gathered to avenge their leader nonetheless it displayed confidence in a leader. This separated its mentality from that of the insurgent crowd on Saturday. Thus the formation and reformation of crowds in Karachi was a microcosm of a larger process which played on and generated a contradictory consciousness. The question here is not one of the fickle-mindedness of a sub-proletrariat.[101] It is rather one that probes the problematic of the complexity of human consciousness which evolved through numerous social intricacies in a multidimensional national movement. However, the tackling of that question, which is open, calls for much wider generalizations lying beyond the purview of this particular study.

NOTES

Acknowledgements: I must thank Sabyasachi Bhattacharya and Majid Hayat Siddiqui, for encouraging me and criticizing this paper at various stages.

  † For a history of the INA see the following. Hugh Toye, *The Springing Tiger*, Bombay, 1962; K.K. Ghosh, *The Indian National Army*, (Meerut, 1969) is by far the most comprehensive work on the subject. Articles by Sehgal, Dhillon, and Bose in part V of N.R. Ray et al. (eds), *Challenge: A Saga of India's Struggle for Freedom*, New Delhi, 1984. The statements of the INA officers on trial were published by the All India INA Enquiry and Relief Committee as *The I.N.A. Speaks*, Delhi, 1946. Netaji was looking and planning for a 'proper psychological moment for a revolution'. For his ideas and moves in 1940–3 see Subhas Chandra Bose, *The Indian Struggle*, Bombay, 1967, especially pp. 357–463. On the Royal Indian Navy (henceforth RIN) see S. Banerjee, *The R.I.N. Strike*, Delhi, 1954. B.C. Dutt, *Mutiny of the Innocents*, Bombay, 1971. Anil Roy, 'Karachi Chapter', in N.R. Ray et al. (eds), *Challenge*, and Anirudh Deshpande, 'The Royal Indian Navy Uprising and Popular Protest,' 1946, unpublished MPhil dissertation submitted to the Centre for Historical Studies, JNU, 1987.

  1. Fortnightly Report (henceforth FR), second half of February 1946, Sindh, Home-Department-Political, 18/2/1946, National Archives of India (henceforth NAI).

2. That the INA influenced the evolution of nationalist consciousness in various sections of the Indian armed forces after the War is evinced by the FR for Sindh between August 1945 and February 1946 as well as the *Transfer of Power*, vol. VI (eds) Nicholas, Mansergh, and Penderel Moon, London, 1970–83.

3. Anil Roy, 'Karachi Chapter', (hereafter KC), p. 606, in N.R. Ray et al. (eds), *Challenge*, New Delhi, 1984.

4. Ibid.

5. S. Banerjee, *The R.I.N. Strike*, Delhi, 1954, p. 83, and the evidence of Chatterjee in Karachi Statements, a file containing petitions to the RIN Mutiny Commission of Enquiry, serial number 14, RIN Mutiny Papers, NAI.

6. KC, p. 607.

7. Ibid., p. 608 and Intelligence Bureau (IB) Home Department report titled 'Mutiny in the RIN and concerned disturbances' (February 1946, Sindh) (hereafter IB1), Home-Political, 5/14/46, NAI complied by K.R. Eates, DSP, Sindh CID.

8. IB1.

9. There were five shore establishments in Karachi situated in Manora: HMIS *Monze*—Local Naval Defence Base, HMIS *Himalaya*—Gunnery School, HMIS *Bahadur* and *Dilwar*—Boy's Training Schools, and HMIS *Chamak*—Radar Training School.

10. IB1.

11. The impact of the INA on postwar polities has been noted well by K.K. Ghosh, *The Indian National Army*, Meerut, 1969, pp. 198–251.

12. KC, p. 609.

13. Ibid., pp. 609–10.

14. KC, p. 610, and I.B. Central Intelligence Officer's report on 'The recent disturbances in Karachi for Home Department's information' (hereafter IB2), Home-Political, 5/14/46, NAI.

15. FR (Sindh), second half of February 1946.

16. Sir Francis Mudie (Governor of Sindh) to Wavell, 27.2.46, in N. Mansergh (ed.) *The Transfer of Power*, 1942–7, vol. VI, London, 1976, pp. 1071–4 (hereafter *TOP*).

17. KC, p. 610, 'lal salam' means red salute, a communist greeting.

18. KC, p. 612 and IB1.

19. This paragraph is based on KC, pp. 613–14.

20. KC, p. 615.

21. *TOP*, pp. 1071–2.

22. During the Quit India movement Sindh, Punjab, the North West Frontier Province, and many areas of south India were quiet compared to western Maharashtra, eastern United Provinces, and Bihar.

23. Francis G. Hutchins, *India's Revolution*, Massachusetts, 1973, p. 237.

24. *The Gazeteer of the Province of Sind B, Volume I Karachi District* (hereafter *GKD*), compiled by J.W. Smyth I.C.S., Bombay, 1919, p. 101, describes

Pir Mangho, popularly called Mugger Pir, a religious shrine, ten miles north of Karachi in the following words: 'When the Pir died and was buried, his grave became a place of pilgrimage for pious Muslims from all parts of the country. But it is also a resort of Hindu devotees, who call it Lala Jasraj. This double character is common among the shrines of Sind: The Mussalman Lal Shahbaz is the Hindu Raja Bhartari and the Mussalman Kawaja Khizr is the Hindu Jinda Pir.

25. FR (Sindh), first half of February 1946, Home-Political, 18/2/46, NAI.
26. FR (Sindh), second half of October 1945, Home-Political, 18/10/45, NAI.
27. H. Dow (Governor of Sindh) to Wavell, 3.11.45, in *TOP*, p. 438. After October 1945 the Congress consistently supported the INA men, and Congress attempts to defend them were widely propagated.
28. IB1.
29. IB2 and *Dawn*, 23 February 1946.
30. *The Tribune*, 22 February 1946.
31. IB2.
32. This 1200 feet long screw-pipe bridge was built in 1865.
33. FR (Sindh), second half of February 1946.
34. *The Tribune*, 23 February 1946.
35. Firing occurred on Friday. This may influenced the sensibilities aroused in devout Muslims in the town. According to *GKD*, p. 60, at Manora there was (and probably is) a tomb of a 'wonder-working Pir' which attracted crowds to an annual fair.
36. *Dawn*, 23 February 1946.
37. *The Tribune*, 23 February 1946.
38. IB2.
39. IB1.
40. IB1.
41. IB1.
42. Ibid.
43. IB2.
44. Ibid.
45. FR (Sindh), second half of February, Home-Political, 18/2/46, NAI.
46. IB2.
47. Forewarning from Bombay was thankfully acknowledged by Mudie. See *TOP*, p. 1072.
48. FR (Sindh), second half of February.
49. IB1.
50. IB1.
51. *Inspiring Story of the Historic RIN Uprising*—by a victimized RIN striker, duplicate of a PPH pamphlet in the Archives for the documents of contemporary history, JNU, New Delhi, p. 10.
52. IB2.
53. Sumit Sarkar, 'Popular Movements and National Leadership, 1945–7', *EPW* annual number April 1982, mentions the police strikes of 1946. Wider

generalizations regarding police behaviour during 1939–46 can however be made only after considerable research in this field is undertaken.

54. IB1.
55. IB1.
56. FR (Sindh), second half of February 1946.
57. IB1.
58. Violence in Karachi was not as extreme as in Bombay during the RIN uprising where a virtual upheaval of the 'have nots' occurred. In Karachi, mass participation was in the nature of an extended riot.
59. IB2.
60. The occupation of the Id Gah by foreign troops probably inflamed passions further.
61. IB2.
62. IB1.
63. *TOP*, p. 1072.
64. IB1.
65. *Dawn*, 24 February 1946.
66. Ibid.
67. *Dawn* and *The Tribune*, 25 February 1946.
68. *Political Census of Pakistan, 1961, District Census report Karachi, 1961*, (hereafter *PCP*), pp. 1–41. Social Science Library, JNU, New Delhi.
69. This fits in well with the general student-worker militancy of the period in Indian history.
70. Even the *People's Age* (3 March 1946) which was by and large sympathetic to the Bombay working class mentioned that during 'Bombay's three days of Heroic battle', 'anti-socials' in some localities took 'advantage of (the) situation by organising orgies of loot....and senseless burnings'. An attempt was thus made to dissociate a disciplined working class from some anti-social elements. In any case the question who was 'organizing' loot and what was being looted and why was left unanswered by this organ of the CPI. [Communist Party of India].
71. For example, to describe the crowd, the *Bombay Chronicle*, 24 February 1946 used terms such as 'frenzied crowds' and 'hooligans'. The crowd action was called a 'thoughtless orgy of violence'. Similar vocabulary characterized the *Times of India* reports.
72. Georges Lefebvre, 'Revolutionary Crowds', in Jeffry Kaplow (ed.), *New Perspectives on the French Revolution: Readings in Historical Sociology*, London, 1965, p. 175.
73. Sumit Sarkar in, 'Popular Movements and National Leadership, 1945–7', describes the postwar conditions and tensions. Lefebvre in, 'Revolutionary Crowds', writes that 'no gathering' apart from lines formed outside bakery doors in large cities is more apt to be suddenly transformed into 'an assembly of rioters'.
74. Lefebvre, 'Revolutionary Crowds', p. 185.

75. In times of social crisis feeling of imminent change often becomes generalized and the so called 'lower orders' too partake of this. Conditions in India from 1942 to 1947 were also critical and uncertain in many ways and the Indian crowd too participated in history within this context.

76. Lefebvre, 'Revolutionary Crowds', p. 179, writes: Every human aggregate forms within society. It is true that, to become a part of it, the individual must provisionally break away from the social group to which he normally belongs; but he cannot for all that completely throw off the collective mentality of the group. The idea and feelings which it involves are only pushed into the back of his consciousness. The degree to which this repression occurs repression occurs depends upon the degree of heterogeneity in the aggregate.

77. See the brilliant discussion on the images, prejudices, ideas, and reality relating to crowds in George Rude, *Crowds in History*, New York, 1964. See E.J. Hobsbawm, *Bandits*, Harmondsworth, 1985, for a general formulation of popular notion of crime. While disagreeing with some of the author's presumptions we nevertheless believe that amongst popular groups (both urban and rural) conceptions of 'straight' and 'bent' exist.

78. This usually refers to massacre, mutilation, rape, and other such activities.

79. In contrast a few months later the complexion of crowd activity was completely transformed. This shows that crowds, like other, and purportedly more conscious social aggregates, are prone to a change in mentality. Instincts of varying types can be aroused by different movements the creation of which depends upon factors often beyond the control of crowds.

80. Lefebvre, 'Revolutionary Crowds', p. 180 writes that the 'sudden awakening of the group consciousness, provoked by a violent emotion, gives the aggregate a new character which could be called the 'state of crowd'.

81. Jan Vansina, *Oral Tradition as History*, London, 1985, p. 6.

82. Ranajit Guha has analysed the role of rumour in peasant insurgency in colonial India on the basis of pioneering works by Allport and postman, Lefebvre, Hobsbawm, Rude and Prasad in his *Elementary Aspects of Peasant Insurgency in Colonial India*, Delhi, 1983, pp. 251–77 Valuable analyses of rumours are to be found also in Shahid Amin, 'Gandhi as Mahatma: Gorakhpur District, Eastern UP, 1921–28,' in Ranajit Guha ed., *Subaltern Studies III*, Delhi, 1984, and Anand A. Yang. 'A Conversion of Rumours: The Language of Popular Mentalities in Late Nineteenth Century Colonial India', in of *Journal of Social History*, V, 20, Number 3. 1987.

83. IB1.

84. Here news is listed with rumour because most probably the newspaper accounts, due to official restrictions, were based on rumour. In that case rumour by becoming news rejuvenated itself.

85. These preceded the RIN uprising.

86. E.J. Hobsbawm, *Bandits*, pp. 27–28.
87. For a sharp insight into the Congress image during the post–1945 period see D.D. Kosambi, *Exasperating Essays*, Pune, 1986, especially pp. 16–17.
88. *The R.I.N. Strike*, pp. 120–1.
89. IB1.
90. IB1 reports that newspapers were spreading 'alarmist' news.
91. Lefebvre, 'Revolutionary Crowds', mentions suspicion, fear, panic and hope as essential attributes of situations involving crowds in action. George Rude, *The Crowd in the French Revolution*, Oxford, 1959, pp. 221–5 writes that, 'one of the most constant elements contributing to certain states of collective mentality, at all times and all places...is the element of panic-fear propagated by rumour', and that this panic arises from a 'threat, real or imaginary, to three matters of vital moment—to property, life, and the means of subsistence'. In Karachi, especially around the harbour, on 22 and 23 February 1946 these elements were more than present.
92. For instance the Baluch Regimental Centre was situated in Karachi.
93. Banerjee, *The R.I.N. Strike*, p. 87 tells us that British troops were used after the Baluch and Gurkha troops disobeyed orders. However his claim that the entire Indian army in Karachi during those days was on the brink of an armed rebellion can only be settled after more rigorous research. *The Inspiring Story of the Historic RIN Uprising*, p. 9, says that two platoons of the Baluch Regiment refused to board the *Hindustan* on 21 February.
94. *TOP*, p. 1072.
95. Visual impacts often produce images of the adversary. If an enemy appears very strong, given varying conditions, the psychological implications of the appearance may vary. In Bombay and Karachi during the RIN uprising the appearance of state power, though menacing, seems to have spurred the collective resolve and solidarity of the working class.
96. IB1.
97. This relay was printed by all newspapers and in books and articles on the RIN revolt.
98. IB2 and *TOP*, p. 1072.
99. IB2.
100. *TOP*, p. 1072.
101. E.J. Hobsbawm, *Primitive Rebels*, New York, 1965, pp. 108–25 has written instructively on the 'city mob' as a sub-proletarian and 'fickle' minded group. The Indian proletariat has not freed itself from this 'fickle' mindedness which Hobsbawm associates with a largely pre-industrial sub-proletariat. The Indian case, by no means exceptional, raises the problem of defining proletarian class consciousness in the Indian as well as the general context.

Select Bibliography

GENERAL WORKS

Bandyopadhyay, Sekhar. *From Plassey to Partition: A History of Modern India*. New Delhi: Orient Longman, 2004.

Bose, Sugata and Ayesha Jalal. *Modern South Asia: History, Culture, Political Economy*. London, New York: Routledge, 1998.

Brown, Judith. *Modern India: The Origins of an Asian Democracy*. New York: Oxford University Press, 1985.

Chandra, Bipan, Aditya Mukherjee, K.N. Panikkar, Mridula Mukherjee, and Sucheta Mahajan. *India's Struggle for Independence*. New Delhi: Penguin Books, 1989.

Jeffrey, Robin. (ed.). *India: Rebellion to Republic, Selected Writings, 1857–1990*. New Delhi: Sterling Publishers, 1990.

Kulke, H. and D. Rothermund. *History of India*. London and New York: Routledge, 1998.

Kumar, Ravinder. *The Making of a Nation: Essays in Indian History and Politics*. New Delhi: Manohar, 1989.

Low, D.A. (ed.). *Congress and the Raj: Facets of the Indian Struggle 1917–47*. New Delhi: Oxford University Press, 2004.

Masselos, Jim. *Indian Nationalism: An History*. Revised edition, Delhi: Sterling, 1985.

Metcalf, Barbara Daly and Thomas Metcalf. *A Concise History of India*. Cambridge: Cambridge University Press, 2002.

Robb, Peter. *A History of India*. Basingstoke: Palgrave, 2002.

Rothermund, D. *The Phases of Indian Nationalism and Other Essays*. Bombay: Nachiketa Publications, 1970.

Sarkar, Sumit. *Modern India, 1885–1947*. 2nd edition, Basingstoke: Macmillan, 1989.

Sisson, R. and S. Wolpert, (eds). *Congress and Indian Nationalism: The Pre-Independence Phase*. Berkeley and Los Angeles: University of California Press, 1988.

Stein, Burton. *A History of India*. Oxford: Blackwell, 1998.

Suntharalingam, R. *Indian Nationalism: An Historical Analysis*. New Delhi: Vikas Publishing House, 1983.

Wolpert, Stanley. *A New History of India.* 6th edition, New York: Oxford University Press, 2000.

NATIONALISM BEFORE GANDHI

Argov, D. *Moderates and Extremists in the Indian Nationalist Movement 1883–1920.* London: Asia Publishing House, 1967.

Barrier, N.G. 'The Arya Samaj and Congress Politics in the Punjab 1894–1907'. *Journal of Asian Studies*, 26 (3), 1967, pp. 363–79.

Basu, Aparna. *The Growth of Education and Political Development in India 1898–1920.* New Delhi: Oxford University Press, 1974.

Bayly, C.A. *The Local Roots of Indian Politics, Allahabad 1880–1920.* Oxford: Clarendon, 1975.

Brass, Paul. *Language, Religion and Politics in North India.* London: Cambridge University Press, 1974.

Cashman, Richard I. 'The Political Recruitment of the God Ganapati'. *The Indian Economic and Social History Review,* 7 (3), 1970, pp. 347–73.

———. *The Myth of the Lokamanya: Tilak and Mass Politics in Maharashtra.* Berkeley: University of California Press, 1975.

Chandra, Bipan. *The Rise and Growth of Economic Nationalism in India.* New Delhi: Peoples' Publishing House, 1966.

———. *Nationalism and Colonialism in Modern India.* New Delhi: Orient Longman, 1979.

Charlesworth, Neil. 'The Myth of the Deccan Riots'. *Modern Asian Studies,* 6 (4), 1972, pp. 401–21.

———. *Peasants and Imperial Rule: Agriculture and Agrarian Society in the Bombay Presidency, 1850–1935.* Cambridge: Cambridge University Press, 1985.

Chatterjee, Partha. *Nationalist Thought and the Colonial World: A Derivative Discourse?.* London: Zed Books, 1986.

———. *The Nation and its Fragments: Colonial and Postcolonial Histories.* Princeton, New Jersey: Princeton University Press, 1993.

Dalmia, Vasudha. *The Nationalization of Hindu Traditions: Bharatendu Harschandra and Nineteenth-century Banaras.* New Delhi: Oxford University Press, 1997.

Desai, A.R. *Social Background of Indian Nationalism.* 3rd edition, Bombay: Popular Book Depot, 1959.

——— (ed.). *Peasant Struggles in India.* New Delhi: Oxford University Press, 1979.

Dobbin, Christine. *Urban Leadership in Western India: Politics and Communities in Bombay City 1840–1885.* London: Oxford University Press, 1972.

Fuchs, Stephen. *Godmen on the Warpath: A Study of Messianic Movements in India,* New Delhi: Munshilal Manoharlal Publishers Pvt Ltd, 1992.

Gallagher, J., G. Johnson, and A. Seal (eds). *Locality, Province and Nation: Essays on Indian Politics 1870 to 1940,* Cambridge: Cambridge University Press, 1973.

Gordon, L.A. *Bengal: the Nationalist Movement 1876–1940.* New York, London: Columbia University Press, 1974.

Guha, Ranajit. *Elementary Aspects of Peasant Insurgency in Colonial India.* New Delhi: Oxford University Press, second impression, 1994.

Hardiman, David. (ed.). *Peasant Resistance in India 1858–1914.* New Delhi: Oxford University Press, 1993.

Heehs, P. *The Bomb in Bengal: The Rise of Revolutionary Terrorism in India 1900–1910.* New Delhi: Oxford University Press, 1993.

_____. *Nationalism, Terrorism, Communalism: Essays in Modern Indian History.* New Delhi: Oxford University Press, 1998.

Heimsath, C.H. *Indian Nationalism and Hindu Social Reform,* Princeton: Princeton University Press, 1964.

Hill, John L. (ed.). *The Congress and Indian Nationalism.* London: Curzon Press, 1991.

Johnson, Gordon. *Provincial Politics and Indian Nationalism. Bombay and the Indian National Congress.* Cambridge: Cambridge University Press, 1973.

Jones, K.W. *The New Cambridge History of India, III.1. Socio-Religious Reform Movements in British India.* Cambridge: Cambridge University Press, 1994.

Kaviraj, S. *The Unhappy Consciousness: Bankimchandra Chattopadhyay and the Formation of Nationalist Discourse in India.* New Delhi: Oxford University Press, 1995.

King, Christopher R. *One Language Two Scripts: The Hindi Movement in Nineteenth Century North India,* paperback edition. New Delhi: Oxford University Press, 1999.

Kling, B.B. *The Blue Mutiny: The Indigo Disturbances in Bengal 1859–1862,* Philadelphia: University of Pennsylvania Press, 1966.

Kumar, Ravinder. *Western India in the Nineteenth Century.* London: Routledge and Kegan Paul, 1968.

Low, D.A. (ed.). *Indian National Congress: Centenary Hindsights.* New Delhi: Oxford University Press, 1988.

McCully, B.T. *English Education and the Origins of Indian Nationalism.* Gloucester, Mass.: Peter Smith, 1966.

McLane, J.R. *Indian Nationalism and the Early Congress.* Princeton, NJ: Princeton University Press, 1977.

Mehrotra, S.R. *The Emergence of the Indian National Congress.* New Delhi: Vikas Publishing House, 1971.

Misra, B.B. *The Indian Middle Classes: Their Growth in Modern Times.* New Delhi: Oxford University Press, 1961.

Nanda, B.R. *Gokhale the Indian Moderates and the British Raj.* New Delhi: Oxford University Press, 1977.

Nanda, B.R.(ed.). *Essays in Modern Indian History.* New Delhi: Oxford University Press, 1980.

Owen, H.F. 'Towards Nationwide Agitation and Organisation: the Home Rule Leagues, 1915–1918', in D.A. Low (ed.), *Soundings in Modern South Asian History.* London: Weidenfeld and Nicolson, 1968, pp. 159–95.

Pandey, Gyanendra. 'Rallying round the Cow: Sectarian Strife in the Bhojpuri Region, c.1888–1917', in R.Guha (ed.), *Subaltern Studies II: Writings on South Asian History and Society.* New Delhi: Oxford University Press, 1983, pp. 60–129.

Panikkar, K.N. *Against Lord and State: Religion and Peasant Uprisings in Malabar, 1836–1921.* New Delhi: Oxford University Press, 1989.

Rag, Pankaj. 'Indian Nationalism 1885–1905: An Overview', *Social Scientist,* 23 (4/6), 1995, pp. 69–97.

Ray, Rajat Kanta. 'Three Interpretaions of Indian Nationalism', in B.R. Nanda (ed.), *Essays in Modern Indian History.* New Delhi: Oxford University Press, 1980, pp. 1–41.

———. *Social Conflict & Political Unrest in Bengal 1875–1927.* New Delhi: Oxford University Press, 1984.

Raychaudhuri,Tapan. *Europe Reconsidered: Perceptions of the West in nineteenth century Bengal.* New Delhi: Oxford University Press, 1989.

———. *Perceptions, Emotions, Sensibilities: Essays on India's Colonial and Post-colonial Experiences.* Bew Delhi: Oxford University Press, 1999.

Robb, Peter. 'The Challenge of Gau Mata: British Policy and Religious Change in India, 1880–1916', *Modern Asian Studies,* 20 (2), 1986, pp. 285–319.

Sarkar, Sumit. *The Swadeshi Movement in Bengal.* New Delhi: Peoples' Publishing House, 1970.

Seal, Anil. *The Emergence of Indian Nationalism: Competition and Collaboration in the Later Nineteenth Century,* Cambridge: Cambridge University Press, 1968.

———. 'Imperialism and Nationalism in India'. *Modern Asian Studies,* 7 (3), 1973.

Sen, Amiya P. *Hindu Revivalism in Bengal 1872–1905.* New Delhi: Oxford University Press, 1993.

Seth, Sanjay. 'Rewriting Histories of Nationalism: The Politics of "Moderate Nationalism" in India, 1870–1905'. *The American Historical Review,* 104 (1), 1999, pp. 95–116.

Southerd, Barbara. 'The Political Strategy of Aurobindo Ghosh: The Utilization of Hindu Religious Symbolism and the Problem of Political Mobilization in Bengal'. *Modern Asian Studies* 14 (3), 1980, pp. 353–76.

Sunthralingam, R. *Politics and nationalist awakening in South India 1852–1891.* Tucson: University of Arizona Press, 1974.

van Schendel, W. 'Madmen of Mymensingh: Peasant Resistance and the Colonial Process in Eastern India, 1824 to 1833'. *The Indian Economic and Social History Review* 22 (2), 1985, pp. 139–73.

Washbrook, David A. *The Emergence of Provincial Politics: The Madras Presidency 1870–1920.* Cambridge: Cambridge University Press, 1976.

Wolpert, Stanley. *Tilak and Gokhale: Revolution and Reform in the Making of Modern India.* Berkeley and Los Angeles: University of California Press, 1962.

GANDHIAN MOVEMENTS

Amin, Shahid. 'Gandhi as Mahatma: Gorakhpur District, Eastern UP, 1921–2', in R. Guha (ed.), *Subaltern Studies III: Writings on South Asian History and Society.* New Delhi: Oxford University Press, 1984, pp. 1–61.

———. *Event, Metaphor, Memory: Chauri Chaura 1922–1992.* Paperback edition, Delhi: Oxford University Press, 1996.

Arnold, David. *The Congress in Tamilnad, Nationalist Politics in South India 1919–1937.* New Delhi: Manohar, 1977.

———. *Gandhi.* London: Longman, 2001.

Baker, C.J. and D.A. Washbrook. *South India: Political Institutions and Political Change 1880–1940.* Delhi: Macmillan, 1975, pp. 98–149.

Baker, C., Johnson, G., and A. Seal (eds). *Power Profit and Politics: Essays on Imperialism, and Change in Twentieth Century India*, published in *Modern Asian Studies*, 15 (3), 1981.

Baker, D.E.U. *Changing Political Leadership in an Indian Province: The Central Provinces and Berar 1919–1939*. New Delhi: Oxford University Press, 1979.

———. *Baghelkhand, or the Tigers' Lair: Region and Nation in Indian History*. New Delhi: Oxford University Press. 2007.

Baruah, Sanjib. *India Against Itself: Assam and the Politics of Nationality*. New Delhi, Oxford University Press, 1999.

Broomfield, John H. *Elite Conflict in a Plural Society: Twentieth-Century Bengal*. Berkeley and Los Angeles: University of California Press, 1968.

Brown, Judith M. *Gandhi's Rise to Power. Indian Politics 1915–1921*. Cambridge: Cambridge University Press, 1972.

———. *Gandhi and Civil Disobedience: The Mahatma in Indian Politics, 1928–1934*. Cambridge: Cambridge University Press, 1977.

———. *Gandhi: Prisoner of Hope*. New Haven and London: Yale University Press, 1989.

———. *Nehru*. Harlow: Longman, 2000.

Dalton, Dennis. *Mahatma Gandhi: Nonviolent Power in Action*. New York: Columbia University Press, 1993.

Damodaran, Vinita. *Broken Promises: Popular Protest, Indian Nationalism and the Congress Party in Bihar, 1935–1946*. New Delhi: Oxford University Press, 1992.

Dhanagare, D.N. *Peasant Movements in India 1920–1950*. New Delhi: Oxford University Press, 1991.

Gallagher, J., G.Johnson, and A. Seal (eds). *Locality, Province and Nation: Essays on Indian Politics 1870 to 1940*. Cambridge: Cambridge University Press, 1973.

Gopal, S. *Jawaharlal Nehru: A Biography*. Volume One, 1889–1947. London: Jonathan Cape, 1975.

Gopalankutty, K. 'Mobilisation against the State and not against the landlords: The Civil Disobedience Movement in Malabar'. *The Indian Economic and Social History Review*, 26 (4), 1989, pp. 459–80.

Gordon, R. 'The Hindu Mahasabha and the Indian National Congress, 1915 to 1926', *Modern Asian Studies*, 9 (2), 1975.

Guha, A. *From Planter Raj to Swaraj: Freedom Struggle and Electoral Politics in Assam 1826–1947*. New Delhi: Peoples Publishing House, 1977.

Guha, Ramchandra. *The Unquiet Woods: Ecological Change and Peasant Resistance in the Himalaya*. Delhi: Oxford University Press, 1991.
_____. 'Forestry and Social Protest in British Kumaun, c. 1893–1921', in R.Guha (ed.), *Subaltern Studies IV: Writings on South Asian history and Society*. Paperback edition, New Delhi: Oxford University Press, 1994, pp. 54–100.
Guha, Ranajit (ed.). *Subaltern Studies I: Writings on South Asian History and Society*, New Delhi: Oxford University Press, 1982.
_____. 'Discipline and Mobilize', in P.Chatterjee and G.Pandey (eds), *Subaltern Studies VII: Writings on South Asian History and Society*. Delhi: Oxford Uiversity Press, 1992, pp. 69–120.
_____. *Dominance without Hegemony: History and Power in Colonial India*. Cambridge, Mass: Harvard University Press, 1998.
Hardiman, David. *Peasant Nationalists of Gujarat Kheda District 1917–1934*. New Delhi: Oxford University Press, 1981.
Henningham, Stephen. *Peasant Movements in Colonial India North Bihar 1917–42*. Canberra: Australian National University, 1982.
_____. 'Quit India in Bihar and the Eastern United Provinces: The Dual Revolt', in R.Guha (ed.), *Subaltern Studies II: Writings on South Asian History and Society*. New Delhi: Oxford University Press, 1983. pp. 130–79.
Hutchins, F.G. *India's Revolution: Gandhi and the Quit India Movement*. Cambridge: Harvard University Press, 1973.
Krishan, Shri. 'Peasant mobilisation, political organisations and modes of interaction: The Bombay countryside 1934–1941'. *The Indian Economic and Social History Review*, 32 (4), 1995, pp. 429–46.
_____. 'Crowd vigour and social identity: The Quit India Movement in western India'. *The Indian Economic and Social History Review*, 33 (4), 1996, pp. 459–79.
Krishna, G. The Development of the Indian National Congress as a Mass Organisation, 1918–1923'. *Journal of Asian Studies*, 25 (3), 1966, pp. 413–30.
Kudaisya, Gyanesh. *Region, Nation, "Heartland": Uttar Pradesh in India's Body Politic*. New Delhi: Sage Publications, 2006.
Kumar, Kapil (ed.). *Congress and Classes: Nationalism, Workers and Peasants*. New Delhi, Manohar, 1988.
_____. *Peasants in Revolt: Tenants, Landlords, Congress and the Raj in Oudh, 1886–1922*. New Delhi: Manohar, 1984.
Kumar, Ravinder. (ed.), *Essays on Gandhian Politics. The Rowlatt Satyagraha of 1919*. Oxford: Clarendon Press, 1971.

Markovits, Claude. *The Un-Gandhian Gandhi: The Life and Afterlife of the Mahatma*. Delhi, Permanent Black. 2003.

Menon, Vishalakshi. *From Movement to Government: The Congress in Uttar Pradesh, 1937–42*. New Delhi: Sage Publications, 2002.

Minault, Gail. *The Khilafat Movement: Religious Symbolism and Political Mobilization in India*. New Delhi: Oxford University Press, 1982.

Mukherjee, Mridula. *Peasants in India's Non-violent Revolution: Practice and Theory*. New Delhi: Sage Publications, 2004.

Pandey, Gyanendra. *The Ascendancy of the Congress in Uttar Pradesh 1926–1934: The Imperfect Mobilization*. New Delhi: Oxford University Prss, 1978.

_____ (ed.). *The Indian Nation in 1942*. Calcutta: K.P.Baghi & Co, 1988.

Parekh, Bhikhu. *Colonialism, Tradition and Reform: An Analysis of Gandhi's Political Discourse*, New Delhi, Newbury Park, London: Sage Publications, 1989.

_____. *Gandhi's Political Philosophy: A Critical Examination*. Notre Dame, Indiana: University of Notre Dame Press, 1989.

Pati, Biswamoy. 'The climax of popular protest: The Quit India Movement in Orissa'. *The Indian Economic and Social History Review*, 29 (1), 1992, pp. 1–35.

_____. *Resisting Domination: Peasants, Tribals and the National Movement in Orissa 1920–50*. New Delhi: Manohar, 1993.

Pouchepadass, J. 'Local leaders and the intelligentsia in the Champaran styagraha (1917): A study in peasant mobilization'. *Contributions to Indian Sociology*, New Series, 8, 1974, pp. 67–87.

_____. *Champaran and Gandhi: Planters, Peasants and Gandhian Politics*. New Delhi: Oxford University Press, 1999.

Sarkar, Tanika. *Bengal 1928–1934: The Politics of Protest*. Delhi: Oxford University Press, 1987.

Tomlinson, B.R. *The Indian National Congress and the Raj, 1929–1942: The Penultimate Phase*. London: Macmillan, 1976.

Wolpert, Stanley. *Gandhi's Passion: The Life and Legacy of Mahatma Gandhi*. Oxford: Oxford University Press, 2001.

Zacharia, Benjamin. *Nehru*. London: Routledge, 2003.

Nationalism and Religious Identities

Ahmed, A. *Jinnah, Pakistan and Islamic Identity: The Search for Saladin*, London, New York: Routledge, 1997.

Ahmed, Rafiuddin. *The Bengal Muslims 1871–1906: A Quest for Identity*. Paperback edition, New Delhi: Oxford University Press, 1996.

Ahsan, A. 'The Partition in Retrospect: A Primordial Divide', in A. Singh (ed.), *The Partition in Retrospect*. New Delhi: Anamika, 2000, pp. 287–310.

Andersen, Walter K. and Shridhar D. Damle. *The Brotherhood in Saffron—The Rashtriya Swayam-Sevak Sangh and Hindu Revialisim*. New Delhi, Sage Publications, 1999.

Basu, Tapan, Pradip Datta, Sumit Sarkar, Tanika Sarkar, and Sambuddha Sen. *Khaki Shorts Saffron Flags: A Crtique of the Hindu Right*. New Delhi, Orient Longman, 1999.

Batabyal, Rakesh. *Communalism in Bengal: From Famine to Noakhali, 1943–47*, New Delhi: Sage Publications, 2005.

Burke, S.M. (ed.). *Jinnah: Speeches and Statements*. Karachi: Oxford University Press, 2004.

Bidwai, Praful, Harbans Mukhia, and Achin Vanaik (eds). *Religion, Religiosity and Communalism*. New Delhi, Manohar, 1996,

Chakrabarty, Bidyut. *Communal Identity in India: Its Construction and Articulation in the Twentieth Century*. New Delhi, Oxford University Press, 2003.

Chandra, Bipan. *Communalism in Modern India*. Second revised edition. New Delhi: Vikas Publishing House, 1993.

Chatterji, Joya: *Bengal Divided: Hindu Communalism and Partition, 1932–1947*. Cambridge: Cambridge University Press, 1995.

Das, Suranjan. *Communal Riots in Bengal 1905–1947*. New Delhi: Oxford University Press, 1991.

Datta, Pradip Kumar. *Carving Blocs: Communal Ideology in Early Twentieth-century Bengal*. New Delhi: Oxford University Press, 1999.

Eaton, Richard M. *The Rise of Islam and the Bengal Frontier 1204–1760*. Berkeley, Los Angeles, London: University of California Press, 1993.

Freitag, Sandria B. *Collective Action and Community: Public Arenas and the Emergence of Communalism in North India*. Berkeley, Los Angeles, Oxford: University of California Press, 1989.

Ghosh, Papiya. 'The making of the Congress Muslim stereotype: Bihar, 1937–39'. The *Indian Economic and Social History Review*, 28 (4), 1991, pp. 417–34.

Gilmartin, D. *Empire and Islam: Punjab and the Making of Pakistan*. Berkeley, Los Angeles, London: University of California Press, 1988.

Hansen, Thomas B. *The Saffron Wave: Democracy and Hindu Nationalism in Modern India*. New Delhi: Oxford University Press, 1999.

Hardiman, David. 'Purifying the nation: The Arya Samaj in Gujarat 1895–1930'. *The Indian Economic and Social History Review*, 44 (1), 2007, pp. 41–65.

Hasan, Mushirul. (ed.). *Communal and Pan-Islamic Trends in Colonial India*. New Delhi: Manohar, 1985.

——. 'The Muslim Mass Contact Campaign: Analysis of a Strategy of Political Mobilization', in R. Sisson and S. Wolpert (eds), *Congress and Indian Nationalism: The Pre-Independence Phase*. Berkeley and Los Angeles: California University Press, 1988, pp. 198–222.

—— (ed.) *India's Partition: Process, Strategy and Mobilization*. Delhi: Oxford University Press, 1993, pp. 1–43.

—— (ed.) *India Partitioned: The Other Face of Freedom*, 2 volumes, New Delhi: Roli Books, 1995.

——. 'The Myth of Unity: Colonial and National Narratives', in D. Ludden (ed.), *Making India Hindu: Religion, Community and the Politics of Democracy in India*. New Delhi: Oxford University Press, 1996, pp. 185–208.

Hashmi, T.I. *Pakistan as a Peasant Utopia: The Communalization of Class Politics in East Bengal, 1920–1947*, Boulder, Colorado: Westview Press, 1992.

Jaffrelot, Christophe. *The Hindu Nationalist Movement and Indian Politics 1925 to the 1990s*. London: Hurst & Company, 1996.

—— (ed.). *Hindu Nationalism: A Reader*. Princeton, NJ.: Princeton University Press, 2007.

Jalal, Ayesha. *The Sole Spokesman: Jinnah, the Muslim League and the Demand for Pakistan*. Cambridge: Cambridge University Press, 1985.

——. 'Exploding Communalism: The Politics of Muslim Identity in South Asia', in S. Bose and A. Jalal (eds), *Nationalism, Democracy and Development: State and Politics in India*. New Delhi: Oxford University Press, 1997, pp. 76–103.

——. *Self and Sovereignty: Individual and Community in South Asian Islam since 1850*. London and New York: Routledge, 2000.

Juergensmeyer, Mark. *Religious Nationalism Confronts the Secular State*. New Delhi: Oxford University Press, 1998.

Kaura, Uma. *Muslims and Indian Nationalism: The Emergence of Demand for India's Partition 1928–1940*. New Delhi: South Asia Books, 1977.

Kishwar, Madhu. *Religion at the Service of Nationalism and Other Essays*. New Delhi, Oxford University Press, 1998.

Kuwajima, Sho. *Muslims, Nationalism and the Partition: 1946 Provincial Elections in India*. New Delhi: Manohar, 1998.

Lelyveld, David. *Aligarh's First Generation: Muslim Solidarity in British India*. Princeton, NJ: Princeton University Press, 1978.

Ludden, David (ed.). *Making India Hindu—Religion, Community, and the Politics of Democracy in India*. New Delhi, Oxford University Press, 1999,

Malik, Hafeez. 'Sir Sayyid Ahmad Khan's Contribution to the Development of Muslim Nationalism in India'. *Modern Asian Studies*, 4(2), 1970, pp. 129–147.

Mayaram, Shail. *Resisting Regimes: Myth, Memory and the Shaping of a Muslim Identity*. New Delhi: Oxford University Press, 1997.

Moore, R.J. *The Crisis of Indian Unity, 1917–1940*. New Delhi: Oxford University Press, 1974.

_____. *Endgames of Empire: Studies of Britain's Indian Problem*. New Delhi: Oxford University Press, 1988.

Murshid, Tazeen M. *The Sacred and the Secular: Bengal Muslim Discourses, 1871–1977*. Calcutta: Oxford University Press, 1995.

Nigam, Aditya. *The Insurrection of Little Selves: The Crisis of Secular-Nationalism in India*. New Delhi: Oxford University Press. 2006.

Page, David. *Prelude to Partition: The Indian Muslims and the Imperial System of Control, 1920–1932*. New Delhi: Oxford University Press, 1982.

Pandey, Gyanendra. *The Construction of Communalism in Colonial North India*. New Delhi: Oxford University Press, 1992.

_____. *Remembering Partition: Violence, Nationalism and History in India*. Cambridge: Cambridge University Press, 2001.

Sen, Shila. *Muslim Politics in Bengal 1937–47*. New Delhi: Impex India, 1976.

Shaikh, F. *Community and Consensus in Islam: Muslim Representation in Colonial India, 1860–1947*. Cambridge: Cambridge University Press, 1989.

Singh, Anita I. *The Origins of the Partition of India 1936–1947*. New Delhi: Oxford University Press, 1987.

Talbot, Ian. *Provincial Politics and the Pakistan Movement*. Karachi: Oxford University Press, 1988.

_____. *Khizr Tiwana, the Punjab Unionist Party and the Partition of India*. Richmond, Surrey: Curzon, 1996.

_____. *Freedom's Cry: Popular Dimension in the Pakistan Movement and Partition Experience in North-West India*. Karachi: Oxford University Press, 1996.

Van der Veer, Peter. *Religious Nationalism: Hindus and Muslims in India*. Berkeley, Los Angeles, London: University of California Press, 1994.

Vanaik, Achin. *The Furies of Indian Communalism: Religion, Modernity and Secularization*. London, New York: Verso, 1997.

Wolpert, Stanley. *Jinnah of Pakistan*. New York: Oxford University Press, 1984.

Wood, Conrad. *The Moplah Rebellion and Its Genesis*. New Delhi: People's Publishing House, 1987.

Zavos, John. *The Emergence of Hindu Nationalism in India*. New Delhi, Oxford University Press, 2000.

NON-BRAHMAN AND DALIT MOVEMENTS

Aloysius, G. *Nationalism Without A Nation in India*. New Delhi: Oxford University Press, 1997.

Ambedkar, B.R. *What Congress and Gandhi Have Done to the Untouchables*. Bombay: Thacker & Co. Ltd., 1945.

_____. *The Essential Writings of B.R. Ambedkar*, edited by Valerian Rodrigues. New Delhi: Oxford University Press, 2001.

Bandyopadhyay, Sekhar. *Caste, Protest and Identity in Colonial India: The Namasudras of Bengal, 1872–1947*. Richmond, Surrey: Curzon Press, 1997.

Banerjee, D.N. *Crusade Against Untouchability: Gandhian Movement for Uplift of Harijans in India*. New Delhi: Nehru Memorial Museum and Library, 2006.

Bayly, Susan. *Caste, Society and Politics in India from the Eighteenth Century to the Modern Age. The New Cambridge History of India IV. 3*. Cambridge: Cambridge University Press, 1999.

Carroll, L. 'Colonial Perceptions of Indian Society and the Emergence of Caste(s) Associations'. *Journal of Asian Studies*, 37 (2), 1978, pp. 233–50.

Constable, P. 'Early Dalit Literature and Culture in Late Nineteenth and Early Twentieth Century Western India'. *Modern Asian Studies*, 31 (2), 1997. pp. 317–38.

_____. 'Sitting on the school verandah: The ideology and practice of "untouchable" educational protest in late nineteenth-century western India'. *The Indian Economic and Social History Review*, 37 (4), 2000, pp. 383–422.

Deshpande, Prachi. 'Caste as Maratha: Social categories, colonial policy and identity in early twentieth-century Maharashtra'. *The Indian Economic and Social History Review,* 41 (1), 2004, pp. 7–32.

Galanter, M. *Competing Equalities: Law and Backward Classes in India.* Berkeley and Los Angeles: University of California Press, 1984.

Geetha, V. and S.V. Rajadurai. *Towards a Non-Brahmin Millennium: From Iyothee Thass to Periyar.* Calcutta: Samya, 1998.

Gooptu, Nandini. *The Politics of the Urban Poor in Early Twentieth Century India.* Cambridge: Cambridge University Press, 2001.

Gore, M.S. *The Social Context of an Ideology: Ambedkar's Political and Social Thought.* New Delhi, Thousand Oaks, London: Sage Publications, 1993.

Hardgrave, Robert L. *The Nadars of Tamilnad,* Berkeley and Los Angeles: University of California Press, 1969.

Ilaiah, Kancha. *Why I am not a Hindu: A Sudra Critique of Hindutva, Philosophy, Culture and Political Economy.* New Delhi: Samya, 1998.

_____. 'Towards Dalitaisation of the Nation', in P. Chatterjee (ed.), *Wages of Freedom: Fifty Years of the Indian Nation State.* New Delhi: Oxford University Press, 1998.

_____. *Buffalo Nationalism: A Critique of Spiritual Fascism.* Kolkata: Samya, 2004.

Irschick, E.F. *Politics and Social Conflict in South India: The Non-Brahman Movement and Tamil Separatism 1916–1929.* Berkeley and Los Angeles: University of California Press, 1969.

Jaffrelot, Christophe. *Dr Ambedkar and Untouchability: Analysing and Fighting Caste.* Delhi: Permanent Black, 2005.

_____. *India's Silent Revolution: The Rise of the Lower Castes.* London: C. Hurst, 2002.

Jeffrey, Robin. 'The Social Origins of a Caste Association, 1875–1905: The Founding of the S.N.D.P.Yogam', *South Asia,* 4, 1974 pp. 39–59.

Juergensmeyer, Mark. *Religion as Social Vision: The Movement against Untouchability in 20th Century Punjab.* Berkeley and Los Angeles: University of California Press, 1982.

Kumar, Ravinder. 'Gandhi, Ambedkar and the Poona Pact, 1932', in J.Masselos (ed.), *Struggling and Ruling: The Indian National Congress 1885–1985.* New Delhi: Sterling, 1987, pp. 87–101.

Lynch, Owen. *The Politics of Untouchability: Social Mobility and Social Change in a City of India.* New York: Columbia University Press, 1969.

Mani, Braj Ranjan. *Debrahmanising History: Dominance and Resistance in Indian Society*. New Delhi, Manohar. 2005.

Mendelsohn, Oliver and Marika Vicziany. *The Untouchables: Subordination, Poverty and the State in Modern India*. Cambridge: Cambridge University Press, 1998.

Menon, Dilip. *Caste, Nationalism and Communism in South India, Malabar 1900–1948*, Cambridge: Cambridge University Press, 1994.

———. *The Blindness of Insight: Essays on Caste in Modern India*. Pondicherry: Navayana Publications, 2006.

Mudaliar, Chandra Y. 'The Non-Brahmin Movement in Kolhapur'. *The Indian Economic and Social History Review*, 15 (1), 1978, pp. 1–19.

O'Hanlon, R. *Caste, Conflict and Ideology: Mahatma Jotirao Phule and Low Caste Protest in Nineteenth Century Western India*. Cambridge: Cambridge University Press, 1985.

———. 'Congress and the non-Brahmans in Western India: The Problem of Popular Politics', in John L. Hill (ed.), *The Congress and Indian Nationalism: Historical Perspectives*. London: Curzon Press, 1991.

Omvedt, Gail. 'Jotirao Phule and the Ideology of Social Revolution in India'. *Economic and Political Weekly*, 6 (37), 11 September 1971, pp. 1969–79.

———. *Cultural Revolt in a Colonial Society: The Non Brahman Movement in Western India: 1873 to 1930*. Bombay: Scientific Socialist Education Trust, 1976.

———. *Dalits and the Democratic Revolution: Dr Ambedkar and the Dalit Movement in Colonial India*. New Delhi, Thousand Oaks, London: Sage Publications, 1994.

Pandian, M.S.S. 'Denationalising' the Past: 'Nation' in E.V.Ramaswamy's Political Discourse'. *Economic and Political Weeekly*, 28 (42), 16 October 1993, pp. 2282–7.

———. 'Notes on the Transformation of "Dravidian" Ideology: Tamilnadu, c. 1900–1940'. *Social Scientist,* 22 (5–6), 1994, pp. 84–104.

———. '"Nation" from Its Margins: Notes on E.V. Ramaswamy's "Impossible" Nation', in R. Bhargava, et.al, (eds), *Multiculturalism, Liberalism and Democracy*. New Delhi: Oxford University Press, 1999, pp. 286–307.

———. *Brahmin and Non-Brahmin: Genealogies of the Tamil Political Present*. New Delhi: Permanent Black, 2007.

Patankar, B. and G. Omvedt, 'The Dalit Liberation Movement in the Colonial Period'. *Economic and Political Weekly,* Annual Number, 14 (7–8), February 1979, pp. 409–24.

Prashad, Vijay. 'The killing of Bala Shah and the birth of Valmiki: Hinduisation and the politics of religion'. *The Indian Economic and Social History Review,* 32 (3), 1995, pp. 287–325.

_____. *Untouchable Freedom: A Social History of a Dalit Community.* New Delhi: Oxford University Press, 2000.

Ramaswamy, Sumathi. *Passions of the Tongue: Language Devotion in Tamil India 1891–1970.* Berkeley, Los Angeles, London: University of California Press, 1997.

Robb, P. (ed.). *Dalit Movements and the Meanings of Labour in India.* New Delhi: Oxford University Press, 1993.

Rudolph, L.I. and S.H. Rudolph. *The Modernity of Tradition—Political Development in India.* Chicago and London: University of Chicago Press, 1967.

Srinivas, M.N. *Social Change in Modern India.* Berkeley and Los Angeles: University of California Press, 1966.

Zelliot, Eleanor. *From Untouchable to Dalit: Essay on Ambedkar Movement.* New Delhi: Manohar, 1993.

_____. 'Congress and the Untouchables, 1917–1950', in R. Sisson and S.Wolpert (eds), *Congress and Indian Nationalism.* New Delhi: Oxford University Press, 1988, pp. 182–97.

Women's Participation

Ali, Aruna Asaf. *The Resurgence of Indian Women.* London: Sangam Books, 1991.

Ali, Azra Asghar. *The Emergence of Feminism Among Indian Muslim Women 1920–1947.* Karachi: Oxford University Press, 2000.

Basu, Aparna and Bharati Ray. *Women's Struggle: A History of the All-India Women's Conference, 1927–1990.* New Delhi: Manohar, 1990.

Basu, Aparna and Anup Taneja (eds), *Breaking out of Invisibility: Women in Indian History.* New Delhi: Indian Council of Historical Research: Northern Book Centre, 2002.

Borthwick, M. *The Changing Role of Women in Bengal. 1849–1905,* Princeton: Princeton University Press, 1984.

Butalia, U. *The Other Side of Silence; Voices from the Partition of India.* Delhi: Penguin Books India, 1998.

Chakravarti, U. *Rewriting History: The Life and Times of Pandita Ramabai*. New Delhi: Kali for Women, 1998.

Chatterjee, Partha. 'Colonialism, Nationalism, and Colonialized Women: The Contest in India'. *American Ethnologist*, 16 (4), 1989, pp. 622–33.

Chowdhury, Indira. *The Frail Hero and Virile History: Gender and the Politics of Culture in Colonial Bengal*. New Delhi: Oxford University Press, 1998.

Custers, Peter. 'Women's Role in Tebhaga Movement', *Economic and Political Weekly*, Review of Women Studies, 31 (43), 23 October 1986, pp. WS-97-104.

———. *Women in Tebhaga Uprising*. London: Pilgrims Publishing, 1987.

Engels, Dagmar. *Beyond Purdah? Women in Bengal 1890–1939*, New Delhi: Oxford University Press, 1996.

Forbes, Geraldine. *Women in Modern India. The New Cambridge History of India*, IV.2. Cambridge: Cambridge University Press, 1998.

Jayawardena, Kumari. *Feminism and Nationalism in the Third World*. London and New Jersey: Zed Books Ltd, 1986.

Jeffery, Patricia and Amrita Basu (eds). *Resisting the Sacred and the Secular: Women's Activism and Politicized Religion in South Asia*. New Delhi: Kali For Women, 1999.

Kasturi, L. and V. Mazumdar (eds). *Women and Indian Nationalism*. New Delhi: Vikas, 1994.

Kishwar, Madhu. 'Gandhi on Women'. *Economic and Political Weekly*, 20 (40), 5 October 1985, pp. 1691–1702.

———. *Off the Beaten Track: Rethinking Gender Justice for Indian Women*. New Delhi: Oxford University Press, 2001.

Lalita, K., Vasantha Kannabiran, Rama Melkote, Uma Maheshwari, Susie Tharu, and Veena Shatrugna—Stree Shakti Sanghatana. *'We Were Making HistoryÖ' Life Stories of Women in the Telengana People's Struggle*. London: Zed Books, 1989.

Menon, Nivedita (ed.). *Gender and Politics in India*. New Delhi: Oxford University Press, 2001.

Menon, Ritu and Kamla Bhasin. *Borders and Boundaries: Women in India's Partition*. New Brunswick: Rutgers University Press, 1998.

Minault, Gail. *The Extended Family: Women and Political Participation in India and Pakistan*. Delhi: Chanakya Publications, 1981.

Murshid, Ghulam. *Reluctant Debutante: Response of Bengali Women to Modernisation 1849–1905*. Rajshahi: Rajshahi University Press, 1983.

SELECT BIBLIOGRAPHY

375

Patel, Sujata. 'Construction and Reconstruction of Woman in Gandhi', in A. Thorner and M. Krishnaraj (eds), *Ideals, Images and Real Lives: Women in Literature and History*. Hyderabad: Orient Longman, 2000, pp. 288–321.

Pearson, Gail. 'Reserved seats—women and the vote in Bombay'. *The Indian Economic and Social History Review*, 20 (1), 1983, pp. 47–66.

Ray, Bharati (ed.). *From the Seams of History: Essays on Indian Women*. New Delhi: Oxford University Press, 1995.

——— (ed.). *Women of India: Colonial and Post-colonial Periods*. New Delhi, Sage Publications, 2005.

Ray, Raka. *Fields of Protest: Women's Movements in India*. New Delhi, Kali for Women, 1999.

Ray, Sangeeta. *En-gendering India: Women and Nation in Colonial and Postcolonial Narratives*. Durham, NC: Duke University Press, 2000.

Sangari, K. and S. Vaid (eds). *Recasting Women*. New Brunswick, NJ: Rutgers University Press, 1990.

Sarkar, Tanika. *Hindu Wife, Hindu Nation: Community, Religion and Cultural Nationalism*. London: Hurst & Co., 2001.

Sinha, Mrinalini. 'Refashioning Mother India: Feminism and Nationalism in Late-Colonial India'. *Feminist Studies*, 26 (3), Autumn 2000, pp. 623–644.

Srilata, K. (ed.), *The Other Half of the Coconut: Women Writing Self-Respect History*. New Delhi, Kali for Women. 2003.

Thapar-Bjorkert, Suruchi. *Women in the Indian National Movement: Unseen Faces and Unheard Voices, 1930–42*. New Delhi: Oxford University Press, 2006.

Capitalists and Nationalism

Bhattacharya, S. 'Cotton Mills and Spinning Wheels: Swadeshi and the Indian Capitalist Class, 1920–22'. *Economic and Political Weekly*, 11 (47), 20 November 1976, pp. 1828–32.

———. 'The Colonial State, Capital and Labour, Bombay 1919–1931', in S. Bhattacharya and R. Thapar (eds), *Situating Indian History for Sarvepalli Gopal*. New Delhi: Oxford University Press, 1986, pp. 171–93.

Chandavarkar, Rajnarayan. *The Origins of Industrial Capitalism in India: Business Strategies and the Working Classes in Bombay, 1900–1940*, Cambridge: Cambridge University Press, 1994.

Chatterji, B. *Trade, Tariffs and Empire: Lancashire and British Policy in India 1919–1939*. New Delhi: Oxford University Press, 1992.

Gordon, A.D.D. *Businessmen and Politics: Rising Nationalism and a Modernising Economy in Bombay, 1918–1933*. New Delhi: Manohar, 1978.

Kudaisya, Medha M. *The Life and Times of G.D. Birla*. New York: Oxford University Press, 2006.

Markovits, C. *Indian Business and Nationalist Politics, 1931–39*. Cambridge: Cambridge University Press, 1985.

Misra, Maria. *Business, Race and Politics in British India c.1850–1960*. Oxford: Clarendon Press, 1999.

Mukherjee, Aditya. 'The Indian Capitalist Class: Aspects of Its Economic, Political and Ideological Development in the Colonial Period, 1927–47', in S.Bhattacharya and R. Thapar (eds), *Situating Indian History for Sarvepalli Gopal*, New Delhi: Oxford University Press, pp. 239–87.

———. *Imperialism, Nationalism and the Indian Capitalist Class, 1920–1947*. New Delhi: Sage, 2002.

Ray, Rajat K. *Industrialization in India: Growth and Conflict in the Private Corporate Sector 1914–47*. New Delhi: Oxford University Press, 1979.

Tripathi, Dwijendra (ed.). *Business and Politics in India: A Historical Perspective*. New Delhi: Manohar, 1991.

———. *The Oxford History of Indian Business*. New Delhi: Oxford University Press, 2004.

WORKING CLASSES AND NATIONALISM

Bahl, Vinay. 'Attitudes of the Indian National Congress Towards the Working Class Struggle in India 1918–1947', in Kapil Kumar (ed.), *Congress and Classes: Nationalism, Workers and Peasants*. New Delhi: Manohar, 1988, pp. 1–33.

———. *The Making of the Indian Working Class: The Case of the Tata Iron and Steel Co., 1880–1946*. New Delhi, Thousand Oaks, London: Sage Publications, 1995.

Basu, Subho. 'Strikes and 'Communal' Riots in Calcutta in the 1890s: Industrial Workers, Bhadalok Nationalist Leadership and the Colonial State'. *Modern Asian Studies*, 32 (4), 1998, pp. 949–83.

Chakrabarty, Dipesh. *Rethinking Working Class History: Bengal 1890–1940*. Princeton: Princeton University Press, 1989.

Chandavarkar, Rajnarayan. *Imperial Power and Popular Politics: Class, Resistance and the State in India, c.1850–1950*. Cambridge: Cambridge University Press, 1998.

Das Gupta, Ranajit. *Labour and Working Class in Eastern India. Studies in Colonial History*. Calcutta: K.P.Bagchi & Co., 1994.

Datta, Partho. 'Strikes in the greater Calcutta region 1918–1924'. *The Indian Economic and Social History Review*, 30 (1), 1993, pp. 57–84.

Ghosh, Parimal. *Colonialism, Class and a History of the Calcutta Jute Millhands 1880–1930*. Chennai: Orient Longman, 2000.

Joshi, Chitra. 'Kanpur Textile Labour: Some Structural Features of Formative Years'. *Economic and Political Weekly*, Special Number, 44 (46), 16 November 1981, pp. 1823–38.

_____. 'Bonds of community, ties of religion: Kanpur textile workers in the early twentieth century'. *The Indian Economic and Social History Review*, 22 (3), 1985, pp. 251–80.

_____. *Lost Worlds: Indian Labour and its Forgotten Histories*. London: Anthem Press, 2005.

Kumar, Nita. 'Labour, capital, and the Congress: Delhi Cloth Mills, 1928–38'. *The Indian Economic and Social History Review*, 26 (1), 1989, pp. 29–59.

Kumar, Ravinder. 'The Bombay Textile Strike, 1919'. *The Indian Economic and Social History Review*, 8 (1), 1971, pp. 1–29.

Morris, M.D. *The Emergence of An Industrial Labor Force in India: A Study of the Bombay Cotton Mills, 1854–1947*. Berkeley and Los Angeles: University of California Press, 1965.

Murphy, E.D. 'Class and Community in India: The Madras Labour Union 1918–21'. *The Indian Economic and Social History Review*, 14 (3), 1977, pp. 291–321.

Patel, Sujata. *The Making of Industrial Relations: The Ahmedabad Textile Industry 1918–1939*. New Delhi: Oxford University Press, 1987.

Sarkar, Sumit. 'Condition and Nature of Subaltern Militancy: Bengal from Swadeshi to Non-Co-operation, 1905–1922', in R.Guha (ed.), *Subaltern Studies III: Writings on South Asian History and Society*, (ed.) R. Guha, New Delhi: Oxford University Press, 1984, pp. 271–320.

Sen, Sukomal. *Working Class in India: History of Emergence and Movement 1830–1970*. Calcutta: K.P. Bagchi & Co., 1977.

Simeon, D. *The Politics of Labour Under Late Colonialism: Workers, Unions and the State in Chota Nagpur 1928–1939*. New Delhi: Manohar, 1995.

Simmons, C.P. 'Recruiting and Organizing an Industrial Labour Force in Colonial India: The Case of the Coal Mining Industry, c.1880–1939'. *The Indian Economic and Social History Review*, 13 (4), 1976, pp. 455–82.

The Restless Forties

Brasted H.V. and C.Bridge. '"15 August 1947": Labour's parting gift to India', in J. Masselos (ed.), *India: Creating a Modern Nation*. New Delhi: Sterling Publishers, 1990, pp. 1–35.
———. 'The Transfer of Power in South Asia: An Historiographical Review'. *South Asia*, New Series, 17 (1), 1994, pp. 93–114.
Chattopadhyay, Gautam. 'The Almost Revolutions: A Case Study of India in February 1946', in B. De (ed.), *Essays in Honour of S.C. Sarkar*. New Delhi: People's Publishing House, 1976, pp. 427–50.
Cooper, A. *Sharecropping and Sharecroppers' Struggle in Bengal 1930–1950*. Calcutta: K.P. Bagchi & Co., 1988.
Desai, A.R. (ed.). *Peasant Struggles in India*. Delhi: Oxford University Press, 1979.
Deshpande, Anirudh. 'Sailors and the Crowd: Popular Protest in Karachi, 1946'. *The Indian Economic and Social History Review*, 26 (1), 1989, pp. 1–27.
Dhanagare, D.N. 1991. *Peasant Movements in India 1920–1950*, New Delhi: Oxford University Press.
Gupta, A.K. (ed.). *Myth and Reality: The Struggle for Freedom in India, 1945–47*. Delhi: Manohar, 1987.
Lalita, K., Vasantha Kannabiran, Rama Melkote, Uma Maheshwari, Susie Tharu, and Veena Shatrugna—Stree Shakti Sanghatana. *'We Were Making History...' Life Stories of Women in the Telengana People's Struggle*. London: Zed Books, 1989.
Mahajan, Sucheta. *Independence and Partition: The Erosion of Colonial Power in India*. New Delhi: Sage Publications, 2000.
Sen, Sunil. *Agrarian Struggle in Bengal 1946–47*. New Delhi: People's Publishing House, 1972.
Sarkar, Sumit. 'Popular Movements and National Leadership, 1945–47'. *Economic and Political Weekly*, Annual Number April, 1982, pp. 677–89.
Singharoy, Debal K. *Peasant Movements in Post-colonial India: Dynamics of Mobilization and Identity*. New Delhi: Sage Publications, 2004.

Index

Contributors

Shahid Amin is Professor, Department of History, University of Delhi, India.

David Arnold is ESRC Professor, University of Warwick, UK.

Vinay Bahl is Associate Professor of Sociology, Pennsylvania College of Technology at Williamsport, USA.

Sekhar Bandyopadhyay is Professor of Asian History, Victoria University of Wellington, New Zealand.

Judith Brown is Beit Professor of Commonwealth History, Balliol College, University of Oxford, UK.

Partha Chatterjee is Professor of Anthropology, Columbia University, USA.

Bipan Chandra is former Professor, Centre for Historical Studies, Jawaharlal Nehru University. He is currently Chairman, National Book Trust, New Delhi, India.

Anirudh Deshpande is at the Department of History, Motilal Nehru College, University of Delhi, India. He was formerly a fellow at the Centre for Contemporary Studies, Nehru Memorial Museum and Library (NMML), New Delhi.

David Hardiman is Professor of History, University of Warwick, UK.

Mushirul Hasan is Vice Chancellor, Jamia Milia Islamia, New Delhi, India.

Ayesha Jalal is Professor of History, Tufts University, Massachusetts, USA.

Madhu Kishwar is Senior Fellow, Centre for the Study of Developing Societies, New Delhi, India.

Gyanendra Pandey is Arts and Sciences Distinguished Professor, Emory University, Atlanta, USA.

M.S.S. Pandian is Visiting Fellow of the Sarai Programme, Centre for the Study of Developing Societies, New Delhi, India.

Rajat K. Ray is Vice Chancellor, Visva Bharati, Santiniketan, India.

Sumit Sarkar is former Professor, Department of History, University of Delhi, India.

Tanika Sarkar is Professor, Centre for Historical Studies, Jawaharlal Nehru University, New Delhi, India.

SANJAY SETH is Professor of Politics, Goldsmiths College, University of London, UK.

BRIAN STODDART was formerly Vice Chancellor (Research), La Trobe University, Melbourne, Australia.

DWIJENDRA TRIPATHI is former Professor of Business and Entrepreneurship, Indian Institute of Management, Ahmedabad, India.

ELEANOR ZELLIOT is Professor Emerita of History, Carleton College, Northfield, Minnesota, USA.